P9-BJB-043

The Cambridge Handbook
of Contemporary
CHINA

CONSULTANTS
Kevin Bucknall
W. J. F. Jenner

MAPS
Val Lyons

The Cambridge Handbook
of Contemporary
CHINA

Colin Mackerras

Key Centre for Asian Languages and Studies
Griffith University

Amanda Yorke

Department of Fine Arts
University of Western Australia

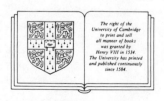

The right of the
University of Cambridge
to print and sell
all manner of books
was granted by
Henry VIII in 1534.
The University has printed
and published continuously
since 1584.

Cambridge University Press

Cambridge
New York Port Chester Melbourne Sydney

Published by the Press Syndicate of the University of Cambridge
The Pitt Building, Trumpington Street, Cambridge CB2 1RP, UK
40 West 20th Street, New York, NY 10011-4211, USA
10 Stamford Road, Oakleigh, Victoria 3166, Australia

© Cambridge University Press 1991
First published 1991
Reprinted (pocket edition) 1991

Printed in Hong Kong by Colorcraft

National Library of Australia cataloguing-in-publication data
Mackerras, Colin, 1939 –
Cambridge handbook of contemporary China.
Bibliography.
Includes index.
ISBN 0 521 38342 0.
ISBN 0 521 38755 8 (pbk.).
1. China – Politics and government – 1976 – .2. China
Social conditions – 1976 – .3. China – Economic
conditions – 1976 – .I. Yorke, Amanda, 1954 – .II.
Title. III. Title: Handbook of contemporary China.
951.059

British Library cataloguing-in-publication data
Mackerras, Colin.
The Cambridge handbook of contemporary China.
1. China Social conditions, 1949 –
I. Title II. Yorke, Amanda
951.05
ISBN 0-521-38342-0
       0-521-38755-8 pbk

Library of Congress cataloguing-in-publication data
Mackerras, Colin.
The Cambridge handbook of contemporary China/by Colin Mackerras
and Amanda Yorke.
Includes bibliographical references and index.
ISBN 0-521-38342-0
ISBN 0-521-38755-8 (pbk.): $40.00
1. China – Handbooks, manuals, etc. I. Yorke, Amanda, 1954 –.
II. Title.
DS706.M24   1990   *73840*
951.05'9 – dc20

HPS

CONTENTS

TABLES
FIGURES
MAPS

FIGURES

MAPS

PREFACE

This work aims to present useful and accurate information, dates and statistics concerning contemporary China in a manageable and accessible form. 'China' has been used to refer to the People's Republic of China, so although Taiwan and Hong Kong are mentioned occasionally, neither of them has been considered systematically or in detail.

Every attempt has been made to keep the information up to date. However, in dealing with contemporary times, it is always necessary to establish a cut-off date. In this case that date is April 30, 1990, since that was when the compilation of the book was completed.

This is a jointly written book. The first of the two named authors compiled Chapters 1, 2, 4, 5, 7 and 9, and contributed substantially to Chapter 8; the second compiled Chapters 3, 6, 8 and 10. Chapter 11 was jointly written. Dr Kevin Bucknall of the Division of Asian and International Studies, Griffith University, carefully examined and revised Chapter 6 and offered advice on all chapters, and Ms Susan Jarvis carried out extensive editorial work on all chapters, contributed substantially to Chapters 8 and 10 and compiled the index, for which both authors express their gratitude.

The two systems of romanization in most widespread use for English-language material are the British-developed Wade–Giles and the *Hanyu pinyin*, which was devised in the 1950s and came into almost universal use in People's Republic of China

foreign-language publications on January 1, 1979. Nowadays both systems are in common use for English-language books published outside China, but for books about the People's Republic of China *pinyin* has become much more standard and is the system we have adopted in this book. The only exceptions are for people who are usually known in the West by names not expressed in standard Chinese, such as Sun Yatsen or Chiang Kaishek. However, in Chapter 3 we have given the Wade–Giles equivalent in parentheses for each biographee's name following its presentation as a heading in *pinyin*.

Below are shown some of the most important differences between the two systems.

Pinyin	Wade–Giles	Approximate English sound
c	ts'	ts
ch	ch'	ch
d	t	d
g	k	g
j	ch	j
k	k'	k
p	p'	p
q	ch'	ch
r	j	r
t	t'	t
x	hs	sh
z	ts	dz
zh	ch	j

ABBREVIATIONS

This list includes only those abbreviations used in this book. A more extensive list of acronyms commonly used in relation to China is provided in the Appendix.

CAAC	Civil Aviation Administration of China
CITIC	China International Trust and Investment Corporation
CCP	Chinese Communist Party
CCPCC	Chinese Communist Party Central Committee
CCYL	Chinese Communist Youth League
CPG	Central People's Government
CPPCC	Chinese People's Political Consultative Conference
DPRK	Democratic People's Republic of Korea
GMD	Guomindang (Kuomintang)
IMAR	Inner Mongolian Autonomous Region
NCNA	New China News Agency
NDYL	New Democratic Youth League
NPC	National People's Congress
PLA	People's Liberation Army
PRC	People's Republic of China
ROC	Republic of China
UN	United Nations
XNA	Xinhua (New China) News Agency

1   CHRONOLOGY

This chronology of significant events in China extends from 1900 to April 1990.[1] The events are divided, for ease of reference, into seven categories: A. Foreign Affairs Events; B. Domestic Political and/or Military Events; C. Economic Events; D. Appointments, Dismissals, etc.; E. Cultural and Social Events; F. Births and Deaths; G. Natural Disasters.

1900   THE BOXER UPRISING

A. Foreign Affairs Events

June 17. Allied troops of Britain, Russia, France, Germany, the United States, Italy, Austria and Japan capture the Dagu forts.

July 3. United States Secretary of State John Hay reiterates the 'open door' policy and calls for the protection of China's territorial integrity and administrative independence.

July 14. A large Allied force seizes the city of Tianjin.

August 14. Allied troops enter Beijing and lift the siege of the legations.

September 30. Russian forces take Shenyang, virtually completing their occupation of Manchuria. The Russian invasion of Manchuria had begun in July.

B. Domestic Political Events

June 20. Troops of the Righteous and Harmonious Militia (*Yihe tuan*)—the Boxers—begin the 'siege of the legations' in Beijing.

August 15. The Empress Dowager Cixi flees following the foreign occupation of Beijing, and takes the Emperor Guangxu with her.

1901

A. Foreign Affairs Events

July 31. The Allied troops begin withdrawing from Beijing, completing the withdrawal on September 17.

September 7. China signs the Boxer protocol with the foreign powers. Terms include payment of an enormous indemnity by China, the denial to Chinese of the right to live in the legation quarter and the razing of the Dagu forts.

D. Appointments, Dismissals, etc.

February 13. At foreign insistence, the imperial court orders punishment, suicide or dismissal for certain officials involved in the Boxer movement.

F. Births and Deaths

November 7. Senior statesman and diplomat Li Hongzhang dies.

1902

A. Foreign Affairs Events

April 18. Russia agrees to withdraw its troops from Manchuria.

C. Economic Events

Motor cars first seen in Shanghai.

1903

C. Economic Events

July 1. The Chinese Eastern Railway formally opens to traffic.

1904

A. Foreign Affairs Events

February 9–10. Russia and Japan declare war on each other over rights in Manchuria and Korea.

February 12. The Chinese court issues an edict declaring itself neutral in the Russo-Japanese war, despite its realization that the war would be fought mainly on Chinese soil.

September 7. British forces led by Francis Young-husband sign the Lhasa Convention with Tibetan representatives. The Convention declares that the Tibetans are to have no dealing with any foreign power without British consent.

E. Cultural and Social Events

March 21. The Shanghai International Committee of the Red Cross is established because of the suffering caused by the Russo-Japanese war.

F. Births and Deaths

August 22. Deng Xiaoping born.

1905

A. Foreign Affairs Events

March 10. The Russo-Japanese Battle of Shenyang (Mukden) ends in a major Japanese victory, and in the Japanese occupation of Shenyang.

September 5. The Treaty of Portsmouth is signed, ending the Russo-Japanese war. Chinese sovereignty in Manchuria is restored, but Japan takes over the lease on the Liaodong Peninsula and the Chinese Eastern Railway previously held by Russia.

B. Domestic Political Events

August 20. A meeting in Tokyo formally establishes the Chinese United League (*Tongmeng hui*), adopts a constitution and elects Sun Yatsen as its president.

C. Economic Events

November 13. Completion of the Beijing–Hankou railway line.

E. Cultural and Social Events

May 26–September 27. China's first modern boycott, against American products, is held in Shanghai, Guangzhou, Nanjing and other major cities.

September 2. The court issues an edict that the traditional examinations be discontinued at all levels.

November 26. *The People's Tribune (Minbao)* begins publication in Tokyo as the organ of

the United League, including Sun Yatsen's 'Three Principles of the People'.

1906

B. Domestic Political Events

November 6. The court reorganizes the government, including the expansion of the traditional Six Boards into eleven ministries, one of the new ministries being the Ministry of Finance.

E. Cultural and Social Events

September 20. The court issues an edict banning opium.

1907

A. Foreign Affairs Events

August 31. Britain and Russia sign a convention on Tibet, by which each nation recognizes Chinese sovereignty in Tibet and agrees not to interfere in Tibetan affairs.

B. Domestic Political Events

April 20. Manchuria is divided into three provinces: Fengtian, Jilin and Heilongjiang.

September 20. An imperial edict orders that a National Assembly be set up.

C. Economic Events

June 29. The Beijing–Shenyang railway opens to traffic.

E. Cultural and Social Events

June 1–2. In Tokyo, Ouyang Yuqian and others produce the spoken drama *The Black Slave's Cry to Heaven (Heinu yutian lu)*, based on *Uncle Tom's Cabin*: it is the first Western–style spoken drama adapted and fully performed by Chinese in the Chinese language.

F. Births and Deaths

July 15. The female anti-Manchu revolutionary Qiu Jin is beheaded.

1908

A. Foreign Affairs Events

June 23. The United States Congress passes a bill

to return part of the Boxer indemnity to China.

B. Domestic Political Events

August 27. The imperial court accepts a draft constitution, providing for a monarchy with defined powers and a parliament.

December 3. The court proclaims that the constitution will be promulgated and a parliamentary system implemented in 1916.

D. Appointments, Dismissals, etc.

December 2. Puyi ascends the throne as Emperor.

F. Births and Deaths

November 14. Emperor Guangxu dies.

November 15. Empress Dowager Cixi dies.

1909

B. Domestic Political Events

February 5. Preliminary local elections begin to select delegates for provincial assemblies.

October 14. The provincial assemblies of the various provinces convene.

F. Births and Deaths

June 23. Li Xiannian born.

October 4. Statesman Zhang Zhidong dies.

1910

B. Domestic Political Events

February 12. Chinese imperial troops occupy Lhasa, the Tibetan capital.

April 18. The Chinese Ministry of Foreign Affairs issues a statement of its formal claim to sovereignty over Tibet.

October 3. The National Assembly convenes.

C. Economic Events

May 23. In Paris, British, German, French and American banks set up the Four-power Consortium to provide loans to the Chinese government.

October 22. The court commands the new Ministry of Finance (see November 6, 1906) to prepare China's first national budget for approval by the National Assembly.

1911   OVERTHROW OF THE MANCHU DYNASTY

B. Domestic Political Events

June 17. The Railway Protection League is established in Sichuan province to protest against the nationalization of the railways.

October 10. A military uprising begins in Wuchang, Hubei province.

October 11. The rebels set up a military government in Wuchang, which is declared independent of the Qing state.

November 4. Shanghai falls to the revolutionaries, following a revolt the preceding day.

November 27. The capital of Sichuan, Chengdu, proclaims independence of the Qing imperial court.

C. Economic Events

May 9. The court nationalizes all China's main railways.

D. Appointments

December 26. Sun Yatsen is elected provisional president of the Republic of China.

1912   BIRTH OF THE REPUBLIC OF CHINA

A. Foreign Affairs Events

November 7. The Chinese Ministry of Foreign Affairs informs Russia of its view that Mongolia is part of China and thus has no right to sign treaties with foreign countries. On November 3, Russia and Mongolia had signed a trade and friendship agreement under which Russia approved Mongolian independence.

B. Domestic Political Events

January 1. The Republic of China (ROC) is officially proclaimed.

March 11. President Sun Yatsen proclaims the revised constitution of the ROC.

August 25. A Congress in Beijing forms the Nationalist Party (*Guomindang*).

C. Economic Events

May 17. The Ministry of Finance reaches agreement on a contract for a large loan from the Four-power Consortium.

June 21. The Tianjin–Pukou railway line opens for traffic, apart from the bridge over the Yellow River (completed mid-November 1912). Pukou lies opposite Nanjing on the bank of the Yangzi River.

D. Appointments, Dismissals, etc.

January 1. Sun Yatsen becomes provisional president of the ROC.

February 12. The Emperor issues an edict of abdication.

February 15. The Senate appoints Yuan Shikai as provisional president of the ROC in place of Sun Yatsen.

August 25. The Nationalist Party's Congress elects Sun Yatsen as the Party's first chairman.

1913

A. Foreign Affairs Events

October 6. Britain, Russia, France, Japan and nine other countries notify the Ministry of Foreign Affairs of their recognition of Yuan Shikai's government.

B. Domestic Political Events

July 12. The 'Second Revolution' begins with the declaration of independence from Yuan Shikai by Li Liejun's revolutionary army in Jiangxi province. Many provinces follow this lead.

April 8. The National Assembly, including both the Senate and House of Representatives, holds its inaugural meeting, with almost half the delegates being members of the Nationalist Party.

September 1. Troops loyal to Yuan Shikai retake Nanjing after overcoming strong resistance. This action signals the end of the 'Second Revolution'.

November 4. Yuan Shikai orders that the Nationalist Party be dissolved.

D. Appointments, Dismissals, etc.

October 6. Under pressure, the National Assembly elects Yuan Shikai as president of the

ROC. He is formally inaugurated on October 10.

F. Births and Deaths

March 22. Revolutionary leader Song Jiaoren dies after being shot by an assassin on March 20.

1914

A. Foreign Affairs Events

July 3. At the Simla Conference, which had opened on October 25, 1913, chaired by Sir A. H. McMahon, Britain and Tibet conclude the Simla Convention. Under it Britain recognizes the autonomy of Tibet. China never ratifies the Convention.

August 6. Yuan Shikai declares China's neutrality in World War I, which broke out on July 28.

September 2. Japan begins an invasion of Shandong province.

November 7. Japanese forces seize Qingdao, Shandong province, forcing the German garrison to surrender.

November 10. Germany formally hands Qingdao over to the Japanese.

B. Domestic Political Events

January 10. Yuan Shikai suspends both houses of the National Assembly.

E. Cultural and Social Events

February 7. Regulations for ceremonies to sacrifice to Heaven and commemorate Confucius are promulgated.

1915

A. Foreign Affairs Events

January 26. The Japanese Minister to Beijing, Hioki Eki, presents the Twenty-one Demands to the Chinese Ministry of Foreign Affairs.

May 25. The Sino-Japanese Treaties are signed, based on the Twenty-one Demands.

B. Domestic Political Events

December 31. Yuan Shikai orders that the following year be the first of the Hongxian reign period. The Presidential Palace is renamed the New China Palace. Both events signal Yuan Shikai's intention to ascend the throne as Emperor.

E. Cultural and Social Events

September 15. The radical journal *Youth Magazine (Qingnian zazhi)* begins publication, edited by Chen Duxiu. From September 1, 1916 it appears under the title *New Youth (Xin qingnian)*.

F. Births and Deaths

November 20. Hu Yaobang born.

1916

B. Domestic Political Events

March 22. Following a storm of domestic and international protest, Yuan Shikai abandons his plan to become Emperor.

June 20. Li Yuanhong restores the ROC Provisional Constitution of March 11, 1912.

August 1. The National Assembly, suspended in 1914, reconvenes.

D. Appointments, Dismissals, etc.

June 7. Li Yuanhong succeeds Yuan Shikai as president.

F. Births and Deaths

June 6. Yuan Shikai dies.

1917

A. Foreign Affairs Events

August 14. China declares war on Germany and Austria–Hungary.

B. Domestic Political, Military Events

September 10. Sun Yatsen sets up the ROC Military Government in Guangzhou.

October 6. Civil war breaks out between the Beijing and Guangzhou governments.

D. Appointments, Dismissals, etc.

July 1. Zhang Xun, Kang Youwei and others restore the former Manchu Emperor, Puyi, to the throne in Beijing, but he abdicates later the same month.

September 10. Sun Yatsen is inaugurated as Generalissimo of the ROC Military Government.

1918

A. Foreign Affairs Events

November 11. World War I ends.

B. Domestic Political Events

November 16. The Beijing government orders a truce in its civil war with the Guangzhou Military Government.

November 22. The Guangzhou Military Government orders a ceasefire.

C. Economic Events

September 28. Japan's series of large loans to China reaches a peak with the last of the 'Nishihara loans', three contracts, each for 20 million yen, signed by the Chinese Minister in Tokyo, Zhang Zongxiang, with a syndicate of Japanese banks.

D. Appointments, Dismissals, etc.

May 4. Sun Yatsen resigns as Generalissimo of the ROC Military Government in Guangzhou, signalling a warlord takeover of that government.

October 10. Xu Shichang is inaugurated as president of the Beijing government.

E. Cultural and Social Events

April 18. Mao Zedong and other revolutionaries set up the New People's Study Society in Changsha, Hunan province.

May 15. Lu Xun's short story *Diary of a Madman (Kuangren riji)* is published in *New Youth*.

1919 THE MAY FOURTH MOVEMENT

A. Foreign Affairs Events

April 30. At the Paris Peace Conference the major powers decide to accept Japan's demands for the transfer of all previous German interests in Shandong.

June 28. The Chinese delegation refuses to take part in the signing of the Treaty of Versailles that ends World War I.

July 25. The Soviet Assistant People's Commissar for Foreign Affairs, Leo Karakhan, issues the first 'Karakhan Manifesto', renouncing all territory seized by Russia from China under the Tsars, extraterritoriality and Boxer indemnity payments.

B. Domestic Political Events

May 4. Thousands of students demonstrate in Beijing against China's treatment by the Paris Peace Conference. The May Fourth Movement begins.

June 5. Workers strike in Shanghai in response to the arrest of many hundreds of students protesting against China's treatment at the Paris Peace Conference on June 3 and 4. The strike spreads to other cities, reaching a climax on June 10.

E. Cultural and Social Events

April 6. *Weekly Critic (Meizhou pinglun)* publishes 'The Manifesto of the Communist Party' ('Gongchan dang de xuanyan') by Marx and Engels.

F. Births and Deaths

November. Zhao Ziyang born in Henan province.

1920

A. Foreign Affairs Events

June 29. China joins the League of Nations.

September 27. The second Karakhan Manifesto is issued by Soviet Russia, renouncing extraterritoriality and other rights forced on China by the Tsars.

E. Cultural and Social Events

October 12. The British philosopher Bertrand Russell arrives in Shanghai for a lecture tour of China, which lasts about a year.

G. Natural Disasters

December 16. Earthquakes in Gansu and other parts of north China result in several hundred thousand casualties.

1921

B. Domestic Political Events

April 7. The Guangzhou National Assembly appoints Sun Yatsen as ROC president, adopts the ROC government organizational plan and determines to confront the Beijing regime headed by Xu Shichang.

D. Appointments, Dismissals, etc.

May 5. Sun Yatsen formally takes up the position of Extraordinary President of the ROC, with its capital in Guangzhou. His intention is to carry out a northern expedition to unite the country.

G. Natural Disasters

Drought-famine reaches a peak in north China, resulting in more than 500 000 deaths in this and the previous year.

1922

A. Foreign Affairs Events

February 4. China and Japan sign a treaty in Washington on the Shandong question.

February 6. The Washington Conference, which had begun on November 12, 1921, concludes with the signature of the Nine Power Treaty. Among provisions relating to China are respect for China's sovereignty and territorial integrity.

B. Domestic Political Events

February 3. Sun Yatsen orders the launching of the Northern Expedition to reunify the country. However, a conflict between Sun Yatsen and the warlord Governor of Guangdong, Chen Jiongming, aborts the Northern Expedition by the middle of the year and results in Sun's fleeing Guangzhou on August 9.

D. Appointments, Dismissals, etc.

June 11. Li Yuanhong again becomes president of the Beijing government.

E. Cultural and Social Events

January 13–March 5. The Hong Kong seamen's strike takes place.

May 1–6. The All-China Labour Federation holds its first congress in Guangzhou.

November 1. A presidential mandate promulgates a new education system, including the provision for four years' compulsory education.

1923

A. Foreign Affairs Events

January 26. Sun Yatsen and the Soviet representative, Adolf Joffe, issue a joint communiqué in Shanghai.

D. Appointments, Dismissals, etc.

March 2. Sun Yatsen becomes Generalissimo of a new government in Guangzhou.

March 17. Sun Yatsen appoints Chiang Kaishek as Chief-of-Staff of the Guangzhou government.

E. Cultural and Social Events

December 4–9. A major railway strike occurs on the Beijing–Hankou railway, but is put down by the army.

1924

A. Foreign Affairs Events

May 31. The Sino-Soviet Agreement is signed: China recognizes the Soviet Union, and the Soviet Union renounces extraterritoriality and the remainder of the Boxer indemnity.

November 26. The Great People's Assembly of the Mongolian People's Republic adopts a constitution which proclaims Mongolia as an independent People's Republic, not part of China.

B. Domestic Political Events

January 20–30. The First National Congress of the Nationalist Party takes place in Guangzhou, with Sun Yatsen in the chair.

1925

A. Foreign Affairs Events

June 24. The Ministry of Foreign Affairs of the Beijing government sends a note to the American, British and other foreign legations asking that China's treaty relations be put on an equitable basis.

B. Domestic Political Events

May 30. British official police fire on a demonstration in Shanghai, killing at least nine students and wounding and arresting many others. This 'May Thirtieth Incident' leads on to a series of strikes, demonstrations and disturbances, aimed at least in part against the British in China.

July 1. The National Government of the Republic of China (ROC) is formally established in Guangzhou.

F. Births and Deaths

March 12. Sun Yatsen dies in Beijing.

August 20. The National Government's Minister of Finance, Liao Zhongkai, is assassinated in Guangzhou.

1926

B. Domestic Political Events

January 1–19. The Second Congress of the Nationalist Party is held in Guangzhou.

March 20. Chiang Kaishek begins his campaign against the CCP with the '*Zhongshan* incident'. He arrests Li Zhilong, the captain of the *SS Zhongshan* and a member of the CCP, and captures the *Zhongshan*.

July 1. Chiang Kaishek orders the launching of the Northern Expedition to reunify the country.

D. Appointments, Dismissals, etc.

June 5. The National Government appoints Chiang Kaishek as Commander-in-Chief, National Revolutionary Army.

1927   CHIANG KAISHEK'S SHANGHAI COUP

A. Foreign Affairs Events

March 15. The British concessions in Hankou and Jiujiang are formally handed over to the Chinese.

December 14. The National Government breaks off diplomatic relations with the Soviet Union.

B. Domestic Political, Military Events

March 21. Shanghai workers begin armed revolution and a general strike. The next day they set up a workers' government.

March 22. The National Revolutionary Army enters Shanghai on its Northern Expedition.

April 12. Chiang Kaishek carries out an anti-CCP coup in Shanghai and begins a large-scale massacre of communists.

April 18. Chiang Kaishek establishes his National Government in Nanjing.

August 1. Ye Ting, Zhou Enlai and others lead a communist military uprising in Nanchang, Jiangxi province, and seize the city. August 1, 1927 is still regarded as the birthday of the Red Army because of this event. The CCP-led troops are forced to leave the city on August 5.

December 11–13. A CCP-led armed uprising in Guangzhou results in the setting up of a soviet government, the Guangzhou Commune. The uprising is suppressed with considerable bloodshed.

D. Appointments, Dismissals, etc.

August 7. A Chinese Communist Party Central Committee (CCPCC) meeting in Hankou dismisses Chen Duxiu as Secretary-General, replacing him with Qu Qiubai.

E. Cultural and Social Events

January 4–February 5. Mao Zedong undertakes an investigation into the peasant movement in several counties of Hunan province.

February 19–24. The All-China General Trade Union calls a general strike in Shanghai, one of many strikes which take place at about this time.

April 12. Chiang Kaishek orders attacks against Shanghai's trade unions. His troops disarm workers and suppress labour organizations and demonstrations, resulting in the death of many workers.

October 16. In Zhoukoudian, near Beijing, the first tooth of Beijing Man (*Sinanthropus pekinensis*) is discovered.

F. Births and Deaths

March 31. Kang Youwei dies.

April 28. CCP pioneer Li Dazhao is executed in Beijing.

1928

A. Foreign Affairs Events

May 3. Japanese troops fight against Chinese in Ji'nan, Shandong province. The event turns into a massacre, with heavy Chinese civilian and military casualties.

B. Domestic Political Events

June 6. The National Revolutionary Army's Northern Expedition seizes Beijing.

June 28. Beijing is renamed Beiping.

December 29. Zhang Xueliang, who has seized power in Manchuria in succession to his late father Zhang Zuolin, formally pledges loyalty to the National Government. This act signals the completion of the reunification of China, which Chiang Kaishek had aimed to achieve through the Northern Expedition.

C. Economic Events

November 1. The National Government's Central Bank of China opens in Shanghai.

D. Appointments, Dismissals, etc.

October 10. Chiang Kaishek is formally inaugurated as chairman of the National Government.

F. Births and Deaths

June 4. Manchurian warlord Zhang Zuolin is killed when his special train is blown up by Japanese agents on the way to Shenyang.

1929

A. Foreign Affairs Events

March 28. China and Japan sign an agreement on the Ji'nan incident of May 3, 1928. China promises to protect Japanese lives and property in China and Japan agrees to withdraw all troops within two months.

May 20. Japan completes the withdrawal of its troops from Shandong.

July 10. Chinese authorities in the north-east

seize the Chinese Eastern Railway from the Soviet Union.

December 22. China and the Soviet Union sign the Khabarovsk Protocol, under which the Chinese Eastern Railway is returned to the Soviet Union.

B. Domestic Political Events

March 15–28. The Third Congress of the Nationalist Party takes place in Nanjing.

D. Appointments, Dismissals, etc.

March 27. The Third National Congress of the Nationalist Party elects a Central Executive Committee including Chiang Kaishek, Hu Hanmin and Wang Jingwei.

E. Cultural and Social Events

February 1. The Nationalist Party's official *Central Daily (Zhongyang ribao)* begins publication in Nanjing.

December 2. Pei Wenzhong unearths the first Beijing Man skull at Zhoukoudian.

F. Births and Deaths

January 19. Liang Qichao dies.

1930

B. Domestic Political, Military Events

May 1. Chiang Kaishek declares war against warlords Feng Yuxiang and Yan Xishan.

July 27. CCP troops under Peng Dehuai take Changsha, capital of Hunan province.

August 5. Peng Dehuai's troops retreat from Changsha.

October 9. Chiang Kaishek's troops seize Luoyang in Henan province, winning the civil war against Feng Yuxiang and Yan Xishan.

C. Economic Events

October 20. The Chinese National Aviation Corporation begins an air service from Shanghai to Hankou.

D. Appointments, Dismissals, etc.

March 1. Wang Jingwei is expelled from the Nationalist Party.

E. Cultural and Social Events

March 2. The League of Left-Wing Writers is established in Shanghai.

G. Natural Disasters

The great drought-famine of 1928–30 in Gansu, Shaanxi, Shanxi, Henan and other parts of northern China reaches its height. Shaanxi and Gansu are worst affected, with a writer in the *Times Monthly (Shishi yuebao)* estimating deaths in Shaanxi alone at three million people.

1931

A. Foreign Affairs Events

September 18. Japanese troops occupy a Chinese barracks outside Shenyang, or Mukden: the Mukden Incident. They occupy Shenyang the following day. Further Japanese encroachments in Manchuria take place over the following months, and by the end of 1931 there are no major Chinese strongholds left in Manchuria.

B. Domestic Political Events

November 7. The Chinese Soviet Republic is established by the CCP with its capital in Ruijin, Jiangxi province.

D. Appointments, Dismissals, etc.

November 27. Mao Zedong is appointed as chairman of the government of the Chinese Soviet Republic.

E. Cultural and Social Events

March 15. *Singsong Girl Red Peony (Genü Hong Mudan)*, China's first cinema 'talkie', has its première.

F. Births and Deaths

November 19. Poet Xu Zhimo dies.

G. Natural Disasters

July 28. Catastrophic flooding occurs when the Yangzi River bursts its banks in Hankou. On August 19, the flood waters at Hankou reach their highest point since record-taking began in the 1860s.

1932

A. Foreign Affairs Events

January 28. Japanese forces attack Shanghai; they clash with Chinese troops and the Battle of Shanghai begins. Japanese withdrawal of all those troops taking part in the the Battle of Shanghai begins on May 6 and is completed by May 31.

April 15. The Chinese Soviet Republic formally declares war against Japan.

December 12. China and the Soviet Union announce resumption of diplomatic relations.

B. Domestic Political Events

March 9. The Japanese-sponsored state of Manzhouguo (Manchukuo), which claims independence from China, is formally set up in Manchuria, with its capital in Changchun, Jilin province.

D. Appointments, Dismissals, etc.

March 9. Former Emperor Puyi is inaugurated as Chief Executive of Manzhouguo.

E. Cultural and Social Events

November 1. The Ministry of Education lays down standard curricula for all kindergartens and schools throughout China.

1933

A. Foreign Affairs Events

February 24. The League of Nations Assembly resolves that its members shall refuse to recognize Manzhouguo. On March 27, Japan announces its withdrawal from the League because of its failure to recognize Manzhouguo.

May 31. Under the Tanggu Truce, the Japanese agree to withdraw to the Great Wall, but China relinquishes control of Heilongjiang, Jilin, Fengtian and Jehol provinces to Japan.

G. Natural Disasters

August 23. The Yellow River (Huanghe) bursts its dykes in Shandong, resulting in devastating floods.

1934

A. Foreign Affairs Events

April 17. Japan declares that it opposes all foreign technical, financial or military aid to China other than its own.

B. Domestic Political Events

October 16. As Chiang Kaishek's Fifth Encirclement Campaign closes in on Ruijin, the capital of the CCP's Chinese Soviet Republic, the Red Army's First Front Army, led by Mao Zedong and Zhu De, begins to move west on the Long March.

November 10. Troops of the Fifth Encirclement Campaign enter Ruijin.

D. Appointments, Dismissals, etc.

March 1. Puyi ascends the throne as Emperor of Manzhouguo in Changchun.

E. Cultural and Social Events

February 19. Chiang Kaishek launches his New Life Movement, to promote Confucian virtues.

G. Natural Disasters

August 31. A government statement reports fourteen provinces affected by serious drought and thirteen by floods, reflecting the worst combination of floods and drought for several decades.

1935

B. Domestic Political Events

October 20. Mao Zedong and his Red Army followers meet with the Fifteenth Red Army Corps in Wuqizhen, northern Shaanxi, ending the Long March.

C. Economic Events

November 3. The Ministry of Finance promulgates regulations to reform the monetary system.

E. Cultural and Social Events

April. Cao Yu's first and most famous drama, *Thunderstorm (Leiyu)*, is premiered in Tokyo. Completed in 1933, it was first published late in 1934 in the *Literary Quarterly (Wenxue jikan)* and as a book by

Shanghai's Cultural Life Press in January 1935.

December 9. Student demonstrations begin in Beiping, protesting against Japanese imperialism and the government's weakness in resisting it. Many students are arrested or wounded and one is killed. Demonstrations spread to other cities.

F. Births and Deaths

June 18. Former CCP head Qu Qiubai is executed at Nanchang, Jiangxi province.

July 6. The Fourteenth Dalai Lama is born.

July 17. The revolutionary musician Nie Er dies.

G. Natural Disasters

July. Devastating flooding occurs along the middle reaches of the Yangzi River and, in Shandong, along the Yellow River.

1936

A. Foreign Affairs Events

November 29. Italy recognizes Manzhouguo.

B. Domestic Political Events

December 12. The Xi'an Incident. Chiang Kaishek is captured by his generals, Yang Hucheng and Zhang Xueliang, who want an end to the civil war against the CCP and effective resistance to Japan.

Mid–late December. The CCP moves its headquarters to Yan'an in northern Shaanxi.

December 25. Chiang Kaishek is released, acknowledging the need to resist Japan.

C. Economic Events

September 1. The Guangzhou–Hankou railway opens to traffic.

E. Cultural and Social Events

Early in the year. Lao She's short novel *Camel Xiangzi (Luotuo Xiangzi)* is published in instalments in *Wind of the Universe (Yuzhou Feng)*.

F. Births and Deaths

October 19. Famous writer Lu Xun dies.

1937   OUTBREAK OF WAR AGAINST JAPAN

A. Foreign Affairs Events

July 7. Japanese soldiers fight Chinese troops near the Lugou (Marco Polo) Bridge outside Beiping. The action sparks the Sino-Japanese War. By the end of July, Beiping and Tianjin have fallen to the Japanese.

December 13. With the Japanese occupation of Nanjing, the rape of Nanjing, in which many thousands of people are killed, begins.

B. Domestic Political Events

August 22. As part of the policy of forming a united front against Japan, the CCP's Red Army is formally redesignated the Eighth Route Army of the National Army.

November 20. Chiang Kaishek's government formally announces the removal of its capital to Chongqing in inland Sichuan province.

E. Cultural and Social Events

April 1. The CCP's New China News Agency is established in Yan'an.

1938

A. Foreign Affairs Events

February 20. Germany recognizes Manzhouguo.

October 21. Guangzhou falls to the Japanese.

October 26. Wuhan falls to the Japanese.

B. Domestic Events

June 7. Nationalist troops burst Yellow River dykes near Zhengzhou, Henan province, to prevent the southern movement of Japanese troops. As a result, the river floods disastrously, drowning many people and causing incalculable damage. Flooding is so severe that the river changes course, but the dykes remain unrepaired due to the war.

November 12. In the false belief that the Japanese have occupied Changsha, capital of Hunan province, the authorities send people to set the city on fire. Over the next few days an enormous fire kills innumerable people and causes destruction all over the city.

C. Economic Events

December 2. The 'Burma Road' is completed from Kunming, capital of Yunnan province, to the Burmese border at Wanding.

1939

A. Foreign Affairs Events

June 16. The Sino-Soviet Commercial Treaty is concluded.

December 30. Wang Jingwei and the Japanese secretly initial terms on which Wang Jingwei will set up a central government subservient to Japan.

B. Domestic Political and Military Events

September 29–October 6. China wins the first Battle of Changsha.

E. Cultural and Social Events

December 8. Pope Pius XII lifts the ban preventing Chinese Catholics from taking part in ancestral rites and ceremonies in honour of Confucius.

December 21. Mao Zedong makes his speech 'In Memory of Norman Bethune'.

F. Births and Deaths

December 4. Wu Peifu dies in Beiping.

1940

A. Foreign Affairs Events

March 30. The United States Secretary of State, Cordell Hull, announces the refusal of the United States to recognize Wang Jingwei's government.

June 26–July 2. The Emperor of Manzhouguo, Puyi, visits Japan.

November 30. Japan recognizes the regime of Wang Jingwei. He signs a treaty with Japan which leaves the main power with Japan.

B. Domestic Political Events

March 30. Wang Jingwei's pro-Japanese government is formally established in Nanjing.

September 6. Chiang Kaishek's government for-

mally declares Chongqing as the wartime capital.

D. Appointments, Dismissals, etc.

February 22. The Fourteenth Dalai Lama is enthroned in Lhasa.

March 30. Wang Jingwei is inaugurated as head of the pro-Japanese government in Nanjing.

F. Births and Deaths

March 5. Cai Yuanpei dies in Hong Kong.

1941

A. Foreign Affairs Events

January 4–15. The Southern Anhui Incident inflicts great damage on the CCP's New Fourth Army and ends the united front between the CCP and the Nationalists.

July 1. Germany and Italy formally recognize the Japanese-sponsored government of Wang Jingwei. The next day, Chiang Kaishek's government breaks off diplomatic relations with Germany and Italy.

December 9. Chiang Kaishek's government declares war on Japan, Germany and Italy following the Japanese attack on Pearl Harbour on December 7.

December 25. The Japanese complete their occupation of Hong Kong.

B. Domestic Political and Military Events

September 7–October 8. China wins the second Battle of Changsha.

December 24. The third Battle of Changsha begins.

G. Natural Disasters

January. The Yellow River bursts its dykes in Henan, resulting in floods in Henan, Anhui and Jiangxi which affect millions of people.

1942

A. Foreign Affairs Events

January 1. China signs the Declaration of the United Nations in Washington.

June 2. China and the United States conclude the Sino-American Lend-Lease Agreement in Washington.

B. Domestic Political and Military Events

January 15. China wins the third Battle of Changsha.

D. Appointments, Dismissals, etc.

March 4. The American General Joseph Stilwell becomes Chief-of-Staff of the China theatre of war.

E. Cultural and Social Events

May 2 and 23. Mao Zedong makes two speeches to the Yan'an Forum on Literature and Art.

F. Births and Deaths

May 27. The former CCP leader Chen Duxiu dies in Sichuan.

1943

A. Foreign Affairs Events

January 9. Wang Jingwei's regime declares war against the United States and Britain.

January 11. Sino-American and Sino-British treaties provide for the abolition of extraterritoriality.

December 1. The Cairo Declaration is issued. It results from the Cairo Conference, for which Chiang Kaishek had been in Cairo from November 21 to December 1. The Declaration states that Manchuria and Taiwan will be restored to China after the war and that 'in due course Korea shall become free and independent'.

D. Appointments, Dismissals, etc.

March. Mao Zedong is elected chairman of the CCPCC's Politburo.

E. Cultural and Social Events

March 10. Chiang Kaishek's book *China's Destiny (Zhongguo zhi mingyun)* is published in Chongqing.

F. Births and Deaths

August 1. Lin Sen, chairman of Chiang Kaishek's government, dies in Chongqing.

September 27. Mao Zemin, Mao Zedong's younger brother, is executed for trying to overthrow Sheng Shicai, the chairman of Xinjiang.

G. Natural Disasters

Catastrophic drought-famine in Henan, Shaanxi, Hubei, Guangdong, Shandong, Sichuan and other provinces kills millions of people.

1944

A. Foreign Affairs Events

July 1–23. The United Nations Monetary and Financial Conference is held at Bretton Woods in the United States, with China participating. On July 19, China is named one of the directors of the proposed World Bank.

B. Domestic Political and Military Events

April 18. The Japanese attack the Yellow River's defences near Zhengzhou and thus begin a general offensive from north to south China, known as the Trans-Continental Offensive, which lasts until almost the end of 1944 and gives Japan effective control over a continuous railway from Vietnam to Korea.

June 18. Changsha falls to the Japanese in their Trans-Continental Offensive.

D. Appointments, Dismissals, etc.

October 19. Chiang Kaishek is informed of General Stilwell's recall from China, an action which Chiang himself had demanded.

F. Births and Deaths

November 10. Wang Jingwei dies in Japan.

1945   JAPAN SURRENDERS

A. Foreign Affairs Events

February 4–11. The Yalta Conference.

April 25. The United Nations Conference on International Organization opens in San Francisco, with China participating. On June 26, the participating nations, including China, sign the United Nations Charter.

August 14. The Sino-Soviet Treaty of Friendship and Alliance is signed in Moscow.

B. Domestic Political and Military Events

August 9. An enormous Soviet force enters Manchuria.

September 9. The Japanese surrender in the China theatre is formally accepted in Nanjing.

C. Economic Events

January 23. Formal inauguration of the Chinese National Relief and Rehabilitation Administration.

E. Cultural and Social Events

April. Premiere of the revolutionary opera *The White-Haired Girl (Baimao nü)* in Yan'an.

November 25 and following days. Students of the South-west Associated University in Kunming, Yunnan, demonstrate against civil war and hold a strike. On December 1, about 400 armed agents and police raid the university, killing four students and wounding more than ten. Two leaders of the raiding party are executed on December 11.

F. Births and Deaths

September 17. Writer Yu Dafu is killed by Japanese police.

October 30. Composer Xian Xinghai dies in Moscow.

1946

A. Foreign Affairs Events

January 5. Chiang Kaishek's government formally recognizes the independence of Outer Mongolia.

May 3. Apart from Lüda, Soviet troops complete their withdrawal from the north-eastern provinces of China.

November 4. A Sino-American Treaty of Friendship, Commerce and Navigation is signed.

B. Domestic Political and Military Events

May 1. The CCP's armed forces are formally designated as the People's Liberation Army (PLA).

May 5. The national capital is formally transferred from Chongqing back to Nanjing.

June 26. The launching of an offensive by Chiang Kaishek's forces against CCP-held areas in Hubei and Henan signals the outbreak of civil war between the Guomindang and the CCP.

December 25. The Constitution of the Republic of China is adopted.

E. Cultural and Social Events

October 1. The CCP's first film studio, the Northeast Film Studio, is formally established in Xingshan, Heilongjiang.

December 24. A Beijing University student is raped by a group of American soldiers. This results in student demonstrations against the United States throughout China for about a month.

F. Births and Deaths

July 15. Wen Yiduo, writer and Democratic League leader, is assassinated in Kunming.

G. Natural Disasters

A *Liberation Daily* report claims that a major famine in Hunan has killed four million people through starvation and resultant disease.

1947

B. Domestic Political and Military Events

March 19. Guomindang forces take Yan'an, the CCP headquarters.

May 13. PLA troops under Lin Biao launch a large-scale offensive in the north-east provinces.

June 30. A large PLA force commanded by Liu Bocheng crosses the Yellow River in Shandong to the south-west, beginning a nationwide offensive.

C. Economic Events

May 2–9. Rice riots break out in many cities; serious food shortages have resulted from galloping inflation.

March 15. Repair work on the Yellow River dykes is completed. As a result, the Yellow River changes back to its pre-1938 course. (See *B. Domestic Events,* June 7, 1938).

E. Cultural and Social Events

May 4. A new student–worker movement begins in Shanghai, spreading quickly throughout the country. It protests against hunger, high prices, persecution and civil war.

1948

A. Foreign Affairs Events

April 2. The American Congress passes the *China Aid Act*, which grants US$338 million to China.

B. Domestic Political and Military Events

May 1. The CCP calls for the Political Consultative Conference to be convened.

September 12. The PLA launches the Liaoxi–Shenyang campaign in the northeast under Lin Biao; it is the first of the three main campaigns of the War of Liberation. The campaign ends on November 2 with the capture of Shenyang.

November 6. The PLA under Chen Yi launches the Huaihai campaign, the second of the three main campaigns of the War of Liberation.

November 29. The PLA under Lin Biao and others begins its third main campaign of the War of Liberation, the Beiping–Tianjin campaign.

C. Economic Events

August 19. Chiang Kaishek promulgates the Financial and Economy Emergency Discipline Regulations, an unsuccessful attempt to control runaway inflation.

E. Cultural and Social Events

June 15. *People's Daily (Renmin ribao)* begins publication in Shijiazhuang.

F. Births and Deaths

September 1. Feng Yuxiang dies near Odessa, in the Soviet Union.

1949   DEFEAT OF THE GUOMINDANG; MAO AND THE CCP ASSUME POWER

A. Foreign Affairs Events

July 1. Mao Zedong declares in his 'On the People's Democratic Dictatorship' ('Lun renmin minzhu zhuanzheng'), published on this day, that China will 'lean to one side', that of the Soviet Union.

August 5. The United States State Department publishes its China White Paper, *United States Relations with China*, in Washington.

December 16. Mao Zedong arrives in Moscow and meets Stalin on his first trip outside China.

B. Domestic Political and Military Events

January 10. The Huaihai campaign ends in a PLA victory.

January 15. Tianjin falls to the PLA.

January 31. The PLA peacefully takes over Beiping, concluding the Tianjin–Beiping campaign.

April 23. Chiang Kaishek's capital, Nanjing, falls to the PLA.

May 27. Shanghai falls to the PLA.

September 21–30. The Chinese People's Political Consultative Conference (CPPCC) takes place in Beiping/Beijing. On September 27, it renames Beiping 'Beijing' and declares it China's capital. On September 29 it adopts the Common Programme, a provisional constitution which stipulates the policies of the Central People's Government (CPG).

October 1. The People's Republic of China (PRC) is formally established.

C. Economic Events

December 21–30. Beijing hosts a National Agricultural Production Conference to make plans for the following year.

D. Appointments, Dismissals, etc.

August 27. Gao Gang is inaugurated as chairman

of the North-east People's Government, established the same day.

September 30. The CPPCC elects Mao Zedong as chairman of the CPG.

October 1. The CPG Council, at its first meeting, appoints Zhou Enlai as the CPG's premier of the Government Administrative Council and Minister of Foreign Affairs, Mao Zedong as chairman of the CPG's Revolutionary Military Affairs Committee, and Zhu De as commander-in-chief of the PLA.

E. Cultural and Social Events

March 15. *People's Daily* formally moves to Beiping.

Spring. Socialist China's first feature film *Bridge (Qiao)* is released from the North-east Film Studio, being among a series of eight feature films with revolutionary content produced by that studio between August 1948 and June 1949.

March 24–April 3. The first National Women's Congress takes place in Beiping.

April 1. Military police beat up students taking part in a demonstration in Nanjing, killing two and injuring over 100.

June 16. *Guangming Daily (Guangming ribao)* begins publication.

July 2–19. The first National Congress of Literature and Art Workers takes place in Beiping, and establishes the Federation of Literature and Art Circles of China.

October. The periodical *People's Literature (Renmin wenxue)* begins publication.

October 5. The Sino-Soviet Friendship Association is established with Liu Shaoqi as president.

November 15. The *New China Monthly (Xinhua yuebao)* begins publication in Beijing.

1950

A. Foreign Affairs Events

February 14. The Sino-Soviet Treaty of Friendship, Alliance and Mutual Assistance is signed in Moscow.

March 4. Mao Zedong arrives back in Beijing from Moscow.

June 28. Mao Zedong denounces the United States for aggression in Korea, where war had broken out on June 25, and in Taiwan.

October 25. The Chinese People's Volunteers publicly enter Korea in support of the troops of the Democratic People's Republic of Korea (DPRK).

December 28. The CPG orders the appropriation of all United States property and the freezing of all American assets in China.

B. Domestic Political and Military Events

October 19. PLA forces take Changdu, in Xikang, as they advance towards Tibet.

October 30. In a note to India, China states that 'Tibet is an integral part of Chinese territory' and that the Tibetan problem is a 'domestic problem' for China.

C. Economic Events

March 22. The CPG orders that the Bank of China be brought under the control of the People's Bank.

E. Cultural and Social Events

January 1. The English-language fortnightly *People's China* begins publication in Beijing.

March. The North-east Film Studio issues the film *The White-Haired Girl (Baimao nü)*, based on the song opera of the same name.

April 2. The Central Drama Institute (*Zhongyang xiju xueyuan*) is formally set up.

April 4. The Central Conservatorium of Music (*Zhongyang yinyue xueyuan*) is set up.

May 1. The CPG promulgates the *Marriage Law of the PRC*.

June 29. The CPG promulgates the *Trade Union Law of the PRC*.

June 30. The CPG promulgates the *Agrarian Reform Law of the PRC*.

1951

A. Foreign Affairs Events

January 4. Chinese People's Volunteers and DPRK troops take Seoul.

February 1. The UN General Assembly condemns China as an aggressor in Korea.

B. Domestic Political Events

May 23. The Agreement of the CPG and the Local Government of Tibet on Measures for the Liberation of Tibet is signed in Beijing. It recognizes Tibet as part of the PRC, but gives the Tibetans the right to regional autonomy.

October 24. The Dalai Lama cables Mao Zedong, signifying his support for the May 23 Agreement.

D. Appointments, Dismissals, etc.

February 28. Peng Zhen is made Mayor of Beijing.

E. Cultural and Social Events

February 26. The CPG promulgates the Labour Insurance Regulations of the PRC.

October 12. Volume I of *The Selected Works of Mao Zedong (Mao Zedong xuanji)* is published in Beijing.

Autumn. The English-language periodical *Chinese Literature* begins publication in Beijing.

F. Births and Deaths

May. Mao Zedong's son Mao Anying is killed in the Korean War.

1952

A. Foreign Affairs Events

March 8. Zhou Enlai denounces the United States for intrusions by its aircraft in China's air space and for using germ warfare in northeast China.

December 31. The transfer of the Chinese Changchun railway by the Soviet Union to China is formally completed.

B. Domestic Political Events

January 1. Mao Zedong calls for struggle against corruption, waste and bureaucratism (the Three-Antis Movement).

February 1. The CPG launches the Five-Antis Movement against five types of corruption.

June 15. The *People's Daily* announces the 'victorious completion' of the Five-Antis Movement. The Three-Antis Movement also ends soon afterwards.

C. Economic Events

September 29. The long-projected Longhai railway, linking Jiangsu with Lanzhou, capital of Gansu province, opens to traffic.

December 24. Zhou Enlai announces that a Five-year Plan will begin in 1953.

D. Appointments, Dismissals, etc.

October 10. Gao Gang is appointed chairman of the newly established State Planning Commission.

E. Cultural and Social Events

July 5. The New China News Agency (NCNA) announces the virtual completion of land reform.

October 6–November 14. The First National Festival of Classical and Folk Drama is held in Beijing.

1953

A. Foreign Affairs Events

July 27. The Korean armistice is signed.

B. Domestic Political Events

March 1. Mao Zedong promulgates the *Electoral Law of the PRC*.

C. Economic Events

January 1. A *People's Daily* editorial announces the beginning of the First Five-year Plan as one of the tasks for 1953.

June 30–July 1. The PRC's first census is taken.

December 16. The CCPCC adopts a resolution in favour of developing Agricultural Producers' Co operatives.

E. Cultural and Social Events

May 30–June 3. The inaugural Conference of the Chinese Buddhist Association.

August 21–October 6. The Chinese Youth and Children Corps is renamed the Chinese Young Pioneers.

September 23–October 6. Second National Congress of Literature and Art Workers.

F. Births and Deaths

September 26. Painter Xu Beihong dies.

1954

A. Foreign Affairs Events

April 20–August 1. Premier Zhou Enlai visits many countries in Europe and Asia for various diplomatic purposes.

June 28. In India, Zhou Enlai and Indian Prime Minister Jawaharlal Nehru agree to the five principles of peaceful co-existence in a joint communiqué.

July 21. In Geneva, China's representative Zhou Enlai agrees to the Final Declaration of the Geneva Conference on Indochina.

October 12. A visiting Soviet delegation, led by Party First Secretary Nikita Khrushchev, and CPG leaders issue several joint communiqués, including one that the Soviet Union will withdraw all its troops from Lüshun before May 31, 1955.

October 19–30. Indian Prime Minister Nehru visits China.

C. Economic Events

January 31. Formal inauguration of direct Beijing–Moscow passenger rail service.

June 3. Direct passenger rail service from Beijing to Pyongyang, capital of the DPRK, begins.

December 25. Ceremonies mark the formal opening to traffic of the Qinghai–Tibet and Xikang–Tibet highways, linking Lhasa with Xining and Yaan respectively.

D. Appointments, Dismissals, etc.

March 31. Gao Gang and Rao Shushi are expelled

from the CCP and dismissed from all posts.

September 27. The First NPC elects Mao Zedong as chairman of the PRC and Liu Shaoqi as chairman of the NPC's Standing Committee; it also approves Mao's recommendation to appoint Zhou Enlai premier of the State Council.

E. Cultural and Social Events

December 31. Mao Zedong has regulations proclaimed setting up urban residents' committees and street offices.

F. Births and Deaths

Spring. Gao Gang commits suicide.

G. Natural Disasters

August 4. NCNA reports the level of the Yangzi River at Wuhan to be even higher than in 1931, an indication of extremely severe flooding.

1955

A. Foreign Affairs Events

April 18–24. Zhou Enlai heads the Chinese delegation at the Afro-Asian Conference held in Bandung, Indonesia, addressing the plenary session on April 19.

April 22. The Sino-Indonesian Treaty Concerning the Question of Dual Nationality is signed in Bandung.

August 1. Sino-American talks at ambassadorial level begin in Geneva.

B. Domestic Political and Military Events

February 26. PLA troops capture the Nanjishan Islands, thus completing the liberation of a series of islands off the coast of Zhejiang.

C. Economic Events

March 1. The People's Bank begins issuing a new people's currency at the rate of 10 000 old to one new yuan. The bank announces the completion of the changeover on June 10.

July 30. The NPC adopts the First Five-year Plan for the Development of the National Economy (1953–57).

D. Appointments, Dismissals, etc.

March 9. The Dalai Lama is appointed chairman

of the Preparatory Committee for the Tibetan Autonomous Region.

May 25. Writer and poet Hu Feng is expelled from all posts in literature and art circles for bourgeois and idealist thinking on literature and art.

October 1. Saifudin is appointed chairman of the Xinjiang Uygur Autonomous Region, set up on this day at a ceremony in Ürümqi.

E. Cultural and Social Events

January 10. The Peking Opera Company of China is formally set up.

May 1. Newspapers in Beijing and Tianjin begin to use the first batch of simplified characters.

July 18. Hu Feng is arrested as a counter-revolutionary.

December. The first volume of Lenin's complete works, *Liening quanji,* is published; the remaining thirty-seven volumes follow by 1959.

F. Births and Deaths

August 29. Dramatist Hong Shen dies.

1956

A. Foreign Affairs Events

February 25. At a closed session of the Twentieth Congress of the Communist Party of the Soviet Union, Khrushchev criticizes Stalin, denouncing the personality cult.

September 30–October 14. Indonesian President Sukarno visits the PRC.

November 1. The Chinese government issues a statement denouncing British and French aggression against Egypt.

November 6. Zhou Enlai cables congratulations and support to Janos Kadar. Soviet troops had just entered Hungary and Budapest to replace the government of Imre Nagy with that of Kadar.

B. Domestic Political Events

April 25. Mao Zedong makes his speech 'On the Ten Major Relationships'.

C. Economic Events

March 17. Mao Zedong orders that the Model Regulations for the Agricultural Producers' Co-operatives be promulgated.

July 13. The 668 km Baoji–Chengdu railway, linking north-west and south-west China, is formally inaugurated.

D. Appointments, Dismissals, etc.

September 26. The Eighth Congress of the CCP elects the Eighth CCPCC, including Mao Zedong as chairman.

September 28. The First Plenum of the Eighth CCPCC elects Liu Shaoqi, Zhou Enlai, Zhu De and Chen Yun as deputy chairmen of the CCPCC, and Deng Xiaoping as secretary-general.

E. Cultural and Social Events

January 1. The *Liberation Army Daily (Jiefang jun bao)* begins publication.

May 2. Mao Zedong calls for greater artistic and academic freedom with the slogan 'let a hundred flowers bloom, and a hundred schools of thought contend'.

October. The magazine *Chinese Cinema (Zhongguo dianying)* begins publication.

G. Natural Disasters

Late May–early June. Severe flooding strikes Henan, Anhui and Jiangsu.

1957

A. Foreign Affairs Events

October 15. Sino-Soviet Agreement on New Technology for National Defence. According to a Chinese statement of August 15, 1963, the Soviet Union had promised China a sample atomic bomb under this agreement.

November 2–21. Mao Zedong heads a Chinese delegation to the Soviet Union. On November 17, Mao Zedong declares in Moscow that 'the east wind is prevailing over the west wind'.

B. Domestic Political Events

February 27. Mao Zedong makes his speech 'On

the Correct Handling of Contradictions among the People'.

May 1–June 7. Open criticisms of the CCP reach their height in the period of the 'Hundred Flowers'.

June 8. An editorial in the *People's Daily* states that rightists are trying to overthrow the CCP. This signals the end of the Hundred Flowers Movement and the beginning of an Anti-Rightist Campaign.

C. Economic Events

October 15. The road–railway bridge over the Yangzi River at Wuhan is formally opened. The bridge links the Beijing–Wuhan and Wuhan–Guangzhou lines, creating the Beijing–Guangzhou railway.

E. Cultural and Social Events

January. The periodical *Poetry (Shikan)* begins publication.

May 15. The Ministry of Public Health issues directives in favour of contraception, and relaxing the limitations on sterilization and abortion operations.

July. The literary periodical *Harvest (Shouhuo)* begins publication.

July 15–August 2. A conference establishes the Chinese Catholic Patriotic Association. It recognizes the Pope's authority in religious matters, but not over political issues.

December. The novel *Keep the Red Flag Flying (Hongqi pu)* by Liang Bin is published.

December 2–12. The Eighth All-China Labour Congress is held in Beijing.

F. Births and Deaths

September 16. Painter Qi Baishi dies in Beijing.

1958   THE GREAT LEAP FORWARD

A. Foreign Affairs Events

July 31–August 3. Nikita Khrushchev, First Secretary of the Communist Party of the Soviet Union, visits China. On the last day he and Mao Zedong issue a joint communiqué expressing unanimity on all matters, but making no mention of Taiwan.

October 6. The Chinese announce the suspension of the bombardment of the offshore island of Quemoy, begun on August 23.

October 26. The Chinese People's Volunteers complete their withdrawal from Korea.

B. Domestic Political Events

March 5. The Guangxi Zhuang autonomous region is established.

April 29. The Sputnik Federated Co-operative, China's first people's commune, is established in Henan province.

May 5–23. The Second Session of the Eighth Congress of the CCP endorses the Great Leap Forward.

August 29. An enlarged conference of the CCPCC's Politburo, the Beidaihe Conference, adopts a decision in favour of establishing people's communes in the countryside. In less than two months, all rural China has been organized into 26 000 communes.

October 25. The Ningxia Hui autonomous region is established.

November 28–December 10. The Sixth Plenum of the Eighth CCPCC, held in Wuchang, reverses some of the most radical policies of the Great Leap Forward.

C. Economic Events

January 1. The Second Five-year Plan (1958–62) moves into operation, but is overtaken and superseded by the Great Leap Forward.

D. Appointments, Dismissals, etc.

February 11. Mao Zedong appoints Chen Yi as Foreign Minister, replacing Zhou Enlai.

E. Cultural and Social Events

January. The novel *The Song of Youth (Qingchun zhi ge)* by Yang Mo is published.

March. Tian Han's spoken drama *Guan Hanqing* is published in the periodical *Play-Scripts (Juben)*.

March 4. *Peking Review* begins publication.

June 1. *Red Flag (Hongqi)* begins publication.

June 29. Pope Pius XII issues the encyclical *Ad Apostolorum Principis*, in which he condemns the Church of the Catholic Patriotic Association and declares its bishops invalid.

September 2. Beijing Television begins broadcasting.

F. Births and Deaths

March 9. Peking Opera performer Cheng Yanqiu dies.

October 17. Chinese literature specialist Zheng Zhenduo dies in an aircraft accident.

1959

A. Foreign Affairs Events

February 9–12. Ho Chi Minh, president of the Democratic Republic of Vietnam, visits Beijing.

October 21. An armed clash between Chinese and Indian border guards on their mutual border in Ladakh results in casualties on both sides.

B. Domestic Political Events

March. On March 10, armed rebellion begins against the Chinese government in Lhasa. By March 23, the revolt is suppressed in Lhasa, and on March 31, the Dalai Lama enters India.

April 28. The First Session of the Second National People's Congress (NPC) directs that democratic reforms be carried out in Tibet.

June 5. The International Commission of Jurists issues a statement in Geneva that 'deliberate violation of fundamental human rights' has taken place in Tibet.

C. Economic Events

February 7. The Guizhou–Guangxi railway, linking Guiyang to Liuzhou, opens to traffic.

November 1. The Luoyang Tractor Plant, China's first such factory, is completed.

D. Appointments, Dismissals, etc.

March 28. The State Council appoints the Bainqen (Panchen) Lama to chair the Preparatory Committee for the Tibetan autonomous region.

April 27. The NPC appoints Liu Shaoqi as president of the PRC in succession to Mao Zedong, with Song Qingling and Dong Biwu as deputies.

August 16. The Lushan Plenum dismisses Peng Dehuai.

September 17. President Liu Shaoqi proclaims the appointment of Lin Biao as Minister of National Defence (replacing Peng Dehuai).

E. Cultural and Social Events

September. The Guangdong People's Press publishes Ouyang Shan's novel *Three Family Lane (Sanjia xiang)*.

September 9–October 3. The PRC's First National Games take place.

G. Natural Disasters

June. Serious flooding occurs in Guangdong.

July–August. Extremely serious drought reaches a peak in vast areas of China, affecting about 30 per cent of China's land under cultivation.

1960

A. Foreign Affairs Events

April 16. An exchange of polemics between China and the Soviet Union begins with an article in *Red Flag* warning against changing Lenin's notion of the nature of imperialism.

April 25. In New Delhi, Zhou Enlai and Indian Prime Minister Nehru sign a joint communiqué that both governments should study problems on their mutual border.

May 31. In Ulan Bator, Zhou Enlai and Mongolian Prime Minister Y. Tsedenbal sign the Sino-Mongolian Treaty of Friendship and Mutual Assistance.

July 16. The Soviet Union notifies China of its decision to withdraw all its experts from China within a month.

October 1. In Beijing, Burmese Prime Minister U Nu and Zhou Enlai sign the Sino-Burmese Boundary Treaty.

December 19. The Sino-Cambodian Treaty of

Friendship and Mutual Non-aggression is signed in Beijing.

C. Economic Events

April 21. The double-track railway bridge over the Yellow River at Zhengzhou, Henan province, is formally opened to traffic.

E. Cultural and Social Events

March 17. The Catholic Bishop of Shanghai, Gong Pinmei, is sentenced to life imprisonment.

May 25. Chinese mountaineers reach the summit of Mt Everest (Jomo Lungma) for the first time.

F. Births and Deaths

May 23. Former Shanxi warlord Yan Xishan dies.

May 29. Politburo member Lin Boqu dies.

G. Natural Disasters

December 29. NCNA claims the 1960 natural disasters—drought, floods, typhoons and insect pests—as the worst for a century. It claims that over half China's total farmland has been affected and states that only Tibet and Xinjiang have escaped the disasters. Widespread and extremely serious famine results.

1961

A. Foreign Affairs Events

April 1. The Sino-Indonesian Treaty of Friendship is signed in Jakarta.

May 16. At the fourteen-nation Geneva Conference on Laos, Foreign Minister Chen Yi demands the abolition of the South-east Asian Treaty Organization.

June 13–15. Indonesian President Sukarno visits China, and ratification of the Sino-Indonesian Treaty of Friendship is exchanged on June 14.

July 11. In Beijing, Zhou Enlai and Kim Il Sung sign the Sino-Korean Treaty of Friendship, Co-operation and Mutual Assistance.

October 5. In Beijing, Liu Shaoqi and King Mahendra Bir Bikram Shah Deva of Nepal sign the Sino-Nepalese Boundary Treaty.

October 19. At the Twenty-second Congress of the Communist Party of the Soviet Union in Moscow, Zhou Enlai defends Albania, publicly censured by Khrushchev two days earlier.

December 15. The United Nations General Assembly adopts a resolution that the PRC's admission should be regarded as an 'important question' requiring a two-thirds majority. China denounces the resolution on December 21.

E. Cultural and Social Events

January 9. The original version of Wu Han's play, *Hai Rui's Dismissal (Hai Rui baguan)*, is published in the periodical *Beijing Literature and Art (Beijing wenyi)*.

April 4–14. The Twenty-sixth World Table Tennis Championships take place in Beijing, with Chinese players winning both the men's and women's singles titles.

July 1. The Museum of Chinese History and the Museum of the Chinese Revolution are both opened in the same building in the centre of Beijing.

December. China Youth Press publishes the novel *Red Crag (Hong yan)* by Luo Guangbin and Yan Yiyan.

F. Births and Deaths

August 8. Peking Opera performer Mei Lanfang dies.

G. Natural Disasters

March 6. A spokesman for the Central Meteorological Bureau claims that the 1959–60 drought was among the worst in more than three centuries, and the worst since 1877. Meanwhile, drought persists in Shandong, Henan, Hebei, Shanxi and Shaanxi, and floods ravage Guangdong, Fujian, Zhejiang and Jiangxi, causing widespread and serious continuing famine, resulting in the death of millions from starvation.

1962

A. Foreign Affairs Events

July 23. In Geneva, China, the Soviet Union, the

United States, Britain and other states sign the Declaration on the Neutrality of Laos.

October 11. A serious clash occurs at Tseng Jong on the Sino-Indian border. The next day Nehru states that he has instructed the Indian army to free Indian territory of Chinese troops.

October 20. Chinese troops launch major offensives on the Sino-Indian border.

November 9. In Beijing, Liao Chengzhi and Takasaki Tatsunosuke sign a memorandum for long-term and comprehensive trade between China and Japan: the Liao–Takasaki memorandum. Trade established through this memorandum is later known as 'L–T trade'.

November 20. China declares a unilateral ceasefire in the Sino-Indian war and announces that its troops will withdraw behind the 'line of actual control' as of November 1959.

December 26. The Sino-Mongolian Boundary Treaty is signed in Beijing.

B. Domestic Political Events

September 24. Mao Zedong makes a speech at the Eighth CCPCC's Tenth Plenum, calling for greater emphasis on class struggle. The plenum marks the beginning of the Socialist Education Movement.

E. Cultural and Social Events

January 6–19. The Chinese Catholic Patriotic Association holds its Second National Conference, at which it determines 'to shake off the control of the Vatican'.

August. The People's Literary Press publishes the last of fourteen volumes of *Ba Jin's Collected Works (Ba Jin wenji)*, the first having been released in March 1958. Deng Tuo's *Evening Talks at Yanshan (Yanshan yehua)*, a collection of essays originally appearing in three Beijing newspapers from March 1961 to September 1962, is published in four volumes.

F. Births and Deaths

February 24. Hu Shi dies.

September 21. Actor and dramatist Ouyang Yuqian dies.

1963

A. Foreign Affairs Events

May 16. In Hanoi, Liu Shaoqi and Ho Chi Minh sign a joint statement which includes an attack on revisionism and calls for struggle against 'imperialism headed by the United States'.

June 14. The CCP writes a long and strongly anti-Soviet and anti-revisionist letter to the Soviet Communist Party on the 'general line of the international Communist movement'.

July 5. Sino-Soviet talks open in Moscow in an unsuccessful attempt to resolve the bilateral differences. Deng Xiaoping and Peng Zhen lead the Chinese delegation.

July 31. The Chinese government issues a statement supporting the total destruction of nuclear weapons and denouncing the Partial Nuclear Test Ban Treaty, initialled on July 25.

November 22. The Sino-Afghan Boundary Treaty is signed in Beijing.

December 14–31. Zhou Enlai and Chen Yi visit the United Arab Republic, Algeria and Morocco in a large-scale African tour.

B. Domestic Political Events

May 20. A Central Work Conference held in Hangzhou issues the 'First Ten Points'. Drafted by Mao Zedong and stressing class struggle, the action is designed to give impetus to the Rural Socialist Education Movement in the countryside.

September. The CCPCC issues the Later Ten Points on the Socialist Education Movement in the countryside, drafted by Peng Zhen.

E. Cultural and Social Events

April 3–26. A meeting of heads of CCP Cultural Bureaux discusses the content of dramas and literary works. A circular by Jiang Qing 'on Suspending the Performance of

Ghost Plays' is distributed, calling for the banning of traditional drama.

December. The People's Literary Press publishes *Poems of Chairman Mao (Mao zhuxi shici)*.

F. Births and Deaths

August 9. Economist Ji Chaoding dies.

1964

A. Foreign Affairs Events

January 9. Zhou Enlai and Chen Yi arrive in Tunis from Albania to continue their large-scale African tour. They visit Tunisia, Ghana, Mali, Guinea, Sudan, Ethiopia and Somalia, leaving on February 4.

August 6. The Chinese government protests against the United States' bombing of northern Vietnam the day before and denounces the United States for fabricating the Tongking Gulf incidents of August 2 and 4. It states that aggression against Vietnam is equivalent to aggression against China.

April 29. The inaugural flight of the Pakistan International Airline to China lands in Shanghai.

B. Domestic Political Events

February 1. *People's Daily* launches a campaign to 'learn from the PLA'.

September 10. The 'Revised Later Ten Points' are issued, ushering in a new phase in the Rural Socialist Education Movement.

October 16. China carries out her first nuclear test; the Chinese government declares that China will never be the first to use nuclear weapons.

December 21–January 4, 1965. The First Session of the Third NPC is held in Beijing.

E. Cultural and Social Events

June 5–July 31. The Festival of Peking Operas on Contemporary Themes is held in Beijing.

September. The first part of *Bright Sunny Skies (Yanyang tian)*, a novel by Haoran, is published in Beijing, with the second part following in March 1966.

October 2. *The East is Red (Dongfang hong)*, a

'large-scale historical poem with music and dancing', is premiered in Beijing.

1965

A. Foreign Affairs Events

February 11. Soviet Prime Minister Aleksei Kosygin meets Mao Zedong and Liu Shaoqi when he visits Beijing on his return trip from Hanoi to Moscow.

March 12. The Chinese government denounces the arrival of American marines in Vietnam on March 8 and 9.

June 2–8. Zhou Enlai visits Pakistan and Tanzania. On June 5, he declares in Dar-es-Salaam that Africa, Asia and Latin America are ripe for revolution.

June 19. Zhou Enlai and Chen Yi arrive in Cairo on their way to attend the Second Afro-Asian Conference. This was to start in Algiers on June 29, but never took place because of a change of government in Algiers.

November 4. The PRC Embassy in Jakarta protests over a raid on the Chinese consulate in Medan the day before and the persecution of Chinese in Indonesia in general. This was the first of many such protests by the PRC Embassy and signalled a drastic decline in Sino-Indonesian relations since the coup of October 1 which brought Suharto and the army to power.

B. Domestic Political Events

January 14. A Central Work Conference held by the Politburo of the CCP's Central Committee adopts 'The Twenty-three Articles on the Socialist Education Movement'.

May 14. China carries out a second atomic explosion.

September 3. *Red Flag* publishes Lin Biao's article 'Long Live the Victory of the People's War' to commemorate the twentieth anniversary of the War of Resistance against Japan.

September 9. The Tibetan autonomous region is formally established.

D. Appointments, Dismissals, etc.

September 8. Ngapo Ngawang Jigme is elected chairman of the Tibetan autonomous region.

E. Cultural and Social Events

June 1. The decision abolishing ranks in the PLA comes into effect.

June 26. Mao Zedong issues an instruction to put stress on the rural areas in the field of medical and health work.

November 10. In the Shanghai newspaper *Wenhui bao,* Yao Wenyuan denounces Wu Han's drama *Hai Rui's Dismissal* as an anti-Party poisonous weed. The article leads on to fierce denunciations in the press of this and other literary works in the following months.

December. Jin Jingmai's novel *The Song of Ouyang Hai (Ouyang Hai zhi ge)* is published in Beijing.

F. Births and Deaths

April 9. Vice-premier Ke Qingshi dies.

June 18. Musician An Bo dies.

December 21. Educationalist Huang Yanpei dies.

1966   OUTBREAK OF THE CULTURAL REVOLUTION

A. Foreign Affairs Events

February 24. Ghanaian President K. Nkrumah is overthrown the same day as he begins a visit to China. The event signals a deterioration in relations between China and Ghana, the most important of several African countries to split with China in 1966.

April 15. A large-scale anti-Chinese demonstration takes place at the Chinese Embassy in Jakarta, with demonstrators ransacking the building.

B. Domestic Political Events

May 7. Mao Zedong writes to Lin Biao calling on the PLA to be 'a great school': the May 7 directive.

May 9. China carries out a nuclear test, its first containing thermonuclear material.

May 16. The Politburo announces its decision to set up the Cultural Revolution Group, and calls for attacks on 'all representatives of the bourgeoisie who have infiltrated the Party, government, army and cultural world'.

July 16. Surrounded by enormous publicity, Mao Zedong takes a swim in the Yangzi River at Wuhan, confounding speculation that he is ill and signifying his willingness to take a lead in the Cultural Revolution.

August 8. The Eleventh Plenum of the Eighth CCPCC adopts its Sixteen Points, a decision in favour of the Cultural Revolution.

August 18. Mao Zedong, Lin Biao, Zhou Enlai and others preside over a gigantic rally in support of the Cultural Revolution in Tiananmen Square in the centre of Beijing. The rally reveals the existence of the Red Guards, the vanguard of the Cultural Revolution until mid-1968. Mao Zedong attends several similar enormous rallies over the next few months.

C. Economic Events

January 1. *People's Daily* declares China to be completely free of foreign debt.

D. Appointments, Dismissals, etc.

May 16. Luo Ruiqing is dismissed as chief of the General Staff of the PLA.

June 3. NCNA announces the decision to appoint Li Xuefeng as first secretary of the Beijing Municipal CCP Committee in place of Peng Zhen, under severe attack as a revisionist in the Cultural Revolution.

July 10. NCNA reveals that Chen Boda is the head of the Cultural Revolution Group.

August 1–12. The Eleventh Plenum of the Eighth CCPCC elects Lin Biao as the only deputy chairman of the Central Committee.

August 31. NCNA reveals that Jiang Qing is Chen Boda's first deputy in the Cultural Revolution Group.

E. Cultural and Social Events

February 2–20. The Forum on the Work in Literature and Art in the Armed Forces, Convened by Jiang Qing on the Instructions of Lin Biao, takes place in Shanghai.

August 20. Red Guards in Beijing begin destroying 'bourgeois and feudal remnants' by forbidding various types of dress and literature, ransacking bookshops, private houses and other places. On August 22 they begin the closure, and often also ransacking, of Beijing's churches and other religious establishments.

September. *Quotations from Chairman Mao Zedong (Mao zhuxi yulu)*, also known as *The Little Red Book*, is published in Shanghai.

F. Births and Deaths

March 22. Philosopher Ai Siqi dies.

May 18. Writer Deng Tuo dies.

August 24. Writer and dramatist Shu Qingchun (pen-name Lao She) dies.

G. Natural Disasters

March 8. Xingtai in Hebei province is shaken by a strong earthquake.

1967

A. Foreign Affairs Events

January 31. The Heilongjiang Provincial Revolutionary Committee is set up. An alliance of revolutionary rebels, the PLA and revolutionary CCP cadres, it becomes the model for the Cultural Revolution's administrative system.

May 15. The Ministry of Foreign Affairs protests to the British chargé d'affaires concerning arrests made in Hong Kong during riots there earlier in May.

August 22. Red Guards attack and ransack the office of the British chargé d'affaires in Beijing, burning down the main building.

September 5. China, Tanzania and Zambia sign an agreement in Beijing under which China will assist in the construction of the Tanzania–Zambia railway.

B. Domestic Political Events

January 23. The CCPCC, Cultural Revolution Group and other bodies issue an urgent notice calling on the PLA to intervene in the Cultural Revolution on the side of the 'broad left-wing masses'.

June 17. China explodes its first hydrogen bomb.

August 4. A rally in Wuhan celebrates the victory of the central forces in a civil war which had broken out in the city about two weeks earlier, after Zhou Enlai had attempted, on August 20 and 21, to mediate a complicated struggle between factions supporting and opposing Chen Zaidao, the regional commander of the Wuhan Military Region.

D. Appointments, Dismissals, etc.

January 31. Pan Fusheng is inaugurated as chairman of the Heilongjiang Provincial Revolutionary Committee.

August 4. Zeng Siyu replaces Chen Zaidao as commander of the Wuhan Military Region.

E. Cultural and Social Events

December 25. NCNA reports the number of copies of *Quotations from Chairman Mao Zedong* published in China at 350 million.

F. Births and Deaths

June 22. Li Lisan dies.

August 15. Former Finance Minister Kong Xiangxi (H. H. Kung) dies in the United States.

October 17. The last Emperor, Puyi, dies.

1968

A. Foreign Affairs Events

August 23. China strongly denounces the Soviet Union for its invasion of Czechoslovakia, which began during the night of August 20–21.

B. Domestic Political and Military Events

June 13. The CCPCC cables, demanding an end to violent clashes on the railway at Liuzhou in Guangxi, where the system has come to a halt and military materials on their way to Vietnam have been stolen.

July 28. In the early hours of the morning, Mao Zedong and others meet with Red Guard leaders and criticize their indulging in armed struggle. The meeting signals the effective end of the most radical phase of the Cultural Revolution.

September 7. A rally in Beijing celebrates the setting up of revolutionary committees in all provinces, municipalities and autonomous regions, except Taiwan.

C. Economic Events

October 1. The rail section of the bridge over the Yangzi River at Nanjing is formally opened to traffic. The road section is formally opened on December 29.

D. Appointments, Dismissals, etc.

October 31. The communiqué of the Twelfth Plenum of the Eighth CCPCC announces that Liu Shaoqi has been expelled from the CCP once and for all and dismissed from all posts both inside and outside the Party.

E. Cultural and Social Events

December 22. A Mao directive urging that 'educated young people' be sent to the countryside for 're-education by the poor and lower middle peasants' is broadcast.

F. Births and Deaths

November 28. Mao's former teacher and current CCPCC member Xu Teli dies.

December 10. Playwright Tian Han dies.

December 18. Historian Jian Bozan dies.

December 26. Peking Opera actor Xun Huisheng dies.

1969

A. Foreign Affairs Events

March 2. An armed clash takes place between Chinese and Soviet forces at Zhenbao (Damansky) Island in the Ussuri River on the eastern border.

March 15. A second major clash takes place on Zhenbao Island.

June 10. A major clash takes place between Chinese and Soviet forces on the Sino-Soviet border at Yumin in Xinjiang, the most serious of many clashes on the western border at about this time.

June 14. Zhou Enlai sends a statement of support to Huynh Tan Phat, president of the Provisional Revolutionary Government of the Republic of South Vietnam, set up on June 6.

July 21. The United States government announces the lifting of many of the restrictions which have prevented travel to China on American passports.

September 11. Zhou Enlai and Soviet Prime Minister Kosygin meet at Beijing airport and discuss a number of matters, including the Sino-Soviet border.

October 8. The Chinese Foreign Ministry calls for 'a new equal Sino-Soviet treaty to replace the old unequal Sino-Russian treaties', until the conclusion of which it proposes that the status quo should be maintained.

December 22. A partial lifting of the United States trade embargo against China takes effect. Among other points, it allows American tourists to make unlimited private purchases of Chinese goods.

B. Domestic Political Events

April 14. The Ninth CCP Congress adopts a new CCP Constitution which reaffirms Marxism–Leninism–Mao Zedong thought as the theoretical basis of the Party.

September 23. China carries out its first successful underground nuclear test.

D. Appointments, Dismissals, etc.

April 28. The First Plenum of the Ninth CCPCC elects Mao Zedong as chairman and Lin Biao as vice-chairman of the Politburo. Also on the Standing Committee are Chen Boda, Zhou Enlai and Kang Sheng.

E. Cultural and Social Events

October 29. *Red Flag* publishes the first of the revised scripts of the 'model dramas': *Taking Tiger Mountain by Strategy (Zhiqu Weihu shan)*.

F. Births and Deaths

January 30. Former vice-president and then president of the ROC, Li Zongren, dies in Beijing.

April 23. Film director Zheng Junli dies.

June 9. He Long dies.

July 29. Historian and CCPCC member Fan Wenlan dies in Beijing.

October 11. Historian Wu Han dies.

November 12. Former PRC president Liu Shaoqi dies in Kaifeng in prison.

1970

A. Foreign Affairs Events

May 4. Norodom Sihanouk, overthrown as head of the Cambodian state by a coup d'état on March 18, sets up his Royal Government of National Union of Kampuchea in Beijing. On the same day, the Chinese government denounces the United States troop movements into Cambodia, which were announced by United States President Nixon on April 30, as a 'provocation to the Chinese people'.

May 5. China formally recognizes Sihanouk's Royal Government of National Union of Kampuchea.

B. Domestic Political Events

April 24. The first Chinese space satellite is successfully launched into orbit.

August 23–25. At the Second Plenum of the Ninth CCPCC, held on Lushan, Jiangxi province, several supporters of Lin Biao oppose an instruction of Mao Zedong, causing him to doubt Lin's loyalty.

November 24–December 4. The Third Hunan Provincial CCP Congress takes place; it is the first Party congress at provincial level since the Cultural Revolution began.

C. Economic Events

July 1. The Chengdu–Kunming railway is formally opened to traffic.

D. Appointments, Dismissals, etc.

December 13. NCNA reports that Hua Guofeng was elected first secretary of the Hunan Provincial CCP Committee by the Third Hunan Provincial CCP Congress.

E. Cultural and Social Events

May 1. The 'model drama' *The Red Lantern (Hongdeng ji)* is published in *Red Flag*.

F. Births and Deaths

March 29. Anna Louise Strong, American writer, friend of Mao Zedong and resident of China, dies.

September 20. Deputy Minister of Foreign Affairs Gong Peng dies.

September 23. Writer Zhao Shuli dies.

1971

A. Foreign Affairs Events

March 15. The United States State Department announces that all restrictions on travel by American citizens to China have been lifted.

April 10–17. An American table tennis team visits China, the first United States group at official or semi-official level to visit the country for many years. Zhou Enlai receives the delegation on April 14.

July 9–11. United States President Nixon's Assistant for National Security Affairs, Dr Henry Kissinger, visits Beijing secretly, holding talks with Zhou Enlai.

July 15. United States President Nixon announces that he has accepted an invitation from Zhou Enlai to visit China before May 1972.

September 29–October 1. Minister of Foreign Trade Bai Xiangguo leads a delegation to France, the first PRC group at full ministerial level to visit Western Europe since 1949.

October 25. The PRC is admitted to the United Nations.

B. Domestic Political Events

September 12. Lin Biao's alleged assassination attempt against Mao Zedong fails.

D. Appointments, Dismissals, etc.

January 10. Zhang Chunqiao is elected first secretary of the Shanghai Municipal CCP Committee.

E. Cultural and Social Events

January 27. The colour films of the 'model' dramas *The Red Lantern* and *The Red Detachment of Women (Hongse niangzi jun)* are given premiere showings.

November. The People's Literary Press publishes *Li Bai and Du Fu (Li Bai yu Du Fu)* by Guo Moruo, the first book on classical literature to be released in China since before the Cultural Revolution.

December 1. NCNA reports that over 340 well-preserved bronzes from about the eleventh century BC were excavated in September 1967.

F. Births and Deaths

April 29. CCPCC member Li Siguang dies.

June 21. Historian Chen Yuan dies in Beijing.

September 13. CCP vice-chairman Lin Biao is killed—in an air crash, according to official Chinese sources.

1972

A. Foreign Affairs Events

February 21–28. United States President Nixon visits China. On the last day a joint Sino-US communiqué is issued in Shanghai which declares, among other points, that the United States does not challenge the position held by all Chinese 'on either side of the Taiwan Strait' that 'there is but one China and that Taiwan is a part of China'.

August 16. Japanese air services between Japan and Shanghai begin.

September 9. China contracts with the United States Boeing Aircraft Corporation to buy ten 707 civilian jet airliners.

September 25–30. Japanese Prime Minister Tanaka Kakuei visits China.

December 29. China signs a contract with the Tokyo Engineering Company of Japan to purchase an ethylene manufacturing plant, the first whole-factory import by China for many years.

B. Domestic Political Events

July 28. Reuter reports that the Chinese government has, through its embassy in Algiers, given the official Chinese account of the Lin Biao affair for the first time.

August 1. *Red Flag* carries an important article giving the first theoretical account of the fall of Lin Biao: class enemies emerge every few years within the Party and will continue to do so.

C. Economic Events

October 1. The longest highway bridge over the Yellow River, at Beizhen in Shandong province, is formally opened to traffic.

E. Cultural and Social Events

May. The People's Literary Press publishes *The Bright Golden Road (Jinguang dadao)*, a novel by Haoran.

July 31. NCNA reports the excavation of a well-preserved tomb near Changsha; over 2000 years old, it contains a female corpse and burial accessories.

F. Births and Deaths

January 6. Former Minister of Foreign Affairs, Chen Yi, dies.

February 21. First Secretary of the Sichuan Provincial CCP Committee, Zhang Guohua, dies.

March 26. Former Minister of Public Security, Xie Fuzhi, dies.

September 1. He Xiangning dies.

1973

A. Foreign Affairs Events

January 29. Chairman Mao Zedong and others send a message of congratulations to the leaders of the Democratic Republic of Vietnam, the Provisional Revolutionary Government of South Vietnam and others on the signing of the Paris Peace Accords (January 27).

February 22. The United States and China announce their intention to establish a liaison office in each other's capitals. Air services, the first between China and Africa, are inaugurated between Shanghai and Addis Ababa.

June 6–19. The Minister of Foreign Affairs, Ji Pengfei, visits Britain, France, Iran and Pakistan.

September 11–17. The President of France, Georges Pompidou, visits China, the first West European head of state ever to have done so, and meets Chairman Mao on September 12.

B. Domestic Political Events

August 24. On the first day of the Tenth National CCP Congress, Zhou Enlai gives the official version of the Lin Biao affair and Wang Hongwen reports on the revision of the CCP Constitution, saying that cultural revolutions will recur.

D. Appointments, Dismissals, etc.

April 12. Deng Xiaoping is mentioned as a vice-premier.

August 30. The First Plenum of the Tenth CCPCC elects Mao Zedong as chairman and Zhou Enlai, Wang Hongwen, Kang Sheng, Ye Jianying and Li Desheng as deputy chairmen.

E. Cultural and Social Events

April 11–16. The Vienna Philharmonic Orchestra visits China.

September 12. The Philadelphia Orchestra arrives in Beijing for a concert tour of China, led by its conductor, Eugene Ormandy.

September 15. The monthly periodical *Study and Criticism (Xuexi yu pipan)* begins publication in Shanghai.

F. Births and Deaths

July 1. Educator, historian and journalist Zhang Shizhao dies in Hong Kong.

1974

A. Foreign Affairs Events

January 19–20. Chinese troops seize the Xisha Islands from the Republic of Vietnam.

April 10. Deng Xiaoping addresses the United Nations General Assembly. He declares that the United States and the Soviet Union are seeking world hegemony, but that the international situation is favourable to the developing countries, and that China belongs to the Third World.

May 28–June 2. The Malaysian Prime Minister, Tun Abdul Razak, visits China, his visit resulting in the establishment of diplomatic relations.

August 21. At the United Nations World Population Conference held in Bucharest, the Chinese representative, Huang Shuze, attacks the Malthusian theory of the population explosion as a fallacy.

October 29. The Beijing–Karachi–Paris route of the Civil Aviation Administration of China (CAAC) is formally begun.

B. Domestic Political Events

January 1. An editorial in *People's Daily* and other major newspapers declares the criticism of Confucius to be part of the criticism of Lin Biao. This launches a mass movement known as the Campaign to Criticize Lin Biao and Confucius.

C. Economic Events

September 14. NCNA reports the completion of the Danjiang canal project in the vicinity of Xiangyang, Hubei province; this is part of the Danjiangkou water control project.

E. Cultural and Social Events

January 14. *People's Daily* launches a condemnation of Beethoven and Schubert, among other European composers, as bourgeois.

January 30. *People's Daily* launches public criticism of the film *China* directed by the Italian M. Antonioni.

September 1–16. The Asian Games take place in Teheran, with China sending its largest sports team ever to go abroad.

F. Births and Deaths

April 19. Fu Zuoyi dies.

November 29. Former Minister of National Defence, Peng Dehuai, dies.

1975

A. Foreign Affairs Events

April 7. Swissair inaugurates its Zurich–Geneva–Athens–Bombay–Beijing–Shanghai air service.

April 30. Mao Zedong and others cable a message of congratulations to leaders of the Democratic Republic of Vietnam, Provisional Revolutionary Government of South Vietnam and others on the liberation of Saigon, which took place the same day.

June 7–10. Philippines President Ferdinand Marcos visits China, resulting in the establishment of diplomatic relations.

June 30–July 6. Thai Prime Minister Kukrit Pramoj makes a visit to China, resulting in the establishment of diplomatic relations.

December 1–5. American President Gerald Ford visits China and meets Mao Zedong on December 2.

B. Domestic Political Events

May 3. At a meeting of the Politburo, Mao Zedong warns Jiang Qing, Wang Hongwen, Zhang Chunqiao and Yao Wenyuan against 'functioning as a gang of four'.

C. Economic Events

September 15–October 19. The First National Conference on Learning from Dazhai in Agriculture, held in Xiyang, Shanxi province, determines to achieve basic farm mechanization by 1980.

D. Appointments, Dismissals, etc.

January 8–10. The Second Plenum of the Tenth CCPCC elects Deng Xiaoping as deputy chairman of the CCPCC.

December 19. Zhao Ziyang is identified for the first time as first secretary of the Sichuan Provincial Party Committee.

E. Cultural and Social Events

August 23. *Guangming Daily* carries articles attacking the classical novel *Water Margin (Shuihu zhuan)*.

F. Births and Deaths

March 8. Peking Opera actor, Zhou Xinfang, dies.

April 2. Dong Biwu dies.

April 5. Chiang Kaishek dies.

December 16. Kang Sheng dies.

G. Natural Disasters

February 4. A large-scale earthquake strikes the Haicheng–Yingkou region of Liaoning province.

1976 THE DEATH OF MAO ZEDONG AND THE FALL OF THE GANG OF FOUR

A. Foreign Affairs Events

May 27. Pakistan's Prime Minister Z. A. Bhutto meets Mao Zedong, the last high-ranking foreigner to do so and the last of numerous world leaders to visit Mao in the final years of his life.

July 14. The Tanzania–Zambia railway, China's largest foreign aid project, is formally opened to traffic.

October 1. Pravda expresses the willingness of the Soviet Union to restore good relations with China.

B. Domestic Political Events

February 10. A poster campaign commences at Beijing University against 'a capitalist roader', clearly Deng Xiaoping, and gathers momentum over the next months.

April 5. Demonstrators in mourning for Zhou Enlai in Tiananmen Square, central Beijing, clash with police; serious violence erupts: the Tiananmen Incident. Similar incidents occur in numerous other parts of China just after this one.

April 7. NCNA condemns the Tiananmen Incident as a 'counter-revolutionary political incident'.

October 6. Four Politburo members, Jiang Qing, Zhang Chunqiao, Yao Wenyuan and Wang Hongwen, are secretly arrested and imprisoned: the fall of the 'gang of four'.

October 24. A gigantic demonstration takes place in Tiananmen Square in support of Hua Guofeng's appointment as CCP chairman and against the 'gang of four'. Wu De claims that Mao specifically chose Hua as his successor and attacks the 'gang of four' for attempting to split the CCP and seize power.

December 10–27. The Second National Conference on Learning from Dazhai in Agriculture is held in Beijing. Hua Guofeng makes a speech on December 25 claiming that major civil war would have broken out had the 'gang of four' not been suppressed.

December 25. For the first time in the PRC, NCNA publishes Mao Zedong's speech of April 25, 1956, 'On the Ten Major Relationships'.

C. Economic Events

April 23. NCNA reports the sinking of China's deepest oil well to this point, in Sichuan province.

August 23. China's first 50 000-tonne oil tanker, the *West Lake (Xihu)*, is launched in Dalian.

D. Appointments, Dismissals, etc.

February 3. Hua Guofeng is appointed acting premier of the State Council, in succession to Zhou Enlai.

April 7. Hua Guofeng is appointed first deputy chairman of the CCP Central Comittee and premier of the State Council; Deng Xiaoping is dismissed from all posts inside and outside the Party.

October 7. The CCPCC appoints Hua Guofeng as its chairman and also as chairman of its Military Affairs Committee in succession to Mao Zedong.

E. Cultural and Social Events

January. *People's Literature* and *Poetry* both recommence publication after suspension in 1966 and 1964 respectively.

November 5. A *People's Daily* editorial points to a less rigid policy on the arts in the wake of the fall of the 'gang of four'.

F. Births and Deaths

January 8. Premier Zhou Enlai dies of cancer in Beijing.

July 6. NPC Standing Committee chairman Zhu De dies in Beijing.

July 27. Musical composer Ma Ke dies.

September 9. CCP chairman Mao Zedong dies in Beijing at 12.10 am.

G. Natural Disasters

July 28. An extremely severe earthquake strikes the Tangshan–Fengnan area of Hebei province; in terms of human casualties, it is among the worst in world history. The Chinese Seismological Society, at its inaugural meeting in November 1979, reported estimated casualties at 242 000 dead and 164 000 seriously wounded. One contemporary estimate, attributed to the Hebei Provincial CCP Committee and published in Hong Kong's *South China Morning Post* on January 5, 1977, put deaths from the earthquake at 655 237.

1977

A. Foreign Affairs Events

November 1. A *People's Daily* article of over 35 000 characters extols Mao Zedong's theory of the three worlds as 'a major contribution to Marxism–Leninism'.

December 31. The Kampuchean Ambassador in Beijing issues a statement charging Vietnam with having launched systematic aggression against Pol Pot's Kampuchea since September 1977.

B. Domestic Political Events

May 24. The Chairman Mao Memorial Hall is completed in Tiananmen Square, Beijing.

August 18. The Eleventh National Congress of the CCP (held August 12–18) adopts the Party Constitution, under which Marxism–Leninism–Mao Zedong thought remains the 'guiding ideology and theoretical basis' of the CCP.

C. Economic Events

April 20–May 13. The National Conference on Learning from Daqing in Industry is held first in Daqing and later in Beijing.

October 23. It is announced that about 46 per cent of workers and staff will have their wages raised from October 1.

D. Appointments, Dismissals, etc.

July 21. The Third Plenum of the Tenth CCPCC confirms Hua Guofeng as chairman of the CCPCC and its Military Affairs Committee, restores Deng Xiaoping to deputy chairmanship of the CCPCC and other posts, and expels Zhang Chunqiao, Jiang Qing, Yao Wenyuan and Wang Hongwen from the Party, dismissing them from all posts.

August 19. The First Plenum of the Eleventh CCPCC elects five members to the Politburo's Standing Committee: Hua Guofeng, Ye Jianying, Deng Xiaoping, Li Xiannian and Wang Dongxing.

E. Cultural and Social Events

February 15. The opera *The White-Haired Girl* is repremiered after more than ten years' suppression.

April 15. The People's Press publishes Volume V of the *Selected Works of Mao Zedong (Mao Zedong xuanji)*.

F. Births and Deaths

June 17. Literary figure Aying dies.

December 3. Foremost specialist on Chinese theatre history Zhou Yibai dies.

1978 THE THIRD PLENUM INTRODUCES THE POLICIES OF REFORM

A. Foreign Affairs Events

February 16. China and Japan sign a long-term trade agreement, under which exports from each side over the period 1978 to 1985 will total US$10 000 million.

May 24. A spokesman of the State Council accuses Vietnam of persecuting Chinese residents in Vietnam. He declares that over 70 000 of them were expelled to China between early April and mid-May. This statement signals the public split between China and Vietnam.

May 29. Minister of Foreign Affairs Huang Hua tells the Special Session of the United Nations General Assembly on Disarmament that the Soviet Union is 'perniciously taking the offensive' in the arms race.

July 3. The Chinese government informs the Vietnamese government of its decision to cease all economic and technical aid to Vietnam; it also recalls its experts from Vietnam.

August 12. China and Japan sign their Treaty of Peace and Friendship in Beijing.

August 25. A Sino-Vietnamese armed clash occurs at Friendship Pass on their mutual border.

November 8. At a press conference in Bangkok, Deng Xiaoping declares that the Soviet–Vietnamese Treaty of Friendship and Co-operation, signed on November 3, is a threat to China and to peace and security in the Asian–Pacific region.

December 13. The Coca-Cola Co. reaches an agreement with China to sell Coca-Cola there and to open a bottling plant in Shanghai.

December 16 (15 in the United States). China and the United States simultaneously issue a joint communiqué of their decision to establish diplomatic relations as from January 1, 1979.

December 19. In Seattle in the United States, Boeing announces that China has purchased three Boeing 747 airliners.

B. Domestic Political Events

November 19. In the first batch of posters on 'democracy wall' in Beijing, one appears accusing Mao Zedong of supporting and buttressing the 'gang of four'.

December 18–22. The Third Plenum of the Eleventh CCPCC shifts the entire stress of the Party on to socialist modernization.

C. Economic Events

March 5. The Fifth NPC formally approves the Ten-year Plan (1976–85).

October 12. Air services begin between Hong Kong and Guangzhou.

December 18–22. The Third Plenum of the Eleventh CCPCC takes the first steps towards restoring the use of market mechanisms in rural China.

D. Appointments, Dismissals, etc.

March 5. The NPC elects Hua Guofeng as premier of the State Council and Deng Xiaoping, Li Xiannian, Chen Yonggui and others as vice-premiers.

December 22. The Third Plenum of the Eleventh CCPCC announces that Chen Yun has been elected as a deputy chairman of the Central Committee and that Hu Yaobang and others have been elected to the Politburo.

E. Cultural and Social Events

April 22–May 16. The Ministry of Education convenes a National Conference on Education Work in Beijing.

May 27–June 5. The Chinese National Federation of Literature and Art Circles holds a major conference on literature and art.

June 15. Prominent Japanese conductor Seiji Ozawa conducts the Central Symphony Orchestra at a concert in Beijing, the first public concert by a Chinese symphony orchestra conducted by a foreigner since 1949.

September 8–17. The Fourth National Women's Congress is held in Beijing.

September 11. *Chinese Youth (Zhongguo qingnian)* resumes publication after a twelve-year break. It is one of many periodicals to do so at about this time.

October 11–21. The Ninth National Congress of Chinese Trade Unions is held in Beijing.

October 16–26. The Tenth National Congress of the Communist Youth League of China is held in Beijing.

F. Births and Deaths

June 12. Scientist, writer and CCPCC member Guo Moruo dies.

August 3. Luo Ruiqing dies.

G. Natural Disasters

November 2. NCNA reports a nationwide drought in 1978 which is more severe 'in length of time, breadth of scope and seriousness of extent' than the great droughts of 1934, 1959 and 1966.

1979

A. Foreign Affairs Events

January 7. The Chinese government denounces Vietnam for aggression against Democratic Kampuchea. Vietnam had invaded Kampuchea, beginning on December 25, 1978, and took Phnom Penh on January 7, 1979.

January 28–February 5. Deng Xiaoping visits the United States, the first visit there by a senior PRC leader.

February 7. In Tokyo, Deng Xiaoping tells Japanese Prime Minister Ohira Masayoshi that Vietnam must be punished for its invasion of Kampuchea. Deng returns to Beijing the next day.

February 17. Chinese troops launch attacks into Vietnamese territory. Both China and Vietnam issue statements, the Chinese claiming that they want only a peaceful and stable border and will withdraw after counter-attacking the Vietnamese aggressors; the Vietnamese denouncing the Chinese authorities for starting a war of aggression against Vietnam.

March 5. Chinese troops complete the seizure of Langson in Vietnam; China states that its troops will begin withdrawal the same day (March 5).

March 16. Chinese Foreign Minister Huang Hua announces that Chinese troops have completed their withdrawal from Vietnam the same day (March 16).

May 14. An NCNA commentary gives China's case for claiming ownership of the Nansha and Xisha Islands, a claim also made by Vietnam.

October 15–November 6. Hua Guofeng visits France, West Germany, Britain and Italy, the first tour of Western Europe by a PRC head of government.

December 30. The Chinese government issues a statement denouncing the Soviet Union for its invasion of Afghanistan, which began on December 27.

B. Domestic Political Events

July 1. The Second Session of the Fifth NPC adopts seven laws, including China's first *Criminal Law* and the *Organic Law of the Local People's Congresses and Local People's Governments.*

September 29. Ye Jianying denounces the Cultural Revolution as unnecessary, ill-judged and calamitous.

December 6. The Beijing Municipal Revolutionary Committee bans big- or small-character posters in public places, except in one part of one specified park, signifying the end of the 1978–79 pro-democracy movement.

C. Economic Events

July 1. The NPC approves the policy of economic readjustment, which involves scaling down some aspects of the Four Modernizations.

October 4. The China International Trust and Investment Corporation (CITIC) is formally established in Beijing.

D. Appointments, Dismissals, etc.

February 23. Peng Zhen is appointed Director of the Commission for Legal Affairs of the NPC Standing Committee.

E. Cultural and Social Events

January. *Harvest* recommences publication, having been suspended in March 1966 due to the Cultural Revolution.

January 1. All publications appearing in China in languages using the Roman alphabet begin using the *Hanyu pinyin* system of romanization.

Early in the year. The two-part colour film *The Great River Rushes On (Dahe benliu),* directed by Xie Tieli and Chen Huaikai, is screened.

February. Wu Han's play *Hai Rui's Dismissal* is restaged.

June. The literary periodical *The Present (Dangdai)* begins publication.

June 1–5. A national forum on acupuncture is held in Beijing.

June–October. Zhao Zhenkai's short novel *Waves (Bodong)* is published in instalments in the periodical *Today (Jintian).*

October 16. Democracy and human rights activist Wei Jingsheng is sentenced to a prison term of fifteen years for passing on military intelligence to a foreigner, and for counter-revolutionary agitation. (An appeal to a higher court was rejected on November 6.)

October 30–November 16. The Fourth Congress of the Federation of Literature and Art Circles of China takes place in Beijing, the first since 1960.

F. Births and Deaths

September 25. Author Zhou Libo dies in Beijing.

December 3. Former CCP leader Zhang Guotao dies in Toronto.

G. Natural Disasters

July 9. Liyang in Jiangsu province is struck by an earthquake; forty-one people are killed and many houses destroyed.

1980

A. Foreign Affairs Events

March 24. The Chinese Olympic Committee decides to boycott the Moscow summer Olympic Games.

April 17. The International Monetary Fund admits China as a member.

May 15. The World Bank admits China to representation in the World Bank Group.

May 18. China successfully launches its first carrier rocket, to the Pacific Ocean.

October 27. At a banquet in honour of Thai Prime Minister Prem Tinsulanond, who visited China October 27–30, Zhao Ziyang says that 'tension in South-east Asia has been caused entirely by the Soviet-backed Vietnamese invasion and occupation of Kampuchea', and that China supports the stand of the ASEAN countries on the Kampuchean problem.

December 3. The Chinese government makes an unsuccessful attempt to persuade the Dutch government to reconsider its decision of November 29 to sell two submarines to Taiwan.

B. Domestic Political Events

January 1. Six new laws come into operation, including the *Organic Law of the Local People's Congresses and Local People's Governments*, under which the posts of provincial governors and mayors are restored.

February 29. The Fifth Plenum of the Eleventh CCPCC adopts a communiqué which, among many other matters, rehabilitates Liu Shaoqi posthumously.

May 15. A CCPCC circular is published calling for more consideration of Tibet's special needs and more efforts to train Tibetan cadres and those of other minority nationalities.

May 22–31. Hu Yaobang and others make an inspection tour of Tibet.

October 20–December 29. A trial is held in Beijing concerning the activities of the 'gang of four', six other living people and six deceased. The charges fall under four headings, including plotting to overthrow the 'political power of the dictatorship of the proletariat', persecuting many cadres and others, and plotting to assassinate Mao Zedong.

December 22. *People's Daily* declares that Mao Zedong made great mistakes during his last years, and that the Cultural Revolution which he led was a great disaster. How-ever, while convicting him of mistakes, it denies he committed crimes.

C. Economic Events

June 20. The Tibetan government announces new economic policies, including exemption from all taxes on agriculture and animal husbandry for two years.

September 10. The NPC approves the *Income Tax Law Concerning Joint Ventures with Chinese and Foreign Investment of the PRC*, and the *Individual Income Tax Law of the PRC*.

November 4. Inauguration of direct flights between Beijing and Hong Kong.

D. Appointments, Dismissals, etc.

February 29. The Fifth Plenum of the Eleventh CCPCC announces the election of Hu Yaobang as secretary-general of the CCPCC; the election of Hu Yaobang and Zhao Ziyang as members of the Standing Committee of the Politburo; and agreement to the requests of Wang Dongxing, Wu De and others to resign from the Central Committee.

September 10. The Third Session of the Fifth NPC approves many changes in the leadership. They include: Zhao Ziyang's replacing Hua Guofeng as premier of the State Council; the resignation of Deng Xiaoping, Li Xiannian, Chen Yun and others as vice-premiers due to old age; and Chen Yonggui's dismissal as vice-premier.

E. Cultural and Social Events

February 12. The NPC Standing Committee approves regulations for the award of the academic degrees of Bachelor, Master and Doctor.

May. The novel *The Depth of Winter (Long dong)*, by Gu Ligao, is published in Beijing.

August. The PRC's first encyclopedic yearbook, *Chinese Encyclopedic Yearbook 1980 (Zhongguo baike nianjian)*, is published in Beijing and Shanghai.

September 10. The NPC approves the revised *Marriage Law of the PRC*, which, among many other points, raises the marriage age for men to 22 and for women to 20; and the *Nationality Law of the PRC*, which prohibits dual nationality for any Chinese national.

September 20–October 20. The Minority Nationalities Arts Festival is held in Beijing.

F. Births and Deaths

March 8. Poet Li Ji dies.

July 10. Journalist Chen Kehan dies in Beijing.

October 10. Film actor Zhao Dan dies.

December 25. Historian Gu Jiegang dies in Beijing.

G. Natural Disasters

June 26–27. Hurricanes, wind and hail storms strike coastal Zhejiang, killing 151 people and causing severe damage to houses and crops.

1981

A. Foreign Affairs Events

January 7. CAAC formally begins its Beijing–New York air service.

January 19. China asks that Sino-Dutch diplomatic relations be demoted to chargé d'affaires level, because of the Netherlands' public reaffirmation, on January 16, of its decision to sell two submarines to Taiwan. The dispute culminates in the withdrawal of ambassadors on February 27.

July 13. China's delegate, Acting Foreign Minister Han Nianlong, addresses the International Conference on Kampuchea in New York. He calls for an unconditional Vietnamese troop withdrawal within six months and affirms the Kampuchean right to self-determination.

October 21. Premier Zhao Ziyang meets United States President Reagan at the Cancun Summit, an international conference held in Mexico to discuss the North–South relationship.

October 29. In Washington, Foreign Minister Huang Hua criticizes the United States' policy of selling advanced armaments to Taiwan.

December 16. A conference of Chinese and Japanese officials concludes with an announcement of US$1.37 billion of Japanese financial aid to Chinese industry, including the first stage of the Baoshan steel mill.

B. Domestic Political Events

January 25. The special court trying the 'gang of four' and others holds its last session. It condemns Jiang Qing and Zhang Chunqiao to death with two-year reprieves, Wang Hongwen to life imprisonment and the others to long terms of imprisonment.

June 29. The communiqué of the Sixth Plenum of the Eleventh CCPCC re-evaluates the role of the CCP since 1949; it attacks the Cultural Revolution as a total disaster, and criticizes Mao Zedong for initiating and leading the Cultural Revolution, as well as many of the other initiatives he took in his later years.

July 17. Deng Xiaoping criticizes laxity and weakness in CCP leadership, together with a fear of criticizing wrong trends.

September 30. Ye Jianying calls for negotiations, on the basis of reciprocity, with the Guomindang over Taiwan. He states that after reunification, Taiwan could enjoy a high degree of autonomy and retain its own armed forces.

C. Economic Events

November 30–December 1. At the Fourth Session of the Fifth NPC, Zhao Ziyang gives a lengthy report on the economic situation, puts forward ten principles for future economic construction and considers the Sixth Five-year Plan (1981–85) and the country's economic prospects.

D. Appointments, Dismissals, etc.

June 29. The Sixth Plenum of the Eleventh CCPCC announces that Hu Yaobang has replaced Hua Guofeng as chairman of the CCPCC, and Deng Xiaoping as chairman of its Military Commission; it also announces the election of Zhao Ziyang and Hua Guofeng as deputy chairmen of the Central Committee.

E. Cultural and Social Events

January 1. The People's Press publishes Volume I of *Selected Works of Zhou Enlai (Zhou Enlai xuanji)*, with the final volume following on December 14, 1984.

April 20. *Liberation Army Daily* criticizes the film script of *Unrequited Love (Ku lian)* (following Deng Xiaoping's criticism of it in a talk 'with leading comrades' of the PLA's General Political Department on March 27).

June 1. *China Daily*, the PRC's first English-language daily, begins publication.

September 25. At a meeting to commemorate the centenary of Lu Xun's birth, Hu Yaobang criticizes bourgeois liberalization and other 'currently widespread' unhealthy tendencies in literature and art work.

October 1. The salaries of primary and secondary school teachers are increased, effective from this day.

F. Births and Deaths

March 27. Shen Yanbing (pen-name Mao Dun) dies in Beijing.

May 29. Song Qingling dies in Beijing.

G. Natural Disasters

January 24. An earthquake strikes Dawu in Sichuan, killing about 150 people and destroying many houses.

July 9–14. Torrential rain in Sichuan causes serious flooding, killing over 700 people and rendering 150 000 homeless.

1982

A. Foreign Affairs Events

January 12. The Chinese Foreign Ministry protests strongly against the American decision to continue selling fighter aircraft to Taiwan.

March 24. In a major speech in Tashkent, Soviet President Leonid Brezhnev appeals for better Sino-Soviet relations 'on the basis of mutual respect for each other's interests, non-interference in each other's affairs, and mutual benefit'.

April 13. The American government formally notifies Congress of the decision to sell military spare parts to Taiwan. The following day the Chinese Foreign Ministry issues a strong protest against 'this act of infringing upon China's sovereignty'.

May 31–June 5. Zhao Ziyang visits Japan, meeting the Emperor on June 1.

June 11. Chinese Foreign Minister Huang Hua puts forward China's position on disarmament to the Second Special Session of the UN General Assembly on Disarmament.

June 25. *People's Daily* expresses China's strong support for the Coalition Government of Democratic Kampuchea, set up on June 22.

July 26. China protests formally against the publication in Japan of a revised history textbook, which China claims distorts the history of Japanese aggression in China.

August 17. The United States and China sign a joint communiqué on the issue of arms sales to Taiwan. The United States promises that it will not actually increase the level of sales, either in quality or quantity, and states its intention 'gradually to reduce its sale of arms to Taiwan, leading, over a period of time, to a final resolution'.

September 22–26. British Prime Minister Margaret Thatcher visits China. On September 24, China and Britain agree to begin discussions on the future of Hong Kong.

September 26. Soviet President L. Brezhnev calls normalization of relations with China a top priority.

September 27. In Hong Kong, Margaret Thatcher states her belief that the unequal treaties of the nineteenth century are still valid and both sides should continue to abide by them. The Chinese Foreign Ministry strongly criticizes the statement on September 30, arguing that the unequal treaties are invalid; that Hong Kong is part of Chinese territory; and that China will recover Hong Kong when conditions are ripe.

October 14–26. A visit by French Communist Party general secretary Georges Marchais results in the re-establishment of relations between the French Communist Party and the CCP.

November 14. Before leaving Beijing for the funeral of Soviet President Leonid Brezhnev, Chinese Foreign Minister Huang Hua describes Brezhnev as 'an outstanding statesman of the Soviet Union'.

December 20. Zhao Ziyang arrives in Egypt at the beginning of an African tour, leaving Cairo for Algeria on December 24, and going to Morocco on December 27 and to Guinea on December 30.

B. Domestic Political Events

March 2. Zhao Ziyang gives a report on the restructuring of the government, including reducing the current number of vice-premiers from thirteen to two.

July 1. The PRC begins its third national census, basically completing enumeration by July 10. The main figures are released on October 27.

September 6. The Twelfth National Congress of the CCP adopts a new CCP Constitution, under which the position of Party chairman is replaced by that of general secretary, and a Central Advisory Commission is established.

December 20–30. The Eleventh National Congress of the Chinese Communist Youth League is held in Beijing.

C. Economic Events

February 15. The China National Offshore Oil Corporation is officially set up to take charge of the exploitation of offshore petroleum resources, in co-operation with foreign enterprises.

March 8. The NPC Standing Committee adopts provisions for the severe punishment of criminals who do great damage to the national economy.

November 30. Zhao Ziyang gives his report on the Sixth Five-year Plan to the NPC.

D. Appointments, Dismissals, etc.

May 4. As part of the restructuring of the government, the NPC Standing Committee resolves that Wan Li and Yao Yilin will remain vice-premiers, but that the other eleven are to be removed from their posts.

July 27. *People's Daily* reports the dismissal of Yang Yibang, Vice-Minister of Chemical Industry, for corruption and for violating Party discipline.

September 12. The First Plenum of the Twelfth CCPCC elects Hu Yaobang as general secretary and, in addition, Ye Jianying, Deng Xiaoping, Zhao Ziyang, Li Xiannian and Chen Yun as the members of the Politburo's Standing Committee. It also elects Deng Xiaoping as chairman of the Military Commission of the Central Committee.

September 13. The First Plenum of the Twelfth CCPCC approves the election of Deng Xiaoping as chairman of the CCP Central Advisory Commission; and of Chen Yun as first secretary of the Central Commission for Discipline Inspection.

E. Cultural and Social Events

January 10. Volume I of *Selected Works of Liu Shaoqi (Liu Shaoqi xuanji)* is released to the public.

March 12. NCNA reports a promulgation by the CCPCC and the State Council of regulations against the import, duplication, sale and broadcasting of 'reactionary, pornographic and obscene sound and video tape recording products'.

July 25. Five people attempt to hijack an aircraft between Xi'an and Shanghai but are overpowered. All are executed on August 19.

November 5. The drama *Warning Signal (Juedui xinhao)*, by Gao Xingjian, is premiered in Beijing.

F. Births and Deaths

May 10. Demographer Ma Yinchu dies, aged 101 years.

G. Natural Disasters

May 20. Beijing Radio reports that 506 people have been killed in floods in Guangdong province.

July. Floods in Sichuan province result in 718 dead and and over 6000 injured, according to a report of August 20.

1983

A. Foreign Affairs Events

January 1–17. Zhao Ziyang continues his official visit to Africa, arriving in Gabon on January 1, in Zaire on January 2, in the Congo on January 4, in Zambia on January 5, in Zimbabwe on January 9, in Tanzania on January 11 and in Kenya on January 15.

March 18. A United Nations spokesperson announces that Qian Xinzhong, Chinese Minister in Charge of the State Family Planning Commission, is one of the first two winners of the 1983 UN population awards.

April 7. China announces it will halt all Sino-US cultural and sporting exchanges for 1982 and 1983 as a protest against the American government's granting of political asylum to Chinese tennis player Hu Na, who defected to the United States in California in July 1982.

May 3–7. French president François Mitterand visits China.

May 17. A *People's Daily* editorial hails Hu Yaobang's first visit to Eastern Europe as CCP general secretary as a success. Hu had arrived in Bucharest on May 5 and in Belgrade on May 10 for official visits to Romania and Yugoslavia.

June 6. For the first time the PRC participates in a meeting of the International Labour Organization, held in Geneva.

October 1. A Burundi student is beaten up and injured in Beijing by two hotel attendants. The incident provokes African students into demonstrating shortly afterwards. On October 8, the Beijing Municipal Public Security Bureau arrests the two attendants.

October 6. The first group of Soviet tourists for almost twenty years arrives in Beijing.

October 11. China's application to join the International Atomic Energy Agency is approved.

November 23–30. Hu Yaobang visits Japan, the first time a CCP General Secretary has visited a non-socialist country. On November 25 he addresses the Japanese Diet, the first Chinese leader ever to have done so.

November 25. Assistant Foreign Minister Zhu Qizhen lodges a strong protest with the United States Ambassador to China over an appropriations bill passed through the United States Congress on November 17 and 18 which urged that Taiwan should remain a full member of the Asian Development Bank even if the PRC were also admitted. The Chinese government regarded the Congress's action as a revival of the 'two Chinas' plot.

B. Domestic Political Events

January 25. The death sentence on Jiang Qing and Zhang Chunqiao (see January 25, 1981) is commuted to life imprisonment.

March 13. In a speech commemorating the centenary of the death of Karl Marx, Hu Yaobang emphasizes the need for Marxist parties to apply the doctrines of Marx to their own countries.

October 11. The Second Plenum of the Twelfth CCPCC adopts its decision 'on Party Consolidation', beginning a campaign against 'spiritual pollution'.

C. Economic Events

April 10. China's deepest offshore oil well to this point, the Pinghu, is completed in the East China Sea.

July 12. A meeting in Beijing marks the inauguration of the China Petrochemical Corporation.

July 15. Guangdong provincial official sources reveal plans for a very large-scale Pearl River Delta economic zone based on Guangzhou, which will eventually include Hong Kong and Macao.

August 1. New exchange control regulations are promulgated.

September 20. The State Council promulgates 'Regulations for the Implementation of the Law of the PRC on Joint Ventures Using Chinese and Foreign Investment'.

October 31. The first business in China wholly run by Japanese investment, the Sanyō (Shekou) Company, begins operating in Guangdong province.

D. Appointments, Dismissals, etc.

June 18. The Fourth Session of the Sixth NPC elects Li Xiannian as president of the PRC, and Peng Zhen as chairman of the NPC Standing Committee.

November 13. Two editors of *People's Daily* are dismissed in the campaign against 'spiritual pollution'.

E. Cultural and Social Events

January 28. *Play-Scripts* publishes the newly written Sichuan opera *The Scholar of Bashan (Bashan xiucai)* by Wei Minglun and Nan Guo.

May 5. The premiere of Arthur Miller's play *Death of a Salesman* takes place, directed by the author himself.

May 27. China confers doctoral degrees on the first batch of postgraduate research students trained in China by its own educators.

July 1. The People's Press publishes the *Selected Works of Deng Xiaoping (Deng Xiaoping xuanji)*.

July 15. *People's Daily* reveals that in Anyang, Henan province, police had seized a gang on November 25, 1982 for engaging in kidnapping and selling women and children. Later investigations by police in Sichuan, Henan, Shandong and Gansu provinces resulted in the arrest of over fifty people. The gang had kidnapped more than 150 women; between February 1980 and their arrest its members had taken in about 14 000 yuan.

July 25. The secretary of the CCP's Central Commission for Discipline Inspection, Han Guang, reveals that economic crimes, including smuggling, graft, bribery, speculation and fraud, have reached a record high since the founding of the PRC.

August 1. The People's Press publishes the *Selected Works of Zhu De (Zhu De xuanji)*.

September 2–12. The Fifth National Women's Congress is held in Beijing.

September 18–October 1. China's Fifth National Games are held in Shanghai.

December 22. The feminist drama *A Friend Comes in a Time of Need (Fengyu guren lai)*, by Bai Fengxi, is premiered in Beijing.

December 26. Several events, including the publication by the People's Press of *The Selected Letters of Mao Zedong (Mao Zedong shuxin xuanji)*, mark the ninetieth anniversary of Mao Zedong's birth.

F. Births and Deaths

January 17. Wang Zhong, Party official and public security deputy director in Shantou, Guangdong province, is executed for large-scale smuggling.

February 22. Economist Sun Yefang dies.

June 10. Sino-Japanese relations authority Liao Chengzhi dies of a heart attack.

September 22. Former Foreign Minister Qiao Guanhua dies.

September 30. Tan Zhenlin, vice-chairman of the Central Advisory Commission of the CCP, dies.

G. Natural Disasters, Accidents

July 21. A State Council directive on flood prevention makes reference to a serious situation along the Yangzi River and dangerously high water levels in other rivers, such as the Yellow, Huai and Hai. Serious flooding is reported in many parts of China, especially Sichuan, at about this time.

September 14. A collision between a passenger jet and a military training aircraft at Guilin airport results in eleven deaths.

1984

A. Foreign Affairs Events

January 1. China formally becomes a member of the International Atomic Energy Agency.

January 10. Zhao Ziyang arrives in Washington for an official visit to the United States, leaving the United States for Canada on January 16.

January 11. China issues a statement of support for the proposal, issued by the Democratic People's Republic of Korea in Pyongyang on January 10, for tripartite talks between the United States and the northern and southern parts of Korea, to ease tension on the Korean peninsula and to promote peaceful reunification.

January 16–23. Zhao Ziyang visits Canada, the first Chinese premier to do so.

February 1. China and the Netherlands agree to upgrade their relations to ambassadorial level, after the Netherlands decides not to grant a permit for the further export of arms to Taiwan (see January 19, 1981).

April 26–May 1. United States President Reagan pays an official visit to China.

May 30–June 16. Zhao Ziyang makes a visit to Western Europe, which takes him to France (May 30–June 3), Belgium (June 3–6), Sweden (June 6–8), Denmark (June 8–10), Norway (June 10–13) and Italy (June 13–16).

August 14. China protests to the Republic of Korea over the early release, on August 13, and immediate 'expulsion' to Taiwan of six persons who in May 1983 had hijacked a Chinese aircraft to Seoul.

October 11. Deng Xiaoping tells a delegation of the Japanese Kōmei Party that China's policy of openness to the outside world will not change either in this or even the next century.

December 19. In Beijing, British Prime Minister Margaret Thatcher and Chinese Premier Zhao Ziyang sign the Sino-British Joint Declaration on Hong Kong (already initialled on September 26). It states that sovereignty will be resumed by the PRC over Hong Kong with effect from July 1, 1997. However, for fifty years, Hong Kong 'will enjoy a high degree of autonomy, except in foreign and defence affairs', as well as 'executive, legislative and independent judicial power', with the current laws remaining basically unchanged.

December 21–29. First Deputy Chairman of the Council of Ministers of the Soviet Union, Ivan Arkhipov, visits China, the highest-ranking Soviet leader to do so since before the Cultural Revolution. On December 23, Zhao Ziyang welcomes him as 'an old friend of China'.

B. Domestic Political Events

June 22–23. Deng Xiaoping meets with business and other leaders from Hong Kong. He tells them that China's policy on Hong Kong is firm and that Hong Kong's current socio-economic system 'will remain unchanged after China resumes the exercise of its sovereignty over Hong Kong in 1997': the 'one country, two systems' formula.

June 30. The Central Commission for Guiding Party Rectification issues Central Circular No. 9 on the process of Party consolidation. It requires that all units involved in rectification should undertake three months of 'rectification and correction' after the stage of 'comparison and examination'.

July 20. *People's Daily* reports a decision by the CCPCC that a 'major decentralization' of power should be implemented.

October 30. The State Bureau of Nuclear Safety is formally established.

November 27. Yang Jingren, head of the CCP's United Front Work Department, tells three representatives of the Dalai Lama in Beijing that he is welcome to return to China, either on a short- or long-term basis, but requiring, among other points, that he and his followers 'will contribute to upholding China's unity and promoting solidarity between the Han and Tibetan nationalities, and among all nationalities, and the modernization programme'.

December 7. A *People's Daily* article calls for the study of the general laws and methodology of Marxism, but deplores regarding Marxism as dogma. It states that 'we cannot look to the books of Marx or Lenin to solve our problems today'; the last four words were amended the following day to 'solve *all* our problems today'.

C. Economic Events

July. Measures aimed at stimulating the Tibetan economy take effect, including the shifting of emphasis from agriculture to animal husbandry, the provision by the People's Bank of China of more interest-free and low-interest loans for Tibet, and exemption from taxation for some enterprises there.

August 7. The 476 km South Xinjiang railway, linking Turpan and Korla, is opened to traffic.

September 1. NCNA reports that China's first nuclear reactor has been declared operational.

October 20. The Third Plenum of the Twelfth CCPCC adopts its decision 'on reform of the economic structure'. It shifts the focus of reform to urban enterprises, calls for the conscious application of the law of value and for the establishment of a rational price system, and urges 'a deep-going transformation of the socialist superstructure' through 'the separation of the functions of government and enterprises as well as simpler and decentralized administration'.

E. Cultural and Social Events

February 15. The first volume of *Selected Works of Chen Yun (Chen Yun xuanji)* is published, with Volume II following on July 15.

March 12. The Standing Committee of the Sixth NPC adopts the *Patent Law of the PRC* to encourage inventions and creations and to protect patent rights for them.

April 8. China launches its first experimental communications satellite.

April 28. The newly written historical Peking opera *The Spirit of Daming (Daming hun)* is published in *Play-Scripts*.

May 7. NCNA announces that in future all Chinese over the age of 16 will be required to carry identity cards.

May 31. The Second Session of the Sixth NPC adopts the *Law on Regional Autonomy for Minority Nationalities of the PRC*.

July. The Sichuan People's Press publishes *Ba Jin's Selected Works (Ba Jin xuanji)* in ten volumes.

July. The periodical *Shanghai Literature (Shanghai wenxue)* publishes Acheng's short novel *King of Chess (Qiwang)*.

July 28. At the 23rd Summer Olympic Games in Los Angeles, China wins the first gold medal of the Games and the first ever won by China when marksman Xu Haifeng wins the free pistol shooting event.

August. The Authors' Press publishes Wang Meng's novel *In Yili, The Light-coloured Grey Eyes (Zai Yili, danse hui de yanzhu)*.

F. Births and Deaths

February 5. Senior General Su Yu dies.

April 19. He Zizhen, Mao Zedong's former wife, dies.

May 17. Educator and social scientist Cheng Fangwu dies.

August 11. Theoretician Li Weihan dies.

1985

A. Foreign Affairs Events

February 7. China's first trade centre in Western Europe is opened in Hamburg.

March 13. Li Peng attends the funeral of the Soviet President Konstantin Chernenko in Moscow. The next day he meets Mikhail Gorbachev, the new Soviet Party general secretary, and shares with him the hope for major improvements in Sino-Soviet relations.

March 21. The Standing Committee of the Sixth NPC adopts the *Foreign Economic Contract Law of the PRC*.

March 30. The American Agency for International Development announces its decision to cut US$10 million from its donation to the United Nations Fund for Population Activities, apparently because of the UN Fund's support for China's population and abortion policies.

April 24–25. Chinese Foreign Minister Wu Xueqian takes part in celebrations in Bandung, Indonesia, marking the thirtieth anniversary of the Asian–African Conference. He is the first high-ranking Chinese leader to visit Indonesia since the suspension of relations in 1967.

May 15. Direct air services between China and Singapore begin.

June 8. A Chinese government statement denounces American attacks on China's family planning program as interference in its domestic policies. The statement disputes allegations that the population policies infringe upon human rights.

October 28–November 12. Premier Zhao Ziyang makes a visit to Colombia, Brazil, Argentina and Venezuela, the first ever trip by a Chinese premier to Latin America.

B. Domestic Political Events

March 7. In a speech at a national science conference, Deng Xiaoping claims that high ideals, including a belief in Marxism and communism, and discipline are the two main guarantees for building socialism with Chinese characteristics.

June 4. Deng Xiaoping, chairman of the Central Military Commission, announces China's intention to reduce the size of its army by one million within two years.

September 18–23. A National Conference of the CCP takes place, with closing session speeches by Deng Xiaoping, Chen Yun and Li Xiannian.

C. Economic Events

March 13. The State Council releases a decision calling for an immediate end to the illegal price rises which have disrupted the market.

March 27. Zhao Ziyang's report on the work of the government, given at the Third Session of the Sixth NPC, emphasizes that the two major tasks in the reform of China's economic structure in 1985 are changes in the wage and price systems.

September 23. The National Conference adopts the CCPCC's Proposal for the Seventh Five-year Plan for National Economic and Social Development (1986–90).

D. Appointments, Dismissals, etc.

March 21. Chen Muhua is appointed president of the People's Bank of China; Zheng Tuobin replaces her as Minister of Foreign Economic Relations and Trade.

June 18. The NPC Standing Committee announces the appointment of nine new ministers, including Li Peng as Minister in Charge of the State Education Commission; all ministers have received a higher education degree.

July 13. China announces that Deng Liqun has been dismissed as the head of the CCP Propaganda Department in favour of Zhu Houze.

July 30. A CCPCC report is released stating that the Hainan Administrative Region Party vice-secretary and Hainan People's Government head Lei Yu and his colleague Chen Yuyi have been dismissed for organizing a large-scale smuggling network for the corrupt import and resale of cars, minibuses, television sets, video recorders and motorcycles.

September 16. The Fourth Plenum of the Twelfth CCPCC approves the resignations of sixty-four of its members (18 per cent of the total) on the grounds of old age. Among these are ten members of the Politburo, including Ye Jianying, Wang Zhen, Li Desheng and Deng Yingchao.

September 24. The Fifth Plenum of the Twelfth CCPCC elects six new members to the Politburo: Tian Jiyun, Qiao Shi, Li Peng, Wu Xueqian, Hu Qili and Yao Yilin; they replace the ten who had sent their resignations to the Fourth Plenum. The appointments implement a policy of putting younger and better educated people into senior leadership positions.

E. Cultural and Social Events

May 1. The PLA begins to wear new uniforms which clearly distinguish between officers and ordinary soldiers.

May 19. China's defeat by Hong Kong in a football match in Beijing results in a destructive riot, the most serious over a sporting loss since 1949, and the sentence (on June 18) of five people to prison terms ranging from four to thirty months.

May 28. The CCPCC's 'Decision on the Reform of the Educational System' is released by NCNA. The Decision calls for education to be geared to the modernization program, the world and the future and urges the universalization and improvement of basic education.

October 18. The Bolshoi Ballet performs in Beijing for the first time for more than two decades.

November 20. Students march in Beijing to oppose Japanese politico-economic influence in China.

December 10. Some 4000 students rally in Beijing in support of the open-door policy.

December 22. In China's first public antinuclear demonstration, several hundred students, including many Uygurs, protest in central Beijing against nuclear testing in Xinjiang.

F. Births and Deaths

June 8. Literary and art critic Hu Feng dies.

June 12. Mathematician Hua Luogeng dies in Tokyo.

August 12. General Xiao Hua dies.

October 22. Xu Shiyou, vice-chairman of the CCP's Central Advisory Commission, dies.

G. Natural Disasters, Accidents

April 18. A severe earthquake strikes Yunnan province, killing twenty-two people and injuring many more.

July–August. Torrential rains and flooding in Liaoning, Guizhou and Sichuan kill some 1000 people, leave thousands homeless and inundate millions of hectares of farmland.

July 30. A typhoon strikes Zhejiang province. On August 7, the Ministry of Civil Affairs puts the death toll at 177.

August 23. An earthquake strikes Xinjiang, killing some sixty people and injuring over 100.

December 24. The main dam of the Tianshengqiao Hydroelectric Power Station in Guangxi collapses while still under construction. Fifty-five workers are buried and forty-eight other people killed.

1986

A. Foreign Affairs Events

March 10. China becomes a member of the Asian Development Bank.

March 17. In Beijing the Coalition Government of Democratic Kampuchea puts forward an eight-point proposal to solve the Kampuchean problem. It involves a two-phase Vietnamese troop withdrawal, with the establishment of a quadripartite government after the completion of the first phase, consisting of the three groups of the coalition and the pro-Vietnamese Heng Samrin group, with Norodom Sihanouk as president.

March 18. Hu Yaobang expresses China's support for the eight-point proposal on Kampuchea put forward the preceding day.

March 21. Premier Zhao Ziyang announces that China has ceased atmospheric nuclear tests and will not undertake them in the future.

April 7. United States President Reagan formally notifies the United States Congress of an agreement with China for the sale of high-technology electronic aviation equipment worth $550 million to help China's military modernization.

July 12. An armed clash takes place along the Sino-Soviet border, but both countries adopt a low-key attitude towards it.

July 28. In a major policy speech in Vladivostok, the Soviet leader Mikhail Gorbachev calls for a good-neighbourly atmosphere in Sino-Soviet relations and for the Sino-Soviet border to 'become a line of peace and friendship in the near future'.

September 2. Deng Xiaoping gives an interview to Mike Wallace of the American Columbia Broadcasting System, telecast in the United States on September 7. He says that if Mr Gorbachev 'takes a solid step' towards removing the three major obstacles to Sino-Soviet relations, in particular urging Vietnam to withdraw its troops from Kampuchea, he is prepared to go 'to any place in the Soviet Union' to meet him.

September 20–October 5. The 10th Asian Games take place in Seoul; China participates and wins the most gold medals of any country.

September 28–30. The first secretary of the Polish Communist Party Central Committee, Wojcieck Jaruzelski, visits China, the first high-ranking Polish official to do so for over two decades.

October 12–18. British Queen Elizabeth II visits China.

October 21–26. Erich Honecker, general secretary of the German Democratic Republic's Society Unity Party and chairman of the State Council, visits China, the first high-ranking East German party and state official to do so.

B. Domestic Political Events

May 3. The Commander of a Taiwanese China Airlines Boeing 747, Wang Xijue, lands his plane in Guangzhou. On May 6 he flies to Beijing where he joins relations.

September 28. The Sixth Plenum of the Twelfth CCPCC adopts a resolution 'on the guiding principles for building a socialist society with an advanced culture and ideology'. Among many other points, it attacks 'bourgeois liberalization' which it defines as a trend 'negating the socialist system in favour of capitalism'.

C. Economic Events

March 25. At the NPC, Zhao Ziyang gives a report on the Seventh Five-year Plan, adopted on April 12.

April 12. The NPC adopts the *Law on Enterprises Operated Exclusively with Foreign Capital*.

May 26–29. In Tianjin a conference of mayors of fourteen cities and regions decides to establish a special economic region around the Bohai.

August 3. NCNA reports that the Shenyang Explosion-Prevention Equipment Factory has been declared bankrupt, the first bankruptcy case in the history of the PRC.

September 15. The CCPCC and State Council issue regulations on the implementation of a responsibility system in publicly-owned industrial enterprises, which gives more power to factory directors.

September 26. The Shanghai Stock Market reopens, for the first time since Liberation.

October 11. State Council provisions to encourage foreign investment come into effect.

December 2. The NPC Standing Committee approves the *Bankruptcy Law* for trial implementation.

E. Cultural and Social Events

First quarter. Wei Minglun's *Pan Jinlian*, a controversial 'drama of the absurd' in the Sichuan opera style, is published in *The Dramatist (Xijujia)*.

April 21. The NPC adopts the *Law of the PRC on Compulsory Education*, which stipulates nine years' compulsory education in the cities and developed areas by 1990 and almost everywhere by the end of the century.

May 5. NCNA reports that the People's Press has simultaneously published all fifty volumes of the first Chinese edition of the *Complete Works of Marx and Engels (Makesi Engesi quanji)*.

May 24–25. A clash between African and Chinese students at Tianjin University leaves several people injured.

July 5–7. The first national Chinese conference of lawyers takes place in Beijing. On the last day the Chinese National Lawyers' Association is set up.

November 28. The Ministry of Public Security promulgates the 'Detailed Rules for Implementation of the Regulations for Residents' Identification Cards of the PRC'.

December 5. Several thousand students march in Hefei, the capital of Anhui province, demanding the seizure of greater democracy, an early major rally in a series of student demonstrations in many Chinese cities in November, and especially December. Later Chinese reports claim that the then vice-president of the Chinese University of Science and Technology in Hefei, Fang Lizhi, had sparked the rally through a speech the preceding evening in which he said that democracy is not granted but won.

December 19–21. Large-scale demonstrations for greater democracy take place in Shanghai, involving tens of thousands of students and others. They continue on December 22, but with fewer participants, authorities having warned that permission would be required for further rallies.

December 23. In Beijing, some 4000 students demonstrate for an end to authoritarianism.

December 26. The Beijing Municipal People's Congress Standing Committee bans student demonstrations lacking police approval.

December 30. The vice-minister of the State Education Commission, He Dongchang,

comments on the recent student demonstrations at a press conference of Chinese and foreign journalists. He claims that only a very small proportion of students took part in the demonstrations, that no students were arrested, and that all those arrested were not students but others who were taking advantage of the demonstrations to commit acts against China's constitution.

F. Births and Deaths

February 19. Chen Xiaomeng and two other children of senior cadres are executed for rape and other crimes in Shanghai: this is a demonstration of the government's willingness to treat everybody equally before the law, no matter what their connections.

March 4. Author Ding Ling dies.

March 26. Former Dazhai 'model' peasant Chen Yonggui dies.

May 3. Linguist and educator Wang Li dies.

July 29. Nuclear scientist Deng Jiaxian dies.

October 7. Marshal Liu Bocheng dies.

October 22. Marshal Ye Jianying dies.

December 28. Huang Kecheng dies.

G. Natural Disasters

July 11. Typhoons begin in south-east China; in Guangdong province alone they result in the deaths of 172 people and cause injuries to 1250.

1987

A. Foreign Affairs Events

January 8. Several hundred African students march to the headquarters of the African diplomatic quarter in Beijing to protest against racist attitudes towards them as expressed in a letter written by a body calling itself the Chinese Students Association.

March 26. Chinese and Portuguese representatives initial a joint declaration that sovereignty over Macao will be transferred to the PRC on December 20, 1999, and that thereafter it will be administered as the Macao Special Administrative Region on the basis of the 'one country, two systems' principle.

April 13. In Beijing, the Portuguese Prime Minister Anibal Cavaco Silva and Zhao Ziyang sign the Joint Declaration on the Question of Macao on the transfer of the sovereignty of Macao to the PRC.

June 4–21. Zhao Ziyang makes a major tour of Eastern Europe, arriving in Poland on June 4, East Germany on June 8, Czechoslovakia on June 11, Hungary on June 14 and Bulgaria on June 18.

October 6. The United States Senate unanimously condemns China's actions in Tibet. The vote follows the appearance of Tibet's Dalai Lama before two United States Congressional bodies on September 21, during which he called for the designation of Tibet as a 'zone of peace' and denounced Chinese policies and actions there.

October 8. The Chinese NPC Foreign Affairs Committee responds to the United States Senate vote of October 6 and other United States Congressional moves on Tibet by demanding strongly that the United States Congress should stop all its interference in China's internal affairs.

B. Domestic Political Events

January 1. A *People's Daily* editorial attacks bourgeois liberalization, and asserts that the fundamental guarantee to ensure the success of China's reform lies in the 'four cardinal principles': adherence to the leadership of the CCP, to Marxism–Leninism–Mao Zedong thought, to the people's democratic dictatorship, and to the socialist road.

January 6. A *People's Daily* editorial states that the recent student demonstrations have now subsided and that they demonstrate the need to oppose bourgeois liberalization and uphold the 'four cardinal principles'.

October 25. In his keynote speech to the Thirteenth Congress of the CCP (held October 25–November 1), Zhao Ziyang states that China is now in the 'primary stage of socialism', which began in the 1950s and would last at least a century 'to the time when socialist modernization will have been in the main accomplished'.

November 24. The NPC Standing Committee adopts the *Organic Law of the Village Committees of the PRC*, defining the character, functions and tasks of the village committees. Village committees are to be established as self-managing mass organizations throughout rural China.

C. Economic Events

February 25. A meeting in Beijing marks the inauguration of the State Commission of the Machine Industry.

March 25. In his report on the work of the government to the NPC, Zhao Ziyang criticizes the failure of total supply to meet social demand, and excessive price rises.

December 1. Rationing of pork and sugar is reintroduced in Beijing, a move followed quickly by the administrations of Shanghai, Tianjin and other major cities.

December 28. A ceremony marks the formal opening of the new Shanghai Railway Station.

D. Appointments, Dismissals, etc.

January 13. Writer Wang Ruofang is expelled from the CCP for advocating bourgeois liberalization and opposing the 'four cardinal principles'.

January 16. Hu Yaobang resigns as general secretary of the CCP in favour of Zhao Ziyang.

January 17. Fang Lizhi is expelled from the CCP for the same reasons as Wang Ruofang four days earlier (see also December 5, 1986).

January 24. It is announced that *People's Daily* reporter Liu Binyan has been expelled from the CCP for advocating bourgeois liberalization and opposing the 'four cardinal principles'.

June 6. Yang Zhong is dismissed as Minister of Forestry because of the catastrophic forest fires in the north-east (see below, *G. Natural Disasters*, May 6).

November 2. The First Plenum of the Thirteenth CCPCC confirms Zhao Ziyang as CCP general secretary. In addition, it appoints Li Peng, Qiao Shi, Hu Qili and Yao Yilin to the Politburo Standing Committee. Chen Yun is elected chairman of the Central Advisory Commission and Deng Xiaoping chairman of the CCPCC's Military Commission.

November 24. The NPC Standing Committee approves Zhao Ziyang's resignation as premier and his replacement by Li Peng as acting premier.

E. Cultural and Social Events

July 3. *People's Daily* reports that any CCP member who takes bribes, however small, will be expelled. It notes the view of the CCP Central Discipline Inspection Commission that the practice of taking and asking for bribes has become rampant in some areas.

September 1. China's first Institute of Tibetan Buddhism officially opens in Beijing.

September 5–25. The first China Art Festival takes place in Beijing, featuring over forty performances of all kinds, as well as fine art exhibitions and mass cultural activities.

September 27. Demonstrations, mainly by monks, begin in Lhasa in favour of Tibetan independence; some demonstrators are arrested.

October 1. Demonstrations by some 2000 monks and others in Lhasa in favour of Tibetan independence lead to clashes with authorities and the death of at least six people, with NCNA claiming (on October 10) that at least fifty foreigners were directly involved.

October 6. Some eighty monks from three of Tibet's main monasteries march through Lhasa calling for independence for Tibet.

F. Births and Deaths

December 27. Long-time China resident from New Zealand, Rewi Alley, dies.

G. Natural Disasters

May 6. A gigantic forest fire breaks out in Heilongjiang province; it later spreads to Inner Mongolia. The fire is extinguished on May 26, but revives two days later. Rain and firefighters finally extinguish it on June 2. It kills some 200 people, leaves more than 50 000 homeless, and burns an area of over one million hectares, causing incalculable damage to the environment.

May 20. Torrential rains begin in Guangdong causing severe flooding over the following days. Some hundred people are later reported killed and many thousands of houses destroyed, as well as 158 000 hectares of farmland swamped.

1988

A. Foreign Affairs Events

April 15. Through a Foreign Ministry spokesman, China welcomes the Geneva Agreement on Afghanistan, signed the day before, which stipulates the withdrawal of all Soviet forces by February 15, 1989.

July 1. The Foreign Ministry issues a four-point statement on Kampuchea, including a freeze on all Kampuchean forces, after a Vietnamese withdrawal and the establishment of a provisional quadripartite government 'so that the Kampuchean people may conduct a free election without outside interference and threat of force'.

September 17. In an interview with an American delegation the day after a major speech given by Gorbachev in Krasnoyarsk, Li Peng states that China is willing to normalize relations with the Soviet Union but does not expect the two countries to be as closely aligned again as they were in the 1950s.

September 17–October 2. China takes part in the Twenty-fourth Olympic Games, held in Seoul, Republic of Korea, despite its lack of recognition of the Republic of Korea, and even though the China-recognized Democratic People's Republic of Korea had made an unsuccessful attempt to co-host the Games.

October 17. In Beijing, Deng Xiaoping tells visiting Romanian President Nicolae Ceausescu that a Sino-Soviet summit might take place in 1989.

November 10–24. Li Peng makes his first overseas trip as premier, visiting Thailand, Australia and New Zealand.

December 1–3. Qian Qichen visits the Soviet Union, the first time a Chinese Foreign Minister has done so since Zhou Enlai in 1956, and holds intensive talks with his Soviet counterpart Eduard Shevardnadze.

December 19–23. Rajiv Gandhi visits China, the first Indian Prime Minister to do so for thirty-four years, meeting Deng Xiaoping on December 21.

B. Domestic Political Events

January 14. The CCPCC sends a message of condolence to the Guomindang Central Committee on the death of Jiang Jingguo.

March 5. Lamas and others demonstrate in Lhasa for independence on the last day of the traditional Tibetan Grand Summons Ceremony.

March 25. Li Peng gives the report on the work of the government on the first day of the First Session of the Seventh NPC.

April 13. The NPC adopts a resolution formally upgrading Hainan to the status of a province, and also making it a special economic zone, at this point China's largest.

June 15. At the European Parliament in Strasbourg, the Dalai Lama proposes that Tibet should become a self-governing political entity in association with China.

December 10. Lamas and others demonstrate in Lhasa for Tibetan independence. At least one person is killed by police.

C. Economic Events

January 22. NCNA releases Zhao Ziyang's outline of a strategy for economic growth based on speeding up the development of urban coastal areas to become centres of export-oriented industries.

July 3. Li Peng signs regulations designed to encourage investment on the mainland from Taiwan.

August 15–17. A Politburo meeting in Beidaihe decides to allow prices for most commodities to be regulated by the market. The decision results in panic buying in the second half of August, creating accelerated inflation.

August 30. The State Council issues an urgent directive in an effort to control serious inflation.

September 26. Zhao Ziyang gives a report to the Third Plenum of the Twelfth CCPCC, in which he states that among the key economic tasks in the next two years are 'cutting back social total demand and checking inflation'.

December 21. The Datong Locomotive Plant in Shanxi turns out its last steam locomotive, marking the end of China's history of steam engine production.

D. Appointments, Dismissals, etc.

March 5. The Railways Minister Ding Guan'gen resigns because of the air crash of January 18, rail disaster of January 24 (see *G. Natural Disasters*, under those dates) and other disasters.

April 8. The NPC elects Yang Shangkun as PRC president (replacing Li Xiannian) and Wang Zhen as vice-president (replacing Ulanfu); Wan Li is elected chairman of the Standing Committee of the NPC (replacing Peng Zhen); and Deng Xiaoping is re-elected chairman of the Central Military Commission.

April 9. The NPC confirms Li Peng as premier of the State Council.

April 12. In the new State Council, elected on this day by the NPC, Wu Xueqian becomes a vice-premier and Qian Qichen replaces him as Minister of Foreign Affairs.

E. Cultural and Social Events

March 10. The Chinese mainland's first test-tube baby is born in Beijing.

March 17. The Ministry of Public Security announces the seizure of 4.5 kg of heroin in Shanghai from March 9 to 13.

June 3. Students demonstrate in protest against the death of Chai Qingfeng (see *F. Births and Deaths*, under June 2); in the next few days wall posters put forward such demands as press freedom, higher priority for education and a better legal system.

July 1. The journal *Seeking Truth from Facts (Qiushi)* replaces *Red Flag (Hongqi)*.

July 21. Li Peng promulgates a nineteen-article set of labour regulations for the protection of female workers, adopted by the State Council on June 28 and due to be put into effect on September 1.

October 16. Beijing's electron-positron collider is successfully completed, with the collision of an enormous mass of positron and electron particles travelling at the speed of light in an underground laboratory in Beijing.

October 22–28. The Eleventh National Congress of the All-China Federation of Trade Unions is held in Beijing, representing 93 365 000 trade union members.

November 8. The NPC Standing Committee adopts a law on the protection of wildlife, to take effect on March 1, 1989. At the Fifth Conference of the China Federation of Literary and Art Circles, Hu Qili gives a major speech on literature and art policies. He calls for the application of the 'four cardinal principles', but not in a stereotyped manner, and for freedom both of literary creation and criticism.

December 22. China's first exhibition of nude paintings opens in Beijing (closing on January 8, 1989).

December 24. A clash erupts between African students and Chinese college employees at the Hehai University in Nanjing. Trouble continues in the following days, with the Africans denouncing the Chinese as racist.

F. Births and Deaths

January 13. Taiwan's President Jiang Jingguo dies.

February 16. Educator, writer, publisher and social activist Ye Shengtao dies in Beijing.

May 10. Writer Shen Congwen dies.

June 2. Postgraduate student Chai Qingfeng is murdered near Beijing University.

June 22. Writer Xiao Jun dies.

October 3. Long-time China resident, the American George Hatem, dies in Beijing.

December 8. Inner Mongolian CCP leader Ulanfu dies.

G. Natural Disasters, Accidents

January 18. A passenger airliner crashes near Chongqing, Sichuan province, killing all ninety-eight passengers and ten crew.

January 24. The Kunming–Shanghai express is derailed and overturned nearly 350 km from Kunming, killing at least ninety people and injuring others.

May 26. *China Daily* reports that severe flooding in the last few days in southern China, especially Fujian province, has killed 117 people and injured nearly 500 others.

July 29–30. Zhejiang suffers its worst floods in four decades. Over 200 people are killed and nearly 500 reported missing, with enormous destruction to property.

August 8. A typhoon strikes Hangzhou and other parts of Zhejiang province; it eventually results in the deaths of 110 people, injuries to well over 1000, and massive destruction to property and crops.

November 6. Severe earthquakes shake the southwest of Yunnan province; deaths total some 730 and about 3500 people are seriously injured, with over 400 000 houses destroyed and another 700 000 damaged.

1989 THE BEIJING MASSACRE

A. Foreign Affairs Events

February 1–4. Eduard Shevardnadze visits China, the first Soviet Foreign Minister to do so since 1959.

February 11–13. Pakistani Prime Minister Benazir Bhutto visits China.

February 25–26. George Bush makes his first trip to China as United States President.

May 15–18. Mikhail Gorbachev makes the first visit of a Soviet leader to China since 1959.

May 16. Gorbachev and Deng Xiaoping hold a meeting in the Great Hall of the People, after which Deng Xiaoping announces that Sino-Soviet relations are 'normalized'.

May 18. The Sino-Soviet Joint Communiqué is issued in Beijing. The two sides agree that 'the Sino-Soviet high level meeting symbolized the normalization of relations between the two countries' but that the normalization of Sino-Soviet relations is not directed at any third country. On Kampuchea the two sides agree that, with the withdrawal of Vietnamese troops, 'the countries concerned should gradually reduce and eventually stop all their military aid to any of the parties in Kampuchea'.

June 5. In protest against the Beijing massacre of June 3–4. United States President Bush announces suspension of all government-to-government sales and commercial export of weapons, and of all visits between senior American and Chinese military officials.

June 7. A Chinese Foreign Ministry announcement denounces United States President Bush's announcement of June 5 as unacceptable pressure on the Chinese government. An official statement describes the United States sanctuary given to dissident Fang Lizhi on June 5 as 'interference in China's internal affairs'.

June 22. Ji Pengfei, Director of the Hong Kong and Macao Affairs Office, declares on China Central Television that the Chinese government will persist in its policies on Hong Kong and Macao, including adherence to the Sino-British and Sino-Portuguese Joint Declarations (see respectively under *A. Foreign Affairs Events,* December 19, 1984 and April 13, 1987) and the concept of 'one country, two systems'.

June 26. The World Bank announces that it will defer consideration of seven new development loans to China worth US$780.2 million because of the massacre and continuing repression.

July 15. Leaders of the seven major industrial capitalist nations—the United States, Japan, France, West Germany, Britain, Italy and Canada—meeting in Paris to discuss world economic problems against the background of celebrations to commemorate the bicentenary of the storming of the Bastille (July 14, 1789) and the French Revolution—issue a political declaration which includes condemnation of China for its suppression of the pro-democracy movement. However, no new measures or economic sanctions are announced.

July 17. A *People's Daily* editorial rejects the Paris declaration of July 15 as unfair, since it was necessary for China to suppress the counter-revolutionary rebellion.

July 18. Japan Air Lines in Beijing receives a letter, dated July 13, from a group calling itself the 'Blood-bright Dare-to-Die Squad', threatening reprisals unless Japan ceases its economic invasion of China and its support for the CCP.

October 31. Deng Xiaoping meets former United States President Richard Nixon and tells him that China was 'the victim' in the recent turmoil and counter-revolutionary rebellion and it is 'unfair to make accusations against her'.

November 6. Deng Xiaoping holds talks with the DPRK President Kim Il Sung during a three-day unofficial visit to China by Kim (November 5–7).

November 13. Deng Xiaoping meets a Japanese business delegation and calls it his last meeting with guests in an official capacity.

November 14–21. Li Peng undertakes his first overseas trip since the June 4 incident: to Pakistan (November 14–18), Bangladesh and Nepal.

December 10. During a twenty-five-hour visit to China, Brent Scowcroft, the National Security Adviser to the United States President, meets Deng Xiaoping and tells him that President Bush still regards him as a friend.

December 11. China formally protests to the Norwegian government over its participation in the December 10 ceremony to award the Dalai Lama the 1989 Nobel Peace Prize. China denounces Norway for 'open support for the activities of the Dalai Lama's clique aimed at splitting China and gross interference in China's internal affairs'.

December 26. The Chinese Foreign Ministry announces that China will 'continue to maintain and develop its friendly relations with Romania', where the day before the previous president and vice-president, Nicolae and Elena Ceausescu, had been executed.

B. Domestic Political Events

March 5–7. Anti-Chinese demonstrations take place in Lhasa; serious violence erupts between police and demonstrators, with looting of Han Chinese houses and shops, making the scale of trouble the worst since 1959. The State Council declares martial law on March 7, to take effect from midnight the same day.

April 22. Official mourning is held in central Beijing for Hu Yaobang. Many thousands of students demonstrate in Tiananmen Square to mourn him, and also to demand his rehabilitation as well as democratic reforms. This demonstration forms a climax to a series of such demonstrations for democracy sparked off by the death of Hu Yaobang a week before.

April 26. An editorial in *People's Daily*, following the line laid down in a speech by Deng Xiaoping the preceding day, criticizes the student demonstrations and declares the situation to be 'a grave political struggle facing the whole Party and Chinese citizens of all nationalities'.

April 27. An enormous demonstration, with well over 100 000 student and other participants, takes place in Beijing in direct defiance of a government ban. The demands of the students include press freedom, government accountability and a crackdown on Party corruption.

May 4. Another enormous demonstration takes place in Beijing, with much smaller ones in several other cities, in commemoration of the May Fourth Movement of 1919. The demonstrations also put forward several demands, including democracy and press freedom. No violence or arrests result.

May 13. A large-scale rally for democracy and freedom converges on Tiananmen Square in the heart of Beijing. Students declare they will remain in occupation of the square until their pro-democracy demands are met, and about 1000 students begin a hunger strike.

May 18. Li Peng holds a televised meeting with representatives of the striking students at the Great Hall of the People, including the Uygur Wuerkaixi from Beijing Teachers' University and Wang Dan from Beijing University.

May 19. Early in the morning Zhao Ziyang appears in Tiananmen Square to express sympathy with hunger-striking demonstrators, his last public appearance before the Beijing massacre of June 3–4.

May 20. The State Council declares martial law in parts of Beijing to take effect from 10 am the same day. Mass demonstrations continue in Beijing, with opposition to the imposition of martial law and demands for the overthrow of Li Peng being central issues. The army refuses to take action against the crowds, while people erect barricades to prevent its advance towards Tiananmen Square.

May 25. A pro-democracy demonstration of some 100 000 workers and intellectuals takes place in Beijing demanding the resignation of the premier, Li Peng, who appears on television announcing that his government is in full control of the situation and will press ahead with reform.

June 2. Three people are killed by a police jeep in Beijing. The incident is regarded by the students as a deliberate foretaste of a massacre, but is claimed by the government to be an accident.

June 3. Crowds of people, especially students, again prevent mainly-unarmed soldiers from entering Tiananmen Square by erecting barricades and other means. According to the government, leaders of the student movement incite the mobs to kill soldiers; this, together with other actions, marks the beginning of a 'counter-revolutionary rebellion'.

June 3–4. The Beijing massacre. Troops of the 27th Army of the PLA and the People's Armed Police move along the Chang'an Boulevard in Beijing to Tiananmen Square to clear the square of demonstrators. The first violence erupts at about 10 pm on June 3 and continues at intervals throughout the night and following morning. Troops force their way through barricades set up by ordinary people, and fire on the crowds, sometimes indiscriminately. Casualties run into many thousands, with deaths probably somewhere between 1000 and 3000. By midday on June 4, troops have sealed off Tiananmen Square.

June 4. In Chengdu, PLA troops advance into the square at the centre of the city to clear it of student protesters. Some 300 people are killed.

June 5. The CCPCC and the State Council claim initial victory against a counter-revolutionary riot instigated by a handful of people aimed at 'negating the leadership of the CCP, destroying the socialist system and overthrowing the People's Republic'.

June 6. In Shanghai, eight people are killed when an express train runs into a human barricade trying to prevent soldiers from entering the city. About thirty others sustain fatal injuries.

June 9. Deng Xiaoping, Yang Shangkun, Li Peng, Qiao Shi, Wan Li, Yao Yilin, Wang Zhen, Peng Zhen and other leaders appear at a televised meeting in central Beijing to praise the military action of June 3–4. Leaders notable by their absence include Zhao Ziyang, Tian Jiyun and Hu Qili. Deng Xiaoping's speech commends the troops for suppressing 'counter-revolutionaries trying to overthrow the CCP' and for putting down 'the counter-revolutionary rebellion'. He also pledges continuation of the reform and open-door policies adopted at the end of 1978.

June 10. Chinese official media announce that 'martial law troops' have arrested over 400 people in Beijing, Hebei, Tianjin and Shanghai 'in order to protect Beijing'. This is the start of an extensive series of arrests.

June 16. In a speech to the new Politburo Standing Committee, Deng Xiaoping refers to three generations of the Chinese leadership core: Mao Zedong heading the first one, himself the second and Jiang Zemin the third. He also makes reference to attacking corruption to strengthen the country, amongst other tasks.

June 24. The Fourth Plenum of the Thirteenth CCPCC adopts a communiqué reaffirming the policies of reform adopted by and since the Third Plenum of the Eleventh CCPCC (December 1978) and the 'one focus and two basic points' established at the Thirteenth CCP Congress. The 'one focus' is the stress on economic development as the nation's central task, while the two basic points are adherence to the four cardinal principles (see under January 1, 1987) and persevering with reform and the open-door policy.

June 30. Mayor of Beijing Chen Xitong gives a

'report on checking the turmoil and quelling the counter-revolutionary rebellion', in which he includes a detailed statement in defence of the government's account of the events of April, May and June. Its essence is that the government was forced to put down a counter-revolutionary rebellion. Among numerous other points he gives some casualty figures: in the several days of the rebellion several dozen soldiers, armed police and public security officers were killed, and more than 6000 injured. During the 'counter-attack' of June 3–4, more than 3000 civilians were wounded and over 200, including thirty-six college students, were killed.

August 15. A government circular announces a policy under which economic criminals who surrender themselves to the authorities before October 31 will be dealt with leniently.

October 31. A ten-week period of clemency for economic criminals ends, with nearly 36 200 people involved in graft, bribery, profiteering, speculation and other economic offences having turned themselves over to the judicial authorities.

C. Economic Events

March 20. In his opening speech to the Second Session of the Seventh NPC, Premier Li Peng sharply criticizes his own government for allowing the economy to become overheated. He says that inflation and excessive price hikes are the main problems faced by China in its modernization drive.

July 11. An air route opens linking Ürümqi, in the Xinjiang Uygur autonomous region, and Alma-Ata, capital of the Soviet Union's Kazakh Soviet Socialist Republic.

August 1. A Boeing-757 aircraft, the first of three imported from the United States by Shanghai Airlines, arrives at Shanghai airport.

August 8. Tianjin signs a contract leasing 5.3 square kilometres of land to the MGM Development Company, a United States-based corporation, the largest foreign contract for China since the Beijing massacre.

October 1. A railway linking Shangqiu, Henan with Fuyang, Anhui opens to traffic.

November 9. The Thirteenth CCPCC's Fifth Plenum issues a communiqué which places emphasis on the economy. It expresses satisfaction over successes achieved in the cooling of the country's overheated economy in the past year, but points to several priority targets, the first being to slow down inflation and bring down the national rate of retail price rises to under 10 per cent.

November 14. A State Statistical Bureau official announces that China suspended 18 000 construction projects in the first nine months of 1989.

D. Appointments, Dismissals, etc.

June 24. The Fourth Plenum of the Thirteenth CCPCC dismisses Zhao Ziyang from all leading posts in the Party and elects Jiang Zemin to replace him as general secretary.

September 4. The Standing Committee of the NPC accepts Wang Meng's resignation as Minister of Culture and appoints He Jingzhi to replace him, in an acting capacity.

September 14. The Ministry of Supervision announces the dismissal of the governor of Hainan Province, Liang Xiang, for the abuse of power for personal gain.

November 9. The Fifth Plenum endorses Deng Xiaoping's request to resign the chairmanship of the CCPCC's Military Commission. It appoints Jiang Zemin to replace him as chairman and appoints Yang Shangkun as first vice-chairman, Liu Huaqing as vice-chairman and Yang Baibing as secretary. It appoints Yang Baibing as a new member of the CCPCC's Secretariat.

E. Cultural and Social Events

Early March. The People's Press and the Central Documents Press publish the *Biography of Zhou Enlai (Zhou Enlai zhuan)* as the first in a series of major political biographies of the main communist leaders.

May 5. Some 2000 Moslems in Lanzhou, capital of Gansu, demonstrate against a book on sexual customs published in Shanghai earlier in the year. They argue that the book is insulting to Islam, and demand respect for their beliefs and punishment for the book's authors.

May 12. Some 2000 Moslem students in Beijing demonstrate against the book on sexual customs, since it is 'full of slander against the Moslems'.

May 18. Several thousand fundamentalist Moslems from the Ürümqi Koranic Studies Institute and supporters demonstrate in Ürümqi, demanding the suppression of the book on sexual customs.

May 30. Students erect the statue of the *Goddess of Democracy (Minzhu nüshen)*, modelled on the Statue of Liberty, in Tiananmen Square.

July 21. A State Education Commission spokesman announces the Chinese government's intention to cut the 1989 student intakes into colleges and universities by 5 per cent—that is, from an originally planned 640 000 to about 610 000.

August 4. NCNA reports that the Xi'an Muslim Cultural Training University, designed for students from the Islamic minority nationalities, has begun to enrol students.

August 24. A *People's Daily* editorial promises to punish according to law only those students who took the lead in organizing the recent demonstrations. It promises that those who only took part, or expressed extreme opinions, including participation in hunger strikes, will not be punished. In a national teleconference, Li Ruihuan calls for the campaign against pornography to be combined with efforts to reinvigorate literature and art, and liven up the people's cultural and recreational life, and for reactionary publications advocating bourgeois liberalization to be curbed.

November 14. China publishes a statement attacking the International Labour Organization for allegations of the suppression of the independent trade union movement and mass arrests and repression of workers. The statement claims the allegations are unfounded and represent an interference in China's internal affairs.

F. Births and Deaths

January 28. The Tenth Bainqen (Panchen) Lama dies in Xigaze, Tibet.

February 28. International affairs expert Huan Xiang dies.

April 15. Former CCP General Secretary Hu Yaobang dies of a heart attack in Beijing.

June 21. Xu Guoming and two other men are executed in Shanghai for setting fire to the train which on June 6 had run into a human barricade trying to prevent soldiers from entering the city.

July 31. Zhou Yang, former president of the China Federation of Literature and Art Circles, dies in Beijing.

August 27. Former Uygur Xinjiang leader Burhan Shahidi dies in Beijing.

September 20. Cultural Revolution leader Chen Boda dies, aged 85.

December 6. Painter Li Keran dies in Beijing, aged 82.

G. Natural Disasters

July 7. Heavy, continuous and torrential rains begin falling in Sichuan province, resulting in very serious flooding in twenty counties and prefectures in the province. Many hundreds of people are killed, large areas of farmland are damaged or destroyed, and millions of people are affected by the ensuing floods. Other provinces seriously affected by flooding from early to mid-July include Anhui, Hubei, Jiangsu and Zhejiang. In the last province, 2.62 million people are affected, more than 300 villages are ruined and 10 000 houses are destroyed.

August 16. *People's Daily* quotes a report by the Ministry of Water Resources as saying that vast areas of China have experienced irregular rainfall and over ten million hectares have been hit by severe drought since July. Worst affected is Shandong province, in which four million people have had problems finding drinking water.

October 18–19. Earthquakes shake the border areas of Shanxi, Hebei and Inner Mongolia, killing at least twenty-nine people and injuring more than 150, many seriously.

1990

A. Foreign Affairs Events

January 25. The United States Senate votes to uphold a veto by President Bush on a bill which would have barred deportation of Chinese students once their American visas expired.

February 2. United States President Bush nullifies the sale by Mamco Manufacturing of Seattle to China National Aero-Technology Import and Export Corporation on the grounds that the latter is a military-related agency of the Chinese government.

April 23–26. Li Peng pays an official visit to the Soviet Union, the first by a top Chinese leader for twenty-six years.

B. Domestic Political Events

January 10. Li Peng announces the State Council's decision to lift martial law in Beijing as from January 11.

February 7. A CCPCC document on relations between the eight democratic parties and the CCP is made public, having been issued on December 30, 1989. It declares that the democratic parties should take part in state power under the leadership of the CCP.

March 20. In his opening speech at the Third Session of the Seventh NPC, Li Peng emphasizes stability and adhering to the socialist road.

April 4. President Yang Shangkun promulgates the Basic Law of the Hong Kong Special Administrative Region of the People's Republic of China, adopted by the Seventh NPC on the same day and scheduled to take effect as of July 1, 1997.

April 5–6. Disturbances described in a local official television broadcast as an 'armed counter-revolutionary rebellion', and attributed to the Islamic Party of East Turkestan, occur in Akto county in the Kizilsu Kirghiz autonomous prefecture, Xinjiang. According to the broadcast, the disturbances are aimed at establishing a separatist Islamic republic but are suppressed by the People's Armed Police, resulting in at least twenty-two deaths, including that of the leader of the rebellion.

April 30. Premier Li Peng signs an order lifting martial law in Lhasa, Tibet, to take effect the following day.

C. Economic Events

January 16. Further economic points from the Thirteenth CCPCC's Fifth Plenum are announced: China faces inflation, imbalances in supply and demand, an irrational economic structure and an undesirable economic order. CCP and government officials are called on to cut overall demand and national consumption.

February 2. The United States Export–Import Bank grants a loan of US$10 million to China's National Offshore Oil Corporation.

April 7. In Xichang, Sichuan, a Chinese carrier rocket launches Asia's first regional communications satellite, American-made Asiasat 1.

D. Appointments, Dismissals, etc.

February 13. NCNA announces that on February 1 the State Council and the CCP's Central Military Commission appointed PLA Major-General Zhou Yushu as commander of the People's Armed Police in place of Li Lianxiu. The move is one of several representing a reorganization of the top echelons of the People's Armed Police.

March 21. The NPC endorses Deng Xiaoping's request to resign the chairmanship of the State Military Commission, replacing him with Jiang Zemin.

E. Cultural and Social Events

January 10. In a speech at a national seminar on cultural affairs, Li Ruihuan emphasizes China's cultural and historical heritage and attacks 'wholesale Westernization'.

January 17. At a working conference of the State Education Commission, Jiang Zemin calls for the strengthening of the teaching of patriotism, national integrity and Chinese history. Li Tieying, Minister in Charge of the State Education Commission, calls for greater emphasis on ideology and the strengthening of CCP leadership in the education system.

January 18. A Ministry of Public Security spokesman announces the release of 573 lawbreakers from the student movement of April–June 1989 because of their willingness to confess and reform.

G. Natural Disasters

April 26. An earthquake measuring 6.9 on the Richter scale kills at least 126 people and destroys thousands of houses in South Qinghai Tibetan autonomous prefecture in Qinghai province.

2 POLITICS

THE PARTY

Although there are eight 'democratic parties' (*minzhu dangpai*) still in existence in China in addition to the Chinese Communist Party (CCP), only the CCP holds any real power. The eight 'democratic parties' are the Revolutionary Committee of the Chinese Nationalist Party (*Zhongguo guomin dang geming weiyuanhui*), the China Democratic League (*Zhongguo minzhu tongmeng*), the China Democratic National Construction Association (*Zhongguo minzhu jianguo hui*), the China Association for Promoting Democracy (*Zhongguo minzhu cujin hui*), the Chinese Peasants' and Workers' Democratic Party (*Zhongguo nonggong minzhu dang*), the China Zhi Gong Dang (*Zhongguo zhigong dang*), the September Third Society (*Jiu san xuehui*), and the Taiwan Democratic Self-Government League (*Taiwan minzhu zizhi tongmeng*)

The 'democratic parties' are in no sense opposition parties and they take part in a united front: on May 5, 1948 they responded to the CCP's invitation to hold the Chinese People's Political Consultative Conference, the meeting which in September 1949 decided to establish the People's Republic of China. In theory the CCP still promises to consult with the 'democratic parties' and accept political supervision from them; however, they really have no choice but to accept the CCP's leadership. The reality is that they survive on sufferance from the CCP and could be immediately crushed if they refused to do the CCP's bidding.

The Chinese Communist Party is the leading organ in society. It sees itself as the vanguard of the proletariat and its role is to lay down policy, which the state then implements.

The highest body of the Party is the National Party Congress. There have been thirteen of these in the history of the Party, as listed in Table 2.1.

Table 2.1 The National Congresses of the Chinese Communist Party

National CCP Congress	Opening and closing dates	Place held
First	July 23–31, 1921	Shanghai and (on the last day only) Jiaxing, Zhejiang
Second	July 16–23, 1922	Shanghai
Third	June 12–20, 1923	Guangzhou
Fourth	January 11–22, 1925	Shanghai
Fifth	April 27–May 9, 1927	Hankou
Sixth	June 18–July 11, 1928	Moscow
Seventh	April 23–June 11, 1945	Yan'an
Eighth (First Session)	September 15–26, 1956	Beijing
Eighth (Second Session)	May 5–23, 1958	Beijing
Ninth	April 1–24, 1969	Beijing
Tenth	August 24–28, 1973	Beijing
Eleventh	August 12–18, 1977	Beijing
Twelfth	September 1–11, 1982	Beijing
Thirteenth	October 25–November 1, 1987	Beijing

Each Congress elects its own Central Committee, which meets in full session from time to time. These plenary sessions, or plenums as they are usually termed, often reach decisions of crucial importance for the PRC. The Thirteenth Party Congress elected a Central Committee of 175 full members and 110 alternate members. The number of each Central Committee is that of the National Party Congress which selected its members.

Table 2.2 Plenary Sessions of the Central Committee of the Chinese Communist Party

Central Committee	Plenum	Dates	Place held
First	—	—	—
Second	—	—	—
Third	—	—	—
Fourth	—	—	—
Emergency Conference of the CCPCC		August 7, 1927	Hankou
Fifth	—	—	—
Sixth	No first plenum		
	Second	Six days at the end of June (probably June 25–30), 1929, the resolution being issued on July 9, 1929	Shanghai
	Third	September 24–28, 1930	Shanghai
	Fourth	January 7–13, 1931	Shanghai
	Fifth	January 18–26, 1934	Ruijin, Jiangxi
	Sixth	September 29–November 6, 1938	Yan'an
	Seventh	May 21, 1944–April 20, 1945	Yan'an
Seventh	First	June 19, 1945	Yan'an
	Second	March 5–13, 1949	Pingshan, Hebei
	Third	June 6–9, 1950	Beijing
	Fourth	February 6–10, 1954	Beijing
	Sixth	October 4–11, 1955	Beijing
Eighth	First	September 28, 1956	Beijing
	Second	November 10–15, 1956	Beijing
	Third	September 20–October 9, 1957	Beijing
	Fifth	May 25, 1958	Beijing
	Sixth	November 28–December 10, 1958	Wuchang
	Seventh	April 2–5, 1959	Shanghai
	Eighth	August 2–16, 1959	Lushan, Jiangxi
	Ninth	January 14–18, 1961	Beijing
	Tenth	September 24–27, 1962	Beijing
	Eleventh	August 1–12, 1966	Beijing
	Twelfth	October 13–31, 1968	Beijing
Ninth	First	April 28, 1969	Beijing
	Second	August 23–September 6, 1970	Lushan, Jiangxi
Tenth	First	August 30, 1973	Beijing
	Second	January 8–10, 1975	Beijing
	Third	July 16–21, 1977	Beijing
Eleventh	First	August 19, 1977	Beijing
	Second	February 18–23, 1978	Beijing
	Third	December 18–22, 1978	Beijing
	Fourth	September 25–28, 1979	Beijing
	Fifth	February 23–29, 1980	Beijing
	Sixth	June 27–29, 1981	Beijing

Central Committee	Plenum	Dates	Place held
Twelfth	First	September 12–13, 1982	Beijing
	Second	October 11–12, 1983	Beijing
	Third	October 20, 1984	Beijing
	Fourth	September 16, 1985	Beijing
	Fifth	September 24, 1985	Beijing
	Sixth	September 28, 1986	Beijing
Thirteenth	First	November 2, 1987	Beijing
	Second	March 15–19, 1988	Beijing
	Third	September 26–30, 1988	Beijing
	Fourth	June 23–24, 1989	Beijing
	Fifth	November 6–9, 1989	Beijing
	Sixth	March 9–12, 1990	Beijing

The First Plenum of the Central Committee is held immediately after its election by the retiring Party Congress. This meeting elects the Political Bureau, or Politburo, which carries on the work of the Central Committee when the latter body is not in session. The First Plenum of the Thirteenth Central Committee elected seventeen full members to the Politburo: (listed in alphabetical order) Hu Qili, Hu Yaobang, Jiang Zemin, Li Peng, Li Ruihuan, Li Tieying, Li Ximing, Qiao Shi, Qin Jiwei, Song Ping, Tian Jiyun, Wan Li, Wu Xueqian, Yang Rudai, Yang Shangkun, Yao Yilin and Zhao Ziyang; and one alternate member: Ding Guan'gen. More information on all these leaders is given in Chapter 3.

Even more select than the Politburo is the Standing Committee of the Politburo, also elected by the Central Committee. In theory, and also largely in practice, this small body contains the most influential and powerful people in China. The composition of the Politburo Standing Committees elected by the First Plenums of the Central Committees since the Eighth Central Committee in 1956, that being the first after Liberation, has been as follows:

- *Eighth:* Mao Zedong, Liu Shaoqi, Zhou Enlai, Zhu De, Chen Yun and Deng Xiaoping
- *Ninth:* Mao Zedong, Lin Biao, Zhou Enlai, Chen Boda and Kang Sheng
- *Tenth:* Mao Zedong, Zhou Enlai, Wang Hongwen, Kang Sheng, Ye Jianying, Li Desheng, Zhang Chunqiao, Zhu De and Dong Biwu
- *Eleventh:* Hua Guofeng, Ye Jianying, Deng Xiaoping, Li Xiannian and Wang Dongxing
- *Twelfth:* Hu Yaobang, Ye Jianying, Deng Xiaoping, Li Xiannian, Chen Yun and Zhao Ziyang

- *Thirteenth:* Zhao Ziyang, Li Peng, Hu Qili, Qiao Shi and Yao Yilin.

Political disturbances have sometimes brought about changes in the composition of the Standing Committee of the Politburo, even between National Party Congresses. For example, on June 24, 1989 the Fourth Plenum of the Thirteenth Central Committee dismissed Zhao Ziyang and Hu Qili and replaced them with Jiang Zemin, Song Ping and Li Ruihuan.

Mao Zedong was elected chairman at a meeting of the Politburo in March 1943 and from that time until his death on September 9, 1976 was regarded as chairman both of the Central Committee and of the whole CCP. His deputy, Hua Guofeng, became acting chairman and, on October 7, 1976, following the arrest and fall of the 'gang of four' the preceding day, he was appointed as chairman to succeed Mao Zedong. This was confirmed by the Third Plenum of the Tenth Central Committee and the First Plenum of the Eleventh. On June 29, 1981 the Sixth Plenum of the Eleventh Central Committee replaced Hua Guofeng with Hu Yaobang as chairman, but the post was abolished by the Twelfth CCP Congress in September 1982, formally making the secretary-general the highest position within the CCP. Secretary-generals since the Twelfth Congress have been:

- Hu Yaobang, dismissed on January 16, 1987
- Zhao Ziyang, appointed by the Politburo on January 16, 1987 and confirmed by the First Plenum of the Thirteenth Congress in November 1987 but in effect dismissed in May 1989
- Jiang Zemin, appointed by the Fourth Plenum of the Thirteenth Central Committee on June 24, 1989.

A crucially important body is the Military Commission of the Party Central Committee, which supervises the organizational links between the Party and the army. The First Plenum of the Thirteenth Congress appointed Deng Xiaoping as its chairman, and it was mainly this position which enabled Deng to carry out the suppression of student demonstrators

adopted by the Twelfth Congress put it. The Commission functions as a council of elders. Initially Deng Xiaoping was the chairman of this body, but he retired from the post in favour of Chen Yun at the First Plenum of the Thirteenth Congress.

The other significant body is the Central Commission for Discipline Inspection. As its name sug-

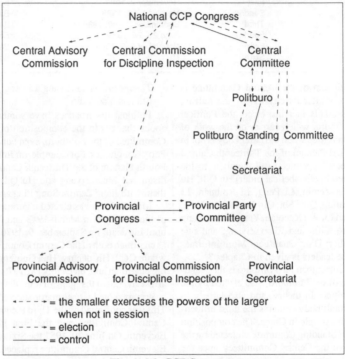

Figure 2.1 CCP Structure

which led to the Beijing massacre of the night of June 3–4, 1989. On September 4, 1989, Deng Xiaoping wrote to the Central Committee requesting permission to resign from this position, and on November 9, 1989, the Fifth Plenum endorsed his request. It appointed Jiang Zemin to replace him as chairman.

Two other central Party bodies have assumed great importance in the 1980s. One is the Central Advisory Commission, set up by the Twelfth Congress in 1982 'to act as political assistant and consultant to the Central Committee', as the Constitution

gests, its rationale is to inspect discipline, which especially includes the curbing of corruption. This has become a very pressing need in the last few years, which have seen the substantial growth of corruption within the Party. Corruption has been more or less endemic to the Chinese bureaucracy for thousands of years. The CCP did manage to curb it successfully in the early years of its rule, but the economic reforms begun in the late 1970s helped open the way for a major return of corruption, because they enabled power-holders to use their influence to gain money, jobs for their relations and various privileges for themselves and their families. Nepotism, bribery, graft and embezzlement have thus once again become very common indeed. Between 1983 and 1986 some 40 000 members of the Party were expelled for corrupt practices, and in 1987 alone the figure was 109 000. Quite a few people have been prosecuted and condemned by the law courts, including some of very high rank. According to the president of the Supreme People's Court, Ren Jianxin, reporting to the National People's Congress on March 29, 1989, the Supreme People's Court in 1988 sentenced 111

embezzlers and bribe-takers to death or life imprisonment and 5642 to prison terms. Of these 5642, 66.54 per cent, or 3754 people, were members of the CCP.

The CCP structure is in evidence everywhere in China, with branches right down to the lowest level. The province-level structures follow the central structure closely, but on a smaller scale. County-level CCP structures are also similar. In the 1950s a policy of periodic transfer of county CCP secretaries was implemented, and this was revived in 1984. Table 2.3 shows CCP membership figures since 1921.

Table 2.3 Figures of membership of the Chinese Communist Party

Year	Number of members	Year	Number of members
1921	57	1949 (end)	4 500 000
1922 (July)	123	1950 (mid)	5 000 000
1923 (June)	432	1950 (end)	5 821 604
1925 (early)	950	1951 (mid)	5 800 000
1927 (April)	57 967	1951 (end)	5 762 293
1927 (later)	10 000	1952 (end)	6 001 698
1928	40 000	1953 (mid)	6 000 000
1930	122 318	1953 (end)	6 612 254
1933	300 000	1954 (early)	6 500 000
1934	300 000	1954 (end)	7 859 473
1937	40 000	1955 (end)	9 393 394
1940	800 000	1956 (mid)	10 734 384
1941	763 447	1957 (mid)	12 720 000
1942	736 151	1959 (mid)	13 960 000
1944	853 420	1961 (mid)	17 000 000
1945 (April)	1 211 128	1966	20 000 000
1946	1 348 320	1973 (August)	28 000 000
1947 (Jan.)	2 200 000	1977 (August)	35 000 000 +
1947 (end)	2 759 456	1982 (Sept.)	39 000 000
1948 (mid)	3 000 000	1984 (July)	40 000 000
1948 (end)	3 065 533	1986 (end)	46 011 951
1949 (Oct.)	4 488 080	1989 (early)	47 755 000
		1989 (August)	48 000 000

Note: The source for the figures from 1921 to 1961 is Franz Schurmann, *Ideology and Organization in Communist China* (University of California Press, Berkeley, Los Angeles, London, second enlarged edition 1968), p. 129. Most of the later figures were released in connection with major Party meetings, in particular Party Congresses. They are recorded in *Peking Review* and its successor *Beijing Review* XVI, 35 and 36 (September 7, 1973), p. 18; XX, 35 (August 26, 1977), p. 6; XXV, 37 (September 13, 1982), p. 5; XXVII, 29 (July 16, 1984), p. 7; XXX, 44 (November 2–8, 1987), p. 5; XXXII, 23 (June 5–11, 1989), p. 26; and XXXII, 36 (September 4–10, 1989), p. 5.

For the early 1989 figure, further breakdowns are given. Workers made up 17.1 per cent of membership, workers in farming, animal husbandry and fisheries 39.5 per cent, cadres 27.7 per cent, army members 2.8 per cent and retirees 2.6 per cent.

Party members below 35 years of age made up 27 per cent, those between 36 and 55 years of age, 30 per cent; and those over 56 years, 20 per cent. The average age of members was 43 years.

Party members with senior school education made up 28.5 per cent of the total, those with junior secondary school education made up 29 per cent, those with primary school education 34.8 per cent and illiterates 7.7 per cent.

Females made up 14.2 per cent of Party membership, and minority nationality members made up 5.5 per cent.

The formal decision to establish the PRC was taken by the first meeting of the Chinese People's Political Consultative Conference (CPPCC) in September 1949. This body continued to play a united-front role in politics until the Cultural Revolution, which abolished it. It resumed this role when its Fifth National Committee met for its First Session in Beijing from February 24 to March 8, 1978. The CPPCC's Constitution (1978) specifies it as 'an organization of the revolutionary united front under the leadership of the CCP'. There have been seven CPPCC National Committees, formed in 1949, 1954, 1959, 1965, 1978, 1983 and 1988. The CPPCC contains members of the eight 'democratic parties', as well as a few CCP members. There were forty representatives of the CCP in the 1954 National Committee, or 7.2 per cent of the total of 729 members, and seventy-six in the 1983 National Committee, or 3.7 per cent of the total of 2039.[1]

THE GOVERNMENT

The Chinese government bureaucracy mirrors that of the Party in many respects. The most important government body is the National People's Congress (NPC), which is like a parliament. In theory, the NPC is elected for a term of five years, and is supposed to meet every year. However, during the Cultural Revolution years, from 1966 to 1976, there was only one meeting of the NPC, held in January 1975. Since the reforms of the late 1970s, the NPC has again begun to meet every year. The NPC has its own Standing Committee, a permanent body which carries out NPC work when it is not in session.

Meetings of the NPC

First NPC
    First Session, September 15–28, 1954
    Second Session, July 5–30, 1955
    Third Session, June 15–30, 1956
    Fourth Session, June 26–July 15, 1957
    Fifth Session, February 1–24, 1958

Second NPC
    First Session, April 18–28, 1959
    Second Session, March 30–April 10, 1960
    Third Session, March 27–April 16, 1962
    Fourth Session, November 17–December 3, 1963

Third NPC
    First Session, December 21, 1964–January 4, 1965

Fourth NPC
    First Session, January 13–17, 1975

Fifth NPC
    First Session, February 26–March 5, 1978
    Second Session, June 18–July 1, 1979
    Third Session, August 30–September 10, 1980
    Fourth Session, November 30–December 13, 1981
    Fifth Session, November 26–December 10, 1982

Sixth NPC
    First Session, June 6–21, 1983
    Second Session, May 15–31, 1984
    Third Session, March 27–April 10, 1985
    Fourth Session, March 25–April 12, 1986
    Fifth Session, March 25–April 11, 1987

Seventh NPC
    First Session, March 25–April 13, 1988
    Second Session, March 20–April 4, 1989
    Third Session, March 20–April 4, 1990

Table 2.4 Numbers of deputies to the NPC

	First NPC	Second NPC	Third NPC	Fourth NPC	Fifth NPC	Sixth NPC	Seventh NPC
Total	1226	1226	3040	2885	3497	2978	2970
Female	147	150	542	653	742	632	634
Percentage	12.0	12.2	17.8	22.6	21.2	21.2	21.3
From minority nationalities	178	179	372	270	381	403	445
Percentage	14.5	14.6	12.2	9.4	10.9	13.5	15

Note: The main sources are The Chinese Academy of Social Sciences, edited for Pergamon Press by C. V. James, *Information China, The Comprehensive and Authoritative Reference Source of New China, Volume I* (Pergamon Press, Oxford, New York, 1989), p. 392; and *Beijing Review* XXXI, 13 (March 28–April 3, 1989), p. 7.

Among the members of the Seventh NPC, 684 (23.03 per cent) are workers and peasants, 697 (23.47 per cent) are intellectuals, 733 (24.68 per cent) are Party or government officials, 267 (8.99 per cent) are in the army and 49 (1.65 per cent) are returned overseas Chinese. Of the total 2970 members, 1986 (or 66.87 per cent) belong to the CCP, and the others are either members of other parties or have no party affiliations. The average age of the deputies is 52.9. Of the new deputies, 56 per cent have received higher education.

One of the tasks of the NPC is to adopt the PRC Constitution. There have been four of these since 1949, adopted respectively on September 20, 1954, January 17, 1975, March 5, 1978 and December 4, 1982.

The NPC also elects the president of the PRC. The following have held the office of president of the PRC (or president of the Central People's Government before the adoption of the 1954 Constitution). The date shown is the date of election to that post by the NPC.

- Mao Zedong, September 27, 1954 (Chairman of the Central People's Government from September 30, 1949)
- Liu Shaoqi, April 27, 1959
- Li Xiannian, June 18, 1983
- Yang Shangkun, April 8, 1988.

Liu Shaoqi became Mao's chief rival and opponent at the time of the Cultural Revolution. This led Mao not only to arrange for Liu Shaoqi's dismissal and humiliation—he was dismissed from all posts by the Twelfth Plenum of the Eighth Central Committee

in October 1968—but also to abolish the post itself. The decision to abolish the post was taken at the Second Plenum of the Ninth Central Committee, and there is no mention of it in the 1975 Constitution. Liu was posthumously rehabilitated in February 1980, and the post of PRC president was restored in the 1982 Constitution.

The office of president is not normally as powerful for the government as that of premier of the State Council (or premier of the Government Administrative Council before the adoption of the 1954 Constitution), a position equivalent to that of the prime minister in the Westminster system. It is the premier who carries out the day-to-day work of the government.

The NPC has the power to elect the chairman of the Central Military Commission, the president of the Supreme Court and the procurator-general of the Supreme People's Procuratorate. It decides on the choice of the premier, but the nomination is made by the president of the PRC. It also decides on the choice of the vice-premiers, state councillors and ministers of the government, on the nomination of the premier. The following have occupied the position of premier (shown with the date of appointment by the NPC):

- Zhou Enlai, September 27, 1954 (premier of the Government Administrative Council from October 1, 1949)
- Hua Guofeng, March 5, 1978 (Hua became acting premier on February 3, 1976 following the death of Zhou Enlai the preceding month, and was confirmed in the position by the Politburo on April 7, 1976)

- Zhao Ziyang, September 10, 1980
- Li Peng, April 9, 1988 (On November 24, 1987, the National People's Congress Standing Committee approved Zhao Ziyang's resignation as premier after he became Party general secretary, together with his replacement by Li Peng as acting premier.)

Among other powers given to the NPC are those enabling it to enact or amend laws, to examine and approve the state budget, to approve, change or negate decisions of its Standing Committee, to decide on the establishment of provinces, autonomous regions, municipalities and special administrative regions, and to decide on questions of war and peace.

There are six permanent committees set up by the NPC: the Nationalities Committee, the Law Committee, the Finance and Economic Committee, the Education, Science, Culture and Public Health Committee, the Foreign Affairs Committee and the Overseas Chinese Committee. When the NPC is not in session, these committees work under the direction of the Standing Committee of the NPC.

The State Council, also termed the Central People's Government, is the highest organ of state administration. It is headed by the premier, and consists in addition of vice-premiers, state councillors, ministers in charge of ministries and others. It generally meets once a month and its Standing Committee, comprising the premier, vice-premiers, secretary-general and state councillors, holds a meeting twice a week.

The First Session of the Seventh NPC of 1988 appointed forty-four members of the State Council, including three vice-premiers and thirty-nine ministers. These were: Premier Li Peng; Vice-Premiers Yao Yilin, Tian Jiyun and Wu Xueqian; State Councillors Li Tieying, Qin Jiwei, Wang Bingqian, Song Jian, Wang Fang, Zou Jiahua, Li Guixian, Chen Xitong and Chen Junsheng; Secretary-General Chen Junsheng; Minister of Foreign Affairs Qian Qichen; Minister of National Defence Qin Jiwei; Minister of the State Planning Commission Yao Yilin; Minister of the State Commission for Restructuring the Economy Li Peng; Minister of the State Education Commission Li Tieying; Minister of the State Science and Technology Commission Song Jian; Minister of the State Commission of Science, Technology and In-

dustry for National Defence Ding Henggao; Minister of the State Nationalities Affairs Commission Ismail Amat; Minister of Public Security Wang Fang; Minister of State Security Jia Chunwang; Minister of Supervision Wei Jianxing; Minister of Civil Affairs Cui Naifu; Minister of Justice Cai Cheng; Minister of Finance Wang Bingqian; Minister of Personnel Zhao Dongwan; Minister of Labour Luo Gan; Minister of Geology and Mineral Resources Zhu Xun; Minister of Construction Lin Hanxiong; Minister of Energy Resources Huang Yicheng; Minister of Railways Li Senmao; Minister of Communications Qian Yongchang; Minister of the Machine-Building and Electronics Industry Zou Jiahua; Minister of the Aeronautics and Astronautics Industry Lin Zongtang; Minister of the Metallurgical Industry Qi Yuanjing; Minister of the Chemical Industry Qin Zhongda; Minister of Light Industry Zeng Xianlin; Minister of the Textile Industry Wu Wenying; Minister of Posts and Telecommunications Yang Taifang; Minister of Water Resources Yang Zhenhuai; Minister of Agriculture He Kang; Minister of Forestry Gao Dezhan; Minister of Commerce Hu Ping; Minister of Foreign Economic Relations and Trade Zheng Tuobin; Minister of Materials Liu Suinian; Minister of Culture Wang Meng; Minister of Radio, Film and Television Ai Zhisheng; Minister of Public Health Chen Minzhang; Minister of the State Physical Culture and Sports Commission Li Menghua; Minister of the State Family Planning Commission Peng Peiyun; Governor of the People's Bank of China Li Guixian; and Auditor-General of the Auditing Administration Lu Peijian. Information on many of these people is given in Chapter 3.

The name most often mentioned as 'China's senior leader' is Deng Xiaoping. At one time, he occupied many Party and state positions. However, he resigned as vice-premier in 1980 due to old age, and retired even from the Party Central Committee itself at the time of the Thirteenth Party Congress in 1987. Deng's September 4, 1989 letter requesting permission to retire from the chairmanship of the CCPCC's Military Commission also announced his intention to retire from the State Military Commission. This was accepted by the NPC on March 21, 1990. The extent of his powers is known to have remained enormous after his retirement from the Central Committee, and he has probably remained extremely influential, even after stepping down from the Military Commissions.

The members of the NPC are elected according to the *Electoral Law* of 1979. However, there are no general elections in China; instead, small elections take place at various levels, and at different times. These elect representatives for their particular level, and it is the representatives who make the choices for the higher levels, going up to the NPC. Thus, though all citizens have the right to vote, they do not decide and may not necessarily influence who becomes a member of the NPC. Under the 1979 *Electoral Law*, which was adopted by the NPC on July 1, 1979, more than one person can stand for election, and surprise candidates with no backing from the CCP have occasionally won. On the whole, however, the CCP candidates have a very much better chance of success than any others, and elections which could result in the ousting of CCP power remained inconceivable in China in 1990.

Government exists at the regional level as well as centrally. The highest level, apart from the central level, is the provincial. There are three kinds of area at provincial level: the provinces, the autonomous regions and the municipalities directly under the central government. The autonomous regions are established for the minority nationalities, and reflect the formal policy, though not reality, that the minority nationalities should enjoy autonomy (see Chapter 9). There are three municipalities directly under the central government: Beijing, Shanghai and Tianjin.

Under the 1982 Constitution, the types of administrative unit below provincial level are autonomous prefectures, counties, autonomous counties, cities, municipal districts, townships, nationality townships and towns. The townships replace the people's communes specified in the 1975 and 1978 Constitutions. The autonomous prefectures and autonomous counties are self-governing according to policy.

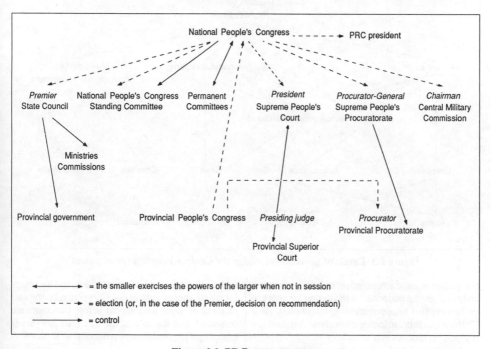

Figure 2.2 PRC state structure

On July 1, 1979, the NPC adopted the *Organic Law of the Local People's Congresses and Local People's Governments*, which came into effect on January 1, 1980. The structures introduced by this law replaced those of the Cultural Revolution. For example, the revolutionary committees which were emphasized during the Cultural Revolution were abolished. The local government structure reflects the central structure closely, with units having their own people's congress and corresponding standing committee. The provincial people's congresses are empowered to pass their own local legislation. Their term of office is five years.

Under the 1982 Constitution, the government head of all autonomous regions, autonomous prefectures and autonomous counties must be a citizen of one of the nationalities represented, or of the nationality exercising regional autonomy. In the people's

provinces, autonomous regions and municipalities under the PRC central government. Within these twenty-nine province-level units, there were 350 cities (not including Beijing, Shanghai or Tianjin), 2017 units at county level and 629 municipal districts. The provinces have changed very slightly over the years. In April 1988, Hainan, until then part of Guangdong province, was upgraded to provincial level, to bring the total number of province-level units (not including Taiwan) to thirty.

THE LEGAL SYSTEM

The Chinese legal system has three arms: the public security organs, the people's procuratorate and the people's courts. The public security arm is responsible for investigating crime and detaining suspects, the procuratorate for approval of arrests and establishing an *a priori* case against suspects, and for

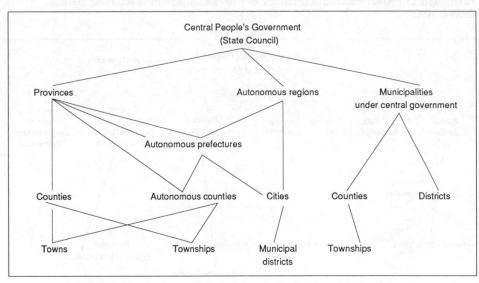

Figure 2.3 Levels of government under the Central People's Government

congresses of these autonomous regions, prefectures and counties, the nationalities inhabiting the area are by law entitled to appropriate representation. (See Chapter 9 for more information on these autonomous regions, prefectures and counties.)

As of the end of 1986, there were twenty-nine

initiating and sustaining prosecutions, and the courts for the passing of judgments. Consequently, the vast majority of those who appear before the courts are convicted, and the role of their defence lawyers is more to get the punishment reduced than to establish their innocence.

The Supreme People's Court and Supreme People's Procuratorate are responsible to the National People's Congress and its Standing Committee. Both people's courts and procuratorates exist at various levels. Apart from the Supreme People's Court, the hierarchy of the courts moves down through the higher, intermediate, basic and special people's courts.

The formal law system suffered almost to the point of total destruction during the Cultural Revolution. However, the Third Plenum of the Eleventh Central Committee in 1978 called for the re-establishment of a formal law system and the 1980s saw an enormous expansion of the legal system, to cover not only criminal matters, but also a wide variety of civil matters, such as commercial law, contract law and family law, especially divorce. The policy of openness to the outside world has resulted in many civil disputes arising from such areas as foreign trade, joint ventures, maritime transportation, collision of ships, capital construction, insurance, patent rights, trademarks and copyright. However, in a report to the NPC on April 2, 1988, the president of the Supreme People's Court, Zheng Tianxiang, acknowledged problems in dealing with civil and, in particular, economic cases. He said that court decisions failed to be enforced in about 30 per cent of cases involving economic disputes in 1987 and in some provinces the rate was higher than 40 per cent.

Article 78 of the 1954 Constitution states that: 'The people's courts administer justice independently and are subject only to law.' Article 126 of the 1982 Constitution states that: 'The people's courts shall, in accordance with the law, exercise judicial power independently and are not subject to interference by administrative organs, public organizations, or individuals.' Neither the 1975 nor the 1978 Constitution makes any mention of the independence of the law system.

The Anti-Rightist Campaign of 1957 saw the greater subordination of the law system to the Party, and during the Cultural Revolution period from 1966 to 1976 there was a complete withdrawal of all vestiges of legal independence. Until the Beijing massacre of June 1989, the 1980s witnessed a general trend towards reviving and recognizing the principle that the law should be independent of the Party or state. In practice, however, both the state and individual leaders have continued to use the law system to promote the Party's, the state's or their own political power. The period following the Beijing massacre has seen blatant use of the legal system to buttress the political power of the Party and government leadership.

The nature of the legal system in the People's Republic has meant that the legal profession has always been small and relatively powerless, with a correspondingly low social status. In 1957 there were about 2100 lawyers in the whole country, a figure which rose to about 3000 by 1960. During the Cultural Revolution, the legal profession was all but destroyed; however, the legal reforms of the late 1970s brought about its revival. As of late 1980 there were 380 legal advisory offices in China, with some 3000 lawyers. These figures grew rapidly until the mid-1980s, but then remained fairly steady, and even began to fall (see Table 2.5).

Table 2.5 Legal personnel

	1982	1984	1985	1986	1988
Legal advisory offices	1 500	2 773	3 131	3 198	—
Legal workers	6 800	20 090	31 629	21 546	31 000
Professional	5 500	10 262	13 411	—	—
Part-time	1 300	9 828	18 218	—	—
Notaries		8 330	13 403	14 537	15 000
Professional		4 947	6 830	7 491	—
Part-time		3 383	6 573	7 046	—
Mediators		4 576 000	4 739 000	6 087 000	6 000 000

Note: The main sources for these figures are State Statistical Bureau, comp., *Zhongguo tongji nianjian 1986 (Statistical Yearbook of China 1986)* (Statistical Press of China, Beijing, 1986), p. 801 and *Statistical Yearbook of China 1987,* p. 836.

It is a long-standing tradition, which is still very much in evidence today, to try to settle cases through mediation and keep them out of the law courts. This explains the large number of 'mediators' in China. Table 2.6 presents some statistics on some of the main categories of cases mediated.

- From August 1983 to the end of 1987, the courts at all levels handled nearly 1.7 million criminal cases and passed judgment on two million people, of whom 38 per cent were sentenced to death, life imprisonment or more than five years in prison; 0.7 per cent were acquitted.

Table 2.6 Cases mediated

Category	1984	1985	1986
Marriage	1 143 742	1 072 116	1 223 836
Housing, residential base	1 063 962	1 035 618	1 107 453
Inheritance	204 391	206 943	262 408
Family provision, alimony, etc.	378 764	347 377	404 356
Debts	260 339	254 669	333 102
Production management	1 129 176	900 093	725 889
Loss compensation	654 195	570 595	535 584
Others	1 914 014	1 945 501	2 714 421

CRIME AND PUNISHMENT

Although crime rates are still quite low by world standards, the incidence of official corruption was a major factor leading to their increase in China in the 1980s. Statistical information was incomparably better for the 1980s than for any other period in PRC history, but is still deficient. It is often unclear precisely what the statistics mean or what they include, and the categories are frequently vague.

Table 2.7 Criminal statistics 1986

Classification of crime	Arrests (persons)	Prosecutions (cases)
Counter-revolution	620	368
Endangering public security	10 861	10 304
Undermining economic order	7 965	5 647
Infringing personal rights	75 958	67 304
Violating property	217 692	143 273
Disrupting social administration	34 353	22 070
Disrupting marriage and family	1 014	1 170
Dereliction of duty	6 066	5 862
Other	1 074	1 221

In his report of April 2, 1988 to the NPC, Supreme People's Court President Zheng Tianxiang revealed the following facts and figures on crime in China:

- The crime rate was 7.4 per 10 000 in 1981 and 1982, but fell to about 5 per 10 000 for four years after that; this rate was still higher than during the 1950s.

- More than 90 per cent of the life imprisonment or death sentences were given for 40.5 per cent of the 690 000 cases of murder, rape, robbery, bombing and hooliganism.
- In 1987 there were 365 000 cases involving economic disputes, eight times the 1983 figure. In 1987, a total of 77 386 cases of embezzlement, bribery, smuggling, speculation and fraud were uncovered, 54.4 per cent more than in the previous year.

In a speech on May 8, 1989, Supreme People's Court President Ren Jianxin acknowledged a serious rise in the incidence of crime in recent months. The number of criminals sentenced in the first three months of the year was 94 800, 14 per cent up on the same period in 1988, and the number of those sentenced to death, death with reprieve or life imprisonment during the same period had increased by nearly 17 per cent over the same period of 1988. There was a 78.7 per cent increase in serious theft, with robberies up by 59.98 per cent and murders by 13.05 per cent. Ren expressed alarm at the incidence of criminal gangs, crimes along main railway lines and train robberies, abduction of women and children, prostitution, drug trafficking and vagrancy.[2]

Official investigation of tax evasion and fraud revealed that 7.6 billion yuan had been misappropriated during the first nine months of 1987, a rise of 18.8 per cent from 6.4 billion yuan over the same period in 1986. In this period a total of 786 cases involving sums of over one million yuan had been brought to the authorities' attention, roughly 600 more cases than were handled in 1986. The State Auditing Administration had found cases of 'tax evasion, fraud, massive over-spending on capital construction, forced donations and waste due to bureaucracy' and losses caused by bureaucrats and corrupt officials of 530 million yuan.

On March 20, 1989, at the Second Session of the Seventh NPC, Li Peng called on procuratorial departments to 'shift the focus of their work to investigating and punishing graft, bribery, extortion, extravagance, waste and abuse of power for personal gain'. The reason was the alarming growth in corruption. At the same session of the Congress, Liu Fuzhi, procurator-in-chief of the Supreme People's Procuratorate, reported that the Supreme People's Procuratorate had examined more than 66 300 cases of economic crime in 1988, representing an 11 per cent increase over the preceding year. Among the 1988 cases, 69 per cent, or 45 700 charges, were of bribery and embezzlement, including 2900 cases involving more than 10 000 yuan.

In descending order of severity, the types of punishment meted out in the Chinese legal system are: death sentence, death sentence with reprieve, life imprisonment, imprisonment for varying periods and supervision. Accessory penalties include fines, deprivation of political rights and forfeiture of property. The most famous case of 'death sentence with reprieve' is that of Jiang Qing and Zhang Chunqiao, members of the 'gang of four'. They were given death sentences with two-year reprieves which were then commuted to life imprisonment (see Chapter 1 under *B. Domestic Political Events*, January 25, 1981 and January 25, 1983). A consistent policy has been 'leniency for those who confess, severity for those who remain obdurate'.

Imprisonment is combined with reform through labour and 'ideological education' or indoctrination. To detain a criminal, a written judgment or warrant is in theory necessary. Prison authorities are armed and may use their arms if criminals rebel or attempt escape. Female prisoners are controlled by female warders. They are not allowed to keep their children in prison, but all criminals may receive their relations twice a month. If a female criminal is unable to find anybody to look after her children, the state takes responsibility for finding appropriate residences, orphanages or kindergartens.

Minor criminals who are judged to be exempt from responsibility are subjected to 'rehabilitation through labour', usually for periods of one to three years. Political education and productive labour are features of this form of punishment. People are instructed in a job and payment is given for their work, either to the prisoner or to relations.

Those sentenced to 'supervision' are placed under the supervision of the public security or the people at their place of work for a specified period of time. Although this form of punishment does not involve imprisonment, it is considered a humiliation both by those affected and by their relations.

Work–study schools are semi-coercive organizations which educate and reform juvenile delinquents who have committed minor offences. Most inmates are teenagers under fifteen years of age whom their parents, teachers or unit-leaders are unable to handle. Like other Chinese corrective institutions they combine labour with education or indoctrination. Since they are semi-coercive only, the parents pay tuition and living expenses.

The Chinese legal and penal system has been the target of serious criticism by foreign and international human rights organizations. A major crackdown on crime, which involved public mass trials and summary executions, began in 1983. The number of executions which has resulted is very unclear, and foreign estimates to mid-1985 range from 5000 to 10 000.

Even before the crisis of 1989, Amnesty International charged that China had hundreds of thousands of political prisoners. It was among a number of international and non-Chinese organizations which claimed a very serious worsening of the legal and human rights situation following the Beijing massacre of June 1989. In particular, it made allegations about and denounced punishments inflicted for no other 'crime' than disagreeing with the ideas of the government.

Chinese authorities have generally denied foreign reports of human rights violations, especially those concerning purely political prisoners; instead they have placed their main emphasis on arguing that national sovereignty forbids interference in China's domestic affairs. The United States State Department's 'Human Rights Report of 1989', issued on February 21, 1990, had a great deal to say about a wide range of violations of human rights in China, especially in connection with the suppression of the pro-democracy movement from early June and with the situation in Tibet. The Chinese authorities denied the charges, but denounced the United States for interfering in China's internal affairs and violating its national sovereignty.

On the other hand, Chinese sources have themselves conceded serious abuses of power and personal rights by police and other authorities. The Cultural Revolution period of 1966 to 1976 is regularly castigated as a period of savage oppression. The special court trying the 'gang of four' and six others in 1980 (see Chapter 1 under *B. Domestic Political Events*, October 20–December 29) revealed that in the cases mentioned in the indictment alone, 729 511 people had been 'framed and persecuted' and 34 800 had been 'persecuted to death'.

These cases concern a period which is now totally discredited in the official version of history. However, serious abuses have also been acknowledged in 'positive' periods. In September 1986, a Chinese English-language newspaper reported several cases of abuse of police power, including one in which two university professors had been detained by police for no other reason than the wish to take revenge.[3] Such reports were probably only the tip of a rather serious iceberg. The Supreme People's Procuratorate reported an increase in cases of abuse of power in the

first half of 1987 which was 13 per cent more than in the same period the preceding year. These 'cases' included extracting confessions by torture, frameups and unlawful detention, instances of the last evil having doubled over the same period in 1986.[4] On 30 April, 1990, over the British Broadcasting Corporation's 'World Roundup' (broadcast on the Australian Broadcasting Corporation's Radio National) Simon Long reported a Chinese legal official as having admitted many cases of serious abuse in the first quarter of the year, including torture and death in Chinese prisons.

Serious cases of abuse through 'turning a blind eye' on major crime rackets have also been recorded. Late in 1988, a Chinese-language newspaper in Shanghai reported on rings of people who traded in women; the most expensive were slightly mentally retarded, because they worked hard but did what they were told without complaining or trying to run away. One man in Hebei province had been imprisoned for trading in women, but used his connections with authorities to secure an early release and simply reestablished his former trade.[5] The sale of women was acknowledged as being among six types of very serious and widespread crimes targeted for suppression from the autumn of 1989. This suggests that, before then, the abuse of power in the form of deliberate laxity in the face of serious crime had become a major problem among police and other authorities. And there is no certainty about the success of the crackdown.

3 EMINENT CONTEMPORARY FIGURES

The following is a highly selective sample of biographies of those Chinese who are, or have recently been, eminent in the PRC in the political, economic, cultural and other fields.[1] For reasons of space and the enormity of the subject, it rigorously excludes all those who died or were rendered politically inoperable before 1980 (e.g. Mao Zedong or the 'gang of four'). Except for most minority nationality members, the names given in parentheses immediately after each heading are the names of the biographees in the Wade–Giles romanization.

Ai Qing (Ai Ch'ing)—b. 1910 Jinhua, Zhejiang province. Studied painting in Hangzhou and Paris 1929–32. Returned to Shanghai and joined the League of Left-wing Artists in 1932, then imprisoned for over four years: began winning fame for poetry while in prison in 1933. Went to Yan'an 1941–45. Took over Beijing's Central Academy of Fine Arts as army representative in 1949. Visited the Soviet Union, Chile and Brazil in the early 1950s. Banished during the 1957 'Anti-Rightist campaign'; again heavily criticized and sent to the countryside during the Cultural Revolution until returning to Beijing for medical treatment in 1973. Again allowed to publish in 1978 and identified as editor of *Poetry* magazine in 1979. Elected vice-chairman, Writers' Association and PEN Centre, 1979 and 1982; Standing Committee member, Sixth NPC 1983–88; and vice-president, International Cultural Exchange Centre under Peng Chong and honorary president, Prose Poetry Society 1984. Since 1979 has visited Europe, the United States, Japan and Singapore; in 1985 was awarded French *Commandeur dans l' ordre des 'Arts et Lettres'*. Poems include 'Dayan River—My Nurse' ('Dayan he—wode baomu') 1933 and 'In Praise of Light' ('Guangde zan'ge') 1978; collections of poems include *Collection of Acclamations (Huanhu ji)* 1950; *The Red Star of the Precious Stone (Baoshi de hong xing)* 1953; and *Spring (Chuntian)* 1956.

Aisin Giorro Pujie—b. 1907. Younger brother of last Manchu emperor, gaoled as war criminal 1945–59. Shanghai deputy, Fifth NPC 1978; Liaoning deputy, Standing Committee member and Nationalities Affairs Committee vice-chairman, Sixth NPC 1983 and deputy head, NPC's China–Japan Friendship Group since 1985; confirmed in all positions and served on Presidium, Seventh NPC, 1988. Vice-president, Society for Study of Sino-Japanese Relations and honorary director, Welfare Fund for Handicapped since 1986. Married to a Japanese, Hiroko Saga.

Ba Jin (Pa Chin)—b. Li Yaotang, 1904, Chengdu, Sichuan province. Attended Chengdu Foreign Languages School. Studied in France and took a new name, 1926–28. Writer, Shanghai 1928–37, with Lu Xun 1936 and Mao Dun 1937. Engaged in literary work, Kunming, Chongqing, Guilin 1937–49. Elected member First CPPCC; Standing Committee, Association of Literary Workers; and member, Federation of Literature and Art Circles 1949: elected Federation vice-chairman 1960 and again identified in this post 1978–present. Elected vice-chairman, Writers' Association 1953; identified as vice-chairman and subsequently elected first vice-chairman 1979, acting chairman 1980 and chairman 1981–present. Sichuan deputy, First and Second NPCs, 1954 and 1958. Purged as counter-revolutionary 1968.

Identified as executive council member, Welfare Institute 1978. Deputy, Fifth NPC 1978–83. Vice-chairman, Sixth CPPCC, 1983; confirmed Seventh CPPCC 1988 when he also served as Presidium executive chairman. President, PEN Centre and Literature Foundation since 1980 and 1986 respectively. In the 1980s, led delegations to Japan and Western Europe. Publications include: *Trilogy of Love (Aiqing sanbuqu)* 1932–33; *Spring (Chun)* 1937; *Autumn (Qiu)* 1940; *Fire: A Trilogy (Huo)* 1938–43; *Ba Jin's Collected Works (Ba Jin wenji*, 14 volumes) 1958–62.

Bainqen Erdeni Qoigyi Gyancan—1937–89, peasant, Xunhua county, Qinghai province. Succeeded to throne, Qinghai's Gumbun (Ta-drh) monastery, as tenth reincarnation, first Bainqen Lama 1943. By-elected member, CPPCC 1951. Elected honorary chairman, founding session, Buddhist League 1953, and council member, Sino-Soviet Friendship Association 1954. Appointed chairman, Preparatory Committee for Establishment of Tibetan autonomous region 1956; acting chairman 1959–64. Imprisoned Beijing 1967–77. Standing Committee member, Fourth CPPCC and vice-chairman, Fifth CPPCC, 1978 and 1979. Tibetan deputy, Presidium member and chairman, Fifth NPC 1980; vice-chairman, Sixth NPC and Seventh NPC 1983 and 1988; and Presidium executive chairman 1988. Re-elected honorary chairman, Buddhist Association 1980; president, Advanced Tibetan Buddhism Institute since 1988.

Bing Xin (Ping Hsin)—b. 1900 as Xie Wanying Minhou, Fujian province, daughter of high-ranking naval officer. Received a classical education and showed early literary ability. Attended Beijing Bridgeman Girls' School and Yanjing University, graduating in 1923 with a BA. Wrote for the May Fourth Movement 1919. Officer, Student Union and executive secretary, Propaganda Department, Women Students' Federation 1920. Visited United States in 1923. Studied for MA, Wellesley College, Massachusetts 1924–26, then lectured at Yanjing University. Travelled in the United States, Europe and Soviet Union, 1936–37, then lectured at South-west Associated University, Kunming. Appointed to Nationalists'

People's Political Council 1945. Lectured at Tokyo University 1946–54. Fujian deputy, first three NPCs 1954–64. Member, Children's and Juvenile Literature Section, Writers' Association by 1955 and deputy director by 1960; secretary, Writers' Association by 1963. Member, Federation of Literature and Art Circles by 1956. Elected member of the friendship associations of many countries visited in the 1950s and 1960s; member, Asian Solidarity Committee 1956, and council member, Association for Cultural Relations with Foreign Countries 1957. Elected member, Central Committee, Association for Promoting Democracy 1956 and Standing Committee member 1958–59. Elected to Executive Council, Women's Federation 1957. Delegate, peace, writers' and women's conferences during latter half of the 1950s: to India, Switzerland, Hiroshima, Britain, Tashkent, Tokyo and Cairo. Disappeared 1967–72. Fujian deputy, Fifth NPC 1978. Standing Committee member, Fifth–Seventh CPPCC 1978–present and Presidium member 1988. Identified as adviser, Popular Science Writers' Society 1978 and appointed adviser, Writers' Association 1981. Vice-president, Children's Foundation 1981–87. Honorary president, Prose Society 1984–present. Vice-chairman, Federation of Literature and Art Circles and Association for Promoting Democracy 1978–present. Among her publications are: *Superman (Chaoren)*, a collection of short stories published in 1921; *Letters to My Young Readers (Ji xiao duzhe)* and *More Letters to My Young Readers (Zai ji xiao duzhe)*, two series written respectively between 1926 and 1935 and after 1949; two volumes of poetry, and a translation of Kahlil Gibran's *The Prophet* 1936. Her short story *The Empty Nest (Kong chao)* won the state short story award in 1980. Married to Wu Wencao.

Bo Yibo (Po I-po)—b. 1908 Dingxiang, Shanxi province. Attended school Taiyuan and Beijing. While studying at Beijing University in 1925, joined CCP and was imprisoned for over three years. During Sino-Japanese War 1937–45 built up pro-Communist anti-Japanese guerilla force in native province. Elected to CCP Central Committee 1945. Appointed political commissar, North

China Military Region around 1947. Appointed member, Central People's Government Council and Government Administrative Council, and vice-chairman, Financial and Economic Affairs Committee 1949 and Minister of Finance 1949–53. Served in State Planning Commission 1952–59, as vice-chairman 1959. Appointed chairman, Economy Commission, alternate Politburo member, Eighth Party Congress, and vice-premier 1956, first deputy director and then director, Staff Office of Industry and Communications 1959–66. Then purged. Appointed vice-premier and member, State Financial and Economic Commission, and by-elected to Eleventh Central Committee 1979–82; vice-chairman, Central Advisory Commission 1982–present. Minister, State Machine Building Industry Commission 1979–82; state councillor 1982–83 and vice-minister, State Commission for Restructuring the Economic System 1982–88. Beijing deputy, Sixth NPC 1982 and Shanxi deputy and Presidium member, Seventh NPC 1988. Presidium Standing Committee member, Thirteenth Party Congress 1987. Elected honorary chairman, Council for Promotion of International Trade and China Technological Import and Export Corporation 1984 and honorary president, Beijing Garment Association 1984, Self-employed Workers' Association 1986, Industrial Economics Association 1988 and Political Restructuring Research Society 1988. Headed government delegations to Canada and the United States in 1980 and Japan in 1982. Married to Hu Ming.

Cao Yu (Ts'ao Yü)—b. 1910 Tianjin as Wan Jiabao, although his family was from Qianjiang in Hubei province. Studied at Qinghua University, and after graduating in 1931 lectured in drama in China and the United States. Associated with various prestigious cultural organizations both prior to and since the Cultural Revolution. Co-founder of Drama Society 1937. In the pre-Cultural Revolution period, served variously in key posts, Central Drama Institute, Federation of Literature and Art Circles, Writers' Association, Association for Cultural Relations with Foreign Countries, Beijing Literature and Art Association, People's Academy of Dramatic Arts and Sino-Soviet Friendship Association's executive

board. Joined CCP 1965. Has figured prominently in Beijing People's Art and Drama Institute, as director prior to Cultural Revolution and again 1979–present. Visited Prague and Japan in connection with the peace movement. Purged 1966, reappearing as Hubei deputy, Fourth–Sixth NPC 1975–88 and Standing Committee member 1978–83. Identified as vice-president, Dramatists' Association 1978 and elected chairman 1979; elected president, International Theatre Institute's China Centre 1981; vice-president, PEN Centre 1982; and president, Shakespeare Research Foundation 1983. Presidium and Standing Committee member and vice-chairman, Committee for Reunification of the Motherland, Seventh CPPCC 1988. Since 1979 has led dramatists' delegations to Western Europe, the United States and Japan. Married for third time. Among most famous dramatic works are *Thunderstorm (Leiyu)* 1934 and *Sunrise (Richu)* 1935. His post-1949 dramas include *Bright Skies (Minglang de tian)* (1954) and *Wang Zhaojun* (1978).

Chai Zemin (Ch'ai Tse-min)—b. 1915 Wenxi, Shanxi province. Served in Shanyin district, Hebei province 1937–48 and Beijing People's Government 1948–61. Identified as council member, Association for Cultural Relations with Foreign Countries 1954; chairman, Beijing Sports Committee 1954–58, and council member, Institute of Foreign Affairs 1955. Appointed director, Beijing CP Communications Department 1959. Appointed ambassador to Hungary 1961, and subsequently to Guinea, Egypt and Thailand, each for about three years, with break of four years 1967–70 when recalled along with most ambassadors. Appointed chief, United States Liaison Office 1978, and ambassador to United States 1978–82. Vice-president, Institute of Foreign Affairs since 1983 and vice-chairman, Association for Peace and Disarmament since 1988. Presidium and National Committee member and vice-chairman, Foreign Affairs Committee, Seventh CPPCC 1988. Headed delegations to the United States and Western Europe in 1980s. Married to Li Youfeng.

Chen Huangmei (Ch'en Huang-mi)—elected member, Federation of Literature and Art Circles and subsequently re-elected 1953 and 1960. Delegate, First CPPCC 1949. Identified in 4th Field Army as deputy director, Political Department's Propaganda Section, and subsequently in newly formed Central–South Military and Administrative Committee, as deputy director, Cultural Department 1950. Following this, and prior to the Cultural Revolution, held series of key posts, Ministry of Culture Film Bureau, as deputy director 1953–59, acting director 1959–61 and director 1961–63. Vice-minister of Culture 1963–65. During this period also associated with many important cultural groups, such as the Writers' Association, Association for Cultural Relations with Foreign Countries and Movie Artists' Association; also editor, *Literary Gazette (Wenxue zazhi)* and *Cinema Art (Dianying yishu)*. Hubei deputy, Third NPC 1964. Purged 1966. Identified as deputy director, Academy of Social Sciences' Institute of Literature 1979–81; director, 1981–85. Identified as vice-chairman, Writers' Association 1979–present and council member, PEN Centre 1980: vice-president 1982–present. Vice-minister of Culture 1981–82. Presidium and National Committee member, Seventh CPPCC 1988. Has headed delegations of literature and film workers to Eastern and Western Europe and the United States in the 1980s.

Chen Muhua (Ch'en Mu-hua)—b. 1920 Qingtian county, Zhejiang province. Studied building construction, Jiaotong University in Shanghai. Identified as bureau deputy director, General Liaison Office of Economic Relations with Foreign Countries 1962 (State Commission after 1964). Became vice-minister when commission upgraded to ministry 1970, and minister 1977. Elected to Tenth Central Committee 1973 and elevated to alternate Politburo membership 1977–87. Vice-premier 1978–82. Headed many Central Committee campaigns and State Council leading groups. Minister, Family Planning Commission 1981–82, minister, Foreign Trade and Economic Relations 1982–85, and state councillor 1982–87. Served on Presidium Standing Committee, Twelfth and Thirteenth Party Congress, 1982 and 1987. Liaoning deputy, Presidium executive chairman, Standing Committee vice-chairman and chairman, Financial and Eco-

nomic Committee, Seventh NPC 1988. President, People's Bank (under State Council) 1985–88; honorary chairman, Bank of China since 1985; and Chinese governor of both International Monetary Fund and Asian Development Bank since 1985 and 1986, respectively. President, Women's Federation since 1988. Has led countless government, economic and trade delegations to over thirty nations. Although no longer on Politburo, retains vast prestige in traditionally male sphere of banking. Married with two children.

Chen Xian (Ch'en Hsien) — Identified as director, Department for Perspective Planning 1959; director, State Statistical Bureau 1980–82; vice-minister, State Planning Commission 1982; and appointed deputy head, State Council's Leading Group for National Industrial Survey 1984–88 and Co-ordination Group for Economic Development of Ningbo 1985–88; and managing director, Bank of China 1985–88. Chairman, China Technological Import and Export Corporation since 1984. Jiangxi deputy and member, Presidium, Standing Committee and Law Committee, Seventh NPC 1988.

Chen Xian (Ch'en Hsien)—Identified as president, Table Tennis Association 1973–78; deputy team head, World Table Tennis Championship, Belgrade 1973. Disappeared 1973–77. Appointed member, National Games Organizing Committee 1979. Identified as vice-minister, State Physical Culture and Sports Commission 1982–85. Vice-president, Sports Federation since 1979; Chinese and Asian Olympic Committees since at least 1983; and president, Sports Aviation Society since 1986. Since 1978, head, volleyball teams to Soviet Union and World Championships; and deputy head and head, sports delegations, Eighth and Ninth Asian Games. Since 1983, head of three Asian Olympic Council delegations and three Olympic delegations.

Chen Xitong (Ch'en Hsi-t'ung)—b. 1930 Anyue county, Sichuan province. Studied Chinese language, Beijing University. Joined CCP 1949. Served in various minor posts at municipal and county level prior to 1979. Served in Beijing as vice-mayor 1979–83 and mayor 1983–present; CP secretary 1981–87 and deputy secretary

1987–present; director, Planning and Construction Committee 1983; Beijing deputy, Sixth and Seventh NPC 1983 and 1987; and head, Beijing delegations to United States and Japan. Appointed chairman, 1990 Asian Games Organizing Committee and head, Games delegation, Tokyo 1985. Central Committee member, Twelfth Party Congress 1982–present, and Presidium member, Thirteenth Party Congress 1987. State councillor since 1988. Author of a detailed official report, dated June 30, 1989, defending the military action of June 3–4, 1989.

Chen Yun (Ch'en Yün)—b. 1905 as Liao Chengyun, Shanghai, where trained as typesetter, becoming active in trade union movement about 1921. Joined CCP 1925 and together with Liu Shaoqi was leading initiator of May Thirtieth Movement against Japanese. Joined Mao Zedong's group in Jiangxi 1927 and worked in Central Committee's Organization Department. Elected to Sixth Central Committee 1934 (continuing in this post to the present) and joined Long March 1934–35. In Soviet Union 1935–37; after return became head, Central Committee's Organization Department 1938–39 and Rural Work Department 1939–43. Member, Politburo and chairman, Financial and Economic Committee, Shaanxi–Gansu–Ningxia border region 1940–45. Again named director, Organization Department 1943. Held important Party and administrative posts, north-east China 1946–49; appointed member, Government Administrative Council, Minister of Heavy Industry, and chairman, government's Financial and Economic Affairs Committee 1949; and appointed vice-premier 1949. Member, State Planning Commission 1952–54; Shanghai deputy, First NPC, 1954. Acting premier during Zhou Enlai's absence in 1955. Elected to Politburo Standing Committee and vice-chairman, Eighth Central Committee 1956. Elected to these posts again, and as first secretary, Central Committee Commission for Inspecting Discipline, Eleventh Party Congress 1978; confirmed, Twelfth Party Congress 1982. Vice-chairman Fourth NPC 1975; confirmed, Fifth NPC 1978. Again vice-premier 1979–80, and chairman, State Financial and Economic Commission 1979–81.

In 1987 elected Presidium Standing Committee member, Thirteenth Party Congress and chairman, Central Advisory Commission.

Chi Haotian (Ch'ih Hao-t'ien)—identified as major of unit, Nanjing Military Region 1958; later commanded 27th Army, Jinan Military Region. NPC deputy pre-Cultural Revolution. Identified as deputy political commissar, Beijing Military Region 1975, and deputy editor-in-chief, *People's Daily* 1977. Identified as deputy chief, PLA General Staff HQ 1977, and appointed chief 1987. Political commissar, Jinan Military Region 1985–87. By-elected to CCP's Twelfth Central Committee 1985; confirmed, and Presidium member, Thirteenth Party Congress 1987. PLA deputy and Presidium member, Seventh NPC 1988. Member, PRC Central Military Commission since 1988. Son-in-law of President Yang Shangkun.

Deng Xiaoping (Teng Hsiao-p'ing)—b. Guang'an, Sichuan province 1904; later among group of returned students from France who gained great prominence in CCP; joined CCP 1924. After six years of study in France, given assignment by Soviet Union's CP to assist then Party head, Li Lisan, 1926. Set up 7th Red Army, later joining Mao–Zhu forces in their retreat to Jiangxi province. Chief of staff, Peng Dehuai's 3rd Army Corps by 1930, and posted to Ruijin 1931. Director, 1st Army Corps Political Department at beginning of Long March 1934, and army's deputy political commissar by 1936. Elevated to rank of political commissar, 129th Division (later 2nd Field Army), one of army's three divisions, after reorganization of communist forces into 8th Route Army at beginning of Sino-Japanese War 1937. Elected to CCP's Seventh Central Committee 1945. After end Sino-Japanese War 1945, among most prominent authors of Huaihai Campaign leading to communist victory; place in CCP, army and government hierarchies thus secured: became ranking secretary, CCP South-west Bureau, political commissar of both army and military region under its control, and vice-chairman, South-west Administrative Committee 1950–54. Transferred to Beijing and became vice-premier under Zhou Enlai 1952. Played prominent role as

Zhou's general secretary, and as only person to serve on all three committees set up under CCP's most important leaders, Mao, Liu Shaoqi and Zhou, to establish national legislative committee 1953–54. Member, CPPCC Standing Committee 1954–59 and Minister of Finance 1953–54. Briefly removed from office; then apparently victor of a power struggle, subsequently identified as secretary-general, CCP's Central Committee, and elevated to Politburo 1955 (re-elected at Eighth Party Congress 1956). Also reappointed vice-premier under Zhou and vice-chairman, Mao's National Defence Council: confirmed 1959 and 1965. Appointed to uniquely powerful position of first secretary, Secretariat and member, Politburo Standing Committee 1956. Maintained high public profile until Cultural Revolution, when accused of collaborating with Liu Shaoqi, and purged. Restored to vice-premiership 1973–76 and Politburo Standing Committee 1975–76, and again purged 1976–77, then restored to all prior posts. Chief, PLA General Staff and vice-premier 1977–80. Chairman, PRC and CCP's Central Military Commissions 1981–90 and 1983–89, respectively. Re-elected to Politburo Standing Committee, Twelfth Party Congress 1982–87, serving only on Presidium, Thirteenth Party Congress 1987. Honorary president, Song Qingling Foundation since 1982. PLA representative and Presidium member, Seventh NPC 1988. Events subsequent to 1989 'pro-democracy' demonstrations indicate power unscathed, although formally retired as chairman of the two Central Military Commissions. From 1978 headed delegations to seventeen countries, including the United States and Japan. Married to Zhuo Lin, with two sons and two daughters.

Deng Yingchao (Teng Ying-ch'ao)—b. Deng Wenshu 1903, Xingyang, Guanshan county, southern Henan province, to bankrupt landlord. Studied Beijing and Tianjin, graduating Hebei 1st Women's Normal School 1920. Highly active in May Fourth Movement and Awakening Society, and met future husband Zhou Enlai. Joined Socialist Youth League 1924, and GMD and CCP 1925. Went to Guangzhou, then a revolutionary centre, and married Zhou 1925. Appointed communist alternate member, Central Executive Committee, Second GMD Congress, and vice-chairman, GMD government Women's Department 1926–27 until collapse of united front; and head, Women's Department, Sixth CCP Congress 1926. Worked in Shanghai underground 1926–32, and then joined communist base in Ruijin as second most important woman in CCP next to Cai Chang. Elected member, Central Executive Committee, and alternate member, CCP Central Committee (and re-elected to this post at following Congress) 1934. One of few women on Long March 1934–35. Served with husband as communist representative on National Government's First People's Political Council, Hankou and Chongqing 1938–43, then returned Yan'an. After end of war, active in organizing CPPCC. Elected member, CPPCC Standing Committee and Political and Legal Affairs Committee, powerful organ of Zhou's Government Administrative Council (or cabinet) 1949. In the 1950s, served with various social welfare and peace organizations. Henan deputy and Standing Committee member, first three NPCs 1954–75; full member, Eighth Central Committee 1956–85 and elevated to Politburo, Eleventh Central Committee 1978. Held post of second secretary, CCP Women's Work Department and elected vice-chairman, subsequently honorary president, Women's Federation 1978. Second secretary, Central Committee's Commission for Inspecting Discipline 1979–82. Honorary chairman, Nurses' Association since 1981. Elected honorary president, Association for Friendship with Foreign Countries 1982 and adviser 1988. Honorary president, Smedley–Strong–Snow Society and Population Welfare Foundation since 1984 and 1987 respectively. Adviser, China–Japan Personnel Exchange Committee since 1984. Presidium executive chairman and National Committee chairman, Sixth CPPCC 1983. Resigned Politburo and Central Committee posts 1985. Presidium member, Thirteenth Party Congress 1987. Has led delegations to many countries and, during husband's illness in 1970s, received several foreign delegations on his behalf.

Ding Guan'gen (Ting Kuan-ken)—b. 1930, worked as engineer. Deputy secretary-general, NPC Standing Committee 1983–88. Minister for Railways 1985–88 and vice-minister, State Planning Commission 1988–present. Central Committee member, Twelfth Party Congress 1982–present; and alternate Politburo member, Thirteenth Central Committee 1987–present.

Ding Guangxun (Ting Kuang-hsün)—b. 1915, studied theology in Canada and the United States and returned to PRC 1951. Director, Nanjing Union Theological Seminary by 1953; vice-chairman, Council of Self-Administration of Protestant Church by 1962, and bishop and director, Institute of Protestant Theology, Nanjing by 1964. Jiangsu deputy and Standing Committee member, Third NPC 1964. Disappeared 1967–72. Identified as director, Institute of Religion, Nanjing University 1979, and president, Nanjing Union Theological Seminary since 1981. Standing Committee member, Fifth CPPCC 1978–83; re-elected NPC Standing Committee, Fifth and Sixth NPC 1978 and 1983; member, NPC Foreign Affairs Committee 1983 and Presidium, fifth session Sixth NPC 1987; confirmed in all NPC posts at first session, Seventh NPC 1988. President, Christian Council of China and chairman, Three-Self Patriotic Movement Committee of Protestant Churches in China since 1980. Vice-president, Association for Peace and Disarmament since 1985.

Ding Ling (Ting Ling)—1904–86, b. Changde, Hunan province, attending Changsha middle school and subsequently Shanghai University. Joined League of Left-Wing Writers 1930 and CCP 1931. Worked in literary and cultural spheres through 1930s and 1940s. Elected council member, Federation of Literature and Art Circles, North China branch 1948. Became executive council member, Democratic Women's Federation (until 1957); head, Literature and Art Section, Central Committee's Propaganda Department; vice-chairman, Literature and Art Workers' Association; member First CPPCC; member Government Administrative Council's Cultural Educational Commission; council member, Sino-Soviet Friendship Association; and director,

Central Literature Institute 1949. However, throughout 1950s, 1960s and 1970s came repeatedly under attack. Elected vice-chairman, Writers' Association 1953, but resigned in 1955 in protest against further 'rightist' accusation, and dismissed from all posts 1957. In exile on northeast China farm for most of period 1958–76. Imprisoned for five years during Cultural Revolution. Reappeared 1979 when elected to Fifth NPC and announced to be working on new novel. Then considered one of best contemporary Chinese writers. Among publications are *Miss Sophie's Diary (Shafei nüshi riji)* (1928), In *The Dark (Zai heian zhong)* (1928), *Mother (Muqin)* (1933) and *Sunshine Over the Sanggan River (Taiyang zhao zai Sanggan he shang)* (1948).

Fang Lizhi (Fang Li-chih)—b. 1936. Identified as professor, University of Science and Technology, Hefei, 1978 and head of its Astrophysics Department 1979, and vice-president 1985; member, Academy of Sciences' Department of Mathematics and Physics 1985 and vice-president, Astronomical Society from 1986. Since 1978 has visited United States and Western Europe. Expelled from the CCP and dismissed as vice-president of University of Science and Technology for bourgeois liberalization January 1987. China's unofficial Opposition leader prior to 1989 'pro-democracy' demonstrations: took refuge in the American Embassy in Beijing in early June 1989. Released to Britain mid-1990.

Fang Yi (Fang I)—b. 1916 Xiamen, Fujian province. Joined CYL in 1930 and CCP in 1931. Soon afterwards became editor, Shanghai Commercial Press, then imprisoned for several years. Held important posts in Jiangsu–Anhui Border Area Administrative Council 1945–46. Became director, Finance Department, Shandong–Anhui Border Area Government 1946; vice-chairman, Shandong Province People's Government 1949; vice-chairman and director, Fujian Province People's Government and its Finance Department 1949 and 1952, respectively. Held number of key financial posts, East China Military Region and Military and Administrative Council 1949–54 and, concurrently, Fujian Military Region and province 1951–52. Briefly deputy mayor, Shanghai 1952. Vice-minister of Finance 1953–54, and PRC's economic representative, North Vietnam 1956–61. Elected to alternate membership, Eighth Central Committee 1958; confirmed 1969. Vice-chairman, State Planning Commission 1961–Cultural Revolution. Appointed deputy director, Foreign Affairs Office 1961 and director, Bureau for Economic Relations with Foreign Countries 1961. When bureau upgraded, first to commission and then ministry, became chairman 1964–71 and minister 1971–77. Relatively unscathed during Cultural Revolution. Elected to full membership, Tenth–Twelfth Central Committee 1973–87; and Eleventh Central Committee's Politburo and Secretariat 1977–82 and 1980–82, respectively. Became vice-president, Academy of Sciences 1977–79 and president 1979–81; minister, State Science and Technology Commission 1978–84; vice-premier 1978–82; State Financial and Economic Commission 1979–81; state councillor and deputy head, State Council's Leading Group for Scientific Work 1982–88; Presidium member, Thirteenth Party Congress 1987. Presidium executive chairman, National Committee vice-chairman and chairman, Education and Culture Committee, Seventh CPPCC 1988. Honorary president, Society of Non-ferrous Metals and Association for Promotion of International Science and Technology since 1984 and 1988 respectively. In first half of 1960s headed some half-dozen delegations to foreign countries. Since early 1970s has headed delegations to African states and Western Europe, and was a member of Deng Xiaoping's delegation to the United States. Married to Yin Sen.

Fei Xiaotong (Fei Hsiao-t'ung)—b. 1910 Wujiang county, Jiangsu province. Graduated from Social Sciences Department, Beijing's Yanjing University 1933, continued studies in Qinghua University and received PhD from London University. Lectured in United States 1943, on return becoming Professor of Anthropology at Qinghua University. Again briefly abroad, working at London School of Economics in 1946. Appointed council member, Institute of Foreign Affairs 1949. Appointed member, Government Administrative Council's Culture and Education Commission 1949 and Nationalities Affairs Commission 1951–54 (vice-chairman of latter 1957–58); identified as executive secretary, Sino-Soviet Friendship Association 1951–54; council member, Political Science and Law Society 1953. Elected Jiangsu deputy, First NPC 1954; Central Committee member, China Democratic League 1956–58. Also appointed deputy director, State Bureau of Experts Administration 1956. In 1957–58 associated with the Hundred Flowers Movement, and subsequently forced to engage in self-criticism and repent past errors. In 1959 and 1964 elected to Third and Fourth CPPCC; and to Standing Committee, Fifth CPPCC 1978. Disappeared 1967–72. Elected president, Society of Sociology 1979. Has served in Academy of Social Sciences, as deputy director, Institute of Ethnology and Nationalities Affairs Commission since at least 1979 and 1980, respectively; director, Institute of Sociology 1980–83; and honorary director since 1983. Reappointed to State Nationalities Commission 1979–83 and remains its adviser. Re-elected to China Democratic League, as vice-chairman 1979 and chairman 1987. Elected honorary president, Society of World Nationalities Studies and appointed special court judge for Trial of Lin Biao and Jiang Qing Counter-revolutionary Cliques 1980. Elected executive chairman and vice-chairman, Sixth CPPCC 1983. Elected Jiangsu deputy, Sixth and Seventh NPC 1983 and 1988; Presidium member and vice-chairman, Seventh NPC 1988 and vice-chairman, NPC Committee for Drafting Basic Law of Hong Kong SAR since 1983. Honorary president, Western Returned Students' Association, Minority Literatures Foundation and Rural Hygiene Association since 1986. Vice-president, Association for International Understanding since 1988. Has received many international awards and honours. In 1980s visited the United States, India, Japan and Western Europe.

Fu Hao (Fu Hao)—b. 1916 Shaanxi province. Secretary, Central Committee's Social Department in early years. Councillor to embassy, Mongolian People's Republic, 1950–54; commissar, Ministry of Foreign Affairs' Asian Affairs Department

1954–55; councillor and chargé d'affaires to embassy, India 1955–62. Identified as director, Ministry of Foreign Affairs' General Office 1970–72. Chinese representative, Twenty-sixth UN General Assembly 1971. Vice-minister of Foreign Affairs 1972–74; ambassador to North Vietnam 1974–77 and Japan 1977–82. In 1983 elected Shaanxi deputy and vice-chairman, Foreign Affairs Committee, Sixth NPC; confirmed Seventh NPC 1988. Member, Twenty-first Century Committee for China–Japan Friendship since 1984. During 1980s, primarily as NPC delegation member, visited many Western European and Central/South American countries and Japan. Married to Jiao Ling.

Gao Dengbang (Kao Teng-pang)—identified as director, 1st Field Army's Communications Department 1949 and held two similar posts within North-west Military and Administrative Council, later Administrative Council, 1950–54. Director, Ministry of Railways Administrative Office 1954–56 and director, State Government Organs Administrative Bureau 1956–66. Deputy secretary-general, State Council 1959–66, and identified as deputy director, State Council's Staff Office for Foreign Affairs 1966. Denounced 1967; identified as deputy secretary-general, Academy of Sciences 1978. Shaanxi deputy, Fifth, Sixth and Seventh NPCs, and member, Standing Committee and Overseas Chinese Affairs Committee since 1979 and 1983 respectively. Deputy director, CCP Central Committee's General Office since 1980 and vice-chairman, Song Qingling Foundation since 1982.

Gao Yang (Kao Yang)—b. Liaoning province Held various mid-level posts, Shenyang CP 1950. Chairman, Liaodong People's Government 1950–52 and secretary 1953–54. Member, Northeast China People's Government 1951–53 and North-east China Administrative Council 1953–54. Liaoning deputy, first three NPCs 1954, 1958 and 1964. Appointed member, Central Control Commission 1956, and deputy director, Industrial Labour Department 1958, both under Central Committee. Minister of Chemical Industry 1962–67, then disappeared. Vice-chairman, Jilin Revolutionary Committee 1977–79 and

secretary, Jilin CP 1978–79. Minister, State Farms and Land Reclamation 1979–82; first secretary and first political commissar, Hebei CP and Military District respectively, 1982–85. Member, Presidium, Twelfth and Thirteenth Party Congress 1982 and 1987; and member, Central Advisory Commission 1982–present. President, Central Party School since 1987, chairman, China Investment Consultants since 1986; and adviser, Political Restructuring Research Society since 1988.

Geng Biao (Keng Piao)—b. 1909 Liling county, Hunan province. While still a teenager, involved in Party underground, and had joined Workers' and Peasants' Red Army, Ruijin by 1930. Regimental commander, Lin Biao and Nie Rongzhen's 1st Army Corps during Long March 1934–45 (see Nie Rongzhen). Studied and then taught at Red Army Academy, which moved to Yan'an as Anti-Japanese Military and Political Academy. After outbreak of hostilities with Japan 1937, worked in 8th Route Army HQ. Liaison Bureau director, Jin–Cha–Ji Border Region Government by 1944 and chief of staff, Jin–Cha–Ji Military Region 1947. In 1946 given rank of major-general, and still holds this rank. Participated in takeover of Shijiazhuang, Hebei province 1947, temporary CCP HQ until end of war 1949. Distinguished active service record. Ambassador to Sweden 1949–56 and minister to Denmark and Finland 1949–55 (first three non-communist governments to recognize PRC). Ambassador to Pakistan 1956–60. Vice-minister, Foreign Ministry 1960–63, and active in South-east Asian affairs, accompanying three top Chinese officials abroad. Ambassador to Burma (Myanmar) 1963–67. Elected member, CCP Central Committee, Ninth, Tenth and Eleventh Party Congress, 1969, 1973 and 1977 respectively, and elevated to Politburo 1977–82. Appointed vice-premier 1978–82. Hunan deputy, Fifth NPC 1978; confirmed Sixth NPC 1983, and elected vice-chairman, NPC's Standing Committee; chairman, NPC's Foreign Affairs Committee; and executive chairman, all plenums except second, 1984. Standing Committee member, CCP Central Military Commission 1979–82, and Central

Advisory Commission 1982–present. Led Party delegation to Western and Eastern Europe in 1980s. Married to Zhao Lanxiang.

Gu Mu (Ku Mu)—b. 1914 Rongchen county, Shandong province, joining CYL 1931 and CCP 1932. Rose to position of secretary, Central–South Shandong CP Committee prior to 1949. Identified as mayor, Jinan and member, Shandong People's Government 1950–52. Director, Shanghai CP's Propaganda Department 1952–54 and vice-chairman, State Council's Construction Commission 1954–56. Vice-chairman, Economic Commission 1956–65. Deputy director, State Council's Third Staff Office 1957–59. Shandong deputy, Second and Third NPC 1959 and 1964. Director, Department of Industry and Communications, Central Committee's Political Work Department by 1964. Appointed chairman, State Council's Capital Construction Commission 1965; disappeared during Cultural Revolution, then identified as minister, Capital Commission and elected to Tenth Central Committee 1973. Shandong deputy and vice-chairman, Fourth and Fifth NPC 1975 and 1978. Political commissar, PLA Capital Construction Engineering Corps and member, State Financial and Economic Commission 1979–81, and minister, Foreign Investment Control Commission 1979–82; identified as minister, Administrative Commission on Import and Export Affairs 1980–82. Elected to Secretariat, Eleventh Central Commission 1980–85; appointed state councillor and headed several tourism/economic organizations, including three State Council groups 1982–88. Member, Presidium, Twelfth and Thirteenth Party Congress 1982 and 1987. Presidium executive chairman, National Committee vice-chairman and Economic Committee chairman, Seventh CPPCC 1988. Elected honorary chairman, Tourism Association 1986 and honorary president, Association for Promotion of International Science and Technology 1988. Has led four government delegations to Japan since 1979; accompanied Zhao Ziyang's eleven-nation African tour 1982; and headed government delegations to Western Europe and Latin America later in 1980s. Married to Mou Feng.

Han Xu (Han Hsü)—identified as Protocol Department official, Ministry of Foreign Affairs 1959. Councillor, embassy in Soviet Union 1964–65; deputy director, Protocol Department 1969–72 and director 1972–73. Deputy head, PRC Liaison Office in Washington 1973–79; director, America and Oceania Affairs Department, Ministry of Foreign Affairs 1979–82 and vice-minister of Foreign Affairs 1982–85. Elected alternate member, Twelfth and Thirteenth Central Committee 1982 and 1987. Appointed ambassador to United States 1985. Led many government delegations to West Indies during 1980s. Married to Ge Qiyun.

Hao Jianxiu (Hao Chien-hsiu)—b. 1935 Qingdao. While working in Qingdao, in 1951, declared 'National Model Worker in Industry' for new spinning method. Won scholarship to Shandong middle school 1952. Continued studies in Beijing; and elected Executive Committee member, Women's Federation and Democratic Youth League 1953. Shandong deputy, first three NPCs 1954, 1958 and 1964. Studied at East China Institute of Weaving and Spinning 1958–62, graduating as engineer and returning to Qingdao where identified as factory deputy director 1964. Elected member, CYL Central Committee 1964–Cultural Revolution. Appointed factory director 1965. Established in Qingdao Revolutionary Committee 1967–76 and Shandong hierarchy 1973–78. Elected to Eleventh Central Committee 1977; confirmed by Twelfth and Thirteenth Party Congress 1982 and 1987. Identified as Vice-minister of Textile Industry 1978; appointed minister 1981–83. Vice-chairman, Women's Federation 1978–83. Alternate member, CCP Secretariat 1982–85; full member 1985–88; member, State Council's Central Financial and Economic Leading Group 1986–88. Along with Chen Muhua, one of two women on Presidium Standing Committee, Thirteenth Party Congress 1987. Vice-minister, State Planning Commission since 1987 and vice-chairman, State Tourism Committee since 1988. During 1980s visited Japan, South-east Asia and Europe.

He Jingzhi (Ho Ching-chih)—b. 1924 Zaozhuang, Shandong province. Attended primary and middle school. Began publishing poetry in Chongqing newspaper in 1939. Went to Yan'an 1940. Wrote libretto for *The White-Haired Girl (Baimao nü)* with Ding Yi. Later worked in north China. Identified as council member, Writers' Association 1953 and secretary, Playwrights' Association 1962. Disappeared 1967–76. Identified as Vice-minister of Culture 1978–82 and vice-chairman, Writers' Association 1980–85. Appointed deputy director, CCP Central Committee's Propaganda Department 1980. Elected honorary director, Chinese Opera Research Institute 1981 and honorary chairman, Society of Chinese Folk Literature 1987. Central Committee member, Twelfth and Thirteenth Party Congress 1982–present. Appointed Minister of Culture September 1989. Married to Ke Yan.

He Kang (Ho K'ang)—b. 1923 Fujian province. Deputy director, State Council's Office of Experts Administration by 1957. Guangdong deputy, Third NPC 1964. Disappeared 1967–78; then identified as vice-minister of Agriculture and Forestry 1978–79; vice-minister in both Ministry of Agriculture and State Agricultural Commission 1979; and vice-president, Agronomy Society 1980. Served on various central health campaign committees and State Council agricultural committees and commissions (e.g. elected vice-chairman, National Agricultural Zoning Committee 1983). Vice-minister of State Planning Commission 1982–85; Vice-minister of Agriculture, Animal Husbandry and Fisheries (Agriculture from 1988) 1982–83, and minister 1983–present. Central Committee member, Twelfth Party Congress 1982–present, and Presidium member, Thirteenth Party Congress 1987. Vice-chairman and deputy head, State Council's Central Patriotic Health Campaign Committee and Leading Group for National Land Development Fund since 1981 and 1988 respectively. Vice-chairman, Science and Technology Association since 1986 and honorary vice-chairman, Zhongkai Institute of Agricultural Technology since 1987. Deputy head, agricultural delegation to United States 1978 and Yugoslavia 1979. During 1980s has led agricultural delegations to various European and Latin American countries; FAO confer-

ences in Rome 1983 and 1985, and UN special sessions on Africa in Geneva 1986.

He Luting (Ho Lu-t'ing)—b. 1903 Shaoyang, Hunan province, and studied at Shanghai Conservatory. Lectured, Lu Xun Institute of Arts, Yan'an after 1938, and there composed famous anthem *The East Is Red (Dongfang hong)*. Participated in First CPPCC 1949; elected member, Federation of Literature and Art Circles and identified as vice-president, Central College of Music and Musicians' Association 1950. Elected council member, Association for Cultural Relations with Foreign Countries and Shanghai deputy, First NPC 1954. President, Shanghai Conservatory by 1966; then purged. Standing Committee member, Fifth and Sixth CPPCC 1978 and 1983; confirmed by Sixth CPPCC 1983. Vice-chairman, Federation of Literature and Art Circles 1979–present; director, Shanghai Conservatory 1979–86 and honorary director 1986–present; vice-president, Musicians' Association 1979–85, and honorary director 1985–present.

Hou Xianglin (Hou Hsiang-lin)—awarded PhD in United States during 1940s. Identified as member, Academy of Sciences Committee of Technical Sciences 1955; secretary-general, Society of Chemical Engineering 1956; and deputy director, Institute of Petroleum Industry 1962. In 1978 elected member, Fifth CPPCC Standing Committee (confirmed by Sixth CPPCC 1983). Identified as Vice-minister of Petroleum Industry 1978–82, and elected director-general, Petroleum Association 1978. Identified as member, Academy of Sciences' Department of Technology 1979; deputy general manager, China National Petroleum Corporation 1980. Elected to Presidium, Academy of Sciences, 1981 and Presidium, Sixth CPPCC 1983. Identified as chairman, Ministry of Petroleum Industry's Science and Technology Commission 1984; member, Academy of Sciences Department of Chemistry 1985. Considered China's leading petrochemical expert.

Hu Jiwei (Hu Chi-wei)—identified as deputy director, Information Bureau, North-west China Military and Administrative Council 1950. Connected with *People's Daily* 1954 onwards, as chief editor

1977–present. Sichuan deputy, Third, Fifth and Sixth NPCs 1964, 1978 and 1983; Standing Committee member and vice-chairman, Education, Science, Culture and Public Health Committee 1983–88. Elected chairman, Journalists' Association 1980–83; president, Beijing Journalism Studies Society 1980; president, Confederation of Journalism Societies 1984 and vice-chairman, Zou Taofen Foundation 1987. Has headed journalistic delegations to Eastern Bloc countries.

Hu Qiaomu (Hu Ch'iao-mu)—b. 1911 Dingxin, Yancheng county, Jiangsu province. After graduating from Yangzhou middle school 1924, studied for two years at Beijing's Qinghua University and a further year at Hangzhou's Zhejiang University. Active in cultural and propaganda sphere for CCP, Shanghai 1930–37. Involved in youth training activities and became editor, *China Youth*, Yan'an 1938. After Yan'an fell in 1947, accompanied Mao to newly liberated Beijing, and elected to NDYL's Central Committee and Federation of Democratic Youth's National Committee 1949–53. Rose to prominence in CPPCC 1949–54. Served on Government Administrative Council 1949–52. Became editor-in-chief *People's Daily* 1949. Vice-chairman, International Organization of Journalists 1950–56. Published strongly Maoist *Thirty Years of The Communist Party of China* 1951 which, as official Party history, brought him much prestige. Up to 1956 Party Congress prominent in most propaganda and ideological campaigns and key figure in language reform program. Member, Mao's Committee to Draft Constitution 1953–54. Jiangsu deputy and Standing Committee member, first three NPCs 1949–75. Appointed member, Academy of Sciences 1955. Elected member, Central Committee and alternate member, Secretariat, Eighth Party Congress 1956, and subsequently more involved in international communist affairs. Relieved of all posts 1966. Tianjin deputy and Standing Committee member, Fifth NPC 1978. President, Academy of Social Sciences 1978–82. Elected to Eleventh Central Committee 1978, as its deputy secretary-general 1979 and member, Secretariat 1980. Member, Twelfth Central Committee's Politburo 1982–87. At Thirteenth Party Congress 1987 served on Presidium Standing Committee; relinquished all posts and elected to Central Advisory Commission's Standing Committee. Chairman, Beijing Journalism Society 1980–88 and honorary president, Political Science Society 1980–88. Honorary president, Academy of Social Sciences 1982–present, Wildlife Conservation Foundation 1983–present, and Wu Yuzhang Foundation 1986–present. Married to Gu Yu.

Hu Qili (Hu Ch'i-li)—b. 1929 Yulin, Shaanxi province; joined CCP 1948. Graduated Beijing University 1951. Prominent in Students' Federation: identified as vice-chairman 1954, and chairman 1956–65 and 1979–80; CYL: alternate secretary by 1964 and secretary 1978–80; Youth Federation: standing Committee member 1958–65, vice-chairman 1965–79 and chairman 1979–80. Travelled widely as youth delegate 1955–56. Identified as council member, Sino-Latin American Friendship Association and Sino-African Society 1960. Heilongjiang deputy, Third NPC 1964. Dismissed from CYL posts 1966, and attacked as follower of Liu Shaoqi and purged by Red Guards 1967; sent to labour camp in Ningxia. Identified in several Party posts at county and regional level 1975–78. Standing Committee member, Fifth CPPCC 1979–80. Tianjin CP secretary and mayor 1980–82 and deputy, Fifth NPC 1980–83. Director, CCP Central Committee's General Office and member, Twelfth Central Committee 1982–88. Presidium and Politburo Standing Committees member and Secretariat secretary-general, Thirteenth Party Congress 1987. Tianjin deputy, Seventh NPC 1988. Since Cultural Revolution has headed delegations to United States and Western Europe, and accompanied Hu Yaobang to Oceania.

Hu Sheng (Hu Sheng)—b. 1911, Suzhou, Jiangsu province. Studied at Beijing University. Journalist in Chongqing after outbreak of Sino-Japanese War 1937. Served in Education Department, North China People's Government 1948. Engaged in language reform work, Government Administrative Council Publications Administration and Board, Chinese Written Language Reform Committee 1949. Took part in First CPPCC 1949. Elected to Federation of Democratic Youth

1949–53, subsequently serving as vice-chairman, Youth Federation 1958–65. Identified as secretary-general, Central Committee's Propaganda Department 1951 and council member, Peace Council 1958–Cultural Revolution. Shandong deputy, First and Second NPC 1954 and 1958. Appointed member, Academy of Sciences' Department of Philosophy and Social Sciences 1955. In 1957 became member, State Council's Scientific Planning Commission. Identified as deputy director, Political Research Office, Higher Party School 1958 and deputy editor-in-chief, journal *Red Flag (Hong qi)* 1961–66. Shanghai deputy, Third NPC 1964. Purged 1966. Standing Committee member, Fourth and Fifth NPC 1975 and 1978. Identified as deputy secretary-general, Constitution Revision Committee 1982. Elected member, Twelfth Central Committee 1982. Elected director and president, Central Committee's Party History Research Centre and Party Historical Research Society, 1982 and 1983, respectively. Appointed president, Academy of Social Sciences 1985 and president, Postgraduate Institute 1987. Vice-chairman, NPC Committees for Drafting Basic Law of Hong Kong and Macao SARs since 1988 (member of former since 1983). Presidium executive chairman, National Committee vice-chairman and Study Committee chairman, Seventh CPPCC 1988. Elected Presidium, Thirteenth Party Congress 1987.

Hu Yaobang (Hu Yao-pang)—1915–89, b. Liuyang, Hunan. Member, Children's Corps, Autumn Harvest Uprising 1927 and engaged in youth work for Jiangxi Soviet 1933. Took part in Long March 1934–35. Prominent in CYL 1935–36. Attended Anti-Japanese Military and Political Academy, northern Shanxi. Served in 18th Army Corps 1941–48, and briefly in Taiyuan administration after city captured by 2nd Field Army 1949, then rejoined army for assault on Sichuan and subsequently served in north Sichuan 1950–52. Served on CPPCC 1949–64, Sino-Soviet Friendship Association's executive board 1949–54 and NDYL's Central Committee 1949–57. Transferred to Beijing as first secretary, NDYL and led several international youth delegations 1952–57. Shandong deputy and Standing Committee member,

First and Second NPC 1954 and 1958; Sichuan deputy, Third NPC 1964; Anhui deputy and Standing Committee member, Fifth NPC 1978; Beijing deputy, Sixth NPC 1983. Elected to Central Committee, Eighth Party Congress 1956, and Eleventh–Thirteenth Party Congress 1977–89; and elevated to Politburo 1979–89. Identified as vice-president and director, Central Committee's Party School and Organization Department, respectively, 1977–78; and general secretary, Central Committee and director of its Propaganda Department 1979. Elevated to Politburo Standing Committee 1980 and post of CCP Chairman 1981–82, then secretary-general, Central Committee 1982 (the post of chairman having been abolished). Dismissed from the position of secretary-general of the Central Committee in January 1987 for bourgeois liberalization. Served on Presidium Standing Committee, Thirteenth Party Congress 1987. During 1980s visited Europe and Oceania. Married to Li Chao. Hu's death in April 1989 sparked Beijing 'pro-democracy' demonstrations.

Hu Zi'ang (Hu Tzu-ang)—b. c. 1899 Chongqing, Sichuan province. Studied agriculture at Beijing University, then became principal, Sichuan Middle School and worked in various government posts. Left for Hong Kong before communist occupation, and returned to take part in First CPPCC 1949. Member, Government Administrative Council's Financial and Economic Affairs Committee 1949–54. Served in South-west China Military and Administrative Council 1950–53 and South-west China Administrative Council 1953–54; elected deputy mayor, Chongqing 1950 and vice-chairman, Federation of Industry and Commerce 1953. Chongqing deputy, First NPC 1954; Sichuan deputy, Second–Fifth NPC 1958–87, and Standing Committee member, Third–Fifth NPC 1965–87. Elected chairman, executive committee, Federation of Industry and Commerce 1978 and honorary chairman, 1988. Served on Presidium, as executive chairman 1987, and elected vice-chairman, Sixth and Seventh CPPCC 1983 and 1988.

Huan Xiang (Huan Hsiang)—1910–89, b. Zunyi, Guizhou province and raised in Hankou, where attended American missionary school. Studied engineering at Shanghai's Jiaotong University and political science at Japan's Waseda University. Editor-in-chief, army paper *Daily Front* 1937–45. Became deputy editor-in-chief, Shanghai *Wenhui bao* and joined CCP 1947. Deputy secretary-general, First CPPCC; director, Ministry of Foreign Affairs' Western Europe and Africa Department; and secretary, Sino-Soviet Friendship Association 1949–54. Chargé d'affaires, Britain 1954–62; assistant minister of Foreign Affairs 1964–66; ambassador to Belgium, European Community and Luxembourg 1976–78; and vice-president, Academy of Social Sciences 1978–82. Elected president, International Law Society and Adviser, Society of World Economics 1980; honorary president, Society for History of Sino-Foreign Relations 1981; honorary president, Middle East Society; vice-president, Law Society; vice-chairman, Chinese Committee, Council of Chinese and Japanese Non-governmental Personages; and adviser, Academy of Social Sciences 1982. Guizhou deputy and member, Standing Committee and Foreign Affairs Committee, Sixth NPC 1983. Elected honorary president, Society of International Relations; adviser, Institute for Federation German Studies; and secretary-general, State Council's Research Centre of International Problems 1985. During 1980s visited Western Europe, Canada and the United States.

Huang Dingchen (Huang Ting-ch'en)—b. 1901 Haifeng, Guangdong province. Studied medicine, Tokyo University 1921–28. Imprisoned as suspected member CCP 1929–37. Joined Zhigong Party 1947; Standing Committee member 1956–66 and chairman 1979–88. In 1949 took part in First CPPCC. Deputy director, Ministry of Public Health's Medical Administration 1949–66. In 1953 identified as president, Anti-Tuberculosis Association. Guangdong deputy, first three NPCs 1954, 1958 and 1964; re-identified as NPC deputy 1976. Identified as vice-president, Medical Society 1956–66 and Standing Committee member, Federation of Returned Overseas Chinese 1956; became vice-president 1984; and member of Presidium and Standing Committee,

Fifth–Seventh CPPCC 1978–present. Elected president, Anti-Tuberculosis Association 1978; vice-president, International Cultural Exchange Centre 1984; adviser, Association for Advancement of International Friendship 1987; and honorary chairman, Zhigong Party 1988.

Huang Hua (Huang Hua)—b. Wang Rumei, Hebei province 1913. Attended Beijing's Yanjing University mid-1930s. Joined American Edgar Snow's tour of China 1936. CCP head in GMD/CCP talks 1946. Head, Shanghai Foreign Residents' Affairs Department 1950–52. Transferred to Ministry of Foreign Affairs 1953 and appointed director, Western Europe and Africa Department 1954–55 and director, Western Europe Department 1955–59. Appointed ambassador to Ghana 1960–65, United Arab Republic 1966–70, Canada 1971 (only ambassador not recalled for self-criticism during Cultural Revolution). Elected to Tenth Central Committee 1973; confirmed Eleventh and Twelfth Party Congress, 1977 and 1982; resigned 1985 and elected to Standing Committee, Central Advisory Commission. Minister of Foreign Affairs 1976–82. Hebei deputy, Fifth and Sixth NPC 1978 and 1983 and vice-chairman, Sixth NPC. Vice-premier 1980–82 and appointed state councillor 1982. Presidium member, Thirteenth Party Congress 1987. Awarded Mercury International Award for Peace and Co-operation 1982. Elected president, Smedley–Strong–Snow Society 1984, Great Wall Society 1987 and Welfare Institute 1988, and chief adviser, Association for International Friendly Contacts 1988. Has visited approximately forty countries visited since Cultural Revolution including several visits to the United States and Latin America, Western and Eastern Europe, Africa, the Middle East, Japan and India. Married to He Liliang.

Huang Kun (Huang K'un)—b. Zhejiang province. Graduated Yanjing University Physics Department 1941 and received doctorate from Bristol University 1947, continuing research at Edinburgh and Liverpool Universities, returning to China 1951. Appointed member, Academy of Sciences' Department of Mathematics, Physics and Chemistry 1955. Identified as physics professor, Beijing University 1959. Beijing deputy, Third NPC 1964, Presidium and Standing Committee member, 5th–7th CPPCC 1978–present, and Science and Technology Committee member since 1988. Appointed director, Academy's Institute of Semi-conductors 1977–85 and honorary director, 1985. Deputy head, Academy delegation to Sweden and Britain 1978. Elected foreign member, Swedish Royal Academy 1980. Elected Fellow, Third World Academy of Sciences, Trieste 1985 and president, Physics Society 1987.

Ismail Amat (Simayi Aimaiti)—b. 1934 in Uygur community, Qira county, Hotan prefecture, Xinjiang. Active in People's Commune Movement up to 1960. Elected Central Committee member, Tenth Central Committee 1973–present. Identified in Xinjiang as CP secretary 1974–85; Revolutionary Committee vice-chairman 1974–79; Military Region political commissar 1976; and appointed first deputy director, Party School 1977. Elected chairman, Xinjiang People's Government 1979–88. By-elected XAR deputy and Standing Committee member, Fifth NPC 1980; confirmed as deputy 1988. Appointed minister, State Nationalities Affairs Commission 1986. Presidium executive chairman and vice-chairman, National Committee and Nationalities Committee, Seventh CPPCC 1988. NPC delegate to Europe and Japan, and head, Xinjiang delegation to Pakistan and Turkey in 1980s.

Ji Pengfei (Chi P'eng-fei)—b. 1909 Yongji county, Shanxi province, attending middle school there and Xi'an. Graduated Military Medical College, Xi'an. Served under Nationalists as army medical officer in unit which joined communists 1931. During Long March 1934–45 active in Medical Department, CCP Military Commission, subsequently becoming its director. Political director, various units during Sino-Japanese War 1937–45. Head, equivalent to ambassador, of Chinese diplomatic mission to East Berlin, German Democratic Republic 1950–53, and ambassador 1953–55. Appointed council member, Institute of Foreign Affairs 1955 and Vice-minister of Foreign Affairs 1955–71. Visited Morocco, Guinea, Mali, Ghana and Congo 1965, and remained in office despite difficulty during Cultural Revolu-

tion, primarily responsible for African and Asian affairs. Appointed acting Minister of Foreign Affairs 1971 and minister 1972. Elected to Tenth and Eleventh Central Committee 1973 and 1977. Shanxi deputy, Third and Fourth NPC 1964 and 1975: secretary-general 1975–79 and vice-chairman 1975–78; Beijing deputy and vice-chairman, Fifth and Sixth NPC 1978–88 and head, NPC China–Greece Friendship Group 1985–88. Director, Central Committee's International Liaison Department 1979–82; vice-premier 1979–82; secretary-general, State Council 1980–87; and state councillor 1982–88. Member, Presidium, Twelfth and Thirteenth Party Congress 1982 and 1987, and on Standing Committee, Central Advisory Commission 1982–present. Director, State Council's Hong Kong and Macao Affairs Office since 1983; chairman, NPC's Committees for Drafting Basic Law of Hong Kong and Macao SARs since 1988. Latter half of 1970s travelled extensively, primarily as head of friendship delegations to a wide selection of Arabic, Eastern and Western European, Latin American and African countries. Married to Xu Hanbing.

Jia Chunwang (Chia Ch'un-wang)—b. 1938. Served successively at Qinghua University as head, CP Student Department and secretary, CYL up to 1978. Elected Standing Committee member, CYL 1978 and secretary, Beijing CYL 1982; deputy secretary Beijing CP 1984–85. Elected to Twelfth and Thirteenth Central Committee 1985 and 1987, and to latter's Presidium. Appointed Minister of State Security 1985.

Jia Shi (Chia Shih)—held top financial post, Shenyang before becoming deputy director, Ministry of Commerce's Foreign Trade Department 1950. Deputy director, Ministry of Foreign Trade's Second Bureau by 1952, and director by 1958; vice-chairman, Council for Promoting Foreign Trade 1967–69; Vice-minister of Foreign Trade 1964–82. Chairman, Council for Promotion of International Trade and International Economic and Trade Arbitration Commission since 1986 and 1988 respectively. Presidium and Standing Committee member, Seventh CPPCC 1988. Has led or accompanied heads of state on trade delegations to a wide variety of Western and Eastern

European countries, the United States, Latin America, the Middle East and Oceania.

Jia Yibin (Chia I-pin)—served in GMD as vice-chairman, Shanghai Section by 1961; vice-chairman, Central Committee since 1979 and head, Executive Bureau since 1985. Presidium and Standing Committee member, Fifth–Seventh CPPCC, 1978–present, and deputy head, Committee for Reunification of Motherland since 1983. Elected vice-president, International Cultural Exchange Centre 1984.

Jiang Zemin (Chiang Tse-min)—identified as director, North-east Military Region's Military Engineering Department 1950, and subsequently as commercial councillor, Chinese embassy to Soviet Union; assistant minister, First Ministry of Machine Building 1956–59 and vice-chairman, Society of Mechanical Engineering 1960 (re-identified in this post 1978). Identified as vice-minister, Administrative Commission for Import and Export Affairs 1980–82 and vice-minister, State Foreign Investment Commission 1981–82. Tianjin deputy, Sixth NPC 1983. Vice-minister of Electronics Industry 1982–83 and appointed minister 1983. Elected to Twelfth Central Committee 1982, and Thirteenth Party Congress's Presidium and Politburo 1987. Mayor, Shanghai 1985–88; deputy secretary, Shanghai CP 1985–87 and secretary 1987–89; chairman, Shanghai Armaments Committee since 1987; and first secretary, Shanghai Garrison CP since 1988. Replaced Zhao Ziyang as Party secretary-general and Deng Xiaoping as chairman, CCP Central Military Commission, and appointed to Secretariat following Beijing student 'pro-democracy' demonstrations 1989.

Jing Shuping (Ching Shu-p'ing)—b. Zhejiang province 1918. Identified as deputy secretary-general, Federation of Industry and Commerce 1963; disappeared 1966–76. Appointed director, China International Trust and Investment Corporation 1979. Identified as deputy secretary-general, Federation of Industry and Commerce 1979 and Standing Committee member 1985. CPPCC Standing Committee member since 1986; Presidium member and Finance Committee vice-chairman, Seventh CPPCC 1988. President and vice-chairman, China International Economic Consultants Inc. since 1981; director, China International Trust and Investment Corporation since 1988. Member, NPC Committee for Drafting Special Law of Macao SAR since 1988. Has travelled as trade delegate to Western Europe, the United States and Oceania since 1979.

Kang Keqing (K'ang K'e-ch'ing)—b. 1910 Wan'an, Jiangsu province, to fisherman, and given away to poor peasant family. In 1927 joined CYL; in 1928 began organizing Red Army guerilla units. Married Zhu De 1929. Commander, Red Army Women's Department 1933. One of few women on Long March 1934–35. Studied at Party School and Anti-Japanese Military and Political Academy 1936–37; then appointed director, Political Department, 8th Route Army. Elected Standing Committee member, Democratic Women's Federation 1949–57 and secretary 1955–57; and vice-president, new Women's Federation 1957, president 1978 and honorary president 1988. Elected member, Eleventh Central Committee 1977. Elected vice-chairman, Fifth–Seventh CPPCC 1978–present; and Presidium executive chairman and chairman, Women and Youth Committee 1988. Elected executive council member, Welfare Institute 1978, and honorary president since 1988; chairman, Song Qingling Foundation 1982–present. Presidium member, Thirteenth Party Congress 1987.

Lei Jieqiong (Lei Chieh-ch'iung)—b. 1905 Guangdong province. Studied law in United States. Elected member, new Federation of Democratic Women and took part in First CPPCC 1949. Member, Government Administrative Council's Commission of Culture and Education 1949–54. Identified as professor, Yanjing University, Beijing 1951. Elected to First, Second and Third NPC 1954, 1959 and 1964. Identified as deputy director, State Council's Bureau of Foreign Exports Administration 1956. Disappeared 1967–75. Identified as Standing Committee member, China Association for Promoting Democracy 1975–79; vice-chairman 1979–83 and chairman, 1983–present. Standing Committee member, Fifth and Sixth CPPCC, 1978 and 1986. Vice-president, Women's Federation 1978–present. Identified as law professor, Beijing University 1978 and 1984. Vice-mayor Beijing 1979–83. Beijing deputy and vice-chairman, Sixth NPC 1983; and Guangdong deputy, Presidium member, Standing Committee vice-chairman, and vice-chairman, Committee for Drafting Basic Law of Macao SAR, Seventh NPC 1988. Elected vice-president, Association for International Understanding 1981; honorary president, Western Returned Students' Association and Society of Gerontology 1986; and chairman, Association for Promoting Democracy 1987. Has visited Middle East, Asia and Oceania since 1979.

Li Desheng (Li Te-sheng)—b. 1916 Hong'an/Huang'an, Hubei province. Joined 4th Front Army around 1932. Took part in Long March 1934–35. In newly reorganized 8th Route Army became detachment commander 1937, battalion commander 1940 and regimental commander 1943. Forces integrated into Central Plains Field Army 1948, and became commander, 2nd Field Army's 35th Division 1949. Division joined Chinese People's Volunteers in Korea in 1951, where appointed chief of staff, 12th Army 1952. Trained at PLA Military Academy, Nanjing 1954. Promoted to major-general 1955, and identified as commander, 12th Army 1958. In response to Lin Biao's call for military commanders to return to basic service, served for some time as private in 1960. Moderating role and sense of restraint during Cultural Revolution led to appointment as commander, Anhui Military District 1967. Served in Anhui as chairman, Revolutionary Committee 1968–74 and first secretary, new CP Secretariat 1971–74. Elected to Ninth Central Committee and alternate Politburo membership 1969; elevated to Politburo Standing Committee 1973–77. Director, PLA's Political Department 1970–74. Commander, Shenyang Military Region 1974–85, and first secretary of its CP 1977–85. Resigned from Politburo and Central Committee posts and elected to Standing Committee, Central Advisory Commission 1985; confirmed 1987. Elected to Presidium, Thirteenth Party Congress, 1987. Has served as political commissar, PLA National Defence University since 1985 and honorary president, Martial Arts Association and Ice Sports Association since 1988.

Li Ding (Li Ting)—Appointed deputy head, Central Committee's United Front Work Department 1982 and elected vice-president, Association for Advancement of International Friendship 1987. Elected vice-chairman, Federation of Industry and Commerce and CP representative on Presidium Standing Committee and Committee for Reunification of the Motherland, Seventh CPPCC 1988.

Li Menghua (Li Meng-hua)—b. 1922, Hebei province. Member, Youth Federation and Central Committee NDYL 1953. Vice-chairman, Physical Culture and Sports Commission and Athletics Association by 1961; led youth and sports delegations overseas. Tianjin deputy, Fifth NPC 1978. Vice-minister, State Physical Culture and Sports Commission 1978–81 and minister since 1981. President, Athletics Association 1978–79; president, Weiqi Association since 1978; vice-president, Sports Federation from June 1962 and since 1978, and president since 1986. Appointed to National Games Organizing Committee 1979 and Olympic Committee 1986. Elected Central Committee member, Twelfth and Thirteenth Party Congress 1982 and 1987. Since Cultural Revolution has led sports delegations to the United States, Canada, Latin America, Eastern and Western Europe, Africa and Japan.

Li Peng (Li P'eng)—b. 1928 Chengdu, Sichuan province and attended college, probably in Soviet Union, after early education in China. Adopted by Zhou Enlai at age 11. Prior to 1980 held various engineering-related posts, as deputy chief engineer and head, Dispatchers' Office, Northeast Power Bureau; and head, Beijing Telecommunication Administration. Identified as Vice-minister of Power Industry 1979; minister 1981–82; vice–minister, newly established Ministry of Water Conservation and Power 1982–83. Central Committee member, Twelfth Party Congress 1982–present. Vice-premier 1983–88; head, four State Council leading groups 1984–88; and head, Central Flood Control HQ 1986–88. Served on Presidium Standing Committee and elevated to Politburo Standing Committee, Thirteenth Party Congress 1987. Chairman, Environmental Protection Committee since 1984; minister, State

Education Commission since 1985; chairman, Wu Yuzhang Award Foundation since 1986; Presidium member and Beijing deputy, Seventh NPC; minister, State Commission for Restructuring the Economic System; and premier since 1988. During 1980s has visited Eastern and Western Europe, Africa, Japan, the United States and Canada. Married to Zhu Lin.

Li Qi (Li Ch'i)—b. 1918 Hebei province. Appointed adviser, Government Administrative Council 1949. Deputy director, Premier's Office 1955–58. Identified as first secretary, Taiyuan CP 1957–61. Vice-minister of Culture 1963–67 and vice-chairman, Association for Cultural Relations with Foreign Countries 1966–67, and headed friendship/cultural delegations to Cuba, North Korea, the Congo and Guinea. Again identified as cadre, State Council's Science and Education Group 1973–75; cadre, Ministry of Culture 1975–77; Vice-minister of Education 1977–82; and vice-president, Education Society 1978–83. Standing Committee member, Fifth CPPCC 1978–83. Hebei deputy, Sixth and Seventh NPC 1983 and 1988; Standing Committee member 1983–88 and member, Internal and Judicial Affairs Committee 1988–present. Appointed/elected chairman, PRC's National Commission for UNESCO 1979; Central Patriotic Health Campaign Committee 1978; vice-chairman, Sports Federation, and president, Middle School Sports Association 1979; director, CCP's Party Literature Research Centre 1982. Since 1979 has visited Japan, Sri Lanka, the United States and France.

Li Ruihuan (Li Jui-huan)—b. 1934 Beijing. Studied Beijing Architectural Engineering Spare-time Institute for six and a half years. Became leader, Beijing Young Carpenters' Shock Brigade 1959; model worker in 1960 and again in 1979. Identified as vice-chairman, Beijing Trade Union 1973, and director-general, worksite for Beijing's Mao Zedong Memorial Hall 1977. Beijing deputy and Standing Committee member, Fifth NPC 1978. CYL secretary and Youth Federation vice-chairman 1980–81. Identified as deputy mayor, Tianjin 1981–82 and mayor 1982–present; elected Standing Committee member, Tianjin CP 1982; deputy

secretary 1985 and secretary 1987–present, and Tianjin deputy, Sixth NPC 1983; confirmed, and served on Presidium, Seventh NPC 1988. Elected to Twelfth Central Committee 1982. Elevated to Politburo, and served on Presidium, Thirteenth Party Congress 1987 and to Politburo Standing Committee June 1989. Since 1978 has visited the United States, Canada, Latin America, Western Europe and Oceania.

Li Tieying (Li T'ieh-ying)—b. 1936 to Li Weihan, one of earliest CCP Central Committee members. Graduated in solid physics, Mathematics Department, Charles University, Czechoslovakia 1961. Then worked in three Shenyang research institutes and elected labour hero 1978. Identified as secretary, Shenyang CP 1981, and elected secretary, Liaoning province CP 1983–85. Elected alternate member, Twelfth Central Committee 1982 and Presidium and Politburo member, Thirteenth Party Congress 1987. Minister, Electronics Industry 1985–87, State Commission for Restructuring the Economic System 1987–88 and State Education Commission 1988–present; state councillor 1988–present; and chairman, State Council's Central Patriotic Public Health Campaign Committee 1988–present.

Li Xiannian (Li Hsien-nien)—b. 1905, Hong'an/Huang'an, Hubei province and trained as carpenter. Joined GMD's Northern Expedition 1926 and after GMD rift with CCP in 1927, joined CCP. Chairman, Hubei Soviet (Hubei Government 1949 onwards). Army captain and political commissar, Long March 1934–35. Later served as commander, Central China Military Committee and then deputy commander, 4th Field Army. Prominent figure in central–south China 1949–54. Appointed vice-premier, member, National Defence Council and army general, and elected Hubei deputy, First NPC 1954. Politburo member, Eighth–Twelfth Party Congress 1956–87. Minister of Finance 1957–75. Member, CCP Secretariat 1958–Cultural Revolution; director, State Financial and Economic Affairs Bureau 1959–Cultural Revolution; vice-chairman, State Planning Commission 1962–72; Standing Committee member, Politburo 1977–87; Hubei deputy, Fifth NPC 1978; vice-chairman, State Financial and

Economic Commission 1979–81. Served on Presidium and Presidium Standing Committee, Twelfth and Thirteenth Party Congress, 1982 and 1987 respectively. President, PRC 1983–86; Presidium executive chairman and National Committee chairman, Seventh CPPCC 1988. Since 1978 has visited some thirty countries, including a number of African and Asian nations, the United States and Canada, Oceania, Romania and Yugoslavia.

Li Ximing (Li Hsi-ming) — b. 1926 Shulu county, Hebei province. Studied civil engineering and architecture at Qinghua University and once served as secretary, Shijingshan Power Plant CP. Identified as government cadre 1975; Vice-minister of Water Conservancy and Electric Power 1975–79 and acting chairman, Society of Electro-Engineering 1975–78; Vice-minister of Power Industry 1979–82, and Minister of Urban and Rural Construction and Environmental Protection 1982–present. Central Committee member, Twelfth Party Congress 1982–present. Elected vice-chairman, State Council's Central Greening Committee and Central Patriotic Health Campaign Committee 1983; vice-chairman, State Environmental Protection Committee, chairman, Urban Science Society 1984–88; secretary, Beijing CP 1984; and first political commissar, Beijing Garrison 1985. Elevated to Politburo and served on Presidium, Thirteenth Party Congress 1987. Headed several delegations to North Korea.

Li Yimeng (Li I-meng)—b. 1902 Chengdu, Sichuan province. After graduating from Shanghai institution, joined Guo Moruo's Creation Society and started literary career. Joined GMD Northern Expedition 1926 but joined CCP after 1927 GMD/CCP rift and went to Jiangxi Soviet 1933, becoming head, Secret Service Department's Bureau of Political Security. During Long March 1934–35 served in 1st Front Army's Political Department as director, Propaganda Section. Joined Shanghai underground 1938, and New 4th Army 1940. Identified as chairman, Jiangsu–Anhui Border Region Government 1943 and first vice-chairman, Lüda Administrative Office 1949. In association with peace movement, travelled exten-

sively to socialist countries 1951–Cultural Revolution. Sichuan deputy, First NPC 1954. Ambassador to Burma (Myanmar) 1958–63. Appointed deputy director, Staff Office for Foreign Affairs and Institute of Foreign Affairs 1964–66 and 1964–67 respectively. Deputy director, Central Committee's International Liaison Department 1975–82 and adviser, 1982–present. Deputy secretary, Central Committee's Commission for Inspecting Discipline 1978–82. Elected president, Association for International Understanding 1981; Standing Committee member, Central Committee Advisory Commission 1982–present; Presidium member, Thirteenth Party Congress 1987. Since 1987 has headed delegations to Eastern Europe and Japan.

Lin Liyun (Lin Li-yün)—b. 1933 Taizhong city, Taiwan; attended primary and high school Kobe, Japan and returned to China 1952 to study, graduating Beijing University 1956. Identified as council member, Sino-Japanese Friendship Association, Taiwan deputy, Fourth–Seventh NPC 1975–present; Standing Committee member, Fourth NPC 1975–78; member, Overseas Chinese Affairs Committee, Sixth NPC 1986–present; and Presidium member, Seventh NPC 1988. Elected Central Committee member, Ninth Party Congress 1969–present, and Presidium member, Thirteenth Party Congress 1987. Elected vice-president, Women's Federation 1978; president, Taiwan Federation 1981; and vice-president, International Cultural Exchange Centre 1984. Since 1979 has visited Japan, Africa, South-east Asia and Latin America.

Liu Binyan (Liu Pin-yen)—b. 1925 Harbin, Heilongjiang province. Forced to leave school when parents separated. Published first story 1939. Worked as teacher, Tianjin and joined CCP 1944. Started work with Beijing's *Youth Daily* 1951. Labelled 'rightist' after Hundred Flowers Movement and sent to countryside 1957–79. Then rehabilitated and resumed work as reporter. Identified as secretary, Writers' Association 1983–85 and appointed vice-chairman, 1985. In 1987 expelled from the CCP for 'bourgeois liberalization', but remained vice-chairman of Writers' Association. Left China during 1989 crisis. Reportage publications include: *Between Men and Monsters* 1979; *Speaking Out Is Better than Silence* 1980; *Mud Under the White Coat* 1984; and *The Second Kind of Loyalty* 1985.

Liu Bocheng (Liu Po-ch'eng)—1892–1986, b. Kaixian, Sichuan province. Father, a travelling musician, provided some classical education. Then attended military school, 'graduating 1911, and joined CCP 1926. Assisted in Nanchang Uprising 1927 (see Nie Rongzhen). Studied at Soviet Union's Red Army Military Academy 1928–30 and served briefly under then-Party leader Li Lisan. Highly capable soldier, particularly skilled in guerilla warfare. Joined Zhu–Mao forces 1931, serving concurrently as chief of staff, Armed Forces HQ and head, Red Army Academy, Ruijin until Long March 1934–35 when served as chief of staff, 1st Front Army. With outbreak of Sino-Japanese War 1937, became commander, 115th Division, one of 8th Route Army's three divisions, with Deng Xiaoping as political commissar. The 115th Division occupied Hebei, Henan and Shandong 1941. Elected to Seventh Central Committee 1945. Drove wedge between Nationalist forces, Wuhan and Nanjing in central China 1947, and with forces subsequently renamed Central Plains Liberation Army, began decisive Huaihai Campaign with Chen Yi. With forces again renamed as 2nd Field Army, and Chen Yi's 4th Army, pushed across Guizhou and Sichuan to take Nanning 1949, becoming both chairman, Nanning Military Control Commission and mayor. Also made member, Government Administrative Council and Revolutionary Military (later National Defence) Council, as well as being elected to executive board, Sino-Soviet Friendship Association. Then led forces into Yunnan (serving there, in South-west Military Region, as one of three key figures until 1954) and in Tibet 1950–51. Appointed president, PLA Military Academy, Nanjing, 1951–57. Elected member of First NPC Standing Committee 1954; vice-chairman, Second–Fifth NPC Standing Committees 1959 to 1978; and director, PLA General Training Department 1954–57. Subsequently identified as Standing Committee member, CCP Military Affairs Commission 1961. Appointed marshal and decorated with Orders of August 1st, Independence and Freedom, and Liberation. Elevated to Politburo, Eighth Party Congress 1956 and held this post until Twelfth Party Congress, 1982. From 1977, due to near total loss of eyesight, did not take part in public occasions; however, retained great prestige. Married to Wang Ronghua.

Liu Fuzhi (Liu Fu-chih)—b. 1917 Mei county, Guangdong province. Served as deputy head, Security Department, Shanxi–Chahar–Hebei Field Army 1948, and deputy head, Third Office, Central Committee's North China Bureau 1949. Served in Ministry of Public Security, as deputy director, Security's General Office 1949–64 and vice-minister from 1964 and again 1971–73. Disappeared 1967–71 and again 1973–78. Vice-minister of Culture 1978–82. Member, State Council's Birth Planning Leading Group 1978–79, first deputy secretary, NPC Standing Committee's Legal Commission 1979–80 and vice-chairman 1980–82. Minister of Justice 1982–83; Minister of Public Security 1983–85. Identified as president, University of Political Science and Law 1983–85. First political commissar, Chinese People's Armed Police Force 1984–85. Member, Twelfth Central Committee 1982; resigned 1985, and elected to Central Advisory Commission (confirmed 1987). Secretary-general, Central Committee's Political Science and Law Commission since 1982; honorary president, Lawyers' Association since 1986; and procurator-general, Supreme People's Procuratorate since 1988. Guangdong deputy and Presidium member, Seventh NPC 1988.

Liu Haisu (Liu Hai-su)—b. 1896 Jiangsu province. Father joined Taiping Rebellion when young. Received classical education and studied classical literature and history, Shengzheng Academy, acquiring nationalistic ideals. After 1911 Revolution set up first modern Chinese painting academy: Shanghai Academy of Painting and Fine Arts. Lectured at Beijing University 1918. Visited Japan twice, for further study 1919 and as fugitive, with exhibition, 1927. Toured Europe, 1929–31 and 1933–35, and during second tour lectured and gave exhibitions of modern Chinese painting. Several exhibitions South-east Asia

1937–49. In 1981 visited Hong Kong for exhibition and was awarded gold medal by Italian National Academy of Art and identified as president, Nanjing Art Academy: honorary president 1984–present. In 1984 awarded honorary doctorate in Fine Arts by United States' World University and by-elected Standing Committee member, Sixth CPPCC; confirmed, and served on Presidium, Seventh CPPCC 1988.

Liu Huaqing (Liu Hua-ch'ing)—b. 1916 Dawu county, Hubei province. Joined CCP guerilla unit 1932, which became 15th Red Army Corps 1935. Joined CCP 1935. Appointed deputy political commissar, 11th Army 1949. Transferred to Navy 1950 and studied naval affairs Soviet Union 1951–53. Awarded Order of Liberation, first class 1955; appointed rear-admiral 1958. Identified as deputy political commissar, South China Sea Fleet and PLA Navy HQ, 1958 and 1965 respectively. Appointed vice-chairman, Science and Technology Commission for National Defence and member, PLA Cultural Revolutionary Group 1967. Attacked together with fellow commissioner Nie Rongzhen 1968. Again identified as vice-minister, State Science and Technology Commission 1978. Assistant to chief, PLA General Staff 1979–80; deputy chief 1980–82. Elected to Twelfth Central Committee 1982; resigned 1985 and has since served on Central Advisory Commission. Commander, PLA Navy 1982–88. Presidium member, Thirteenth Party Congress 1987. Deputy secretary-general, CCP Central Military Commission 1987–89 and appointed vice-chairman November 1989. PLA deputy, Seventh NPC and Presidium member, first session 1988. Member, PRC Central Military Commission since 1988. Since 1979 has visited many European countries, United States, Egypt and Sudan, Bangladesh and Pakistan, mainly as head of PLA delegations.

Liu Nengyuan (Liu Neng-yüan)—b. 1962. Chairman, Students' Federation and vice-chairman, Youth Federation since 1983. Identified in Beijing University, in Department of Political Economy 1983 and as chairman, Student Union 1984.

Liu Nianzhi (Liu Nien-chih)—b. 1911. Has served as vice-chairman, Federation of Industry and Commerce since 1979. Shanghai deputy, Fifth–Seventh NPC 1978–present; member, Standing Committee and Finance and Economic Committee since 1983. Served as member, Constitution Revision Committee 1980; vice-president, Federation of Returned Overseas Chinese since 1978; and vice-chairman, Shanghai People's Congress since 1983.

Liu Zhenhua (Liu Chen-hua)—b. 1921. Served in 4th Field Army prior to 1950 and then as Political Department director, PLA division; identified as commander, PLA division during Korean War and political commissar, PLA corps 1969. Elected alternate member, Ninth Central Committee 1969 and retained this position until elected to full membership, Twelfth Central Committee 1982. Ambassador to Albania 1971–76 and Vice-minister of Foreign Affairs 1976–79. Identified as deputy political commissar, Shenyang Military Region 1980–82: political commissar and CP secretary 1982–88. Has been secretary, Fushun CP since 1987 and political commissar, Beijing Military Region since 1988. Elected to Presidium and Central Committee, Thirteenth Party Congress 1987. Married to Liu Junxiao.

Ma Hong (Ma Hung)—b. 1920 Dingxiang county, Shanxi province. Identified as deputy secretary-general, Central Committee's North-east Bureau 1951. Member, State Planning Commission 1952–54. Identified as vice-president, Academy of Social Sciences 1979–82 and president 1982–85. Elected vice-president, Society for Study of Distribution of Means of Production and Society on Economics of Capital Construction 1980. Identified as vice-president, Enterprise Management Association 1981, and permanent secretary, State Council's Economic, Technological and Social Development Research Centre from 1981; director-general 1985–present. Adviser, Federation of Economic Societies and China–Japan Personnel Exchange Committee since 1981 and 1985 respectively. Shanxi deputy, Standing Committee member and Finance and Economics Committee vice-chairman, Seventh NPC 1988. During the 1980s headed academy delegations to Asia.

Ma Yi (Ma I)—Identified as cadre, First Ministry of Machine Building 1972, and vice-minister 1973–77. Identified as vice-minister, State Planning Commission 1978; appointed vice-minister, State Economic Commission 1978–c. 85 and adviser 1985–88. Elected vice-chairman, China Technological Import and Export Corporation and National Petrochemical Corporation 1984 and 1986 respectively. Vice-chairman, Federation of Industry and Commerce since 1988. National Committee member and Finance Committee vice-chairman, Seventh CPPCC 1988. Head, numerous scientific and technical delegations to Hungary in 1970s, and economic delegations to Japan, Sweden and Federal Republic of Germany in the 1980s.

Mu Qing (Mu Ch'ing)—b. 1921 Si county, Henan province, of Hui origin. Joined 120th Division, 8th Route Army 1937. Studied literature, Lu Xun Academy, Yan'an 1938. Later assigned to army's 129th Division. Worked as journalist, north-east China 1949. Identified as Shanghai director, Xinhua News Agency (under State Council) 1950 and deputy director, XNA 1959; disappeared 1966–72 and re-identified in last post 1972–82. Also identified as cadre, Central Committee Department 1976–77. Tianjin deputy, Fifth NPC 1978. Elected vice-president, Journalists' Association 1983, honorary president, Photo-Journalism Society 1986 and dean, School of Journalism 1986. Elected CCP Central Committee member Twelfth Party Congress and member, Central Advisory Commission 1987. Director-general, XNA 1988–present. Has headed journalistic/XNA delegations to countries worldwide.

Ngapoi Ngawang Jigme (Apei Awang Jinmei)—b. 1909 in present-day Qinghai province as son of Tibetan aristocrat, governor of Qamdo and commander Tibetan armed forces. Studied in Britain, and upon return in 1932 joined Tibetan Army. As cabinet member under Dalai Lama, advocated reform. While serving as governor of Qamdo 1950, captured by occupying communist forces, but subsequently released and returned to Lhasa. Headed Tibetan delegation to Beijing peace negotiations 1951; member, State Council's Minorities Commission and CPPCC 1951–54,

and vice-chairman, CPPCC 1959–64. Deputy commander Tibet Military Region 1952–77 and member National Defence Council 1954–Cultural Revolution. Appointed lieutenant-general and awarded Order of Liberation first class 1955. Tibetan deputy to all seven NPCs 1954–88; elected Standing Committee member 1965, vice-chairman, Fourth NPC 1975–present; chairman, Nationalities Committee, Sixth NPC 1983–present, and Presidium executive chairman for most sessions, including first session Seventh NPC 1988, 1975–present. Key figure in Preparatory Committee for establishment of Tibetan autonomous region 1956–65, as variously secretary-general, vice-chairman and acting chairman, and accompanied Bainqen Lama on several trips to Beijing. Elected chairman, First People's Congress of Tibet and Presidium executive chairman, first session 1965. Vice-chairman, Tibet's Revolutionary Committee 1968–79. In marked contrast to many other leading figures, made numerous public appearances as NPC representative 1969–74. Chairman, Tibetan Autonomous Region People's Congress 1979–81 and Tibetan Autonomous Region People's Government 1981–present. Honorary president, Buddhist Association since 1980. Head, NPC delegations to Colombia, Guyana, West Indies, Sri Lanka and Nepal early 1980s. Married to Nyapoi Cedan Zhoigar (Apei Caitan Zhouge), vice-president Tibet Women's Federation and vice-chairman Women's Federation

Ni Zhifu (Ni Chih-fu)—b. 1932 Shanghai and attended elementary school for three years from age 13. After this worked in factory, joining trade union 1950 and CCP 1958, and gradually improving position in factory. One of few still thriving who took an active part in the Cultural Revolution. Elected chairman, Beijing Trade Union 1973; Beijing CP secretary 1973–76; vice-chairman, Beijing Revolutionary Committee 1973–78; second secretary, Shanghai CP and first vice-chairman, Shanghai Revolutionary Committee 1976–78; second secretary, Beijing CP 1977; appointed leading secretary, Tianjin CP 1984. Beijing deputy, Fifth NPC 1978; Tianjin deputy, Sixth NPC 1983; Shandong deputy, Presidium member, Credentials Committee member and vice-chairman, Seventh NPC 1988. Member, Constitution Revision Committee 1980. Central Committee member, Ninth Party Congress 1969–present; alternate Politburo member, Tenth Party Congress 1973–77; Politburo member, Eleventh and Twelfth Central Committees 1977–87; and Presidium Standing Committee member, Thirteenth Central Committee 1987. President, Federation of Trade Unions and president, Federation Cadre School 1978–present, and Federation first secretary 1983–present. Travelled extensively as trade union representative to Europe, Japan, India and Africa in 1980s.

Nie Rongzhen (Nieh Jung-chen)—b. 1899 Jiangjing, Sichuan province and attended middle school in Chongqing. Participated in May Fourth Movement 1919 and, after graduating, went to France to study engineering under work-and-study program. Joined Youth League 1922 and CCP 1923. Studied Moscow's Red Army Academy 1924–25. Worked under Zhou Enlai in Military Committee, Guangdong CP, Guangzhou and as instructor and Political Department secretary-general, Whampoa Military Academy 1925–26. Participated in Northern Expedition in GMD 2nd Front Army's 24th Division under Ye Ting 1926. Helped plan Nanchang Uprising in which 24th Division revolted against GMD leadership, and consequently became chief political commissar in Ye's newly organized 11th Army, but after small success forced to flee. Deputy director, Red Army's General Political Department, Chinese Soviet Republic, Ruijin by 1931, and appointed political commissar, Lin Biao's 1st Army Corps in Mao Zedong and Zhu De's 1st Front Army 1932. Elected to Central Executive Committee. Noted for many heroic exploits during Long March 1934–35. Appointed Lin's deputy commander and political commissar when armed forces reorganized as 8th Route Army with Lin commanding one of its three divisions 1937. Subsequently became commander and political commissar, Jin–Cha–Ji Military Region and also, after Lin returned to Yan'an, acting divisional commander. Instrumental in setting up Jin–Cha–Ji Border Region, serving on its Administrative

Committee. In 1943 transferred to Yan'an and elected member, Seventh Central Committee 1945, a position subsequently held until resignation 1985. Engineered fall of Shijiazhuang, a strategically important town and CCP HQ 1947–49, leading to consolidation of this area and Jin–Cha–Ji Border Region into North China Military Region, and consolidation of two regions' CPs into North China Bureau under Bo Yibo. Appointed commander of both region and its forces and Bureau second secretary. With Lin, one of two major figures in capture of Beijing, and immediately became commander, Beijing–Tianjin Garrison 1949–50, mayor Beijing 1949–51 and chairman, Beijing Military Control Commission. Involved in setting up CPPCC and subsequently became a member of this body and the Central People's Government Council which administered China until 1954, and Revolutionary Military Council, on which served as acting chief of staff 1949–54. Held positions in North China People's Government and on Administrative Committee in this period. North China Military Region deputy and Standing Committee member, First NPC 1954; Sichuan deputy, Second and Third NPC 1958–75 and Standing Committee vice-chairman, Fourth and Fifth NPC 1975–80. Appointed one of ten highest ranking marshals and awarded three highest decorations: August 1st, Independence and Freedom, and Liberation first class, 1955. In latter half of 1950s visited many Eastern Bloc countries and important capitals (e.g. Moscow, London, Berne and Prague). Elected vice-premier State Council 1956–74. Appointed chairman, State Council's Scientific Planning Commission (Science and Technology Commission 1958 onwards) 1957–66; chairman, State Council's Science and Technology Commission for National Defence 1967; vice-chairman, CCP and NPC Central Military Commissions 1961–88 and 1983–88, respectively. Identified as Politburo member 1967–69 and re-elected to Eleventh and Twelfth Central Committee's Politburo 1977 and 1982. In 1980 served on Constitution Revision Committee. Presidium member, Thirteenth Party Congress 1987, but resigned Politburo and

Central Committee 1985; however, remains powerful conservative force in opposition to Deng Xiaoping. Married to Zhang Ruihua since about 1930, and had two children by 1938.

Ou Tangliang (Ou T'ang-liang)—b. Guangxi province. Graduated Beijing's Yanjing University. Participated in Communist International Students' Federation 1948. Elected Executive Council alternate member, New Democratic (later Communist Youth) League and Administrative Council member, Federation of Democratic Youth 1949, holding many positions in both. Led youth delegations to Fourth and Fifth World Federation Democratic Youth, Bucharest and Warsaw mid-1950s: Federation council member 1954–62. Elected to National Committee, Peace Council 1950 and secretary-general 1958. Delegate, World Peace Council, Vienna, Stockholm and New Delhi, and conferences on disarmament, Vienna and Moscow, in 1950s and early 1960s. Elected Standing Committee member, Democratic Women's Federation 1953, and again 1958: deputy head, delegation to World Women's Conference, Moscow 1963. Linked with many international friendship associations since 1954 when first elected Standing Committee member, Association for Cultural Relations with Foreign Countries. Elected Guangxi deputy, first three NPCs 1954, 1958 and 1964, and Standing Committee member 1965. NPC delegate to Eastern Bloc countries 1957. Disappeared 1967; identified as cadre, Central Committee's International Liaison Department 1972–82 and adviser, 1982–present. Confirmed in former NPC Standing Committee post 1972–present, as Tianjin deputy, Fifth NPC 1978 and Guangdong deputy, Sixth and Seventh NPC, 1982 and 1988; and member, NPC's Foreign Affairs Committee since 1988. Vice-president, Association for Peace and Disarmament since 1985.

Pagbalha Geleg Namgyai (Pabala Zhoulie Langjie)—b. 1940 Litang county, Sichuan province. Member, Qamdo Tibetan Monastery, and confirmed 1942 as eleventh incarnation of Buddha. Elected deputy director, Qamdo Liberation Committee 1950, and served on Preparatory Committee, Tibetan autonomous region from 1956, as Standing Committee member by 1958, vice-chairman 1960–65, and director, Religious Affairs Committee 1963–65, accompanying Bainqen Lama on several trips to Beijing during this period. Vice-chairman, CPPCC 1959–Cultural Revolution. Member, Tibetan People's Congress and vice-chairman, Tibetan autonomous region 1965–Cultural Revolution. Again identified as vice-chairman, Fourth CPPCC, 1972–present, and Presidium executive chairman since Sixth CPPCC 1983. Vice-chairman, Tibet CPPCC since 1977. Tibetan deputy, Fifth NPC 1978. Vice-chairman, Tibetan People's Government 1979–83 and People's Congress 1983–present. Member Constitution Revision Committee 1980. Vice-president, Buddhist Association since 1980 and identified as honorary president, Tibetan branch, 1982.

Peng Chong (P'eng Ch'ung)—b. 1915 Zhangzhou, Fujian province, joining CYL 1933 and CCP 1934. Worked in Party underground in early 1930s. Later political cadre in 1st Front Army, and appointed political commissar, New 4th Army 1938. Became, concurrently, member of both Fujian and Taiwan CPs, and then appointed secretary-general, Fujian People's Government 1950. Established in Nanjing political, military and government hierarchies 1950–77; appointed deputy mayor 1954 and mayor 1955, first CP secretary 1958–67, political commissar, Nanjing Militia Command 1960, and second political commissar, Nanjing Military Region 1977. Similarly in Jiangsu hierarchy, appointed vice-chairman, Revolutionary Committee 1968–74 and chairman 1974–76, and identified as CP secretary 1974–76. Then transferred to Shanghai: first CP secretary 1979–80 and chairman, Revolutionary Committee 1979; first secretary, Shanghai Garrison CP 1979–80 and mayor 1979–80. Jiangsu deputy, Second and Third NPC 1958 and 1964. Elected alternate member, Ninth and Tenth Central Committee 1969 and 1973; full Central Committee member, Eleventh–Thirteenth Party Congress 1977–present; Politburo 1977–82 and Secretariat 1980–82. Jiangsu deputy and vice-chairman, Fifth–Seventh NPC 1980–present; chairman, Law Committee 1983–1987; Presidium executive chairman 1983–present; deputy secretary-general, Sixth NPC 1983 and secretary-general, Seventh NPC 1988. President, International Cultural Exchange Centre since 1984. Has headed numerous Party and NPC delegations to Europe, Japan, Africa, South-east Asia, Latin America and Australia. Married to Luo Ping.

Peng Zhen (P'eng Chen)—b. c. 1902 Quwo, Shanxi province. Suffered great hardship, only managing to attend middle school after turning 21. While studying joined Socialist Youth League. Joined CCP and helped establish Shanxi Party organization 1923. Labour leader in Taiyuan, provincial capital until 1930; gaoled 1930–35. Appointed secretary, Central Committee's North China Bureau (see Nie Rongzhen)1936–38, and head 1938. Appointed political commissar, Nie's 115th Division 1937, and member, Nie's Border Region Government Council. Appointed vice-president, Central Party School, Yan'an 1941 and president, 1943–44, and head, key Organization Department 1943. Elected to Central Committee, Politburo and possibly Secretariat (equivalent to later Politburo Standing Committee), Seventh Party Congress, Yan'an 1945. Top Party figure in Manchuria after Japanese surrender 1945: as secretary, North-east Bureau 1945–46, and director of its Organization Department 1946. In military hierarchy, became political commissar of both Lin Biao's North-east Democratic Allied Army and North-east Military and Political Academy. Among first top communists to arrive in Beijing 1949: appointed ranking secretary, Beijing CP and elected member, First CPPCC; appointed member, Government Administrative Council and vice-chairman, Council's Political and Legal Affairs Committee. CCP Organization Department head and executive member, Sino-Soviet Friendship Association 1949–54. Appointed chairman, Beijing's Finance and Economics Committee 1950 and mayor 1951; remained top man in CCP and government hierarchies there over next fifteen years. Became member, Central Election Committee to set up government apparatus 1953; elected vice-chairman, First–Third NPC 1954–75 and secretary-general, First–Second NPC 1954–65. Re-elected to Central Committee and Politburo, and made second-rank-

ing secretary in Deng Xiaoping's newly revised Secretariat, Eighth Party Congress 1956. Member, key delegations to Moscow 1960 and 1961, and acting head of latter. As First CCP Secretary of Beijing, among first leaders to be purged in 1966. Reappeared Fifth NPC 1979 as by-elected Beijing deputy, vice-chairman, secretary-general (until 1981) and Legal Commission chairman (until 1980), subsequently serving as chairman, Fifth and Sixth NPC. By-elected Politburo member, Eleventh CCPCC 1979. Secretary, Central Committee's Politics and Law Commission 1983–85. Standing Committee member, Presidium, Thirteenth Party Congress 1987; reappeared in position of prominence after 1989 Beijing 'pro-democracy' demonstrations, being among those at the June 9, 1989 meeting in praise of the military action of June 3–4. Head of Party/NPC delegations to Yugoslavia, North Korea and Japan in 1980s. Married to Zhang Jieqing.

Qian Liren (Ch'ien Li-jen)—b. 1924. Identified as deputy secretary-general, Federation Democratic Youth and Central Committee member, NDYL (later CYL) 1953; secretary-general, Students' Federation 1956. Elected Standing Committee member, Youth Federation 1958 when that body superseded the Federation of Democratic Youth. Identified as head, CYL's International Liaison Department 1959. Led numerous youth delegations to Eastern Europe, Cuba, Africa and Japan in pre-Cultural Revolution period. Disappeared 1967–74. Identified as Standing Committee member, Association for Friendship with Foreign Countries 1975. Permanent UNESCO delegate 1978–81. Deputy director, Central Committee's International Liaison Department and director, 1983–88; Central Committee member and director, *People's Daily* (under Central Committee) 1985–present. Member/head, Party/government delegations to South Asia, Western Europe and Japan in early 1980s.

Qian Qichen (Ch'ien Ch'i-ch'en)—second secretary, embassy to Soviet Union 1960–62. Ambassador to Guinea Bissau 1974–75 and Guinea 1974–76. Identified as director, Ministry of Foreign Affairs' Information Department 1977. Elected Central Committee member, Twelfth

Party Congress 1982–present; appointed Vice-minister for Foreign Affairs 1982–88 and minister 1988–present. Elected vice-chairman, International Year of Peace 1985 and International Year of Shelter for Homeless 1987. Since 1978 head/deputy head, journalistic delegations to the United States and Western Europe; Chinese envoy, Moscow; UN delegate, Tokyo and Bangkok; accompanied Zhao Ziyang to Western Europe; and generally head, government/Party delegations to Japan, Eastern and Western Europe and Latin America.

Qian Sanqiang (Ch'ien San-ch'iang)—son of historian Qian Xuantong. Graduated in physics, Qinghua University, Beijing 1936 and continued studies, *Academia Sinica's* Physics Department. Scholarship student, Paris, accompanied by wife, Dr He Cehui 1937–47. Studied nuclear physics, Curie Institute 1937–44, receiving physics doctorate, University of Paris 1943. In 1946 awarded French Academy of Sciences' Physics Prize for uranium fission technique discovered jointly with He; continued studies under Professor Joliot-Curie 1946–47. Appointed director, Communist World Federation of Scientific Workers 1946. Appointed professor of nuclear physics at Qinghua University on return to China 1948, and director, Physics Department 1950. During this early period involved with youth groups and peace movement, often travelling abroad in this connection to Vienna, Prague, Warsaw and Oslo, and elected to World Peace Council. Deputy director, Academy of Sciences' Institute of Modern Physics (later Atomic Energy) 1950–51 and director, 1951–Cultural Revolution. Appointed member, State Council Scientific Planning Commission 1955 and involved with establishment of Joint Soviet Nuclear Research Centre, Dubna, Soviet Union 1955–60. Member, Academy's Mathematics, Physics and Chemistry (later, Mathematics and Physics) Department 1955–present; Academy secretary-general 1954–61, deputy secretary-general 1961–63. Shandong deputy, First NPC 1954; Heilongjiang deputy, Third NPC 1964. Disappeared 1968–73. Tianjin deputy, Fifth NPC 1978. Identified as vice-president, Physics Society 1978–83, president 1983–87 and honorary

director 1987. Academy secretary-general 1975–78; vice-president 1978–85; and special adviser 1985–88. President, Zhejiang University 1979–84. Deputy director, Committee for Promotion of International Measurement 1979–88; vice-chairman, National Academic Degrees Committee 1980–88; and chairman, National Committee for Unification of Natural Science and Technological Terms 1985–88 (all under State Council). President, Society for Study of Scientific and Technological Policies 1982–88. Vice-chairman, Association for Science and Technology 1980–86 and chairman 1986–present; and chairman, Association's Work Committee for Unification of Natural and Social Sciences 1986–88. Honorary president, Nuclear Society and Nuclear Physics Society since 1980, and Mechanics Society since 1982. Director, Academy's Department of Mathematics and Physics since 1981. Awarded French Remise de la Legion d'Honneur 1985. Presidium and Standing Committee member and Science and Technology Committee vice-chairman, Sixth and Seventh CPPCC 1983 and 1988. Headed Academy's delegations to Australia and Eastern and Western Europe 1977–78 and scientific delegation to the United States 1980.

Qian Weichang (Ch'ien Wei-ch'ang)—b. 1912. Nuclear physicist, apparently assistant to Qian Xuesen, California Institute Technology, before returning to China 1946. Elected to NDYL and Federation Scientific Societies Standing Committees 1949–58 and 1950–58 respectively. Identified as dean of studies, Beijing's Qinghua University 1951–55 and vice-president 1955–58. Board member, Association for Cultural Relations with Foreign Countries 1954–58. Jiangsu deputy, First NPC 1954. Member, Academy of Sciences' newly formed Mathematics, Physics and Chemistry (later, Mathematics and Physics) Department 1955–present and awarded Academy's second prize 1957. Awarded title of Academician by Polish Academy of Sciences 1956. Identified as council member, Mechanics Society 1957. Member, State Council Scientific Planning Commission 1957–58. Due to views expressed in Hundred Flowers Movement, relieved of all posts

1958–60. By-elected Standing Committee member, Fifth CPPCC 1980 and vice-chairman, Sixth CPPCC 1987; confirmed in both posts, and elected Presidium executive chairman, and chairman, Committee for Reunification of Motherland, Seventh CPPCC 1988–present. President, Society for Chinese Language Information Processing 1981–88; developed new method of encoding Chinese characters 1984. Vice-president, Mechanics Society since 1982. President, Shanghai Engineering University and Shanghai University since 1983 and 1986 respectively; vice-chairman, Democratic League since 1983; vice-chairman, NPC Committee for Drafting Basic Law Macao SAR since 1988. Headed scientific delegations to Hong Kong and Britain during 1980s.

Qian Xinzhong (Ch'ien Hsin-chung)—b. 1911, Baoshan county, Shanghai, and studied German in youth. Studied medicine, Tongji University, Shanghai and after graduating worked as physician. Later served as director, 25th Red Army Hospital, and director, Public Health Department, 8th Route Army's 129th Division and, subsequently, 2nd Field Army: 2nd Field Army representative, First CPPCC 1949. Director, Health Department, South-west China Military Region, Military and Administrative Council, and Administrative Council at various times 1950–54. Identified as Standing Committee member, Federation Scientific Societies 1950–58. Postgraduate study, No. 1 Academy of Medical Sciences, Moscow 1952–52. Identified in Ministry of Public Health, as Medical Research Committee member 1955 and vice-minister 1957–79. Identified as member, State Council's Scientific Planning Commission 1957–58, Scientific and Technical Association 1958, Sino-Soviet Committee for Scientific and Technical Co-operation 1959 and Red Cross Society Executive Council 1961: elected chairman 1965. Jiangsu deputy, Third NPC 1964. Purged 1966–72. Reconfirmed as vice-minister, Public Health 1973; minister 1979–82; and adviser 1982. Identified as deputy head, two Central Committee leading groups 1978 and 1979; president, Medical Association 1978–80; and Red Cross Society 1978–85. Shanghai deputy and Standing Committee member,

Fifth and Sixth NPC 1978 and 1983. Minister, State Family Planning Commission 1982–83; joint winner, UN Population Award 1983. Elected chairman, Sports Federation for Disabled 1983 and honorary president, Association for Blind and Deaf Mute 1984. Honorary chairman, Bio-Medical Engineering Society since 1980, and honorary president, Ultrasonic Medicine Society and Red Cross Society since 1984 and 1985 respectively. Elected member, Central Advisory Commission 1988. Has travelled widely, generally as head/deputy head of health delegations, to Eastern Europe, Cuba, North Korea and Egypt late 1950s–early 1960s; Eastern and Western Europe, Africa, Japan and Oceania in 1970s; and the United States, Asia and Latin America in 1980s.

Qian Xuesen (Ch'ien Hsüeh-sen)—b. 1910 Shanghai, and graduated in engineering, Shanghai's Jiaotong University 1934. Scholarship student United States: Master's degree, aeronautics and aerodynamics, Massachusetts Institute of Technology 1935–36 and doctorate, supersonic jet propulsion, California Institute Technology 1936–38. Became assistant professor, Laboratory for Supersonic Research. Worked as director, Rocket Section, United States National Defence Scientific Advisory Board, World War II, with rank of colonel from 1945. At 34, MIT's youngest professor in 1946. Returned briefly to Shanghai and married Jiang Ying, daughter General Jiang Baili 1947. Professor, Californian Institute Technology 1947–49 and director, Guggenheim Jet Propulsion Laboratory 1949–55. Then returned home with wife and two children and became key figure in establishment of Academy of Sciences' Institute of Mechanics. Appointed director 1956 and member, Academy's Mathematics, Physics and Chemistry (later, Mathematics and Physics) Department 1957–present; awarded Academy's Science Award first prize for dissertation written in United States, *Engineering Cybernetics*, 1957. Elected to Second CPPCC 1956, and appointed member, State Council Scientific Planning Commission 1956–58. Elected chairman, Dynamics Society, and Executive Council member, International Federation of Automatic Control 1957. In 1958 joined CCP; elected to newly founded Scientific and Technical Association, and key figure in setting up Automation Society, in which he served as chairman 1961. Guangdong deputy, Second and Third NPC 1958 and 1964, and PLA deputy, Fifth NPC 1978. Appointed director, Mathematics Department, University of Science and Technology 1959. Appointed editor, monthly *Zhongguo Kexue (Scientia Sinica)* 1961. Frequent public appearances during Cultural Revolution 1966–68. Alternate Central Committee member, Ninth Party Congress 1969–85. Placed at top of scientists in PLA's Scientific and Technical (Science, Technology and Industry from 1984) Commission for National Defence 1975; Commission vice-chairman 1978–88 and adviser 1988–present. Identified as vice-chairman of its Scientific (later Science and Technology) Committee 1981–88; president, Mechanics Society 1978–82 and honorary president, 1982–present; honorary president, Astronautics Society and Society of Systems Engineering since 1980; adviser, Energy Research Society since 1981; chairman, Science and Technology Association since 1986. By-elected vice-chairman, Sixth CPPCC 1986; confirmed, and elected Presidium executive chairman and Science and Technology Committee chairman, Seventh CPPCC 1988.

Qiao Shi (Ch'iao Shih)—b. 1925, Dinghai county, Zhejiang province. Joined CCP 1940; served as secretary, Shanghai middle school CP 1942. Became deputy secretary, Shanghai district CP around 1947. In 1950–63 served successively as secretary, Hangzhou CP Youth Committee; under Youth Committee, Central Committee's East China Bureau; and then in various positions in iron and steel industry. Secretary, Afro-Asian Solidarity Committee 1965–Cultural Revolution. Served under Central Committee as deputy bureau chief, bureau chief, deputy director and director, International Liaison Department 1963–82; director, Organization Department; secretary, Political Science and Law Commission 1985–present; and secretary, Central Commission for Discipline Inspection, 1987–present. Vice-premier 1986–88. Elected Central Committee member and alternate Politburo member,

Twelfth Party Congress 1982, and Politburo member 1985; Presidium Standing Committee member and deputy secretary-general, and member, Secretariat and Politburo Standing Committee, Thirteenth Party Congress 1987. Member/head several Party/government delegations to Europe, North Korea and Algeria since 1978.

Qin Jiwei (Ch'in Chi-wei)—b. 1914 Hongan county, Hubei province. Joined CCP 1927, participated in Huanggang Uprising and joined guerilla unit; integrated into Xu Xiangqian's Red Workers' and Peasants' Army 1929. After army reorganized into 4th Front Army 1931, given command of 2nd Company, Pistol Battalion, HQ Forces. Trained at Red Army University, Jiangxi. Participated in Long March under Zhang Guotao's Left Route Column 1934–35. Captured by GMD 1936 but escaped to Yan'an, and attended Anti-Japanese Military and Political Academy 1937–38. Appointed political commissar, first sub-district, Taihang Military District 1939; chief-of-staff and commander by 1944. Appointed commander, 9th Column, Central Plains Army 1948; commander, 15th Corps, 4th Army Group, 2nd Field Army 1949 and concurrently commander, South Yunnan Military District 1950. Appointed divisional commander, Korean War 1951 and commended for distinguished service as commander, Chinese People's Volunteers 15th Army 1952. Appointed commander, Yunnan Military District 1954–58 and commander, Kunming Military District 1958–Cultural Revolution. PLA deputy, Second and Third NPC, 1958 and 1964. Member, National Defence Council 1965–67, then disappeared in Cultural Revolution. Central Committee member, Tenth Party Congress 1973–present. Identified as commander, Chengdu Military District 1974–75. Identified in Beijing Military District 1976–81 as second, then first, political commissar 1976–78 and 1978–79; second, then first, CP secretary 1979–81 and 1981; and commander 1980–88. Alternate Politburo member, Twelfth Party Congress 1982–87, and full Politburo member, Presidium Standing Committee member and deputy secretary-general, Thirteenth Party Congress 1987–present. Elected PLA deputy and Presidium member, Seventh NPC 1988; and appointed state councillor, Minister of National Defence, and member, PRC Central Military Commission 1988. Married to Tang Xianmei.

Qu Wu (Ch'ü Wu)—b. 1898 Weinan county, Shaanxi province. Elected president, Shaanxi Student Union and participated in May Fourth Movement 1919. Studied at Moscow University 1926–29 and served in Nationalist government 1929–49. Retained last post, as mayor of Ürümqi, under PRC until around 1950 and became member, North-west China Military and Administrative Council 1949–53. Deputy secretary-general, Government Administration Council 1950–54. Has held key revolutionary wing GMD posts since 1952: identified as member, Solidarity Committee by 1952 and deputy secretary-general, Central Committee by 1954; elected Central Committee member 1956. Henan deputy, First and Second NPC 1954 and 1958, and Standing Committee deputy secretary-general 1954–58. Standing Committee member, Third and Fourth CPPCC 1959 and 1965. Associated with many cultural delegations and friendship associations: vice-chairman, Association for Cultural Relations with Foreign Countries 1958–65; NPC delegate to Finland, and head, cultural/friendship delegations to Switzerland, Afghanistan, Sudan, Morocco and Hungary. Disappeared 1967–74, then re-identified on Standing Committee, Fourth CPPCC; confirmed, Fifth CPPCC 1978; Presidium executive chairman and National Committee chairman, Sixth and Seventh CPPCC 1983 and 1988, and head, Work Group for Reunification of the Motherland 1983–88. Shaanxi deputy, Fifth NPC 1978. Appointed president, Sino-Soviet Friendship Association 1984. GMD vice-chairman 1979–83, chairman 1983–88 and honorary chairman 1988–present.

Ren Jianxin (Jen Chien-hsin)—travelled widely in 1960s and 1970s: deputy secretary-general and head, economic exhibitions to Japan and Syria, respectively; and head, international law observer groups, Madrid, Hamburg and Bordeaux. Vice-president, International Law Society since 1980 and Chinese president, International Association for Protection of Industrial Property (under State Council) since 1982. Identified in Council for Promotion of International Trade as Department of Legal Affairs director 1980 and Council vice-chairman 1981; secretary-general, China International Economic and Trade Arbitration Commission 1981–86, and honorary chairman 1988–present. Vice-president, Supreme People's Court 1983–88 and president 1988–present. Central Committee member, Thirteenth Party Congress 1987–present. Shanxi deputy and Presidium member, Seventh NPC 1988. In 1980s, head, Supreme People's Court delegations to India, Western Europe, the United States and Latin America.

Rong Yiren (Jung I-jen)—b. 1916 Wuxi, Jiangsu province. Graduated St John's University, Shanghai. Served in Wuxi as assistant manager and then manager, Mow Sing Flour Mill; in Shanghai as director, Feng County and manager, Sanxin Bank and, when PRC founded in 1949, as deputy director, Sangsong Cotton Mills and Fuxin Flour Company, both Rong family concerns. Appointed member, Finance and Economic Affairs Committee, East China Military and Administrative Council (Administrative Council after 1952) 1950–54. Elected member, Shanghai People's Government Council (Shanghai People's Council after 1955) 1950. Appointed director, Sangsong Cotton Mills Administrative Council 1952. Elected vice-chairman, Shanghai Federation of Industry and Commerce 1954. Shanghai deputy, First NPC 1954–Cultural Revolution. Vice-minister, Textile Industry 1959–Cultural Revolution. CPPCC Standing Committee member 1959–Cultural Revolution and again 1972–83, and vice-president, Fifth CPPCC 1978–83. Again Shanghai deputy, Fourth NPC 1975 present; Presidium executive chairman and Standing Committee vice-chairman, Sixth and Seventh NPC 1983 and 1988. Vice-chairman, Federation of Industry and Commerce 1978–88 and chairman 1988–present; managing director, Bank of China 1979–88; chairman, China International Trust and Investment Corporation (Group) 1979–present; member, Constitution Revision Committee 1980; vice-chairman, Song Qingling Foundation 1982–present; awarded honorary doctorate by Hofstra University, New York 1986; chairman, Jinan

University 1986–present; honorary chairman, China International Economic Consultants Inc. 1986–present; honorary chairman, CITIC Industrial Bank 1987–present; and honorary president, Softball Association 1987–present. In 1980s visited, mainly as head economic/trade delegations, the United States, Canada and Latin America, Western Europe, Japan and Singapore, the Middle East and Africa. Married to Yang Jianqing.

Seypidin Äzizi (Saifuding Aze)—b. 1919 of Uygur nationality. Studied political science, Central Asian University, Tashkent and also joined Soviet Union CP, around 1938–42. Important role in founding Nationalist-supported People's Republic of East Turkestan 1945. Instigated break with Nationalists 1947 and renaming of republic as League for Protection of Democracy and Self-Government in Xīnjiang 1948. Member, First CPPCC and Government People's Council; and vice-chairman, Council's Nationalities Affairs Commission 1949–54. Joined CCP and appointed vice-chairman, new North-west China Administrative Council 1950. Relieved of all posts after central government's reorganization 1954; shortly afterwards appointed member, newly established National Defence Council. Xinjiang deputy and vice-chairman, First–Seventh NPC 1954–present. Alternate Central Committee member, Eighth Party Congress 1956; full member, Ninth Party Congress 1969–present; and alternate Politburo member, Tenth and Eleventh Party Congress, 1973–82. Appointed fourth secretary, Xinjiang CP 1950; vice-governor, Xinjiang province 1954; chairman (equivalent to governor), newly formed Xinjiang Uygur autonomous region 1955; CP secretary, Xinjiang Military District, 1955–71; and deputy commander 1955–73. Vice-chairman, Sino-Soviet Friendship Association and Federation of Literature and Art Circles, and chancellor, Xinjiang University, 1954, 1960 and 1964, respectively–Cultural Revolution. During Cultural Revolution appointed vice-chairman, Xinjiang's Revolutionary Committee 1968–73, and chairman 1973–78. Identified as second and first secretary, Xinjiang Military District 1971 and 1973, and appointed first political commissar 1973–78. Director, Xinjiang Party School

1977–78. Presidium executive chairman, Sixth and Seventh NPC 1983 and 1988. Elected honorary president, Minority Writers' Society and Minority Literature Foundation, 1985 and 1986, respectively. Married to Ahyimu.

Shen Qizhen (Shen Ch'i-chen)—identified as head, New 4th Army Medical Department 1946; director, Ministry of Public Health Sanitation Research Institute 1952–Cultural Revolution. Hunan deputy, first three NPCs, 1954, 1958 and 1964. Associated with Academy of Sciences (subsequently Medical Sciences), since 1955 as member, Department of Biology and Geology; and re-identified in Academy of Medical Sciences' Department of Biology 1985. Identified as Academy vice-president 1960, and re-identified in this post 1978–present. Appointed vice-president, Red Cross Society 1979 and vice-chairman, China Peasants' and Workers' Democratic Party 1979–present. Vice-president, International Cultural Exchange Centre 1984–present. Presidium and Standing Committee member, and vice-chairman, Work Group for Health and Medicine (Medical, Health and Sports Committee after 1988), Sixth and Seventh CPPCC 1983 and 1988.

Song Defu (Sung Te-fu)—b. 1946. Joined PLA 1966 and served as squadron leader, platoon leader, company political instructor and youth department head. CYL Standing Committee member since 1982, secretary 1983–85 and first secretary 1985–present. Identified as deputy director, Youth Section, PLA General Political Department 1983. President, Youth Political Institute since 1985. By-elected alternate Central Committee member, Twelfth Party Congress 1985; full Central Committee member, Thirteenth Party Congress, and director, Youth Ideological Education Research Centre since 1987.

Song Jian (Sung Chien)—b. 1932 Rongcheng county, Shandong province. Joined 8th Route Army 1946 and CCP 1947. Studied Harbin Technical University 1951–53; mechanics and automatic control, Bauman Polytechnical Institute and Moscow University 1953–58, and wrote six postgraduate theses 1958–61. Returned to China and engaged in carrier rocket production, Spaceflight Research Institute 1961; appointed director, Research Institute for Development of New Rocket Type and deputy head, Cybernetics Research Office 1962. Lectured at Harvard University, Washington University, Massachusetts Institute of Technology and Minnesota University 1980. Identified as director, Institute of Information Processing and Control 1980 and vice-minister, Seventh Ministry of Machine-building 1981–82. Vice-minister, Space Industry 1982–84. Elected alternate Central Committee member, Twelfth Party Congress 1982 and full member 1985–present; Presidium member, Thirteenth Party Congress 1987. Identified as vice-president, Systems Engineering Society and Population Science Society 1984. Served in three State Council Leading Groups: as deputy head, Scientific Work 1983–88; deputy head, Development of Electronics Industry 1984–88; and head, Scientific Work and Marine Resources 1986–88. Head, Central Group in Charge of Professional Job Designations 1986–88; president, Society of Automation 1980–present.; Minister, State Science and Technology Commission 1984–present; and chairman of its Invention Recommendation and Examination Committee 1984–88. State councillor 1986–present; member, State Planning Commission 1988–present; chairman, State Environmental Protection Committee 1988. In latter half of 1980s visited, mainly as head of scientific/technical delegations, Eastern Europe and the United States.

Song Ping (Sung P'ing)—b. 1917 Ju county, Shandong province. Joined CCP 1937. Studied at Central Party School and Institute of Marxism–Leninism, Yan'an late 1930s, later serving in school and then institute, in latter years as chief, Organization Section and director, Department of Studies. In mid-1940s became secretary-general, Chongqing *Xinhua Daily's* Editorial Department and then served as political secretary to Zhou Enlai in Nanjing. Held departmental posts in Trade Union Council, north-east China to 1955, then became director, State Planning Commission's Labour and Wages Planning Bureau. Identified as Vice-minister of Labour 1957, State Planning Commission 1959, and Planning Committee director, Central Committee's North-west

China Bureau 1960. Identified as secretary, Gansu CP 1973–77 and first secretary 1977–81; vice-chairman, Gansu Revolutionary Committee 1973–77 and chairman 1977–79. First political commissar, Gansu Military District and second political commissar, Lanzhou Military Region 1977–81. Central Committee member, Eleventh Party Congress 1977–present. Gansu deputy, Fifth NPC 1978–present and Presidium executive chairman and deputy secretary-general, first session, Seventh NPC 1988. Again vice-minister, State Planning Commission 1981–83 and minister 1983–87. Elected to Academy of Sciences' Presidium 1981. Appointed deputy director, CCP's Leading Group for Co-ordinating National Scientific Work 1981, and state councillor 1983–88. Served under State Council as deputy head, Zhao Ziyang's Leading Group for Scientific Work and vice-chairman, Wan Li's National Agricultural Zoning Committee 1983–88; vice-chairman, Li Peng's Environmental Protection Committee 1984–88; and head, Leading Group for Economic Information Management 1986–88. Elected deputy secretary-general and Politburo member, Thirteenth Party Congress, and appointed head, Central Committee's Organization Department 1987. Elevated to Politburo Standing Committee following 1989 Beijing 'pro-democracy' demonstrations. In 1980s visited, generally as head of government delegations, the United States, Eastern Europe, Japan, Madagascar and Turkey.

Song Renqiong (Sung Jen-ch'iung)—b. 1909 Liuyang county, Hunan province. Graduated Liuyang High School and joined CCP 1926; later graduated Whampoa Military Academy. Served in 4th Red Army 1927, and under Liu Bocheng 1932. Political commissar, Red Army Cadre Corps, Long March 1934–35 and political commissar, 129th Division, beginning Sino-Japanese War 1937. Lectured at CCP's Central Academy 1943. Alternate member, Seventh Central Committee 1945. Key commander in Hebei during civil war, and became political commissar, 10th Army Corps. Appointed chairman, Nanjing Military Control Commission when Nanjing occupied by Liu Bocheng's 2nd Field Army 1949.

Subsequently held posts in south-west China Party military and administrative hierarchies until recalled to Beijing and appointed member, National Defence Council 1954. Promoted to rank of army general and awarded Orders of August 1st, Independence and Freedom, and Liberation, first class 1955. Elected full Central Committee member and secretary-general, Eighth Party Congress 1956; elevated to alternate Politburo membership 1966. Appointed minister, Third Ministry of Machine-building 1956. Became minister, Second Ministry of Machine-building when Third Ministry incorporated with Second Ministry in 1958. Yunnan deputy, Second NPC 1958. Identified as secretary, Central Committee's North-east China Bureau 1961; political commissar, Shenyang Military Region 1964 and first political commissar 1965. Elected vice-chairman, Fourth CPPCC 1965. Disappeared 1968–74. Elected Sichuan deputy, Fifth NPC and vice-chairman, Fifth CPPCC 1978, and Central Committee member, Eleventh and Twelfth Party Congress 1978 and 1982. Director, Central Committee's Organization Department 1979–83; member, Constitution Revision Committee 1980; member, CCP Secretariat 1980–82, and Politburo member, Twelfth Party Congress 1982–85. Retired from Central Committee and Politburo 1985, and elected vice-chairman, Central Advisory Commission 1985–present. Elected honorary president, Volleyball Association 1984, and adviser, Higher Education Society 1987. Presidium Standing Committee member, Thirteenth Party Congress 1987. Yunnan deputy, Seventh NPC 1988. Married to Zhong Yuelin.

Tang Aoqing (T'ang Ao-ch'ing)—b. 1915. Studied chemistry, Beijing University 1936–40, then taught at National South-west Associated University, Kunming; later did postgraduate studies, Columbia University, United States, returning to China 1950 as specialist in quantum chemistry. Jilin deputy, Second and Third NPC, 1958 and 1964. Identified as deputy director, Academy of Sciences' Jilin Branch 1960, and vice-president, Jilin University 1960–Cultural Revolution. Reappeared in Jilin University as professor, Chemistry Department 1977, 'special-class model worker' 1979, president 1979–88 and director, Institute of Theoretical Chemistry 1982. Member, State Council's Natural Science Award Committee and National Academic Degrees Committee 1980; Presidium member, Academy of Science 1981; winner, Academy's first class science prize 1982, and identified as member, Academy's Department of Chemistry 1985; chairman, Natural Science Foundation Committee 1986–88. President, Chemistry Society; vice-president, Association for International Exchange of Personnel; and vice-chairman, Science and Technology Association since 1986. Elected National Committee member and Science and Technology Committee vice-chairman, Seventh CPPCC 1988.

Tian Jiyun (T'ien Chi-yün)—b. 1929 Feicheng county, Shandong province. Joined CCP 1945. Head, land reform work team 1948. Cadre, Guiyang Military Control Commission and held number of important financial positions in Guizhou province before the Cultural Revolution, then identified as deputy director, Financial and Monetary Division, Office of Financial Affairs, Central Committee's South-west China Bureau. Finance Department director, Sichuan People's Government. State Council deputy secretary-general 1981–83 and secretary-general 1983–85; head, State Council's Commodity Prices Group 1984–88. Elected Central Committee member, Twelfth Party Congress 1982–present, Secretariat member 1985–87 and Politburo member 1985–present; vice-premier 1982–present; and Presidium member, Thirteenth Party Congress 1987. Head, Central Fire Prevention HQ and State Flood Control HQ since 1987 and 1988 respectively. In 1980s member/leader, government delegations to Japan, South Asia, Africa and Western Europe.

Tomur Dawamat (Tiemuer Dawamaiti)—b. 1925, Uygur farmhand until 1949. Became village chief 1950, and joined CCP 1952. Studied Beijing Central Nationalities College 1955–56. First member of Xinjiang Uygur minority to hold post of CP secretary at county level, when appointed secretary, Toksun county 1956; first secretary by 1960, and vice-chairman, Xinjiang autonomous region by 1964. Xinjiang deputy, Third NPC 1964. Elected to Xinjiang's new Revolutionary Committee 1968, but then disappeared 1968–76. Again key figure in Xinjiang by 1978, as vice-chairman, Revolutionary Committee; CP deputy secretary 1978–present; and Xinjiang deputy and Standing Committee member, Fifth NPC 1978–present. Vice-minister, State Nationalities Affairs Commission 1979–82; chairman, XUAR People's Congress 1979–85; and chairman, XUAR People's Government 1985–present. Central Committee member, Twelfth Party Congress 1982–present. In 1980s visited Yugoslavia and Middle East.

Ulanhu (Wulanfu)—1906–88, b. Tumet or Tumd Banner, Inner Mongolia. Most important minority nationalities representative on CCP. Studied at Moscow's Far East University, and met Wang Ruofei (superior in underground CP movement until death 1946). Most dominant figure in Inner Mongolia from time of return from Soviet Union 1930, when he secured a post as personal secretary to Fu Zuoyi, lieutenant of GMD warlord. During this period, active in Mongolian resistance to 1931 Japanese invasion. Elected alternate member, Central Committee, as only non-Han member, Seventh Party Congress, Yan'an 1945. Also became chairman, new communist-backed Inner Mongolia Autonomous Movement Association in Kalgan 1945. When Nationalists took Kalgan 1946, established People's Government in Ulanhot, with himself as chairman and army commander and political commissar. By 1947 had control of Eastern Mongolian Autonomous Government, and subsequently established Inner Mongolia autonomous region. By 1949 was secretary, Central Committee's Inner Mongolian Sub-bureau (and remained CP head there until death); Standing Committee member, First CPPCC Preparatory and National Committees; member, Central People's Government Council; vice-chairman, Nationalities Affairs Commission (and chairman in 1954); and member, Sino-Soviet Friendship Association (and later vice-chairman until his death). Retained posts as commander and political commissar in what later (1954) became Inner Mongolia Military District.

IMAR deputy from establishment of NPC 1954 until his death, and made both vice-premier and member, National Defence Council. Awarded Order of Liberation and appointed to rank of colonel-general 1955. Emerged as one of CCP's leaders at Eighth Party Congress 1956, serving as member, Presidium and Credentials Committee, and alternate member, Politburo, and thenceforth as full member, Central Committee. Appointed president, Inner Mongolia University 1957. Identified as second secretary, Central Committee's North China Bureau 1965. Also elected chairman, Central Committee's Third Inner Mongolian Committee during 1960s; the only Party leader at either provincial or autonomous regional level to simultaneously hold top posts in CCP, government and army hierarchies. Disappeared 1967–73. Elected member, Tenth Central Committee 1973. Standing Committee member, Fourth NPC 1975–death; vice-chairman, Fourth NPC 1975–78; Presidium executive chairman Sixth and Seventh NPC 1983 and 1988; and vice-chairman, Seventh NPC 1988. Identified as director, Central Committee's United Front Work Department 1977. Elected to Politburo, Eleventh Party Congress 1977–85, when resigned Central Committee and Politburo posts. Elected vice-president, Fifth CPPCC 1978–83; vice-president, PRC 1983–death. Honorary president, Greening Foundation 1985–death. Presidium member, Thirteenth Party Congress 1987. Frequently travelled abroad, visiting Eastern Bloc countries, Nepal and Middle East, Australia and New Zealand, Sudan and Turkey. Left widow, Yun Liwen.

Wan Li (Wan Li)—b. 1916 and studied in France during youth; also possibly involved with prominent Beijing youth leaders mid-1930s. Involved in communist liberation of Nanjing and Chongqing 1949–50, and subsequently held important financial posts in both cities. In Chongqing served under South-west Military and Administrative Committee as member, Deng Xiaoping's Finance and Economics Committee and deputy director, Industry Department. Transferred to Beijing as vice-minister, new Ministry of Building 1952–56 and concurrently appointed director, Urban Construction General Bureau 1955–56; then, with redesignation of Bureau as Ministry, became minister 1952–58. Identified as secretary, Beijing CP and elected vice-mayor, Beijing 1958, posts in which subordinate to Peng Zhen. Beijing deputy, Second and Third NPC 1958 and 1964. Disappeared twice during Cultural Revolution decade, first during 1966–71. Identified in successively higher posts in Beijing 1971–74 and as CP secretary 1974–75, and as Minister of Railways 1975–76; disappeared again 1976–77. Elected Central Committee member, Eleventh Party Congress 1977–present. Appointed first secretary, Anhui CP and chairman, Anhui Revolutionary Committee 1977–79; and Anhui Military District first political commissar 1977–80, and first CP secretary 1979–80. Member, Constitution Revision Committee 1980. Vice-premier 1980–88: briefly acting premier 1982 and 1983. Member, CCP Secretariat 1980–82 and member, Politburo, Twelfth Party Congress 1982–present. Minister, State Agricultural Commission 1980–82; chairman, Central Greening Committee 1982–88; chairman, State Council's Greening Committee 1983–present; and chairman, National Agricultural Zoning Committee 1983–88. Vice-chairman, CCP's Central Commission for Guiding Party Consolidation 1983. Chairman, National Committee for Promoting Socialist Ethics 1983–88; head, State Council's Leading Groups for Development of Electronic Computers and LSIC's, and Resettlement of Ex-servicemen and Retired Officers 1983 and 1983, respectively. Honorary president, Bridge Foundation, Tennis Society, Urban Science Society, 1990 Asian Games Organizing Committee, and Literature Foundation since 1980, 1982, 1984, 1985 and 1986, respectively. Awarded Solomon Award, highest international bridge players' award 1985, and Gold Olympic Order by International Olympic Committee 1986. Presidium Standing Committee member, Thirteenth Party Congress 1987. Beijing deputy, Presidium executive chairman and Standing Committee chairman, Seventh NPC 1988. Since 1978 has headed delegations to Japan and the United States and Party delegations to Moscow and Romania.

Wang Bingqian (Wang Ping-ch'ien)—b. 1925 Li county, Hebei province. Joined CCP 1940. Began work in finance and economy 1945. Served in Ministry of Finance, various posts 1949–62, and identified as director, Budget Department 1963. Identified as Vice-minister of Finance 1973–80, and minister 1980–present. President, Accounting Society 1980–88 and honorary president 1988–present. Honorary chairman, China Investment Bank since 1981 and Chinese governor, World Bank since 1986. State councillor since 1983 and served under Council as chairman, Administrative Committee for Underdeveloped Regions Development Fund and Customs Tax Regulations Committee, 1986–88 and 1987–88, respectively. Elected Central Committee member, Twelfth Party Congress 1982. Appointed member, State Planning Commission 1988–present. In 1980s visited, generally as head of World Bank delegations, Washington, Tokyo, Helsinki, Toronto and Mexico.

Wang Daheng (Wang Ta-heng)—b. 1915 and studied King's College, London. Jilin deputy, Third NPC and Fifth NPC 1964 and 1978. Identified as deputy director, Changchun Institute of Optical and Precision Machinery 1978; director 1978–83, and honorary director 1986–present. Identified as vice-chairman, Jilin CPPCC 1979. President, Optical Society 1979–present; elected member, Academy of Sciences' Presidium 1981; director, Academy's Department of Technical Science and Space Science and Technology Centre 1986–present; honorary president, Lighting Society 1987–present; vice-chairman, Science and Technology Association 1988–present; Member, National Committee and Science and Technology Committee, Seventh CPPCC 1988–present.

Wang Fang (Wang Fang)—served as political commissar, 94th Division, 32nd Army, 3rd Field Army 1949. Identified as deputy commander, Hangzhou Air Defence Command 1950. Established in Zhejiang provincial hierarchy over 1950s and early 1960s, becoming vice-governor 1964. Purged and disappeared 1967–77. Vice-chairman, Zhejiang Revolutionary Committee 1977–79. Standing Committee member, Zhejiang province CP by 1978; CP deputy secretary 1978–82 and leading secretary 1982–83. Vice-chairman, Zhejiang People's Congress 1979–83. Identified as first political commissar, Zhejiang Military District 1983. Procurator, Special Procuratorate for trial of Lin Biao and Jiang Qing Counter-revolutionary Cliques 1980. Member, Twelfth Central Committee 1982, and Central Advisory Commission 1987; Presidium member, Thirteenth Party Congress 1987. Appointed Minister of Public Security and first political commissar, Chinese People's Armed Police Force 1987; and state councillor 1988. Visited Hong Kong and North Korea latter half of 1980s. Married to Liu Xin.

Wang Ganchang (Wang Kan-ch'ang)—b. 1907. Studied Qinghua University 1925–29 and Berlin University 1930–34 and awarded PhD, nuclear physics. Returned China. Engaged in research, University of California 1948. Identified as deputy director, Academy of Sciences' Physics Institute 1953–58, and appointed member Academy's new Department of Mathematics, Physics and Chemistry. Elected to September Third Society's Central Committee 1956. Organized research team at Joint Soviet Nuclear Research Centre, Dubna, Soviet Union 1958; deputy director 1959–61 and head, joint Sino-Soviet scientific team responsible for breakthroughs 1960: unscathed by Cultural Revolution as work of vital importance. Deputy director, Academy's Atomic Energy Institute 1958–78; director 1978–86; and honorary director, 1986–present. NPC Standing Committee member, Third–Sixth NPC 1964–88; as Jiangsu deputy, Third and Fourth NPC 1964 and 1975, and Sichuan deputy, Fifth and Sixth NPC 1978 and 1983; member, NPC Education, Science, Culture and Public Health Committee 1983–88. Identified as vice-minister, Second Ministry of Machine Building 1979–82; president, Nuclear Society 1980–84 and honorary president 1984–present. Honorary president, Society of Nuclear Physics 1980–present. Academy Presidium member 1981, and awarded first class prize for natural science 1982. Vice-president, Association for International Exchange of Personnel 1986–present, and leading member, Nuclear Instruments Association 1987–present.

Visited Canada 1979 and Federal Republic of Germany and Switzerland 1985. Has three daughters and two sons.

Wang Guangying (Wang Kuang-ying)—b. Britain; elder brother of Wang Guangmei, Liu Shaoqi's widow. Studied Beijing Experimental Primary School; graduated Furen (Catholic) University, Beijing 1942. Appointed director, Tianjin Modern Chemical Plant 1943 and identified as managing director 1952. Manager, Tianjin Lisheng Knitwear Factory 1950. Identified as member, Tianjin Association of Industry and Commerce 1952; elected chairman 1959. Involved in setting up Federation of Industry and Commerce 1952 onwards, and member, Executive Committee by 1955. Served on Federation of Democratic Youth (Youth Federation from 1959): as Standing Committee member from 1953 and vice-chairman 1958–67. Tianjin deputy, First NPC 1954, and Hebei deputy, Second and Third NPC 1958 and 1964. Disappeared 1967–79. Appointed director, China International Trust and Investment Corporation and elected vice-chairman, China Democratic National Construction Association 1979. By-elected to Fifth CPPCC 1979; served as Presidium executive chairman and vice-chairman, Sixth and Seventh CPPCC 1983 and 1988. Vice-mayor Tianjin 198083; vice-chairman, Federation of Industry and Commerce 1982–present; and chairman, new Everbright Industrial Corporation 1983–present. Appointed honorary director-in-chief, Welfare Fund for Handicapped 1984. Received honorary Doctorate of Law from University of Maryland, United States 1986. Visited Thailand, Brussels, Finland and Japan in 1980s.

Wang Meng (Wang Meng)—b. 1934 Beijing. Joined CCP in 1948. Rose to prominence as writer in the 1950s, first significant work being the novel *Long Live Youth (Qingchun wansui)*. His short novel *The Young Newcomer in the Organization Department (Zuzhi bu xinlai de nianqingren)* (1956) subjected to intense criticism in 1957 as anti-Party and anti-socialist, and became one of the main literary targets of the Anti-rightist Campaign, Wang himself being declared a rightist. Worked as labourer near Beijing; in 1963 sent to Yili in Xinjiang. Rehabilitated in 1978 but not allowed to return to Beijing until 1979. Quickly established himself as outstanding and innovative fiction writer. His short novel *The Butterfly (Hudie)*, published in literary periodical *October (Shiyue)* in 1980 (No. 4), won first prize in the nationwide awards for outstanding short novels. It is innovative for its impressionistic technique and represents a 'literature of questions', as against one of stories. Travelled in the United States for four months in 1980. In December 1981 identified as council member of the Writers' Association and vice-chairman of the Beijing branch of the association in March 1983. Identified as editor-in-chief of *People's Literature (Renmin wenxue)* in July 1983. Elected alternate member, CCPCC by the Twelfth CCP Congress in September 1982. Minister of Culture from early 1986 to September 1989. Has written numerous short stories, short and full-length novels, including, apart from those items already mentioned, the full-length novel *In Yili, The Light-coloured Grey Eyes (Zai Yili, danse hui de yanzhu)*, published in 1984.

Wang Zhen (Wang Chen)—b. 1908 Liuyang county, Hunan province. Attended elementary school for three years, then worked at train station; joined Railway Workers' Association 1924 and CCP 1927. From then onwards involved in organizing armed rebellion, and by 1934 was troop leader under He Long. Took part in Long March 1934–35 and then became brigade commander, 120th Division. During Sino-Japanese War 1937–45, led unit from Shanxi to Guangdong. After war returned to north-west China. Elected alternate Central Committee member, Seventh Party Congress 1945. Important member of Xinjiang military, political and administrative hierarchies 1949–54. Appointed commander and political commissar, PLA Railway Corps 1954; elected PLA deputy, First NPC 1954–59; and appointed member, National Defence Council 1954–Cultural Revolution. Promoted to rank of colonel-general, awarded Orders of August 1st, Independence and Freedom, and Liberation, first class 1955. Minister, State Farms and Reclamation 1956–Cultural Revolution. Elected full Central Committee member, Eighth Party Con-

gress 1956–85. Heilongjiang deputy, Second and Third NPC 1959 and 1964. Criticized as He Long supporter but retained Central Committee post 1966. Vice-premier 1975–80. Politburo member, Eleventh and Twelfth Central Committee 1978–85. Member, State Financial and Economic Commission 1979–81; member, Constitution Revision Committee 1980. Appointed president, Central Party School and adviser, CCP Central Commission for Guiding Party Consolidation 1983; appointed chairman, Chinese Committee, Council of Chinese and Japanese Non-governmental Personages 1983. Hebei deputy, Sixth NPC 1983–88. Appointed honorary director-in-chief, Welfare Fund for Handicapped and honorary president, Association for International Friendly Contacts 1984. Resigned from Central Committee and Politburo posts and elected vice-chairman, Central Advisory Commission 1985–present. However, reappeared in position of prominence after 1989 Beijing 'pro-democracy' demonstrations, being among those at the June 9, 1989 meeting in praise of the military action of June 3–4. Has made trips to Western Europe and several to Japan as head of government/ friendship delegations since 1978.

Wen Jiabao (Wen Chia-pao)—graduated with postgraduate degree, Geology College 1968, and then worked in Geology Department, Gansu Provincial Government. Appointed Reform Research Office director, Ministry of Geology and Mineral Resources 1982–83, and vice-minister 1983–85. Identified as vice-chairman, National Committee on Mineral Reserves 1984–86; alternate member, CCP Secretariat, and Central Committee member, Thirteenth Party Congress 1987. Served on Working Committee for Central Committee Departments, as General Office director since 1986 and secretary since 1988.

Wu Jieping (Wu Chieh-p'ing)—b. 1916. Urologist. Identified as professor, Beijing University 1960, and subsequently became known as eminent medical specialist when he treated President Sukarno for kidney disease, Jakarta 1962. Appointed director, Second Medical College, Beijing 1966. Placed first on list of Chinese medical personnel, and headed delegation to Twenty-ninth World Health Organization, Geneva 1976. Identified as vice-president, Medical Association and Academy of Medical Sciences 1978; Association president and Academy honorary president since 1984 and 1987, respectively. President, Beijing Union Medical College since 1984; vice-chairman, Science and Technology Association since 1986; and vice-chairman, Family Planning Association since 1988. Elected Shanghai deputy and member, Education, Science, Culture and Public Health Committee, Seventh NPC 1988. Since 1979 has headed medical delegations to the United States and Britain.

Wu Xiuquan (Wu Hsiu-ch'üan)—b. 1903 Wuchang, Hubei province. Active as student leader while still in middle school. Studied political and military science, Sun Yatsen University, Soviet Union for five years from the mid-1920s. Then lectured in political science, Fudan University, Shanghai. Red Army HQ staff member and lecturer at Red Army University 1932. Deputy chief-of-staff, 3rd Army Corps 1934, and remained with Corps for Long March 1934–35. Appointed head, Central Committee's Foreign Affairs Department 1936. Transferred to Manchuria under Lin Biao 1945. Appointed chairman, Shenyang Military Control Commission after communist occupation 1948 and member, new People's Government North-east China 1949. Director, Ministry of Foreign Affairs, Soviet Union and Eastern Europe Department 1949–52. Vice-minister, Foreign Affairs 1951–55, and ambassador to Yugoslavia 1955–58. Sichuan deputy, First NPC 1954. Central Committee member, Eighth Party Congress–Cultural Revolution 1956–67. Identified as director, Central Committee's International Liaison Department 1959; deputy director 1964–67. In these posts, frequently member/head, Party/government delegations to Poland, Britain, Romania, Cuba, France, North Korea, Sofia, Budapest, Czechoslovakia, Berlin, Moscow and Albania prior to Cultural Revolution. Member, CPPCC Standing Committee 1965–66; Standing Committee member, Fourth NPC 1975–78; and identified as deputy chief, PLA General Staff 1975–c. 1983. Elected to Eleventh Central Committee 1977–82; Standing Committee member,

CCP's Central Advisory Commission since 1982; and Presidium member, Thirteenth Party Congress 1987. Vice-president, Special Court for Trial of Lin Biao and Jiang Qing Counter-revolutionary Cliques and chief judge, Second Tribunal 1980. Director, Beijing Institute for International Strategic Studies 1980–87. Member, Central Committee's Central Commission for Guiding Party Consolidation 1983. President, Armymen's Association since 1979; vice-president, Western Returned Students' Association since 1986; president, Soviet and Eastern European Studies Society and Sino-Soviet Friendship Association since 1986 and 1987, respectively. Since 1977 has visited, generally as head, military delegations, Eastern and Western Europe, Japan, North Korea and the Philippines. Married to Xu He.

Wu Xueqian (Wu Hsüeh-ch'ien)—b. 1921 Shanghai, and joined CCP 1939. Head, Urban Work Department's Liaison Office under Central Committee's Central China Bureau around 1943. Associated with many youth groups, in positions of prominence by 1950s: Central Committee member, Federation of Democratic Youth 1953–56 and vice-chairman, new Youth Federation 1958–64; Standing Committee member, CYL 1957–Cultural Revolution; and director, both organizations' International Liaison Departments, 1953–58 and 1952–Cultural Revolution, respectively. Youth delegate to fourteen countries during 1950s, including World Youth Festivals in Warsaw and Moscow. Elected council member, Association for Cultural Relations with Foreign Countries by 1954, Sino-African People's Friendship Association 1960, and Institute of Foreign Affairs 1964; member, Sino-Afro-Asian People's Solidarity Committee 1961–65, and vice-chairman 1965; and director, Political Science and Law Association 1964, holding all posts until Cultural Revolution. Visited wide variety of socialist and/or developing countries in Asia, Africa and Eastern Europe, and attended peace conferences, Moscow and Tokyo. Anhui deputy, Third NPC 1964. Important cadre, CCP Central Committee's International Liaison Office (later Department) by c. 1963; disappeared 1967–78;

re-identified in department as deputy director 1978–82. Appointed Vice-minister of Foreign Affairs 1982, and subsequently minister 1982–88. Elected to Fifth CPPCC 1978; as council member, Association for International Understanding 1981. Elected Central Committee member, Twelfth Party Congress 1982, and additionally Presidium Standing Committee and Politburo member, Thirteenth Party Congress 1987. Appointed state councillor 1983–88 and vice-premier 1988–present. Chairman, State Tourism Committee 1988–present. Has headed government delegations to over seventy countries in Africa, Eastern and Western Europe, North and South America, Australasia, Southern Asia, the Middle East and South-east Asia since reappearance. Married to Bi Ling.

Wu Zhichao (Wu Chih-ch'ao)—identified as deputy director, Administrative Bureau for Agricultural People's Communes 1965. Appointed chairman, Shanghai Federation of Industry and Commerce 1979; executive director, China International Trust and Investment Corporation 1979 and permanent director 1988. Elected vice-chairman, China Democratic National Construction Association 1979, and appointed vice-chairman, International Economic Consultants Inc. 1986. Presidium and Standing Committee member, Seventh CPPCC, 1988.

Wu Zuoren (Wu Tso-jen)—b. 1908 Jingxian, Anhui province, and raised in Suzhou. Among most eminent living Chinese artists. As youth, studied under Xu Beihong, Shanghai. Entered French Ecole Nationale Supérieure des Beaux-Arts 1930, and soon afterwards went to Brussels and studied under Alfred Bastien, Académie Royale de Belgique. Returned China 1935. Taught Central University, first in Nanjing 1935–37 and then Chongqing 1937–43. During war years spent much time on Tibetan plateaux of Xikang and Qinghai, and subject-matter reflects this. Identified as council member, Sino-Indian Friendship Association 1952 and member, Federation of Literature and Art Circles until 1953–67. Henan deputy, first three NPCs 1954–75. Identified as vice-chairman, Artists' Association and vice-president, Central Institute of Fine Arts 1954, and president

of Institute by 1958. Delegate to Conference on Disarmament and International Co-operation, Stockholm 1958. Disappeared 1967–73. Re-identified as president, Institute 1978–82: honorary president 1982–present; and vice-chairman, Artists' Association 1979–83: chairman 1983–present. Vice-chairman, Federation of Literature and Art Circles 1979–present. Shanghai deputy, Fourth, Fifth and Sixth NPC 1975, 1978 and 1983, and Presidium and Standing Committee member 1983–88. Elected deputy head, Sino-European Parliament Friendship Group 1986. China Democratic League representative and member, Presidium, Standing Committee and Education and Culture Committee, Seventh CPPCC 1988. Visited Argentina, France and United States. Married to Xiao Shufang.

Xiang Shouzhi (Hsiang Shou-chih)—served as junior cadre, 75th Division, 25th Red Army, Long March 1934–35. Appointed commander, 10th Regiment, 1st Subdistrict under Qin Jiwei, Taihang Military District c. 1941; commander, 44th Division in Qin's 15th Army, 2nd Field Army and divisional commander, Korean War 1950. Identified as military leader, Beijing 1974. Deputy commander, Nanjing Military Region 1977–82, and commander 1982–present; and identified as region's CP secretary 1984. Presidium member, Twelfth Party Congress 1982 and member, Central Advisory Commission 1982–present; PLA deputy, Sixth NPC 1983–88.

Xu Yinsheng (Hsü Yin-sheng)—b. 1939. Represented Shanghai in National Table Tennis Championships 1956. Ranked sixteenth in Twenty-fifth World Table Tennis Championships 1959. Elected vice-chairman, Youth Federation 1965; re-identified in this post 1979–83; vice-president, Table Tennis Association by 1975, and president 1979–present. Elected Asian vice-president, International Table Tennis Association 1975, and identified as vice-president 1982. First vice-minister, Physical Culture and Sports Commission 1977–present; member, National Games Organizing Committee 1979; president, Table Tennis Association 1979–present; member, Central Patriotic Public Health Campaign Committee 1983; vice-president, 1990 Asian Games Organizing Committee 1985–present; vice-president, Sports Federation and Olympic Committee 1986–present; president, Boxing Association 1987–present. Member, four table tennis teams visiting Sweden and Japan, 1960s and early 1970s. Head, eleven table tennis teams, including Thirty-third and Thirty-fifth–Thirty-eighth World Championship teams, mainly to Asian countries, 1970s and 1980s.

Yang Dezhi (Yang Te-chih)—b. 1910 Zhuzhou, Hunan province, and at age of 11 started work as shepherd. Railway labourer, Hengyang 1927 when first came into contact with retreating communist forces from failed Nanchang Uprising, and by following year had joined CCP. Regimental commander, 1st Front Army, taking significant part in Long March 1934–35. Regimental commander, 115th Division at commencement of hostilities with Japan 1937. With troops reorganized as 19th Army Corps, occupied Yinchuan, Ningxia 1947; appointed chairman, Yinchuan Military Control Commission, and commander, Ningxia Military Region. Member, North-west China Military and Administrative Council and Shaanxi People's Government 1950–51. Then transferred with troops to Korea, where appointed successively deputy commander 1951–54 and commander 1954–55, Chinese People's Volunteers. Recalled and appointed to National Defence Council 1955–67. Promoted to lieutenant-general 1955, and spent next four years training at Nanjing Military Academy. Elected alternate Central Committee member, Eighth Party Congress–Cultural Revolution 1956–67. Promoted to colonel-general 1958, appointed commander, Jinan Military Region 1958–73, and established position in Shandong Party hierarchy, becoming first secretary, CP and chairman, Revolutionary Committee by 1971. Shandong deputy, second and third NPC 1958 and 1964, and CCP Central Committee member 1967–85. Identified as commander, Wuhan Military Region 1974–78, and first CP secretary 1976–78. PLA deputy, Fifth NPC, and awarded North Korean Order of Freedom and Independence, first class 1978. Commander and first CP secretary, Kunming Military Region 1979–80; member, Consti-

tution Revision Committee 1980; Vice-minister of National Defence, and member, CCP Secretariat 1980–82. Politburo member, Twelfth Party Congress 1982– 87. Chief of General Staff HQ, PLA 1980–87, and appointed first secretary 1980. Standing Committee member, CCP Central Committee Central Military Commission 1980–87; and deputy secretary-general 1984–87. Member, PRC Central Military Commission 1983–present and deputy secretary-general 1984–present. Standing Committee member, CCP Central Advisory Committee 1987–present; Presidium Standing Committee member, Thirteenth Party Congress 1987. In 1980s visited, generally as head, military delegations, Eastern and Western Europe, the United States and Japan. Married to Shen Gejun.

Yang Rudai (Yang Ju-tai)—b. 1924, attended middle school and later served as rural district head, and secretary, county and prefectural CP. Established in Sichuan provincial hierarchy 1977–83, becoming vice-chairman, Revolutionary Committee 1977–79; vice-governor 1979–83; member, CP Standing Committee 1979–80, secretary 1981–83, and leading secretary 1983–present; first political commissar, Sichuan Military District 1984–present; chairman, Sichuan Armament Committee from 1984; and first secretary, PLA Sichuan Provincial Command CP from 1985. Central Committee member, Twelfth Party Congress 1982–present; served on Presidium and Credentials Committee, and elevated to Politburo, Thirteenth Party Congress 1987.

Yang Shangkun (Yang Shang-k'un)—b. 1907, Shuangjiang, Sichuan province. Attended middle school Chengdu, and joined CYL 1925. Studied Chongqing's Sino-French Institute 1926, then GMD training establishment, working closely with CCP. In 1927 joined CCP, studied in Shanghai and worked as labour organizer under Zhou Enlai, and went to Sun Yatsen University, Moscow 1927–31. Later among Zhou's returned student faction. Worked in CCP's underground, Shanghai 1931–32, and then left for Chinese Soviet Republic, Ruijin, where elected to Republic's Central Executive Committee. Served as director, Political Department, under Zhou in 1st Red Army 1933–37, except for interval of Long

March 1934–35: joined Peng Dehuai's 3rd Army Corps 1934, becoming its political commissar and serving as deputy director, Central Executive Committee's Revolutionary Military Council 1935. Sent to Beijing–Tianjin area, under Central Committee's North China Bureau and probably Liu Shaoqi and Peng Zhen 1937. Secretary-general, 8th Route Army HQ, Yan'an 1940–46. Possibly secretary, North China Bureau and head, its United Front Department 1943 onwards; and head, Central Committee's General Office 1945–Cultural Revolution. Executive board member, Sino-Soviet Friendship Association 1949–54. Standing Committee member, Second and Third CPPCC 1954–64; Sichuan deputy and Standing Committee member, Third NPC 1964. Elected member, Central Committee and Secretariat under Deng Xiaoping, Eighth Party Congress 1956. Also secretary, Committee for Organs Directly Subordinate to Central Committee by 1957. Branded counter-revolutionary revisionist 1966. Identified as second CP secretary and vice-chairman, Guangdong Provincial Revolutionary Committee 1970–79. Elected Standing Committee member, Fifth CPPCC 1979. Vice-governor Guangdong 1979–80; first political commissar, Guangdong Military District 1980. By-elected Guangdong deputy, Presidium member, vice-chairman and secretary-general, Fifth NPC 1980–83, and served as permanent chairman 1981. Identified as secretary-general, Central Committee's Central Military Commission 1981–82. Elected to Central Committee and Politburo, Twelfth and Thirteenth Party Congress 1982 and 1987. Elected permanent vice-chairman and vice-chairman CCP and PRC Central Military Commissions 1982 and 1983, respectively. Member, Central Committee's Leading Group for Party History since 1984. Elected PLA deputy and Presidium member, Seventh NPC 1988. Elected president, PRC 1988. Played major role in 27th Army's suppression of Beijing 'pro-democracy' demonstrations 1989, through family connections: General Chi Haotian, PLA Chief of General Staff, who once commanded 27th Army, and Yang Baibing, director, PLA General Political Department and

new appointee to PRC Central Military Commission, are both very close relations. Since 1979 has visited, mainly as head NPC delegations, Japan, Austria, Romania, the Federal Republic of Germany, the Philippines and North Korea.

Yao Yilin (Yao I-lin)—b. Yao Keguang c. 1917 Guichi county, Anhui province as son of prominent politician and Nationalist supporter during last days of Qing Dynasty. Attended middle school attached to Guanghua University early 1930s and studied history, Beijing's Qinghua University 1934–7. Joined CCP 1935. Became active in anti-Japanese riots 1935 (see Hu Qiaomu), and expelled from university 1937. Worked under Beijing's key party official, Peng Zhen, both at this time and later during Sino-Japanese War 1937–45. Served as secretary-general, Central Committee's North China Bureau; secretary, Tianjin CP; and director, CP Propaganda Department, Hebei, later Hebei–Rehe–Chahar Border Region. Secretary-general, Central Committee's Shanxi–Chahar–Hebei Bureau in Shanxi–Chahar–Hebei (Jin–Cha–Ji) Border Region by 1946. When this and another region subsequently merged to form North China People's Government, appointed member, Finance and Economics Committee and head, its Industry and Commerce Department in Shijiazhuang, new CCP HQ 1948–49. Under new Government Administrative Council or cabinet, appointed Vice-minister of Trade (Commerce after 1952) 1949–60, and minister 1960–Cultural Revolution. Identified as head, Central School for Commercial Cadres 1950. Association with Federation of Co-operatives (later Federation of Supply and Marketing Co-operatives) and China Democratic National Construction Association by 1950, serving on their Standing Committees by at least 1955. Jiangxi deputy and Budget Committee member, First NPC 1954–59. Elected alternate Central Committee member, Eighth Party Congress 1956. Appointed deputy director, State Council's Finance and Trade Office 1959; and deputy director, CCP's Finance and Trade Work Department 1959, acting director 1961, and director, reorganized Finance and Trade Political Department 1964–Cultural Revolution. Disappeared 1967–73, then re-elected alternate

Central Committee member, Tenth Party Congress 1973, and full membership, Eleventh Party Congress 1977–present. Identified as vice-minister, Foreign Trade 1973–77, acting minister 1975 and first deputy minister 1977–78; and Minister of Commerce 1978–79. Secretary-general, State Financial and Economic Commission 1979–81. Served as secretary-general, Central Committee 1979–82, and under Central Committee as director, General Office 1980–82 and member, Secretariat 1980–85. Member, Constitution Revision Committee 1980. Vice-premier 1979–present. Minister, State Planning Commission 1980–present. Alternate member, Politburo 1982–85; full member 1985–87 and Standing Committee member 1987–present. Since Cultural Revolution has headed trade/goodwill delegations to Europe and the Middle East, and visited Japan, the United States and Canada.

Ye Fei (Yeh Fei)—b. Fujian province, and joined CCP 1932. Served in guerilla units during Sino-Japanese War 1937–45. Appointed commander, New 4th Army's 1st Division 1941, and after cessation of hostilities fought Nationalists in Fujian and Jiangsu. Served in number of relatively minor posts in home province and as first vice-chairman, Fujian People's Government and member, Central People's Government Overseas Chinese Affairs Commission until 1952, then appointed member, East China Administrative Council 1952–54. Member, National Defence Council 1954–67. Promoted to colonel-general 1955. Appointed governor, Fujian province 1955–59 and vice-governor 1959–63. During this time held number of posts in Fujian provincial CP: successively secretary 1955–58 and first secretary 1958–67. Fujian deputy, first NPC 1954–59. Alternate member, Central Committee, Eighth Party Congress 1954–67. Identified as commander, Fuzhou Military Region 1961 and political commissar 1964; secretary, Central Committee's East China Bureau 1963; and Minister of Communications 1965, holding all these posts until 1967. Elected to full Central Committee membership, Eleventh Party Congress 1977–85. Identified in Navy as first CP secretary 1979–80, first political commissar 1979–81; and commander

1980–82. By-elected PLA deputy, Fifth–Seventh NPC 1980–present; NPC Presidium executive chairman since 1985; vice-chairman and chairman, Overseas Chinese Affairs Commission, Sixth and Seventh NPC 1983 and 1988. President, Overseas Chinese University since 1983; honorary president, Federation of Returned Overseas Chinese and Society for History of Overseas Chinese since 1984 and 1986, respectively. Since 1977 has led government delegations to Mozambique, North Korea, North and South Yemen, Burma (Myanmar) and Thailand; and communications delegations to Western and Eastern Europe. Daughter Zhifei, b. 1946, sentenced to seventeen years' imprisonment for taking bribes in 1986.

Ye Jianying (Yeh Chien-ying)—1892–1986. b. Mei county, Guangdong province, and spent most of early years in Singapore and Hanoi. Graduated Yunnan Military Academy and lectured Whampoa Military Academy. Commanded division in Northern Expedition. Joined CCP 1926. Studied military science, Moscow 1928–31; then appointed chief-of-staff, Revolutionary Military Council, Jiangxi Soviet and later head, Red Army School. Important role in Long March 1934–35. Chief-of-staff, 8th Route Army during Sino-Japanese War 1937–45 and subsequently, during civil war, deputy chief-of-staff, Communist Armed Forces. Appointed chairman, Beijing Military Control Commission and mayor, Beijing, and became key figure in Guangdong military, Party and administrative hierarchy 1949. Served on Central Government Council, Overseas Chinese Affairs Commission, Revolutionary Military Council and, as vice-chairman, Central–South China Military and Administrative Council 1949–54. PLA deputy and Standing Committee member, First, Second and Third NPC 1954, 1959 and 1965. Vice-chairman, National Defence Council 1954–76. Promoted to PRC's highest rank, marshal, and awarded Orders of August 1st, Independence and Freedom, and Liberation, first class 1955. Travelled abroad from mid-1950s onwards, to Burma (Myanmar), Poland, North Vietnam and North Korea. Elected Central Committee member, Eighth Party Congress 1956–85. Appointed commandant, PLA Academy of Military Sciences 1958. Elevated to Politburo, Eighth Party Central Committee 1966. Appointed vice-chairman, CCP Military Council 1967. Member of Politburo Standing Committees of Tenth, Eleventh and Twelfth Central Committees, 1973–85. Minister of National Defence 1975–78. PLA deputy and Standing Committee chairman, Fifth NPC 1978; permanent chairman, third and fourth sessions, 1980 and 1981, and Presidium member, fourth and fifth sessions, 1981 and 1982. Chairman, Constitution Revision Committee 1980; vice-chairman, CCP Central Military Commission 1983–85. Resigned all posts 1985. Married to Zeng Xianzhi, who died in 1986.

Yu Qiuli (Yü Ch'iu-li)—b. 1914 Ji'an county, Jiangxi province, and joined CCP 1931. Served in 2nd Front Army during Long March 1934–35. Company and battalion commander, 8th Route Army during Sino-Japanese War 1937–45, and later regimental commander and political commissar, Hebei. Assisted in defence of Yan'an in major campaigns during 1947. Served in South-west Military Region as, successively, deputy political commissar, Military and Political Academy; commandant and political commissar, Second Advanced Infantry Academy; and director, Logistics Department 1949–55. Promoted to lieutenant-general and awarded Order of Liberation, first class 1955. Identified as director, General Finance Department, Central Committee's Military Commission 1956, and political commissar, PLA's General Logistics Department 1957–58. Minister, Petroleum Industry 1958–72. Sichuan deputy, Second and Third NPC 1958 and 1964. Appointed vice-chairman, State Planning Commission 1965, and chairman 1972. Elected to Ninth–Twelfth Central Committees 1969, 1973, 1977 and 1982, and as Politburo member, Eleventh and Twelfth Central Committees 1977–1985. Vice-premier 1975–82. Jiangxi deputy, Fifth NPC 1978 and PLA deputy and Presidium member, Sixth NPC 1983. Identified as member, CCP Secretariat and Constitution Revision Committee 1980. Member, State Financial and Economic Commission 1979–81; minister, State

Energy Commission 1980–82; state councillor 1982–83; director, PLA General Political Department 1982–87; deputy secretary-general and member, respectively, CCP and PRC Central Military Commission 1982–87; vice-chairman, CCP Central Commission for Guiding Party Consolidation 1983; honorary director-in-chief, Welfare Fund for Handicapped and honorary president, Basketball Association since 1984; Standing Committee member, CCP Central Advisory Commission 1985–present; Presidium Standing Committee member, Thirteenth Party Congress 1987. Member, government delegation to Western Europe 1979.

Yuan Weimin (Yüan Wei-min)—b. 1939 Suzhou, Jiangsu province. Graduated middle school. Won prominence as player, then leader, National Men's Volleyball Team, in over 200 world competitions 1964–74. Chief coach, Chinese Women's Volleyball Team 1976, and subsequently coach, women's teams visiting Peru and the United States, and the Soviet Union 1984. Named best coach after women's team victory, Volleyball World Cup 1981. Tianjin deputy, Sixth NPC 1983. Vice-minister, Physical Culture and Sports Commission 1977–present; appointed member, National Games Organizing Committee 1979. By-elected alternate member, Twelfth Central Committee 1985, and elected full member, Thirteenth Central Committee 1987–present. Vice-president, Sports Federation, 1990 Asian Games Organizing Committee and Olympic Committee 1986–present.

Zeng Tao (Tseng T'ao)—b. 1914 Jiangsu province. Identified as deputy secretary, Work Committee, Zhenjiang CP, Jiangsu province. Identified as secretary-general, Shanghai People's Council 1956–60 and head, Xinhua (New China) News Agency's Havana Bureau 1960. Secretary-general, State Council's Foreign Affairs Office 1961–62. Ambassador to Algeria 1962 until recalled due to Cultural Revolution, Yugoslavia 1970–73 and France 1973–77. Appointed member, Central Patriotic Health Campaign Committee 1978. Identified as deputy director, and subsequently director, XNA 1978; director-general 1981–82 and adviser from 1982. Identified as sessional deputy secretary-general, Fifth NPC 1982; Henan deputy, and vice-chairman, Foreign Affairs Committee, Sixth and Seventh NPC 1983 and 1988, and deputy secretary-general, several NPC sessions including Seventh NPC's first session 1988. Elected adviser, Association for International Friendship and head, NPC China–European Parliament Friendship Group 1985. Headed journalistic delegation to Western Europe, Egypt and India; deputy head/head, NPC delegations to Latin America and Western Europe. Married to Zhu Liqing.

Zhang Aiping (Chang Ai-p'ing)—b. c. 1909 Sichuan province. Served in 5th Red Army under Peng Dehuai, Hunan 1927–29, and subsequently in 14th Red Army, Jiangsu province. Identified as head, Young Pioneer Corps' Organization Department, Jiangxi province 1931. Served as political commissar, Workers' and Peasants' Red Army, North Shaanxi 1935, and set up guerilla base in Anhui 1939. Identified as deputy commander, 3rd Division, New 4th Army, Jiangsu 1941. Identified as chief of staff, East China Military Region 1948 and 3rd Field Army 1948–54. Served in east China military and administrative hierarchy 1952–54. Appointed member, National Defence Council and deputy chief of PLA General Staff 1954. Promoted to lieutenant-general and awarded Orders of August 1st, Independence and Freedom, and Liberation 1955. Colonel-general by 1958. Elected alternate member, Eighth Central Committee 1958. Prior to Cultural Revolution participated in military delegations to India and Burma (Myanmar). Disappeared 1967–75. Identified as chairman, Scientific and Technological Commission for National Defence 1975. Elected to full Central Committee membership, Eleventh Party Congress 1977–85. Again identified as deputy chief of PLA General Staff 1977–82. PLA deputy and Standing Committee member, Fifth NPC 1978. Member, Constitution Revision Committee 1980. Vice-premier 1980–82. Appointed state councillor 1982. Deputy secretary general and member, respectively, CCP and PRC Central Military Commission 1983–87; Standing Committee member, Central Advisory Commission 1985–present; Presidium member, Thirteenth

Party Congress 1987. Since 1978 has headed military delegations to Sweden, Italy and Brazil and visited the United States and Canada, France and Portugal, Pakistan and Romania. Married to Li Youlan.

Zhang Wenjin (Chang Wen-chin)—b. Beijing 1914. Studied at Yanjing University, Beijing, then Sun Yatsen University, Moscow and finally in Germany. Director, Overseas Chinese Office, Tianjin People's Government by 1952. Deputy director, Ministry of Foreign Affairs' Asian Affairs Department 1954–57 and director 1957–58; appointed director, First Asian Affairs Department 1958. Member numerous government delegations 1954–65: to Geneva, India, Burma (Myanmar), Pakistan, Nepal, New Delhi, Rangoon, Indonesia, Jakarta and Algiers. Ambassador to Pakistan 1966–67. Director, Ministry of Foreign Affairs' Western Europe, America and Australia Department 1967–72, and assistant minister 1972–73. Ambassador to Canada 1973–76. Identified as Vice-minister of Foreign Affairs 1978–83. Awarded Doctorate of Human Letters by University of Nebraska, United States 1985. President, Association for Friendship with Foreign Countries since 1982, and honorary president, Association of Returned Students from Germany since 1988. Tianjin deputy and vice-chairman, Foreign Affairs Committee, Seventh NPC 1988. Since 1973, member, government delegations under Deng Xiaoping, Hua Guofeng and Li Xiannian respectively, to the United States, France, Federal Republic of Germany, Britain and Italy, and Papua New Guinea, Australia and New Zealand. Has made several visits to Geneva, and attended UN sessions in Bangkok and Vienna, generally as delegation head. Head government delegation to Latin America, and friendship delegations to Japan, Austria and Finland. Visited Spain and Portugal. Married to Zhang Ying.

Zhang Zhen (Chang Chen)—b. 1907. Underwent military training, Soviet Union 1935. Served in Central China Military Region 1945. By 1947 army corps chief of staff and commander, 9th Military District, Jiangsu–Shandong Military Region; and additionally appointed deputy chief of staff, East China Field Army. By 1949 deputy chief of staff, later chief of staff, 3rd Field Army. Head, Department G3, PLA General Staff 1952. Promoted to lieutenant-general 1955. Deputy commandant, PLA Military Academy, Nanjing by 1957, and commandant by 1963. Disappeared 1963–73. Identified as deputy commander, Wuhan Military Region 1973. Elected alternate member, Eleventh Central Committee 1977–82 and elevated to full member, Twelfth Central Committee 1982–85. Deputy director, PLA's Logistics Department 1977–78, and director, 1978–80. PLA deputy, Fifth NPC 1978. Deputy chief, PLA General Staff 1980–85. Awarded High Award of Hilal-e-Quaid-i-Azam by Pakistani president 1982. Resigned Central Committee and elected to Central Advisory Commission 1985. Commander, PLA National Defence University since 1985. Consul-general, Leningrad since 1986. Since 1978 has visited Sudan and Turkey as head of military delegations, and Pakistan, the United States and Canada.

Zhao Puchu (Chao Pu-ch'u)—b. c. 1906 Taihu, Anhui province. Director, Huatung Transportation Corporation, Shanghai early in career. Buddhist representative, First CPPCC, and appointed member, Peace Council 1949. Joined Association for Promoting Democracy 1950. Served in various posts, East China Military and Administration Council: as deputy director, Civil Affairs Department 1950–51, and Personnel Department 1951–52. Key figure in establishment of Buddhist Association 1952–53, and elected vice-chairman and secretary-general 1953. Anhui deputy, First NPC 1954. Made several trips to Burma (Myanmar) in connection with Buddhist Association in late 1950s. Attended four World Conferences Against Use of Atomic Bombs, Tokyo, and three World Peace Council sessions, Stockholm and New Delhi; and led four Buddhist delegations to Ceylon, Tokyo, Cambodia and Indonesia late 1950s–early 1960s. Identified as council member, Association for Cultural Relations with Foreign Countries 1954; elected vice-chairman, Sino-Burmese Friendship Association 1959; identified as vice-chairman, Sino-Japanese Friendship Association 1963–83. Elected vice-president, Red Cross Society 1961, and Execu-

tive Council member 1963. Elected to Standing Committee, Fourth CPPCC 1965. Elected vice-chairman, Peace Council 1965. Disappeared 1966–72, then reconfirmed as CPPCC Standing Committee member and cadre, Buddhist Association; Association's acting president 1979–80, and president since 1980. Anhui deputy, Fourth and Fifth NPC 1975 and 1978. Appointed vice-president, Calligraphers' Association 1981. Vice-chairman, Association for Promoting Democracy 1978–87, and chairman, Association's Central Consultative Committee since 1987. Honorary president, Society for Study of Religion since 1979. Re-elected vice-president, Red Cross Society 1979, and honorary president since 1985. Member, Constitution Revision Committee 1980. Identified as director, Institute of Buddhist Theology 1982. Elected Chinese Committee, Council of Chinese and Japanese Non-governmental Personages 1982. Awarded Japan Buddhist Evangelical Association Prize and honorary doctorate from Japan Buddhist University while visiting Japan 1982; and Japanese Niwano Peace Prize 1985. Chairman, Sino-Japanese Friendship Society since 1983; president, Society for Study of Sino-Japanese Relations 1984–85 and honorary president since 1985; Vice-president, Association for Peace and Disarmament since 1985. Presidium executive chairman, National Committee vice-chairman, and chairman, Religious Committee, Fifth, Sixth and Seventh CPPCC; identified 1980 and retained position to present. Head, religious delegations to Japan, the United States and Sri Lanka since 1978.

Zhao Xianshun (Chao Hsien-shun)—identified as deputy commander, Heilongjiang Military District 1974–76, and commander 1976–78. PLA deputy, Fifth and Sixth NPC 1978 and 1983. Identified as deputy commander, Shenyang Military District 1982–85. Commander, Lanzhou Military Area 1985–present. By-elected member, Twelfth Central Committee 1985–present.

Zhao Zhongyao (Chao Chung-yao)—b. 1902. Studied physics, England, Germany and United States, at Cambridge and Halle Universities and Californian Institute of Technology, where he received a doctorate in nuclear physics 1930. Spent twenty-four years in United States specializing in gamma radiation, and was official observer at American atomic bomb tests; returned PRC 1950. Peace delegate, East Berlin and Beijing 1951 and 1952. Zhejiang deputy, first three NPCs 1954, 1958 and 1964, and Standing Committee member, Third NPC 1964. Appointed to Academy of Sciences' new Department of Mathematics, Physics and Chemistry 1955, and re-identified in Department of Mathematics and Physics 1985. Spent years 1955–61 at Joint Soviet Nuclear Research Centre, Dubna, Soviet Union. Appointed deputy director, Academy's Institute of Nuclear Physics 1957, and retained this post through Cultural Revolution period. Shanghai deputy and Standing Committee member, Fourth, Fifth and Sixth NPC, 1975, 1978 and 1983, and Presidium member in most years 1980–88. Identified as president, Nuclear Physics Society 1980; honorary president, Nuclear Physics and Nuclear Society since 1980 and 1984, respectively.

Zhao Ziyang (Chao Tzu-yang)—b. 1919 Hua county, Henan province. Attended elementary school in native town 1928–36 and middle school Kaifeng and Wuhan until 1937. Joined CYL 1932 and CCP 1938. Worked first in Hebei–Shandong and later, Hebei–Shandong–Hunan border region in 1940s, and in South China Sub-bureau, Central Committee's Central–South China Bureau in first half of 1950s. Established in Guangdong hierarchy 1955–67: elected member, Guangdong People's Council 1955; identified as political commissar, Guangdong Military District 1964 and first CP secretary 1965. Denounced as counter-revolutionary revisionist 1967–71. Identified as Inner Mongolia CP secretary and chairman until 1972; then re-identified in Guangdong, as Revolutionary Committee vice-chairman 1972–74 and chairman 1974–75; CP secretary 1973–74 and first secretary 1974–75. Central Committee member, Tenth Party Congress 1973–89; political commissar, Guangzhou Military Region 1975; Presidium member, Fourth NPC 1975. Identified in Sichuan as first CP secretary, Revolutionary Committee chairman, and first political commissar, Chengdu Military Region 1975–80. Elected alternate Politburo member, Eleventh Party

Congress 1977, full member 1979 and Standing Committee member 1980–89. Sichuan deputy, Fifth NPC 1978; vice-president, Fifth CPPCC 1978–80; vice-premier 1978–80 and premier 1980–88. Minister, Commission for Restructuring Economic System 1982–88. Beijing deputy and Presidium member, Sixth and Seventh NPC 1983 and 1988. Head, State Council's Leading Group for Scientific Work 1983–87 and Central Leading Group for Finance and Economy 1986–87. Awarded Gold Mercury International Peace Emblem and Round Table Foundation Children's Peace Prize 1984. Presidium Standing Committee member, Thirteenth Party Congress 1987, and elected CCP secretary-general 1987. Appointed first vice-chairman and vice-chairman, respectively, CCP and PRC Central Military Commissions 1987 and 1988. Relieved of all official posts following 1989 Beijing 'pro-democracy' demonstrations, but not expelled from the CCP. Visited over fifty countries, generally as head, government delegations since Cultural Revolution. Married to Liang Boqi; has four sons and one daughter.

Zhou Peiyuan (Chou P'ei-yüan)—b. 1902 Yixing, Jiangsu province. Physics graduate, Beijing's Qinghua University 1924. Continued studies United States 1925–28, awarded Master's degree from University of Chicago 1927 and doctorate from California Institute of Technology 1928. Made two further trips to the United States, returning in interim to lecture in physics, Qinghua: 1935–36 worked at Princeton's Institute for Advanced Studies, taking part in Einstein's seminar on relativity, and 1943–47 engaged in United States naval research into torpedoes, then returned once more to Qinghua. Elected chairman, Physics Society 1948, and council member, Federation of Scientific Societies 1950, becoming director, Federation's Organization Department 1952. Transferred to Beijing University 1953. Elected to Central Committee, September Third (Science for Democracy) Society 1953. Jiangsu deputy, first four NPCs 1954–78 and Beijing deputy and Standing Committee member, Fifth NPC 1978. Appointed member, Academy of Sciences' new Department of

Mathematics, Physics and Chemistry 1955 (re-identified in this post 1979). Appointed council member and honorary secretary, World Federation of Scientific Workers 1956; council member, new Dynamics Society 1957, vice-chairman 1958. When Society incorporated into Science and Technology Association in 1958, became secretary; vice-chairman 1963–77; chairman 1977–86; and honorary chairman 1986–present. Member, World Peace Council 1958–65. Joined CCP 1959. Member, CPPCC Standing Committee 1959–78. In pre-Cultural Revolution period travelled extensively. Peace delegate, Second and Third World Peace Congresses, Warsaw and Budapest; World Peace Council, New Delhi; and World Conference Against Use of Atomic Bombs, Tokyo. Scientific delegate, World Federation of Scientific Workers, East Berlin, Helsinki, Warsaw, Budapest, Sofia, Geneva, Moscow (as Congress vice-chairman) and Budapest; Ninth International Conference on Applied Mechanics, Brussels; Moscow; First and Seventh Pugwash Conferences, Canada and Moscow; and New Delhi. Head, Academy of Science delegations to Albania and Bucharest. Disappeared 1966–70; identified as vice-chairman, Beijing University Revolutionary Committee 1970 and member, CPPCC Standing Committee 1971. Appointed deputy director, Institute of Foreign Affairs 1972. Identified as president, Beijing University 1978–81, and deputy secretary, Beijing CP 1980. Chairman, Physics Society 1978–83 and honorary chairman 1983–present. Vice-president, Academy of Sciences 1978–81 and Presidium member 1981. Appointed member, Constitution Revision Committee and awarded honorary Doctor of Law degree by Princeton University, United States 1980. Elected vice-chairman, September Third Society 1979–88 and chairman 1988–present. Elected president, Association for Science and Technology 1980–86 and honorary president 1986–present. By-elected vice-chairman, Fifth CPPCC 1980; confirmed, and Presidium executive chairman, Sixth and Seventh CPPCC 1983 and 1988; and chairman, Foreign Affairs Committee since 1988. Elected member, Chinese Committee, Council of Chinese and Japanese

Non-governmental Personages 1983; president, Sino-Polish Friendship Association 1984–present; president, Association for Peace and Disarmament 1985–present; honorary president, Western Returned Students' Association 1986–present; director, International Science and Technology Conference Centre 1986–present; and president, Association for Promotion of International Science and Technology 1988–present. Head, scientific/Academy delegations to Western Europe and United States; educational delegation to the United States; and peace delegate to Eastern Europe since 1974. Married to Wang Dicheng.

Zhou Yang (Chou Yang)—1907–89. b. Zhou Qiying Yiyang county, Hunan province. Graduated Hunan middle school and studied at Shanghai University, then in Japan. Returned to Shanghai 1930; became secretary, League of Left-Wing Writers 1931; joined CPC around 1932. After outbreak of Sino-Japanese War 1937, went to Yan'an. Identified in various positions there, including director, Education Department, Shaanxi–Gansu–Ningxia border region, director, Lu Xun Art Institute and vice-president, North China Associated University. At invitation of left-wing American cultural circles, spent 1946–48 in the United States. Appointed deputy director and director, respectively, Propaganda Departments of both Central Committee and its North China Bureau; Vice-minister of Culture and director, Minister's Art Bureau, as well as holding various other semi-official prestigious posts 1949: elected to First CPPCC, Standing Committee, Association of Literary Workers; and vice-chairman, Federation of Literature and Art Circles. Elected vice-chairman, Writers' Association 1953, and council member, Association for Cultural Relations with Foreign Countries 1954. Guangdong deputy, First NPC 1954. Appointed member, Academy of Sciences' new Philosophy and Social Science Department 1955. Appointed member, State Scientific Planning Commission and elected to alternate membership, Eighth Central Committee 1956. Appointed professor, Central Theatrical Institute 1958. During two decades prior to Cultural Revolution, visited, mainly as head/deputy head writers' delegations, Moscow, New Delhi, Tashkent and Cuba; appointed chairman, Asian–African Society and identified as council member, Sino-Cuban Friendship Association 1962. Disappeared 1966–78. Elected Standing Committee member and director, Cultural Group, Fifth CPPCC 1978. Identified as vice-president, Academy of Social Sciences 1978–80 and director, Academy's Postgraduate Institute 1978–85; vice-chairman, Writers' Association from 1978 and adviser 1985–present; vice-chairman, Federation of Literature and Art Circles 1978–79 and elected chairman in 1979. Elected honorary president, Ancient Literature Theory Society 1979, and Aesthetics Society and Modern Literature Society 1980. Vice-president, Folk Literature and Art Society 1979–80 and president 1980–84; adviser, Lu Xun Studies Society 1979–81 and elected president 1981. Member, Eleventh Central Committee 1979–82 and Central Advisory Commission 1982–85. Member, Constitution Revision Committee 1980. Has headed two writers' delegations to Japan since 1979.

Zhu Xuefan (Chu Hsüeh-fan)—b. 1905 Jiashan, Zhejiang province. Studied at Shanghai Institute of Law, then worked in Shanghai Post Office and became member, Postal Workers' Union. Initially persecuted by GMD, so joined GMD labour leader Lu Jingshi 1927, and after Lu left trade union movement, took over his post as head, trade unions' Arbitration Department and chairman, Postal Workers' Union. Lived in Chongqing during Sino-Japanese War 1937–45. Joined left-wing union movement 1948: elected vice-chairman, Sixth Workers' Congress, Harbin, and became head, Union of Postal Workers. Appointed member, Government Administrative Council's Finance and Economic Affairs Committee 1949, and Minister of Post and Telecommunications 1949–67. Elected to Standing Committee, Revolutionary GMD 1950. Identified as member, Red Cross Society 1950; elected Executive Council member 1961. Guangdong deputy, First NPC, and Standing Committee member, Second CPPCC 1954. Identified as General Council

member, World Federation of Trade Unions 1960; elected Executive Council member 1961. Disappeared 1967–78. Elected vice-president, Federation of Trade Unions 1978. Elected Shandong deputy and Standing Committee member, Fifth NPC, 1978 and vice-chairman 1981. Elected vice-chairman, Revolutionary GMD 1979–88 and chairman 1988–present; chairman, GMD Central Inspection Committee 1987–present. Appointed member, Constitution Revision Committee 1980. Vice-chairman, Children's Foundation, vice-president, Association for International Understanding 1981–present and honorary chairman, Philatelic Society 1982–present. Appointed chairman, 1983 World Communication Year 1982. Shanghai deputy, Presidium executive chairman, Credentials Committee vice-chairman and Standing Committee vice-chairman, Sixth and Seventh NPC 1983 and 1988. Elected adviser, Sun Yatsen Society and appointed honorary director-in-chief, Welfare Fund for Handicapped 1984. Honorary president, Workers' International Exchange Centre 1984–present and Red Cross Society 1985–present. President, Association for Advancement of International Friendship 1987–present. NPC delegate to Japan, Australia and New Zealand since 1979.

Zou Jiahua (Tsou Chia-hua)—b. 1927 Shanghai as son of Zou Caofen, leader of Federation for National Salvation. Received university education. Director, Beijing Power Administration. Elected alternate Central Committee member, Eleventh Party Congress 1977; confirmed, Twelfth Party Congress 1982; and elevated to full member, and served on Presidium, Thirteenth Party Congress 1987. Identified as deputy director, State Office of National Defence Industry 1979–81; and vice-minister, Commission of Science, Technology and Industry for National Defence 1983–85. Minister, Ordnance Industry 1985–86, State Machine-building Industry Commission 1986–88 and Aeronautics and Astronautics Industry 1988–present. Member, Zhang Aiping's military goodwill mission to Sweden and Italy 1978. Son-in-law of Marshal Ye Jianying.

4 BIBLIOGRAPHY

The following classified and annotated bibliography makes no pretence at being comprehensive. Each of the items included has been chosen on the following basis:

1. It is listed in at least one of the following publications: *Books in Print Plus*, R. R. Bowker, New York or London, Summer 1989, Whitaker's *Books in Print*, J. Whitaker & Sons, London, 1988 or *Whitaker's Books in Print 1989*, J. Whitaker & Sons, London, 1989.

2. It is entirely or almost entirely in the English language.

3. It is a book of at least 100 pages; periodicals, journals or newspapers have not been included.

4. It focuses mainly on the People's Republic of China or its foreign relations; comparative works about several countries, works largely about Taiwan or Hong Kong or historical works dealing mainly with the period before 1949 are not included.

5. Its principal concern is one of those aspects of China which are focal to the present book. As a result, topics such as philosophy or ideology, although recognized as extremely important, are not covered and, although a few books *discussing* literature and the arts are included under the heading 'Culture and Society', those which are primarily straight translations of a Chinese literary work or works have been omitted.

A. REFERENCE BOOKS

Bartke, Wolfgang, *Who's Who in the People's Republic of China,* 2nd edn, K. G. Saur, Munich, New York, London, 1987. The first edition of this work was published by M. E. Sharpe, Armonk, New York and The Harvester Press, Sussex, in 1981. It consists mainly of biographies presented in alphabetical order. The biography of each individual is given with posts held and a photograph where possible, followed by activities,

appointments and identifications presented in strict chronological order.

Bartke, Wolfgang and Schier, Peter, *China's New Party Leadership, Biographies and Analysis of the Twelfth Central Committee of the Chinese Communist Party,* M. E. Sharpe, Armonk, 1985. There are three parts to this large and valuable book. By far the longest is the second, which gives biographies in chronological note form of the members and alternate members of the CCP's Twelfth Central Committee. The other two explain and reproduce documents for the Twelfth CCP Congress of 1982 and also explain the structure of the central leadership of the PRC as of early 1984, including how China is governed.

Cheng, Peter P., *Chronology of the People's Republic of China 1970–1979,* Scarecrow Press, Metuchen, N.J. and London, 1986. Each year is preceded by brief commentary on the main events. The chronology itself is extremely detailed, but the events are not categorized. The predecessor to this work, not listed in the books in print works noted above, was Peter Cheng, *A Chronology of the People's Republic of China from October 1, 1949,* Littlefield, Adams & Co., Totowa, N.J., 1972.

China Directory in Pinyin and Chinese, Radiopress, Tokyo, 1971– . This is an annual publication giving extremely detailed information on the administrative structure of China, including the most recent information about who occupies which position. It covers the CCP, the National People's Congress, the State Council and all its various ministries and other organs, academic, economic and mass organizations, and the military. It provides very detailed information about regional as well as central organs, together with a thorough name index.

Chinese Academy of Social Sciences, comp. and trans., edited for Pergamon Press by James, C. V., *Information China, The Comprehensive and*

Authoritative Reference Source of New China, 3 vols, Pergamon Press, Oxford, New York, Beijing, etc., 1989. There are twenty parts to this very large work, dealing with China's land and people, history, sociopolitical structure and law, economy, foreign trade, living standards, the armed forces, sport, education, literature and the arts, the mass media, nationalities, religion and foreign policy. There is considerable information about the past, even though the focus is the PRC, innumerable statistics and a brief bibliography of 'further reading' in European languages, though the books are almost all in English.

Encyclopedia of New China, Foreign Languages Press, Beijing, 1987. This heavy but well produced volume includes sections on 'The Land and the People', 'History', 'Politics', 'Economy' and 'Culture'. Appendixes include the 1982 Constitution and various laws, a 'brief guide to China's leading officials' and a chronology from 1949 to 1980. There are numerous coloured and black-and-white pictures.

Hinton, Harold C. (ed.), *The People's Republic of China, 1979–1984: A Documentary Survey*, 2 vols, Scholarly Resources, Wilmington, Delaware, 1986. This is a comprehensive collection of translated materials which covers all aspects of domestic and foreign policy. It is the successor to a similar five-volume work covering the period 1949 to 1979.

Kaplan, Fredric M. and Sobin, Julian M.; Introduction by John S. Service, *Encyclopedia of China Today*, 3rd rev. edn, Eurasia Press, New York and Hong Kong, 1982. The first edition appeared in 1979. This volume includes an enormous amount of information about contemporary China, aimed at assisting contacts with China. There are sections on government, law, geography, the economic system and various chronologies, as well as on such areas as 'Doing business with the PRC'.

Klein, Donald W. and Clark, Anne B., *Biographic Dictionary of Chinese Communism, 1921–1965*, 2 vols, Harvard University Press, Cambridge, Mass., 1971. This is a highly scholarly work which includes detailed biographies of all those in the history of Chinese communism who had

made a significant impact by 1965. The biographies are in prose, not note, form and documented. They are overwhelmingly factual rather than critical. There are extensive appendixes, including lists showing the fields of work in which the biographees have engaged, as well as a great deal of other information.

Lamb, Malcolm, *Directory of Officials and Organisations in China, 1968–1983*, Contemporary China Centre, Australian National University, Canberra, 1983. China's many governing organizations are listed by category, together with the names of the numerous people who held each post and when. The first two categories are the central CCP and the state structure. There is an extensive index.

Scherer, John L. (ed.), *China: Facts and Figures Annual*, Academic International Press, Gulf Breeze, Florida. This is an annual work which began publication in 1978. It collects an enormous amount of information and a large number of statistics and dates of various sorts. The sections are not totally consistent from year to year, but generally include government, the CCP, the military, population, the economy, agriculture, trade and aid, communications, health, education and welfare.

State Statistical Bureau, People's Republic of China, *Statistical Yearbook of China*, Longman, Hong Kong, Oxford University Press, 1st edn 1986. This statistical yearbook is closely based on the Chinese-language statistical yearbooks. It includes statistics on 'administrative division and natural resources', population, agriculture, industry, energy, transport, posts and telecommunications, trade (both domestic and foreign), finance, prices, people's livelihood, education, culture, sport and other topics. There is a section of explanatory notes.

B. HISTORY OR GENERAL

Barnett, A. Doak and Clough, Ralph N. (eds), *Modernizing China: Post-Mao Reform and Development*, Westview, Boulder, Col., 1986. This looks at the general theme of modernization in China from 1978. It is based on a series of lectures given by Harry Harding , Dwight Perkins, Martin King

Whyte and others at the Johns Hopkins University in 1984 and 1985, and covers political, economic, military, cultural and other aspects.

Benewick, Robert and Wingrove, Paul (eds), *Reforming the Revolution, China in Transition*, Macmillan, London, 1988. This book is an 'attempt to understand the decade since the death of Mao Zedong', a period which is described as 'reforming the revolution' (p. 1). There are fifteen essays, each by a different author, on topics ranging from political structure and reform and the reorganization of the countryside and the urban economy to health, family, literature and foreign relations.

Blecher, Marc, *China: Politics, Economics and Society, Iconoclasm and Innovation in a Revolutionary Socialist Country*, Frances Pinter, London, 1986. This is part of the 'Marxist Regimes Series'. It is a general introduction to the history, government, political economy and foreign policy of the PRC, as part of a comparative analysis. It includes an enlightening chapter on 'society and socialism: class and gender', which argues that the effect of the economic structures and policies of the period 1949 to 1979 was 'heavily egalitarian' (p. 149) but recognizes continuing gender inequality.

Brugger, Bill (ed.), *China Since the 'Gang of Four'*, Croom Helm, London, 1980. This book aims to confront questions about 'the nature of socialism, development theory, freedom of expression and the role of education' (p. 19). Seven authors, all of whom work in Australia, take up such issues as the transformation of the CCP, industrial development, rural policy, education, literature and foreign relations.

Brugger, Bill, *China: Liberation and Transformation 1942–1962* and *China: Radicalism to Revisionism 1962–1979*, Croom Helm, London, Barnes & Noble, Totowa, 1981. This two-volume history of the PRC grew out of Brugger's *Contemporary China*, first published in 1977. The books are designed as textbooks for Chinese politics or history, and each chapter takes up a chronological segment. The author's approach is to acknowledge that China has lessons to teach, in particular the contradiction between freedom and necessity, which are at the core of the Marxist project.

Chan, Anita, Rosen, Stanley and Unger, Jonathan (eds), *On Socialist Democracy and the Chinese Legal System: The Li Yizhe Debates*, M. E. Sharpe, Armonk and London, 1985. 'On Socialist Democracy and the Chinese Legal System' is the title of a dissident manifesto pasted up in Guangzhou on November 10, 1974 by a small group of intellectuals who used the collective penname Li Yizhe. The manifesto attacked the Cultural Revolution and called for democratic reform. In this book the main documents of the ensuing debates are collected, translated and annotated. There is a long explanatory introduction.

Chang King-yuh (ed.), *Perspectives on Development in Mainland China*, Westview, Boulder, Col., 1985. This book grew from a conference held in June 1983 in Virginia, sponsored by the Institute of International Relations in Taibei. The main, but not exclusive, focus is on the post-Mao era. Areas covered include the political process, military problems, economic developments and foreign relations. Several chapters take up comparisons between China and other socialist states.

Chossudovsky, Michel, *Towards Capitalist Restoration? Chinese Socialism after Mao*, Macmillan, Houndmills, Basingstoke, Hampshire and London, St Martin's Press, New York, 1986. This book argues forcefully that China is not only undergoing a capitalist restoration but re-establishing many of the unfortunate features of the pre-1949 era. He believes the Four Modernizations program undermines the foundations of revolutionary socialism, and claims that this is extremely undesirable.

Bonavia, David, *The Chinese*, Penguin, Harmondsworth, 1982. This book was first published in the United States by Lippincott & Crowell in 1980 and has been through many editions. It is a many-sided look at the Chinese people, from the point of view of a journalist highly experienced both in China and the Soviet Union. It is written in an impressionistic but very readable style, and is possibly and best and most influential journalistic and general account of the Chinese, with the focus on the period of reform.

Butterfield, Fox, *China: Alive in the Bitter Sea,* New York Times Books, New York, Hodder and Stoughton, London, 1982. This is an extremely critical book about a wide variety of topics concerning post-Mao China. The author lived for twenty months in Beijing in the early 1980s as a *New York Times* correspondent. He portrays China as totalitarian and notable for its lack of social equality. His Chinese friends initiated him into 'the myriad ways Chinese had invented to ignore, evade, resist, or confound the revolution that Mao had thrust on them. In short, to survive' (p. 7).

Clayre, Alasdair, *The Heart of the Dragon,* Collins/Harvill, London, 1984. This book was planned to accompany the large-scale television series of the same name. Each program covers a theme, such as believing, marrying, eating, working, creating or trading. The focus is the PRC, but there is also an emphasis on history. The language is accessible and the content well informed. There are numerous pictures, most of them in colour.

Dietrich, Craig, *People's China, A Brief History,* Oxford University Press, New York, Oxford, 1986. This highly accessible book aims 'to give the reader a reasonably good idea of the general contours of historical events in China' from 1949 to the mid-1980s, and succeeds admirably. It is well documented with a good bibliography but makes no pretence of being original research. The author is critical but generally very positive about the Chinese revolution.

Dittmer, Lowell, *China's Continuous Revolution: The Post-Liberation Epoch, 1949–1981,* University of California Press, Berkeley and Los Angeles, 1987. This is a theoretical, analytical and narrative book which explores contemporary Chinese politics as a case study of continuous revolution. It is based on a wide variety of sources, both primary and secondary, as well as interviews with recent Chinese emigrés. The author sees China as approaching a post-revolutionary phase from the early 1980s.

Fairbank, John King, *China Watch,* Harvard University Press, Cambridge, Mass. and London, 1987. This is a collection of twenty-five book reviews by a famous and eminent China specialist. He has divided the reviews into five parts, covering relations between the United States and China and continuities in Chinese history, including in the present era.

Fraser, John, *The Chinese: Portrait of a People,* Collins, Toronto, Summit Books, New York, 1980. The author was for two years in the late 1970s the China correspondent for the *Toronto Globe and Mail,* which had an office in Beijing as early as 1959. The section to which the greatest space is devoted is the 'tiny democracy movement' which arose at the end of 1978, and which gave the author a special interest in the question of democracy in China. He is very struck by the Chinese ability to survive against fearsome odds.

Gao Yuan, *Born Red: A Chronicle of the Cultural Revolution,* Stanford University Press, Stanford, 1987. This is an account of how a secondary-school student made revolution during the years 1966 to 1969 and brought disaster both on himself and others. He details how everyone he knew fell victim to the Cultural Revolution. The Foreword, by William A. Joseph, describes it as offering 'a voice that speaks to United States of the human anguish of inhuman events' (p. ix). This is one of a number of such accounts published, especially since the CCP itself denounced the Cultural Revolution.

Garside, Roger, *Coming Alive, China After Mao,* McGraw-Hill, New York, 1981. This is an account of Chinese development from the beginning of 1976 to the early 1980s by somebody who watched events 'at close quarters', his personal experiences being supplemented by substantial written sources. His stated aim is 'to tell the story of how life returned to a nation that had been half-dead' (p. vii). He concludes by stressing the uniqueness of China.

Ginsburg, Norton and Lalor, Bernard A. (eds), *China: The 80s Era,* Westview, Boulder, Col., and London, 1984. This volume is based on a conference held in 1981 at the University of Chicago, which aimed to assess China's problems and prospects. The book gathers together papers on ideological, political, economic, social, demographic, cultural and foreign policies in China since the late

1970s. The introduction, by Ginsburg, integrates the papers and suggests the lines of a research agenda about and for China.

Gittings, John, *China Changes Face, The Road from Revolution*, Oxford University Press, Oxford, 1989. This book covers the history of the PRC, showing the transformations it has undergone. It is suggested that ideologies of substance have disappeared in the 1980s.

Gray, Jack and White, Gordon (eds), *China's New Development Strategy*, Academic Press, London, 1982. This collection of papers from a 1979 conference covers politics, government, industry, trade, rural development and education. The basic purpose of the book is to examine and evaluate the changes in Chinese development strategy after Mao. Jack Gray concludes that there are threats to the new directions from practical problems, cadre inexperience and inflation, among other problems.

Hinton, William, *Shenfan*, Random House, New York, 1983. This is a description of Long Bow Village in Shanxi province, the same village which Hinton covered in his earlier *Fanshen*. Here he takes the story through from 1949 to 1971 using several themes, including the Cultural Revolution and the Dazhai model. The style is similar to *Fanshen* and *Hundred Day War* in its detailed and fascinating microcosmic focus on revolutionary and social processes. Hinton describes his own work as 'a disconcerting chronicle of the rise and decline of a co-operative dream'. He sees the Cultural Revolution as a murderous power struggle, but supports the Dazhai model, claiming that its denunciation as a fraud was based 'on questionable evidence' (p. xxiv).

Hunter, Neale, *Shanghai Journal: An Eyewitness Account of the Cultural Revolution*, Beacon Press, Boston, 1971; Oxford University Press, Hong Kong, 1988. The book is a detailed account of the early stages of the Cultural Revolution in Shanghai as told by somebody who was living there at the time. The author sees the Cultural Revolution as a momentous and complex movement which put China through a self-imposed ordeal by fire. China emerged scarred but stronger and surer of its future. The new edition adds an introduction by the author, which ends with the hope that China will have the word 'love' somewhere on her banner as she heads into the next century.

Leys, Simon, trans. Appleyard, Carol and Goode, Patrick, *The Chairman's New Clothes, Mao and the Cultural Revolution*, Allison and Busby, London, 1981 edn. The French original was published first in 1971 under the title *Les habits neufs du président Mao*, and appeared in English translation in 1977. This work chronicles the Cultural Revolution down to 1969 and is a scathing indictment of this period of Chinese history. Its main analytical statement comes at the beginning: the Cultural Revolution 'was a power struggle waged at the top between a handful of men and behind the smokescreen of a fictitious mass movement' (p. 13).

Leys, Simon, trans. Cox, Steve, *Broken Images, Essays on Chinese Culture and Politics*, St Martin's Press, New York, 1979. Simon Leys (the penname of Pierre Ryckmans, who is acknowledged as holding copyright) has collected articles and essays on contemporary China written by him over the preceding four years. They cover a wide variety of literary, cultural, biographical and general topics, but all share acid hostility to the CCP rulers of China. According to Leys, these people 'have nothing but contempt for the Chinese masses' (p. 106).

Liang Heng and Shapiro, Judith, *After the Nightmare*, Alfred A. Knopf, New York, 1986. Based on travels and renewals of old contacts in 1985, the authors of *Son of the Revolution* (see under *D. Biography*) discuss the China of the 1980s. Despite their recognition of the improvement of living standards, their evaluation is very negative. 'The nightmare was over, Mao was truly dead', but 'it was easy to fear that the seeds of new disasters lay amid the optimism' (p. 240).

MacFarquhar, Roderick, *The Origins of the Cultural Revolution, 1: Contradictions among the People 1956–1957*, Columbia University Press, New York, 1974, 1987; and *The Origins of the Cultural Revolution, 2: The Great Leap Forward 1958–1960*, Columbia University Press, New York, 1983, 1987. This is an extremely detailed, scholarly and illuminating study of Chinese politics in the period leading up to the Cultural Revolution. The books aim to explain the Cultural Revolution, but each volume is self-contained as well as part of the series and each reaches its own conclusions on its period of focus.

MacFarquar, Roderick and Fairbank, John K. (eds), *The Cambridge History of China, Volume 14: The People's Republic, Part 1: The Emergence of Revolutionary China, 1949–1965*, Cambridge University Press, Cambridge, 1987. Itself nearly the last of this multi-volumed history of China, the *Cambridge History of China*, this is the first of two volumes to deal with the PRC period. Its authors take up key issues involved in the history of the first sixteen years and discuss developments in politics, economics, culture, education and foreign relations. The editors divide the period in 1957: the years until then are portrayed as successes; those following as failures.

Maxwell, Neville, and McFarlane, Bruce (eds), *China's Changed Road to Development*, Pergamon, Oxford, 1984. A wide range of topics, including political, economic, population, education and Marxism, is covered by sixteen authors. The 'changed road' is that adopted since 1978. The papers are scholarly and perceptive, mostly based on a conference held in 1982 in Oxford. Each chapter is headed by a useful summary of its main points.

Meisner, Maurice, *Mao's China and After: A History of the People's Republic*, The Free Press, New York, Collier Macmillan, London, 1986. This is actually a revised and updated edition of the same author's *Mao's China*, published in 1977. It is a general history of the PRC from a political scientist's point of view. He has explicitly tried to discuss the history of the PRC in the light of its leaders' own Marxist goals and standards. In the updated edition, the section on the Cultural Revolution has been expanded and revised to take account of recent interpretations. In addition, there is a whole new section on post-Mao China. The general assessment of China under Deng is generally negative.

Morath, Inge and Miller, Arthur, *Chinese Encounters*, Secker & Warburg, London; Farrar, Strauss & Giroux, New York, 1979. This book includes commentary on various aspects of China's arts and society by the famous American playwright Arthur Miller, and photographs by Inge Morath, resulting from a visit in 1978. The comments are critical and perceptive, but what surprised the authors most about China was its 'pervasive beauty' and the 'instinct for aesthetic harmony' of the Chinese (p. 111).

Schell, Orville, *To Get Rich is Glorious, China in the Eighties*, Pantheon Books, New York, 1984; Robin Clark, London, 1985. In two parts, entitled 'The Wind of Wanting to Go It Alone' and 'The New Open Door', Schell discusses the reforms in China and Western influence in a chatty, journalistic style. The book is based on travels in 1983 and 1984. He concludes that the Chinese have temporarily lost touch with that current in their recent history which makes them feel 'humiliated in the face of Western wealth, power, and technological superiority' (p. 210).

Selden, Mark with Eggleston, Patti (eds), *The People's Republic of China: A Documentary History of Revolutionary Change*, Monthly Review Press, New York and London, 1979. Selden has written a very long, interpretive introduction on the theme of the documents: revolutionary change and the period to which they refer, 1946 to 1978. The documents themselves cover several sub-themes, depending on the period, such as 'Land Revolution and the New Democracy, 1946–1952', 'The Two-Line Struggle in City and Countryside, 1959–1965', and 'The Great Proletarian Cultural Revolution, 1966–1976'.

Seymour, James D., *China's Satellite Parties*, M. E. Sharpe, Armonk and London, 1987. This book concerns the history since 1949 of six of those Chinese political parties termed 'democratic parties'. It is based on a Master's thesis of 1961 and research in China in the 1980s. Seymour considers that the 'satellite parties' function as weak interest groups, and are not mere passive tools of the state. 'They are one more indication that while China is not a democracy, neither is it a totalitarian state.' (p. 91)

Terzani, Tiziano, *Behind the Forbidden Door, Travels in China*, Allen & Unwin, London, 1986. The author was the *Der Spiegel* reporter in China from

1980 until March 1984, when he was expelled for his critical reporting. The articles in this book cover a wide range of topics, such as the destruction of the city of Beijing and abuses inherent in the one-child-per-couple policy. The images he portrays of China in this book are negative in the extreme.

Thurston, Anne F., *Enemies of the People: The Ordeal of the Intellectuals in China's Great Cultural Revolution,* Harvard University Press, 1988. This book, based on interviews carried out in China in 1980 and 1981, concerns the sufferings of intellectuals during the Cultural Revolution. The author, whose intention is to view the history of the Cultural Revolution not as politics but as tragedy, presents the Cultural Revolution as 'a failure of morality'.

Tsou Tang, *The Cultural Revolution and post-Mao Reforms: A Historical Perspective,* University of Chicago Press, Chicago, 1986. Here Tang Tsou's essays, written over two decades or so, are collected, together with a new essay giving a general perspective on the history of twentieth-century China. The focus is on the PRC period, especially the Cultural Revolution and after. The book is highly interpretive and the author has much to say both about China and about social science theory, including that relating to political ideology.

Young, Graham (ed.), *China: Dilemmas of Modernisation,* Croom Helm, London, Sydney, Dover, New Hampshire, 1985. The six chapters in this book cover various aspects of China's post-Mao modernization program: the agricultural economy, organization in Chinese industry, technological change, the army, youth and the minority nationalities, together with an introduction. The chapters are based on papers given at a conference on 'Chinese modernization: the latest phase', held early in 1983.

C. POLITICS AND LAW

Amin, Samir, trans. Finkelstein, Norman, *The Future of Maoism,* Monthly Review Press, New York, 1981. This book adopts a very critical posture towards the reforms in China from the point of view of support for Mao's policies. The author sees revisionism, or the Soviet model, as 'the pre-eminent enemy of socialism in the contemporary world' (p. 135) and believes China to be in danger of succumbing to it.

Burns, John P., *Political Participation in Rural China,* University of California Press, Berkeley, 1988. Focusing on the period 1962 to 1984, Burns looks at the theory of modernization which predicts that, in one-party states undergoing economic development, political participation is transformed and expanded. He challenges this for the rural Chinese case, claiming that from 1962 to 1984, 'political participation in rural China was largely restricted to influencing the implementation of a relatively narrow range of economic policies' (p. 59).

Burns, John P. and Rosen, S. (eds), *Policy Conflicts in Post-Mao China, A Documentary Survey, with Analyses,* M. E. Sharpe, Armonk, N.Y. and London, England, 1986. This contains a collection of documents dealing with many aspects of change and conflict. The documents are divided into two categories: 'structure and process' (e.g. ideology, political participation and bureaucracy) and 'policy arenas', such as industry, commerce, agriculture, education and population. In addition to introductory commentary on each section, there is a general introduction which gives the aims of the reader, surveys Chinese politics since 1976 and discusses the use of primary sources in the study of contemporary China.

Chang, Parris, *Power and Policy in China,* Pennsylvania State University Press, University Park, 1975; 2nd enlarged edn, 1978. An excellent study of policy-making processes in China before the Cultural Revolution through an examination of five major policy issues, including the commune movement, the Socialist Education Campaign and the ideological rectification campaign. It concludes that, though Mao's power was enormous, 'other party leaders frequently were able to block his policy or modify its substance' (p. 190).

Cohen, Jerome A., *The Criminal Process in the People's Republic of China 1949–1963: An Introduction,* Harvard University Press, Cambridge, Mass., 1968. This is a pioneering study of

China's legal system as it existed before the Cultural Revolution. A long introduction periodizes China's legal history to 1963 and explains the processes of China's criminal legal system. The main body of the book presents major materials (the vast bulk of them translations of Chinese sources) relevant to the criminal process.

Derbyshire, Ian, *Politics in China: From Mao to Deng*, Chambers, Edinburgh, 1987. This small book provides a brief survey of Chinese history under the PRC, with its primary focus on the late 1970s and 1980s. In addition, there are chapters on the political structure, economic and social developments, and defence and foreign policies. The work is successfully designed as summation, not new research.

Domes, Jürgen, *The Government and Politics of the PRC—A Time of Transition*, Westview, Boulder, Col.,1985. This book provides a very good and comprehensive coverage of China's political economy. The four parts are 'the material and historical framework', 'political institutions', 'the politics of a transitional crisis system' and 'economics, the society, and political perspectives'. The postscript, dated January 14, 1985, sees a strong possibility of 'a return to a Soviet-type system of centralized planning' (p. 258).

Gardner, John, *Chinese Politics and the Succession to Mao*, Macmillan, London and Basingstoke, 1982. The author discusses the failure of Liu Shaoqi and Lin Biao to succeed Mao as planned, but concludes that the early 1980s began to see attempts at proper procedures of succession. Although his cautious optimism has not been validated, he was right to identify the problem of succession as a crucial one in Chinese politics.

Goodman, David S. G., *Centre and province in the People's Republic of China, Sichuan and Guizhou, 1955–1965*, Cambridge University Press, Cambridge, 1986. This book looks at the interaction between the centre and two neighbouring south-western provinces, rich and powerful Sichuan and poor and backward Guizhou, in the decade before the Cultural Revolution. The focus is on the mechanisms of the decision-making process. The author contributes to the debate on the balance of power between centre and province at the time with evidence in favour of a centralist view.

Harding, Harry, *Organizing China: The Problem of Bureaucracy, 1949–1976*, Stanford University Press, Stanford, 1981. This study examines how organizational policy developed down to the death of Mao, showing its impact on the Party and government administration. The author credits the CCP with being able 'to establish a complex network of political organizations that has effectively blanketed a large, diverse and populous nation' (p. 357). He also points to serious problems, such as elitism, abuse of power and corruption, and criticizes the techniques of indoctrination, rectification and mass campaigns.

Lampton, David M. (ed.), *Policy Implementation in Post-Mao China*, University of California Press, Berkeley, Los Angeles and London, 1987. This collection of articles is based on a conference held in 1983. It covers such areas as water management policy, the tax system, the one-child policy and price control policy. The political system is described as 'one in which consensus building and negotiation are central to the political process' (p. 18). At the same time, there are major inefficiencies and irrationalities because 'the logic of the marketplace is at variance with the central needs of China's planners, police, propagandists, and central personnel organs' (p. 22).

Mao Zedong, edited by Kau, Michael Y. M. and Leung, John K., *The Writings of Mao Zedong, 1949–1976, Volume I: September 1949–December 1955*, M. E. Sharpe, Armonk, New York and London, 1986. This is the first volume of a series of six which will translate into English everything reasonably attributable to Mao Zedong that was written between September 1949 and his death. The volume of material contained in *The Selected Works of Mao Tsetung*, published by Beijing's Foreign Languages Press in 1977, is not extensive.

Moody, Peter R. Jr, *Chinese Politics after Mao, Development and Liberalization 1976 to 1983*, Praeger, New York, 1983. The author gives a highly scholarly and thoughtful analysis of the main aspects of the Chinese political culture after Mao. He believes that 'what we are seeing in

China may be a natural evolution within totalitarianism, not a basic change from totalitarianism' (p. 168).

Nathan, Andrew J., *Chinese Democracy*, Alfred A. Knopf, New York, 1985; University of California Press, Berkeley and Los Angeles, 1986. Nathan shows the very short tradition of democracy in China, and the tendency to sacrifice democracy in favour of nationalism. He emphasises the role of propaganda and the media in China, especially since 1949. A long appendix analyzes interviews with Chinese emigrés and travellers who 'provided information for this book that could not have come from any other source' (p. 235).

Nee, Victor and Mozingo, David (eds), *State and Society in Contemporary China*, Cornell University Press, Ithaca, N.Y., 1983. Several political scientists examine the nature and exercise of state power in China and its relationship to society and the economy, as well as the relation between centre and locality. The periods both during and after the Mao Zedong era are considered. One consistent theme is the inadequacy of understanding PRC social history 'in terms of China's bureaucratic heritage or the concept of totalitarianism' (p. 18).

Oldham, John R. (ed.), *China's Legal Development*, M. E. Sharpe, Armonk and London, 1986. This is a collection of articles from the May 1983 issue of the *Columbia Journal of Transnational Law*, which was devoted to China, with an additional extensive piece on Chinese tax law which was published later in the same journal. It includes a comprehensive bibliography of English-language sources on modern Chinese law. Topics covered include economic law and legislation, the teaching of international law in China, Western scholarship on Chinese law and international legal issues, especially legal problems in Sino-United States relations.

Robinson, Thomas W., *The Cultural Revolution in China*, University of California Press, Berkeley, 1971. This is a series of four essays analyzing the Cultural Revolution from a range of different perspectives. They include Maoist theories of policy-making and organization, Zhou Enlai's role in the Cultural Revolution, foreign affairs and the countryside. Robinson's introduction selects as its first generalization that the Cultural Revolution 'did possess several aspects of a genuine revolution' (p. 19).

Ross, Lester and Silk, Mitchell A., *Environmental Law and Policy in the People's Republic of China*, Quorum Books, New York, Westport, London, 1987. This book aims to 'shed light on the actual workings and policy underpinnings of China's environmental administration' (p. ix). There is a short introduction, the main body being devoted to translated Chinese materials, with commentary, on such topics as air and water pollution control, noise control, wildlife and forest protection, and land use and planning. Appendixes give texts of relevant laws, regulations, measures and so on.

Saich, T., *China—Politics and Government*, Macmillan, London; St Martin's Press, New York, 1981. This book contains chapters on China's history from the early twentieth century to the late 1970s, Marxism–Leninism–Mao Zedong Thought, the CCP, the state structure, the army, social control, urban and rural China. There are copious references and suggestions for further reading for each chapter. The author is sceptical of some aspects of the reform policies.

Shue, Vivienne, *The Reach of the State: Sketches of the Chinese Body Politic*, Stanford University Press, Stanford, California, 1988. This is a series of four theoretical essays around the theme of state–society relations with the focus on contemporary China. The author sees Chinese rural society as cellular, with local politics marked as much by negotiation as by coercion. She considers the Dengist governments of the 1980s to be paternalistic and bound to penetrate the 'honeycomb structure' of society for successful modernization. This is a highly challenging work of interpretation.

Teiwes, Frederick C., *Leadership, Legitimacy, and Conflict in China, From a Charismatic Mao to the Politics of Succession*, Macmillan, London and Basingstoke, M. E. Sharpe, Armonk, 1984. This book contains three essays about leadership at the apex of the Chinese system. The author raises questions about conflict in the the Politburo and among the senior leaders. Most of the material concerns Mao Zedong and the changing nature of his authority, but some consideration is also given to the years after 1976. The author predicts, after Deng, 'a long-term trend toward a more Soviet style politics where formal institutional positions and the tradeoff of organizational interests predominate' (pp. 129–30).

Townsend, James R. and Womack, Brantley, *Politics in China,* Little, Brown, Boston, 3rd edn, 1986. This highly scholarly and well documented study has a strong theoretical political science approach. It discusses political structures and processes, value systems and decision-making in the PRC. There are extensive appendixes containing statistical and other information.

Wang, James C. F., Contemporary *Chinese Politics, An Introduction,* Prentice-Hall, Englewood Cliffs, New Jersey, 1985, 1988. Originally published in the United States in 1980, this book exists in several editions. It is well documented but readable, making it a good textbook. It covers contemporary history, ideology and political structures and processes, including mass participation and the politics of modernization, and China's role in world politics. It also includes useful appendixes.

White, Gordon, *Party and Professionals, The Political Role of Teachers in Contemporary China,* M. E. Sharpe, Armonk, 1981. In this theoretical study the theme is politics and power; the case study is the teaching profession. White points to several phases in the political role of teachers, including the first revolution, modernization drive and continuous revolution. He argues that teachers have provided one weight in the political balance which has swung power towards the modernizers, although he believes they are *less central* to the CCP's goal of modernization than professional managers, technicians or engineers. More than half the book is devoted to relevant documents from Chinese sources.

D. BIOGRAPHY

Bachman, David M., *Chen Yun and the Chinese Political System,* Institute of East Asian Studies/ Center for Chinese Studies, University of California, Berkeley, 1985. This biography of one of the PRC's most influential economic leaders gives chronological details of his career down to 1984, and examines Chen's economic thought. The last chapter examines the parts played by Chen, Deng Xiaoping and Zhao Ziyang in the processes of economic reform after 1978. Bachman concludes that while Chen Yun was one of the giants of the Chinese communist movement, he was ultimately not a pivotal figure in the history of the PRC.

Bennett, Gordon A. and Montaperto, Ronald N., *Red Guard, The Political Biography of Dai Hsiao-ai,* George Allen & Unwin, London, 1971; Anchor Books, Doubleday, Garden City, 1972. This is a detailed biography of a Chinese secondary school student's role in the Cultural Revolution from May 1966 until November 1967, when he left for Hong Kong, showing the movement through his eyes. Although he became disillusioned, it was the institutions and personalities which constituted China's political system that he rejected, not the values which it expressed. This work is less intensely negative about the Cultural Revolution than most comparable books.

Cheng, Nien, *Life and Death in Shanghai,* Grafton Books, London, 1986. An autobiographical work focusing attention on seven years spent in prison from 1966 to 1973 during the Cultural Revolution, one of the author's 'crimes' being to defend Liu Shaoqi. This vivid account paints an extremely dark picture of the Cultural Revolution in general and prison life in particular. The real culprit for the iniquity of her imprisonment was 'the evil system under which we all had to live' (p. 321).

Dittmer, Lowell, *Liu Shao-ch'i and the Chinese Cultural Revolution, The Politics of Mass Criticism,* University of California Press, Berkeley, 1974. This is a study of Mao's main target of attack during the Cultural Revolution. The first section is a chronological discussion of Liu's life, the second includes an account of the conflict between Mao and Liu from the point of view of temperaments, styles of work and policies, and in the last part the author develops a theory of mass criticism and the mass line, using Liu Shaoqi as a case study.

Domes, Jürgen, *P'eng Te-huai: The Man and the Image,* Stanford University Press, Stanford, 1985.

This work considers not only Peng Dehuai's political career, but also the attitudes which the CCP leadership has adopted towards him at various times. The author argues that the manipulation of Peng's image for political purposes has become so dominant that 'the actual person does not seem to play an important part' and 'the symbols become thoroughly de-personalized' (p. 150).

Hollingworth, Clare, *Mao and the Men against Him*, Jonathan Cape, London, 1985. Although this deals with all of Mao's career, it is mainly about the post-1949 period. Its focus is the men who opposed Mao and the power struggles caused. The author is a distinguished journalist, and the book is journalistic more than scholarly, lacking documentation.

Liang Heng and Shapiro, Judith, *Son of the Revolution*, Knopf, New York, 1983; Fontana Paperbacks, London, 1984. The autobiography of a man who grew up during the Cultural Revolution years but later married an American. The view of the Cultural Revolution and the Chinese socialist system in general is devastatingly negative.

Rice, Edward E., *Mao's Way*, University of California Press, Berkeley, 1972. This work is a biography of Mao, with the focus on his 'way'. This is seen in terms of campaigns, all conducted 'in an atmosphere of tension' after which 'each was allowed to die down' (p. 478). The book becomes a detailed account of the various power struggles within the CCP, with particular emphasis on the Cultural Revolution.

Schram, Stuart (ed.), *Chairman Mao Talks to the People: Talks and Letters: 1956–1971*, Pantheon Books, New York, 1974, 1975. This book was earlier published in Britain as *Mao Tse-tung Unrehearsed: Talks and Letters 1956–71* by Penguin. It is a collection of Mao's speeches and statements which show the colourful side of his character. The introduction, by Schram, emphasizes two contradictions in Mao. One was between his concern for mass participation and for organization; the other between his pride in China's past and his resolve to change Chinese society and culture along revolutionary lines.

Solomon, Richard H., *Mao's Revolution and the Chinese Political Culture*, University of California Press, Berkeley, 1971. This book is a study of Mao and his personal struggle to change China. It takes a psychological look at Chinese politics, with emphasis on Mao Zedong's temperament, socialization and political culture. It concludes that in the case of Mao's revolution, sentiments of aggression were 'the distinguishing motivational quality of political activity' (p. 522).

Terrill, Ross, *A Biography, Mao*, Harper & Row, New York, 1980. This is a chronological biography of Mao written in a highly readable style. Just over half the book concerns the period after the founding of the PRC. In an epilogue the author evaluates Mao and sums up his career: 'With all his faults, Mao gave China a new start, and gave the twentieth century a fascinating man of politics.' (p. 424)

Terrill, Ross, *The White-Boned Demon: A Biography of Madame Mao Zedong*, Heinemann, London, Morrow, New York, 1984. This popular biography of Jiang Qing is based on unofficial sources such as oral eyewitness accounts and the testimony of those Chinese outside China who knew Jiang Qing. It is a chronological account of Jiang Qing's life down to the legal condemnation passed on her in 1981. Terrill argues that she never regretted anything right to the end, and believed she had accomplished her mission. He foresees the possibility that a new government may at some time reverse the verdict on her.

Wilson, Dick (ed.), *Mao Zedong in the Scales of History, A Preliminary Assessment Organized by the China Quarterly*, Cambridge University Press, Cambridge, 1977. In this work, published soon after Mao's death, eleven leading authorities discuss Mao as philosopher, Marxist, political leader, soldier, teacher and so on. In the introduction, the editor looks at Mao's contributions and message, giving pride of place to 'the unlocking of Marxism–Leninism from its prison of old dogmas' (p. 4).

Yang Zhongmei, trans. Wycoff, William A.; Timothy Cheek (ed.), *Hu Yaobang: A Chinese Biography*, M. E. Sharpe, Armonk, 1988. The main emphasis is on a description of Hu Yaobang's career, together with an assessment of his ideas and character. The study, which is highly laudatory of

Hu, provides an insight into the system of personal patronage of Chinese political leadership.

Yao Ming-le, *The Conspiracy and Murder of Mao's Heir*, Knopf, New York, Collins, London, 1983. This remarkable book, by one writing under a pen-name who claims inside information, states that Mao had Lin Biao murdered on September 12, 1971. It claims that the plane crash of the following day did kill his son, Lin Liguo, but not Lin Biao himself.

Yue Daiyun and Wakeman, Carolyn, *To the Storm: The Odyssey of a Revolutionary Chinese Woman*, University of California Press, Berkeley, 1985. This is the biography of Yue Daiyun, a specialist on literature from Beijing University, from the late 1950s until the late 1970s. Despite her intense loyalty to the Party, she was denounced as a rightist and underwent untold hardships, especially during the Cultural Revolution. Even that nightmare did not extinguish her determination to 'join in the efforts to rebuild the Party', since she remained convinced that it alone could lead China forward (p. 387).

E. FOREIGN RELATIONS

Chen, King C., *China's War With Vietnam, 1979: Issues, Decisions and Implications*, Hoover Institution Press, Stanford University, Stanford, California, 1987. In addition to a detailed account of 'Deng Xiaoping's war', this book contains a good treatment of relations between China and Vietnam from 1949 on. Although the author considers that the 1979 war 'can hardly be justified' and failed to achieve its major political objectives (p. 118), his approach is avowedly China-centred and, like the PRC government, he regards China's action as a counter-attack.

Dreyer, June Teufel (ed.), *Chinese Defense and Foreign Policy*, Paragon House, New York, 1989. The eleven chapters by eleven authors derive from papers presented to the Third Congress of the Professors, World Peace Academy held in Manila in August 1987. Most chapters concern regional issues, especially those in particular bilateral relations. Dreyer has added an integrative Introduction, in which she points out common themes, such as the mutual interaction between China's domestic politics and its international behaviour.

Duiker, William J., *China and Vietnam: The Roots of Conflict*, Institute of East Asian Studies, University of California, Berkeley, 1986. The author bases his work on major documents, as well as interviews in Beijing, Hanoi and Phnom Penh, to offer a chronological examination of Sino-Vietnamese relations from the 1930s to the 1980s. His aim is to explain the poor state of relations in the late 1970s and 1980s, and in particular the causes of the 1979 war. The copious sources include works in English, French and Vietnamese.

Ellison, Herbert J. (ed.), *The Sino-Soviet Conflict, A Global Perspective*, University of Washington Press, Seattle and London, 1982. Based on a conference, this collective work examines Sino-Soviet relations from the point of view of the domestic politics and economies of each country, and the international perspectives of the relationship, including the various regions where China and the Soviet Union have come into competition or conflict. A final section provides overviews on such things as the Sino-Soviet dispute in the 1970s and looks at prospects for the 1980s. The point of view is that of the American right.

Fung, Edmund S. K. and Mackerras, Colin, *From Fear to Friendship, Australia's Policies Towards the People's Republic of China, 1966–82*, University of Queensland Press, St Lucia, 1985. This describes the development of Australia–China relations, and analyzes Australia's policies towards China. There are two parts, entitled 'persistent hostility' and 'a new relationship', the division between the two representing the major break from Australian fear of China to the establishment of a friendly relationship in 1972.

Gurtov, Melvin, and Hwang Byong-Moo, *China under Threat: The Politics of Strategy and Diplomacy*, Johns Hopkins University Press, Baltimore and London, 1980. This book argues that domestic issues have been the main determinants of foreign policy. It examines five case studies between 1950 and 1965 to reach this conclusion, including the Korean War, the Taiwan Strait crisis of 1958, Vietnam, and the Sino-Soviet border clashes of 1969.

Harding, Harry (ed.), *China's Foreign Relations in the 1980s*, Yale University Press, New Haven and London, 1984. This book is 'designed to encourage Americans to take a broader and more balanced view of China' (p. viii). It is a valuable and well integrated series of essays on such topics as 'domestic politics and foreign policy', 'China in the international economy', and 'the PRC as a regional power'. The authors believe that 'China will, over the rest of the century, be neither a close friend nor a bitter foe of the US' (p. xiv).

Harris, Lillian Craig and Worden, Robert L. (eds), *China and the Third World, Champion or Challenger?*, Croom Helm, London, 1986. The emphasis in this multi-authored book is on the very recent past. The authors question the continuing importance of the Third World to Beijing in the period of reform, with one chapter emphasizing Beijing's tendency to view the Third World merely as an adjunct to its relations with the superpowers. The book attacks some commonly held stereotypes about relations between China and the Third World. In particular, Bruce Larkin's chapter on China's global economic role shows China as a competitor with the rest of the Third World for trade and economic aid.

Hart, Thomas G., *Sino-Soviet Relations: Re-examining the Prospects for Normalization*, Gower, Aldershot, Brookfield USA, Hong Kong, Singapore, Sydney, 1987. The author of this small book tries to explain the history and determine the current status of all issues he is able to identify dividing China and the Soviet Union. His approach is issue resolution, but he is very cautious about predicting normalization of relations and sees quite a bit of realpolitik, striving for national-chauvinistic prestige and hypocrisy on both sides.

Hsiao, Gene T. and Witunski, Michael (eds), *Sino-American Normalization and its Policy Implications*, Praeger, New York, 1983. This very large book grew from a conference in Missouri in 1980. It contains a great deal about the history of Sino-American relations in the 1970s and 1980s, as well as commentary on the Taiwan issue, educational exchange and strategic implications. Just over half the book is devoted to appendixes with relevant documents, statements, communiqués, agreements, speeches and so on.

Jacobsen, C. G., *Sino-Soviet Relations since Mao: The Chairman's Legacy*, Praeger, New York, 1981. In this fairly scholarly study, the author examines the causes of friction, the function of Sino-Soviet relations in China's domestic politics, the Sino-Vietnamese war and other factors. He concludes that 'prolonged Deng dominance is likely to see continued Chinese interest in improved Sino-Soviet relations' (p. 156).

Kallgren, Joyce K., Sopiee, Noordin and Djiwandono, Soedjati (eds), *ASEAN and China, An Evolving Relationship*, Institute of East Asian Studies, University of California, Berkeley, 1988. The papers in this book derive from a conference held in January 1987. They cover such topics as the implications for South-east Asia of political leadership in China, China's policy towards ethnic Chinese, China's relations with individual states of South-east Asia and the implications for South-east Asia of the United States–Soviet Union–China relationships. Kallgren's introduction draws attention to the 'cautionary' tone of ASEAN's views of China, which appreciate the benefits to be derived from successful Chinese modernization but are concerned over the pressures which could result from the PRC as a major regional power.

Kapur, Harish (ed.), *As China Sees the World, Perceptions of Chinese Scholars*, Frances Pinter, London, 1987. This book consists of accounts by twenty-nine Chinese scholars of various aspects of post-war and especially contemporary international relations. Topics range from macro-analysis, such as the emergence of superpowers, to Third World crises, such as those in Kampuchea and Central America, and 'patterns of Third World regional integration', such as ASEAN. There is a brief integrative introduction.

Kapur, Harish, *China and the European Economic Community: The New Connection*, Martinus Nijhoff, Dordrecht, Boston and Lancaster, 1986. This book examines China's relations with the European Economic Community, with the aim of exploring the relative importance of economic and political factors in Chinese foreign policy decisions and the way changes are made in Chinese foreign policy. Over two-thirds of the book is devoted to thirty-two documents.

Kapur, Harish (ed.), *The End of an Isolation: China after Mao*, Martinus Nijhoff, Dordrecht, 1985. The main purpose of this book, according to the editor, is to examine and evaluate the changes in Chinese foreign relations since the death of Mao. The first section takes up China's relations with other states, such as the superpowers, Japan and the Third World. The second discusses determinants in Chinese foreign policy, such as security, the international communist movement and self-reliance. There is a focus on change and continuity.

Kim, Samuel S. (ed.), *China and the World: Chinese Foreign Policy in the Post-Mao Era*, Westview, Boulder, Col. and London, 1984. This collective book claims to 'represent a modest step toward remedying the dialogue of the deaf between China scholars and world politics analysts' (p. x). It includes four essays on theoretical issues, four on China's relations with the United States, the Soviet Union and the countries of the Second and Third Worlds, and four others on specific policy areas like China's involvement in the world economy. In the last chapter, Allen Whiting discusses China's foreign policy options and prospects.

Kim, Samuel S., *China, The United Nations, and World Order*, Princeton University Press, Princeton, 1979. This is a thickly documented and scholarly book, which includes a detailed bibliography and numerous appendixes, one of which gives the voting record of the main five countries on resolutions adopted by the Security Council between November 14, 1971 and December 31, 1976. One of the author's main themes is that it is symbolic that China's entry into the United Nations has strengthened it as a forum for the mobilization of world political opinion on major issues of global concern.

Lawson, Eugene K., *The Sino-Vietnamese Conflict*, Praeger, New York, 1984. The chapter on 'the historical perspective' deals mainly with the 'peaceful decade' (1954–64). The focus is the period 1965 to 1975—that is, the years of the Vietnam War leading up to the victory of the communists in South Vietnam—with documentation on how the attitudes of the two states diverged. The author argues that the main conflict was over policy towards the superpowers. By 1975 Vietnam could no longer continue its balancing act. The Vietnam War 'laid the foundations for the postwar conflict between Vietnam and China' (p. 311).

Lee Chae-Jin, *China and Japan: New Economic Diplomacy*, Hoover Institution, Stanford, 1984. This book focuses on three case studies of economic diplomacy, including the Baoshan steel complex. One major conclusion is that China's vast but inefficient bureaucratic system poses a serious obstacle to partnership between China and Japan. On the other hand, the author expects the 'intelligent and resourceful people of China and Japan' to find ways of obtaining 'substantial economic benefits from each other in the future' (p. 146).

Ross, Robert S., *The Indochina Tangle, China's Vietnam Policy 1975–1979*, Columbia University Press, New York, 1988. This is an extremely detailed chronological study of China's Vietnam policy from the communist victory in Indochina to the Sino-Vietnamese war. Based on a range of sources from China, Vietnam, the Soviet Union, Kampuchea and the United States, as well as numerous secondary sources, it focuses on the roots of growing PRC hostility to Vietnam and China's policy objectives *vis-à-vis* Hanoi. The author concludes that the crux of the matter was Sino-Soviet relations: 'It was China's inalterable fate to endure the frustration of confronting a weaker nation [Vietnam] in alliance with its stronger adversary [the Soviet Union]' (p. 266).

Rozman, Gilbert, *The Chinese Debate about Soviet Socialism, 1978–1985*, Princeton University Press, Princeton and Guildford, Surrey, 1987. This study includes both a chronological survey of Chinese writings on the Soviet Union between 1978 and 1985 and a thematic account of the views of Soviet peasants, workers, intellectuals and officials. The author sees China's own conception of Chinese socialism and the relations between China and the Soviet Union as the main determinants of Chinese views of the Soviet Union. He stresses 'persistent, sharp differences between reform and orthodox position' (p. 374).

Segal, Gerald, *Defending China,* Oxford University Press, New York, 1985. This book examines eight main instances in which Beijing has used military force to defend China, including Korea (1950–53), India (1962) and Vietnam (1979). The author argues that the rulers in Beijing acted to defend China with pragmatism and flexibility, but without any grand strategy learned either from Chinese history or revolutionary struggle.

Segal, Gerald and Tow, William T. (eds), *Chinese Defence Policy,* Macmillan, London; University of Illinois Press, Urbana and Chicago, 1984. This collection of papers by eighteen authors is divided into four parts, dealing with sources of strategy, the armed forces, the economic dimension and foreign policy. A main conclusion is that Beijing will pursue its perceptions of its own best interests and balance other countries against each other.

Snow, Philip, *The Star Raft: China's Encounter with Africa,* Weidenfeld and Nicolson, London, New York, 1988; Cornell University Press, Ithaca, 1989. Although this book covers five centuries of China's relations with Africa, about two-thirds of it is devoted to the PRC period. The sources for the contemporary period are Africans involved with China and Chinese archives and officials. The contemporary material is arranged thematically rather than chronologically. The author shows great empathy both with the Chinese and Africans, and is generally positive about China's efforts to befriend Africa, seeing them as often more successful than those of Europe.

Sutter, Robert G., *Chinese Foreign Policy: Developments After Mao,* Praeger, New York, 1986. This work's objectives are to survey recent Chinese foreign policy and to establish an analytical framework to explain the key factors. There are two chapters of historical background—in effect foreign policy under Mao—but most attention is given to the years 1976–84. Western Europe, Latin America and Africa are discussed, but by far the most attention goes to the superpowers and Asia. The author argues that, during the few years following Mao's death, 'China's top foreign policy priority has remained the pragmatic quest for the stable environment needed for effective modernization and development' (p. 10).

Taylor, Robert, *The Sino-Japanese Axis, A New Force in Asia?,* Athlone, London, St Martin's Press, New York, 1985. This is a survey of Sino-Japanese relations with the emphasis on the period after diplomatic relations were established in 1972. Based on Western press reports and translations from Chinese sources, it evaluates the two countries' economic co-operation, among other factors. The author concludes that a Sino-Japanese axis could indeed emerge, bringing a new civilization 'built on Chinese culture and Japanese technology' and that this axis would be to 'the lasting benefit of the people of Asia' (p. 116).

Vertzberger, Yaacov Y. I., *China's Southwestern Strategy: Encirclement and Counterencirclement,* Praeger, New York, 1985. This is a detailed account of Sino-Pakistani relations from 1954 to 1984, including a discussion of the 'informal alliance' and the trade and aid relationship. Other factors, such as the roles of Afghanistan and the United States, are also given attention.

Yahuda, Michael, *Towards the End of Isolationism: China's Foreign Policy after Mao,* Macmillan, London, 1983. This analytical work 'seeks to examine the continuities and changes in China's foreign policy since the death of Mao Zedong' (p. ix). To this end it discusses Mao's legacy and policy after 1976. The author sees a relative, but not total, end to isolation. He believes China's leaders want to extend links with the international economy, but without suffering limitations on 'freedom of international manoeuvre' (p. 247).

F. THE ECONOMY

Barnett, A. Doak, *China's Economy in Global Perspective,* The Brookings Institution, Washington D.C., 1981. This is a very large and scholarly work which focuses particularly on China's international economic policies and performance in the late 1970s and 1980, as well as on its domestic policies. There are five chapters, all extremely long, on China's modernization program, trade, China and the world food and energy systems, and the economic dimension of Sino-American relations. A large amount of statistical data is presented.

Baum, Richard (ed.), *China's Four Modernizations, The New Technological Revolution*, Westview, Boulder, Col., 1980. This book is the result of a 1979 conference in Bermuda. Its focus is the acquisition and use of modern industrial science and technology in China. Various specialists look at such topics as Chinese industry, science and technology policy, energy technology and the modernization of national defence. Each chapter is followed by commentaries from participants. Jeffrey Schultz's conclusion points out that bourgeois ideas will accompany foreign technology and argues that this represents a danger to the socialist order.

Buxbaum, David C. Joseph, Cassondra, E. and Reynolds, Paul D. (eds), *China Trade, Prospects and Perspectives*, Praeger, New York, 1982. This large and scholarly collective work looks at trade from several points of view. It examines the background, the economy, politics and people, selected market sectors such as agriculture, the petroleum industry and the machine-tool industry, and presents some case studies of trade, such as Pullman Kellogg. Finally, it takes up some practical considerations such as contracts. The perspective is heavily American and generally, though cautiously, enthusiastic about trade with China.

Byrd, William, *China's Financial System: The Changing Role of the Banks*, Westview Press, Boulder, Col., 1983. This history of the banking system in the PRC focuses on the changes between 1978 and 1982, when the account finishes. The author shows the interrelationship between financial and fiscal issues. He points to impressive results so far, but also to the formidable problems still to be overcome.

Carter, Colin A. and Zhong Fu-ning, *China's Grain Production and Trade: An Economic Analysis*, Westview Press, Boulder, Col., 1988. The authors use an econometric analysis to propose a new model for estimating grain supply and demand until the year 2000. They conclude that on the basis of current technology China will probably experience annual grain shortfalls of between 20 million and 25 million tonnes.

Chow, Gregory C., *The Chinese Economy*, Harper and Row, New York, London, 1985; World Scientific Publishing Company, Teaneck, N.J., 1987. The author states that the main purpose of this book 'is to apply the basic tools of economic analysis to the economy' of the PRC (p. ix). Intended as an economics textbook, this work includes a good deal of economic theoretical material in addition to a description of the Chinese economy. The first chapters describe how market and planned economies function and how the Chinese economy works. Other chapters analyze the organization and performance of Chinese agriculture, industry and foreign trade and deal with national income, population and consumption.

Croll, Elisabeth, *The Family Rice Bowl*, United Nations Research Institute for Social Development, Geneva/Zed Press, London, 1983. This highly scholarly account focuses on the supply, types and quantity of food in China, with separate chapters covering the cities and country areas. Most attention is given to the period since 1949, but there is a chapter on food consumption in Republican China. There are numerous tables and charts.

Feuchtwang, Stephan, Hussain, Athar and Pairault, Thierry (eds), *Transforming China's Economy in the Eighties*, 2 vols entitled *The Rural Sector, Welfare and Employment* and *Management, Industry and the Urban Sector*, Westview Press, Boulder, Col.,1988. These two volumes contain seventeen essays on such topics as the single-child family policy, the new inheritance law, urban housing policy, ideology and industrialization, and industrial restructuring. The authors are British, French and American specialists on contemporary China. The period of focus is between 1978 and 1985, but there is much attention to historical background going back as far as the 1950s.

Griffin, Keith (ed.), *Institutional Reform and Economic Development in the Chinese Countryside*, Macmillan, London and Basingstoke, 1984. The authors of this collection of essays are mainly development economists with great international experience, rather than sinologists. The major focuses are income distribution and social and economic power. The material was mostly obtained during a visit to China in July and August 1982, but the epilogue is based on a return visit in the summer of 1983. The authors are generally impressed with China's economic growth, especially in comparison with other Third World countries, but are also aware of serious problems.

Howard, Pat, *Breaking the Iron Rice Bowl: Prospects for Socialism in China's Countryside*, M. E. Sharpe, Armonk, New York and London, 1988. This book deals with the rural reforms in the post-Mao era. It is based on the assumption that socialism can be reached only under a truly participatory system in which rural economic units are given greater autonomy and interference by state bureaucrats is limited. It presents a fairly optimistic and favourable analysis of rural reform.

Howe, Christopher, *China's Economy: A Basic Guide*, Paul Elek, London, Basic Books, New York, 1978. This gives an excellent introduction to China's economic system before the period of reform. It covers such areas as population, agriculture, industry, foreign trade and incomes, prices and the standard of living. The author's aim is to provide, on each topic covered, 'the minimum information that a professional or serious student would need to know' (p. xiii).

Lardy, Nicholas R., *Agriculture in China's Modern Economic Development*, Cambridge University Press, Cambridge, 1983. This study of China's agriculture shows its uneven performance and uncertain future. The author takes up issues such as the role of agriculture, planning and allocative efficiency, prices, living standards and the prospects for reform. All but one of the chapters concludes with a summary.

Lee, Peter N. S., *Industrial Management and Economic Reform in China 1949–1984*, Oxford University Press, New York, 1988. This is a systematic analysis of China's industrial system, with much focus on the period of the reforms.

Lin Wei and Chao, Arnold (eds), *China's Economic Reforms*, University of Pennsylvania Press, Philadelphia, 1982. This is a collective book with eleven chapters on China's economic reforms, including market mechanisms, leadership system, industry and agriculture. All contributors are Chinese and they express the official viewpoint. There are numerous tables and statistics, and a very useful glossary of PRC economic terms which gives extensive definitions and explanations.

Lyons, Thomas P., *Economic Integration and Planning in Maoist China*, Columbia University Press, New York, 1987. Maoist China is here understood as the period from 1958 to 1978. The author puts forward the hypothesis that Chinese economic development between 1957 and 1979 showed a tendency towards regional autarky, meaning that economic integration was arrested or retarded.

Nolan, Peter, *The Political Economy of Collective Farms: An Analysis of China's Post-Mao Rural Reforms*, Westview, Boulder, Col., 1988. In the first three chapters the author analyzes the debates over collectivization and the performance of collectives. He argues that the economic failures of collectivization are manifest, and expects that when decollectivization and market reforms occur, the peasants will 'demand democratic rights and ensure that the party "withers away"' through popular pressure from below' (p. 11).

Parish, William L. (ed.), *Chinese Rural Development. The Great Transformation*, M. E. Sharpe, Armonk and London, 1985. This is a collection of papers presented at a conference in 1981, and based on scholarly and field research carried out just after the policies of reform were introduced. It covers such topics as peasant incentives, equality and inequality, and welfare, with substantial focus given to specific areas of China.

Perkins, Dwight and Yusuf, Shahid, *Rural Development in China*, Johns Hopkins University Press, Baltimore and London, 1984. This is a World Bank study which covers the dual economy, agricultural production, organizational changes, income distribution, health care, education and other matters. The authors are critically but favourably impressed with the changes wrought over the period since 1949, especially in areas such as public health.

Perry, Elizabeth J. and Wong, Christine, *The Political Economy of Reform in Post-Mao China,* The Council on East Asian Studies/Harvard University, Cambridge, Mass., and London, 1985. This volume grew from a workshop held at Harvard University in 1983. Its two parts consider agriculture and industry: five of the ten chapters are by economists, the rest by political scientists. One theme to emerge is the interconnection of economics and politics. The editors consider the results of reform to 1983 mixed and the prognosis uncertain.

Porter, Ian, Taylor, Robert P. et al., *China, Long-term Development Issues and Options,* Johns Hopkins University Press, Baltimore and London, 1985. This is a World Bank country study covering agriculture, energy development, international economic strategy, industrial technology, human development and other factors. It is based on two visits to China by an economic mission in 1984. The study takes a calm look at China's serious economic problems, but considers that 'China's long-term development objectives seem attainable in principle, and if recent experience is any guide, there is a good chance that they will be attained in practice.' (p. 20)

Reynolds, Bruce L. (ed. and intro.), *Reform in China: Challenges & Choices: A Summary and Analysis of the CESRRI Survey,* M. E. Sharpe, Armonk, New York and London, 1987. In 1986 the Chinese-language book *Gaige: Women mianlingde tiaozhan yu xuanze (Reform: The Challenges and Choices We Face)* was published from 156 reports produced under the leadership of the China Economic System Reform Research Institute (CESRRI). This is the English edition. It contains eleven chapters, including discussion of the most important achievements of industrial reform, examination of some major problems and presentation of possible future solutions. It contains an enormous amount of data and information.

Riskin, Carl, *China's Political Economy, the Quest for Development since 1949,* Oxford University Press, Oxford, 1987. This is a thickly documented

and extremely scholarly account of China's economic development from 1949 to 1985. Each chapter is designated by period and theme. While the author is impressed with the rise in per capita income in the period of reform, he believes that 'sustaining such growth rates of income will be difficult if not impossible' (p. 376).

Saith, Ashwani (ed.), *The Re-emergence of the Chinese Peasantry,* Croom Helm, London, 1987. The essays in this collective work compare the conditions for the Chinese peasants under collectivization and decollectivization. Most of the writers see decollectivization as having produced much growth, as opposed to the very low living standards of the preceding era, but Ajit Kumar Ghose believes that the rural performance from 1965 to 1975 was remarkable by any standards.

Selden, Mark and Lippit, Victor (eds), *The Transition to Socialism in China,* M. E. Sharpe, New York; Croom Helm, London, 1982. This book came out of a conference on the transition to socialism in China held in Washington D.C. in 1980. A range of scholars examines a series of ideological, economic and political issues connected with the transition to socialism. These include collectivization in the 1950s, the rise and fall of the Dazhai model, the role of the market in a poor socialist country such as China and the Maoist legacy in industry. Although there is much on the post-1978 reforms, the book is more a re-examination of policy under Mao and shows that there has been a shift towards pragmatism, not only in China itself but also among the left in the United States and other advanced capitalist countries.

Solinger, Dorothy J., *Chinese Business under Socialism, The Politics of Domestic Commerce 1949–1980,* University of California Press, Berkeley, 1985. The author sees three policy models towards commerce in the PRC, depending on which group holds power over goods at any particular time. The three essential groups are the radicals, whose concern is issues of class and equality, the bureaucrats, who care about state control, and the marketeers or reformers, concerned with productivity.

Vermeer, Eduard B., *Economic Development in*

Provincial China: The Central Shaanxi Since 1930, Cambridge University Press, Cambridge, 1988. One area, Guanzhong in central Shaanxi, is covered from about 1930 until the 1980s. Through an enormous amount of detail, numerous charts, figures and statistics, the author aims to show the much greater economic success of free markets and privately owned land over socialism.

Volti, Rudi, *Technology, Politics and Society in China*, Westview, Boulder, Col., 1982. Part I traces the development of technological policy in the PRC and considers theoretical and background issues, such as ideological and organizational aspects of technology. Part II takes up sectoral studies of areas such as agricultural, energy and medical technologies. The author concludes by pointing out that 'the Chinese model' has been forgotten, making China look like an ordinary underdeveloped country. However, he also praises China's record of accomplishment, though mixed, in producing a better life for the people.

Walder, Andrew, *Communist Neo-Traditionalism: Work and Authority in Chinese Industry*, University of California Press, Berkeley, Los Angeles and London, 1986. This book puts forward a theory that Chinese authority in the workplace, and indeed 'the national political order' as well, is based not on totalitarian power but on 'communist neo-traditionalism'. This means 'a clientelist system in which public loyalty to the party and its ideology is mingled with personal loyalties between party branch officials and their clients' (p. 6). The basis of this clientelism is not traditional culture or institutions, but rather the structure of 'Communist' industrial organization as it evolved after 1949. The sources for this very scholarly work include government documents and interviews with former Chinese industrial employees living in Hong Kong or the United States.

Walker, Kenneth R., *Food Grain Procurement and Consumption in China*, Cambridge University Press, Cambridge, London and New York, 1984. This work of agroeconomics deals with the years 1953–62 and the late 1970s, but focuses most attention on the 1950s because of the better statistical material available. Over 100 pages are devoted to appendixes. Walker believes the agricultural depression of the 1960s was inevitable due to conditions and policies before 1958. He shows rising national output per head from the 1950s to 1970s, together with decreasing inter-provincial inequality.

Zweig, David, *Agrarian Radicalism in China, 1968–1981*, Harvard University Press, Cambridge, Mass., 1989. Zweig sees the struggle over the degree of collectivization which should occur as one between radicals and moderates. He argues that collectivization turned peasants into 'coolies for rural cadres' and strengthened the power of a voracious state which consumed everything the peasants produced (p. 193).

G. POPULATION

Banister, Judith, *China's Changing Population*, Stanford University Press, Stanford, 1987. A brilliant, highly scholarly and thickly documented book covering the whole period of the PRC, but with more focus on the post-Mao period than any other. It covers fertility decline, mortality, late marriage and birth planning, the one-child family campaign and other relevant matters. The author is critical but broadly positive about the PRC's record in population matters.

Croll, Elisabeth, Davin, Delia and Kane, Penny (eds), *China's One-Child Family Policy*, Macmillan, London, 1985. Based on papers given at a workshop in 1983, this book contains eight chapters by a range of authors on various aspects of the one-child policy, including the policy in the cities and countryside and birth-control methods. There are also comparisons with Singapore. The authors tend to be defensive of the policy, despite recognition of its inherent problems.

Kane, Penny, *The Second Billion, Population and Family Planning in China*, Penguin Books, Ringwood, Victoria, 1987. A sensitive and scholarly work, on a scale somewhat smaller than Banister's, which traces the development of the PRC's population policies in great detail, and also covers family planning in both urban and rural areas. The author considers that China's family-planning program 'has been successful on a scale not previously seen anywhere' (p. 2).

Population Census Office of the State Council of the People's Republic of China and the Institute of Geography of the Chinese Academy of Sciences (eds), *The Population Atlas of China*, Oxford University Press, Hong Kong, 1987. This atlas is based on the 1982 census of the PRC, but also includes material from those of 1953 and 1964. The introduction explains the scope of the maps and charts, population distribution, ethnicity, sex and age, population change, educational level, employment and so on. There is a long appendix giving statistics for population indicators by county and city unit.

Tien, H. Yuan (ed.), *Population Theory in China*, M. E. Sharpe, White Plains, NY; Croom Helm, London, 1980. Most of this book is devoted to translations of Chinese commentaries on population matters, especially three chapters from *Renkou Lilun (Population Theory)*, written by a team headed by Liu Zheng and published in 1977 by the Office of Population Research of the Beijing Economics Institute, later the People's University. There is an explanatory introduction by the editor.

H. THE MINORITY NATIONALITIES

Dessaint, Alain Y., *Minorities of Southwest China, An Introduction to the Yi (Lolo) and Related Peoples and an Annotated Bibliography*, HRAF Press, New Haven, 1980. This work gives an annotated bibliography of eleven of China's southwestern nationalities which the author terms 'Yi peoples', including a short introduction on their languages, history, present condition and ethnography.

Dreyer, June Teufel, *China's Forty Millions, Minority Nationalities and National Integration in the People's Republic of China*, Harvard University Press, Cambridge, Mass. and London, 1976. A pioneering study which traces the PRC's policy towards the minority nationalities down to 1975 against the historical background. The author credits the CCP 'with having made sincere, sustained, and often creative efforts' to deal with the

minorities (p. 276) within a policy of integration and accommodation, not assimilation.

Grunfeld, A. Tom, *The Making of Modern Tibet*, Zed Books, London, M.E. Sharpe, Armonk, 1987. This is an extremely detailed and thoroughly researched account of Tibetan history, with just over half dealing with the period since 1950. Two valuable appendixes discuss Tibet's population and present the various attitudes towards Tibetan independence. The author's aspiration is towards 'disinterested and dispassionate history' (p. 3). This book is considerably less critical of the Chinese and their role in Tibet than most English-language accounts of Tibet.

Harrer, Heinrich, trans. Osers, Ewald, *Return to Tibet*, Penguin, Harmondsworth, 1985. This book was first published in Germany in 1983, and in England by Weidenfeld and Nicolson in 1984. There have been several Penguin imprints. Harrer lived and worked in the old Tibet and wrote of his experiences in his well known *Seven Years in Tibet*. The present book records his impressions, mainly sharply negative, on a return to Tibet in 1982. There is a good deal of historical commentary, but the focus is the present.

Heberer, Thomas, *China and its National Minorities, Autonomy or Assimilation*, M. E. Sharpe, Armonk and London, 1989. This is a very substantial revision of a German-language work published in 1984 by the University of Bremen. It covers problems of the identification of the minority nationalities, the issue of autonomy, the case of Yunnan province, population policies and religion. The author concludes that 'the number of nationalities could be diminished over the long term by deliberate linguistic and cultural assimilation, which would result in increased uniformity among the population' (p. 130).

Lee Chae-Jin, *China's Korean Minority: The Politics of Ethnic Education*, Westview, Boulder, Col. and London, 1986. This book is based on visits to Korean areas of China, written materials and talks with several hundred Koreans. It examines the history of China's Korean nationality and of the policies towards education followed in the the Yanbian Korean autonomous prefecture in Jilin province. The author considers that the

Koreans in China have 'tenaciously sustained a considerable range of ethnically oriented educational opportunities for their children' (p. 141).

Moseley, George V. H. III, *The Consolidation of the South China Frontier*, University of California Press, Berkeley, Los Angeles, London, 1973. The focus here is on the minority nationalities of Yunnan and Guangxi and their integration into the PRC until the Cultural Revolution. The book includes a chapter on the economic aspects of regional autonomy in Guangxi. The author's conclusion is that 'the non-Han peoples have been rather successfully integrated into China's new polity' with the result that the PRC's southern frontier regions 'are not so vulnerable to outside penetration as they once were' (p. 173).

Schwarz, Henry G., *The Minorities of Northern China, A Survey*, Western Washington University, Bellingham, Washington, 1984. This book surveys twenty-one minority nationalities of Northern China. They are divided into the Turkic, Mongolian and Manchu–Tungus groups, and others. For each nationality, details are given on population, location, history, language, recent developments, literature and arts, society and religion. There is an extremely thorough general bibliography as well as one for each nationality covered.

Solinger, Dorothy J., *Regional Government and Political Integration in Southwest China, 1949–1954, A Case Study*, University of California Press, Berkeley, Los Angeles, London, 1977. This is a study of regionalism and the processes of integration in the early PRC years. The case study covers Sichuan, Yunnan, Guizhou and Xikang provinces, all of which include substantial minority populations. In her evaluation of the processes of integration, the author states that 'integration was hindered both because of faults in the bureaucracy and because policy was misapplied' (p. 230).

I. EDUCATION

Cleverley, John, *The School of China, Tradition and Modernity in Chinese Education*, George Allen & Unwin, Sydney, London, Boston, 1985. This book covers all periods of education in China, but it mainly deals with the CCP and PRC, and three of the fifteen chapters concern the period since the death of Mao. The author has used only English-language sources, yet it is both a scholarly and readable account.

Hayhoe, Ruth (ed.), *Contemporary Chinese Education*, M. E. Sharpe, Armonk, Croom Helm, London and Sydney, 1984. The various chapters of this collective book consider the levels of institution from primary to secondary and higher education, as well as teacher training and adult education. The editor's conclusion discusses China's scholarly exchanges with the West since 1977 and assesses their implications for Chinese education. The book has much to say on the structure of the Chinese education system and its relationship with the rest of Chinese society.

Hayhoe, Ruth, *China's Universities and the Open Door*, M. E. Sharpe, Armonk, 1988. The first half of this book deals mainly with China's domestic educational developments, and the second half with China's re-entry into the world community. Hayhoe focuses on the 'fundamental contradiction' between education and knowledge as a tool of political control and a means towards economic modernization. She places great emphasis on the continuities with Confucian knowledge patterns in contemporary China.

Kallgren, Joyce K. and Simon, Denis Fred, *Educational Exchanges: Essays on the Sino-American Experience*, Institute of East Asian Studies, University of California, Berkeley, 1987. A thorough study by thirteen contributors based on conference papers. There is some treatment of the pre-1949 period, but the main coverage is of the PRC, especially the 1980s. Several major controversial issues connected with the exchanges are brought out.

Kwong, Julia, *Cultural Revolution in China's Schools. May 1966–April 1969*, Hoover Institution Press, Stanford, 1988. Based mainly on interviews, this book describes student factionalism in the Cultural Revolution. It concludes that the cult of Mao Zedong filled the vacuum left by the breakdown of tight controls on students, resulting in factionalism and the legitimation of violence.

Montaperto, Ronald N. and Henderson, Jay (eds), *China's Schools in Flux*, M. E. Sharpe, White

Plains, NY, 1979. This is the report of the State Education Leaders Delegation, National Committee on United States–China Relations, which visited China in 1977. It covers many aspects of education, including curriculum, early childhood education and family and community involvement. The delegation's main conclusions concerned the importance attached to education and the high priority given to political education.

Price, R. F., *Education in Modern China*, Routledge & Kegan Paul, London, 1979. This work, originally published as *Education in Communist China* in 1970, covers topics such as the educational aims and ideas of Mao, obstacles to educational reform, the education system, teachers, the impact of the Cultural Revolution and education after Mao. In a chapter on 'the moral–political educators' Price examines the crucial role of political organizations such as the CCP on education.

Rosen, Stanley, *Red Guard Factionalism and the Cultural Revolution in Guangzhou (Canton)*, Westview, Boulder, Col., 1982. This is an analysis of factionalism among secondary school students from 1966 to 1968 in Guangzhou which also includes material on educational aims and student relationships from 1960 to 1966. The main sources are the official press, Red Guard newspapers and interviews carried out in Hong Kong with Chinese emigrés from 1971 to 1976 and in 1980.

Seybolt, Peter J., *Revolutionary Education in China, Documents and Commentary,* International Arts and Sciences Press, White Plains, N.Y., 1973. The documents are grouped under general categories such as 'general directives', 'control of the schools', 'teachers and teaching' and 'higher-level technical training'. Commentary is provided in a substantial introduction, which is positive about Chinese educational efforts and decisively disagrees with those who believed that the Cultural Revolution would irreparably damage China.

Shirk, Susan L., *Competitive Comrades: Career Incentives and Student Strategies in China*, University of California Press, Berkeley, Los Angeles, London, 1982. This study is based mainly on interviews with refugees in Hong Kong. It examines the effects of educational policy on the urban students who went through the system from Liberation through to the late 1970s. The author considers China to be a 'virtuocracy', that being a system where occupational selection is through virtue, not through merit or traditional means. She believed the trend at the time she wrote was towards meritocracy and foresaw the possibility that this could make the youth 'go against the tide' in order to seek the moral reformation of politics.

Unger, Jonathan, *Education under Mao: Class and Competition in Canton Schools, 1960–1980*, Columbia University Press, New York, 1982. This work examines the impact of class policy on the educational opportunities of people in various social groups. The first section covers the 1960s; the second the late 1960s to mid-1970s. The author believes nothing was solved through two decades of educational debate and that from 1960 to 1980 Chinese education went full circle in terms of dilemmas and problems, but lost ground in terms of quality and standards.

J. CULTURE AND SOCIETY

Andors, Phyllis, *The Unfinished Liberation of China Women, 1949–1980*, Indiana University Press, Bloomington; Wheatsheaf Books Sussex, 1983. After a chapter on women in pre-1949 China, this book traces the position of women chronologically from 1950 to 1980. The author is concerned with the relationship between economic development, industrialization and modernization on the one hand and the productive roles and status of women on the other. She argues that the period of the Cultural Revolution and afterwards to 1976 had benefits for women, but criticizes the emphasis on ideology as opposed to analysis of the important structural impediments with which women still had to cope. She considers that there was 'a retreat from the goals of female emancipation in post-Mao China, (p. 169).

Chan, Anita, *Children of Mao, Personality Development and Political Activism in the Red Guard Generation*, University of Washington Press, Seattle; Macmillan, London, 1985. This is an excellent scholarly study of fourteen young Chinese, interviewed by the author, and their development through the Chinese education system and the Cultural Revolution to later disillusionment. All fourteen were found to have authoritarian personalities, perceiving the world in terms of the forces of good and evil. Chan's main conclusion is that their personalities have been imposed on them by the authoritarianism of the system, even though she claims no 'deliberate process of political socialization on the part of the party' (p. 222).

Chan, Anita, Madsen, Richard and Unger, Jonathan, *Chen Village*, University of California Press, Berkeley, 1984. Based on interviews with twenty-six of its inhabitants who had moved to Hong Kong, this study discusses the changes in the lives of the people in a South China farming village from the mid-1960s to the early 1980s. The coverage is chronological, with an emphasis on political campaigns, which 'all too often had been employed to bludgeon a minority of the villagers' and enforce conformity and reticence, with a resulting exhaustion among the peasantry (p. 281).

Chang, Arnold, *Painting in the People's Republic of China, The Politics of Style*, Westview, Boulder, Col., 1980. There are three main chapters: one on policies towards painting, beginning with Mao Zedong's 'Talks at the Yan'an Forum', one giving an overview of art and artists under the PRC, with emphasis on traditional-style ink painting, and one discussing a few specific painters in more detail. Nearly a third of the book is given to reproductions of paintings. The main aesthetic lesson the author draws is 'that artistic styles evolve gradually, and that an artistic revolution must ultimately be carried out by artists, and not by government spokesmen' (p. 77).

Chu, Godwin C. and Hsu Francis L. K. (eds), *Moving a Mountain, Cultural Change in China*, University Press of Hawaii, Honolulu, 1979. This volume is the result of a conference held in Honolulu in 1979 on the subject of cultural change in China. Topics covered include the communication system, political culture and value change. The editors see areas of strong continuity, others of extensive change, and 'perhaps the world's best-co-ordinated communication system' to push change ahead (p. 408). They believe Mao was aware of the need to change China by an ideological approach and knew that the process would take time.

Clark, Paul, *Chinese Cinema, Culture and Politics since 1949*, Cambridge University Press, Cambridge, 1987. After a chapter on 'film and Chinese society before 1949', the author goes on to discuss PRC cinema and its relationship to politics and society period by period, ending with a discussion of the 1984 film *Yellow Earth,* which 'signaled the emergence of a fifth generation of filmmakers and a Chinese New Wave' (p. 184). Other material includes a 'filmography' which lists every film mentioned in the book.

Croll, Elisabeth, *Chinese Women Since Mao*, Zed Press, London, 1983. Chapter topics include peasant women, urban working women, child care, love, marriage and divorce, and the one-child family. The last chapter summarizes the main content. Croll gives the PRC credit for genuine attempts to improve the position of women, but considers that in the process of carrying out its policies, the leadership has focused far too much attention on ideology to the neglect of 'the underlying structures of the political economy' (p. 129).

Croll, Elisabeth, *The Politics of Marriage in Contemporary China*, Cambridge University Press, Cambridge, 1981. Croll is here 'primarily concerned with the processes of change within the institution of marriage' in the PRC (p. ix). There are separate chapters on age at marriage, the ceremonial of marriage and the choice of marriage partners. She has placed much emphasis on the substitution of free-choice marriage for arranged marriage, but also on the difficulties of implementing this reform and on the factors limiting its adoption.

Davin, Delia, *Woman-Work: Women and the Party in Revolutionary China*, Clarendon Press, Oxford, 1976. This is a thorough and detailed account of official policy towards women and the real situation, with emphasis on the 1950s. Topics covered include the Women's Federation, the *Marriage Law* of 1950 and its impact, and the position of women in the urban and rural areas. The overall argument is that a fundamental change has taken place and the position of women has greatly improved, but that shortcomings remain serious everywhere and 'women are still a long way from economic equality with men in the countryside' (p. 19).

Duke, Michael S., *Blooming and Contending: Chinese Literature in the Post-Mao Era*, Indiana University Press, Bloomington, 1985. Duke analyzes the political background and the works of a number of controversial writers of the late 1970s and early 1980s, such as Liu Binyan and Bai Hua. He calls this the period of 'the second "Hundred Flowers" policy' and sees in it a re-emergence of humanism in the Confucian and May Fourth traditions. The younger exponents of post-Mao literature he describes as a 'thinking generation'.

Goldblatt, Howard (ed.), *Chinese Literature for the 1980s, The Fourth Congress of Writers and Artists*, M. E. Sharpe, Armonk and London, 1982. This consists of sixteen speeches delivered at the Fourth Congress of Writers and Artists held in 1979, together with a short introduction by the editor. The speeches, given by Mao Dun, Deng Xiaoping, Bai Hua, Liu Binyan and others, illustrate the thinking of CCP authorities and artists just after the drastic change in policies on the arts which followed the destructive radicalism of the Cultural Revolution.

Goldman, Merle, *China's Intellectuals, Advise and Dissent*, Harvard University Press, Cambridge, Mass. and London, 1981. This highly scholarly and perceptive book traces the role of intellectuals in the PRC state to the late 1970s. The author sees a process of 'advice and dissent' involving 'myth deflation', 'critical judgment' and 'increasing exposure to Western ideas'. She believes the PRC has the opportunity for a new pattern of relationships to emerge between intellectuals and the regime, but a by-product is the undermining of 'the very ideological consensus that Chinese governments have always thought necessary in order to rule' (p. 245).

Goldman, Merle, with Cheek, Timothy and Hamrin, Carol Lee (eds), *China's Intellectuals and the State: In Search of a New Relationship*, Harvard Contemporary China Series No. 3, Harvard University Press, 1987. This deals generally with the relationship between intellectuals and the state in the post-Mao period. It includes studies of individuals, such as 'ideological spokesman' Ai Siqi, historian Jian Bozan, and philosopher–journalist Wang Ruoshui, and groups such as legal professionals, scientists and writers. An integrative introduction characterizes the relationship of the intellectuals to the Party in the Deng Xiaoping era as one of 'limited autonomy' (p. 19).

Goodman, David S. G. (ed.), *Beijing Street Voices. The Poetry and Politics of China's Democracy Movement*, Marion Boyars Publishers, London and Salem, New Hampshire, 1981. Translations of poems which appeared as part of the Democracy Movement in Beijing from November 1978 to April 1979 are presented, accompanied by detailed explanations and commentary and arranged to focus on what they show about the politics and society of the period.

Hamrin, Carol Lee and Cheek, Timothy (eds), *China's Establishment Intellectuals*, M. E. Sharpe, Armonk, New York and London, 1986. This book contains essays on some of the PRC's main intellectuals, including Yang Xianzhen, Sun Yefang, Wu Han, Deng Tuo, Peng Zhen and Bai Hua. There is also one on alienated youth, especially of the 1980s. It (together with the preceding volume but one) aims 'to understand how a changing Chinese Marxism both reflects and shapes the lives of the intelligentsia in China' (p. vii). It explores the motives for collaboration between leading intellectuals and the top CCP leadership, and classifies such specialists as 'establishment intellectuals'.

Johnson, Kay Ann, *Women, the Family and Peasant Revolution in China*, University of Chicago Press, Chicago and London, 1983. This book analyzes CCP policy towards women from the 1920s to 1979, focusing on reforms in marriage, family and kinship practices. It gives considerable attention to the *Marriage Law* of 1950 and to the Campaign to Criticize Lin Biao and Confucius of 1973 and 1974, since the author argues that only then did the CCP and government make serious efforts to bring about family reform and gender equality.

Kinkley, Jeffrey C. (ed.), *After Mao, Chinese Litera-*

ture and Society, 1978–1981, Harvard University Press, Cambridge, Mass., 1985. This is a collection of seven papers given at a conference on contemporary Chinese literature in New York in 1982, with an introduction by the editor. There are three parts: 'Literary Subject Matter', 'Literary Art' and 'The Sociology of Publishing and Reading'. The last and longest chapter discusses the role of fiction on the entertainment and cultural scene and looks at the sources of fiction in society, such as bookshops, libraries, reading rooms and friends.

Mackerras, Colin, *The Performing Arts in Contemporary China*, Routledge & Kegan Paul, London, 1981. The focus here is on the period from 1976 to 1980 and on drama. There is also material on the years down to 1976 and on cinema and music. The author considers that 'successful modernisation cannot fail to bring a deleterious effect on traditional theatre forms' (p. 214).

McDougall, Bonnie S. (ed.), *Popular Chinese Literature and Performing Arts in the People's Republic of China, 1949–1979*, University of California Press, Berkeley, Los Angeles and London, 1984. Although some space is given to the literary and drama practices of the war period of the 1940s, the focus is on the *xiangsheng*, song, cinema, fiction, drama and poetry of the first three decades of the PRC. In her conclusion, McDougall argues a tendency from an author-centred to an audience-centred culture. She distinguishes between the 'popular audience' of the pre-1949 period and the 'mass audience' of the PRC, the latter being 'circumscribed by an authority that is more concerned with what the masses should have than with what they want' (pp. 282–3). She believes 'Yan'an populism' is 'likely to be only a passing phase' in China's cultural history (p. 304).

Mosher, Steven W., *Broken Earth: The Rural Chinese*, The Free Press, New York, 1983. The author lived in and studied a village in Guangdong province in 1979–80 as a postgraduate student of Stanford University. He paints a bleakly negative picture of a corrupt and cruel society there. His attitudes and behaviour, and the publication of this book, proved extremely controversial.

Mosher, Steven W., *Journey to the Forbidden China*, The Free Press, New York, 1985. This book is based on a very short trip of six days by dirt roads through Guangdong, Guangxi and Guizhou during the author's stay in 1979–80. He portrays a shocking level of misery and concludes that the Chinese Communist Party has forgotten and betrayed the peasantry, and even squeezed them on behalf of industry.

Myrdal, Jan, trans. Michael, Maurice, *Report from a Chinese Village*, William Heinemann, London, 1965, Pan Books, London, 1975 edn; Pantheon, New York, 1981. The book consists of interviews with people from the village of Liu Ling in northern Shaanxi province, where the author spent one month in 1962. The interviews are presented in such a way that they tell their own story. For most interviewees there are notes on what others said of them.

Smil, Vaclav, *The Bad Earth, Environmental Degradation in China*, M. E. Sharpe, Armonk, Zed Press, London, 1984. This book brings together substantial information on water, land and biotic resources, on urban and rural conditions, and on official policies on conservation and the environment. As the title suggests, Smil argues that the environment is a disaster area in the PRC due to a variety of factors including population increase, irrational agricultural policies, official stupidity and corruption.

Stacey, Judith, *Patriarchy and Socialist Revolution in China*, University of California Press, Berkeley, 1983. In this book Stacey puts forward a detailed feminist theory explaining the relationship between socialism, the development of the family and women's role in society. She argues that patriarchy survives strongly in China, even though there has been a radical reconstruction of its family system. She claims that the CCP never wanted a women's revolution, but preferred to maintain a stable family system in a patriarchal style.

Tung, Constantine and Mackerras, Colin (eds), *Drama in the People's Republic of China*, State University of New York Press, Albany, 1987. Based on a conference held in Buffalo, New York, in 1984, this collection of papers is divided into four parts: 'Drama on Historical Themes', 'Drama, Ideal and Theory', 'Post-1976 Theater and Drama' and 'Foreign Theaters in China: Two Case Studies'. An introduction by the first of the two editors gives a fairly detailed chronological summation of the relationship between theatre and politics in the PRC.

Whyte, Martin King and Parish, William L., *Urban Life in Contemporary China*, University of Chicago Press, Chicago, 1984. This account has three parts: Urban Political Economy, Family Behaviour and Quality of Life, each of them subdivided into chapters. The authors cover the PRC period but focus more attention on the mid-1970s than any other years. They see some very distinctive features of Chinese urbanism, including strict migration controls and minimal urbanization, despite considerable economic development. They are struck by the *lack* of change in basic elements of Chinese family life: 'There are few signs of the kinds of family disorganization that sometimes accompany urbanism.' (p. 369)

Wolf, Margery, *Revolution Postponed: Women in Contemporary China*, Stanford University Press, Stanford, 1985. This is an excellent study of women in contemporary China, which concludes that, although the position of women has improved greatly under the CCP, the interests of women have always been sacrificed first in any crisis. In the period of reform, 'women are being told to step aside in the interests of the nation' yet again (p. 26). The author is pessimistic about the future.

Young, Marilyn B., *Women in China: Studies in Social Change and Feminism*, University of Michigan Center for Chinese Studies, Ann Arbor, 1973. Female feminist sinologists explore the struggle for women's rights in China. The whole of the twentieth century is covered, as is Taiwan, but the focus is on the PRC. Topics include women in the early communist movement, institutionalized motivation for fertility limitation, and the lessons for women in the Chinese and Soviet revolutions. The main 'lesson' is that 'women must win and hold power themselves' during the revolutionary period, and the author argues that this has not happened either in China or the Soviet Union.

K. GEOGRAPHY

China Handbook Editorial Committee, trans. Liang Liangxing, *Geography*, Foreign Languages Press, Beijing, 1983. This work covers China's territory, topography, climate and rivers and lakes. It then looks at all the provinces, centrally administered municipalities and autonomous regions individually. The approach is factual, rather than interpretive.

Sun Jingzhi (ed.), *The Economic Geography of China*, Oxford University Press, Hong Kong, 1988. This work presents developments in China's economic geography from 1949 to 1980. It is a translation of *Zhongguo jingji dili gailun*, published in Beijing in 1984, and the material has not been updated. There are chapters on industry, agriculture and various means of transport and communications. The book includes fifty-seven maps.

Zhao Songqiao, *Physical Geography of China*, Science Press, Beijing and John Wiley, New York, 1986. This joint production is beautifully produced, with extensive maps, diagrams and photographs. The explanations, which have been reduced in translation from the original Chinese, include a general survey, discussion of climatic and geomorphological features, water, soils and land, together with an account of the major physical regions.

5

FOREIGN RELATIONS

Note: Events which have featured in China's foreign relations since 1949 are given in detail in a special category in Chapter 1, while Chapter 4 devotes a section to the substantial literature on the same topic.

China's overwhelming foreign relations aims since 1949 have been the defence of her own security and interests, and the desire for international respect. Consequently, her dominant concerns have been firstly with the Soviet Union and the United States, secondly with the nations, interests and conflicts of her own region, and thirdly with general international bodies, in particular the United Nations, and issues, including nuclear disarmament. Although China has tried to befriend most of the nations of the Third World, these countries have rarely loomed as large in her thinking as any of the categories of nations and issues mentioned above; nor have they been as important as China's public pronouncements might suggest.

RELATIONS WITH THE SOVIET UNION

The Soviet Union recognized the new PRC on October 2, 1949, the day after it was established. Mao Zedong and Zhou Enlai visited Moscow shortly afterwards and the Sino-Soviet Treaty of Friendship, Alliance and Mutual Assistance was signed in Moscow on February 14, 1950. The excellent relations China enjoyed with the Soviet Union thereafter began to deteriorate after Khrushchev's deStalinization speech at the Twentieth Congress of the Communist Party of the Soviet Union (February 25, 1956). In April 1960, China charged, through an article in its main ideological journal *Red Flag*, that the Soviet Union was changing and negating Lenin's concept of imperialism, and thus began serious polemics with its former ally.

National issues quickly assumed much more importance than ideological ones. The Soviet Union

believed the Great Leap Forward and the establishment of the people's communes in 1958 to be not only unMarxist, but also exercises in madness, and in the summer of 1960 withdrew all its experts from China, causing serious problems for a Chinese economy which was already in dire straits. According to a later Chinese claim, the Soviet Union refused to fulfil a nuclear-sharing agreement it reached with the Chinese leadership in 1957.

The Soviet Union also denounced the Cultural Revolution in strong terms. In 1969 Sino-Soviet relations reached a nadir, with armed clashes along the border. By then China had reached the conclusion that Soviet social imperialism was an even more serious threat to her security and to the peace of the world than United States imperialism.

The death of Mao Zedong in 1976 at first opened the possibility of a thaw in relations, but the Chinese soon let it be known that they still regarded opposition to Soviet interests as the lynchpin of their foreign policy. A long article published in *People's Daily* on November 1, 1977 fulsomely praised Mao Zedong's theory of the 'three worlds', and in foreign policy terms gave top prominence to its anti-Soviet implications. In particular, the article declared that the Soviet Union was 'more ferocious, more reckless and more treacherous' than the United States, and 'the most dangerous source of world war'. In the late 1970s China's relations with the Soviet Union again worsened, due to the Soviet invasion of Afghanistan, which began at the end of 1979, and other factors.

In 1982, the Soviet Union began very tentatively to seek a normalization of relations with China, which responded by setting down 'three obstacles': troops along the Sino-Soviet and Sino-Mongolian borders; Soviet support for Vietnam's occupation of Kampuchea; and the Soviet occupation of Afghanistan. At first progress towards normalization was extremely slow, but it gathered momentum following Mikhail Gorbachev's accession to power in 1985. In his Vladivostok speech of July 28, 1986, he made several concrete proposals to improve relations, including co-operation in space exploration. In mid-May, 1989 Gorbachev made a major visit to Beijing and Shanghai, during which relations were declared 'normalized' in a joint communiqué.

Foreign Minister Qian Qichen's reaction to the disintegration of power of the communist parties in Eastern Europe at the end of 1989 was one of pessimism. He predicted that regional turmoil and world instability would result which, in the final analysis, he believed would 'be unfavourable to the people of all countries'. When Gorbachev was elected as president of the Soviet Union with widely expanded powers in mid-March 1990, his Chinese counterpart, Yang Shangkun, sent him a message of congratulations and called for further improvements in Sino-Soviet relations.

RELATIONS WITH THE UNITED STATES AND THE WEST

The PRC's relations with the main capitalist countries of the world began on a bad footing. In August 1949, even before the establishment of the PRC, the United States government issued a white paper denouncing Mao Zedong's statement of the previous month, that China under the CCP would 'lean to one side', namely that of the Soviet Union. Great Britain, however, recognized the PRC in January 1950.

It was the Korean War of June 1950 to July 1953 which solidified hostility between the PRC and the capitalist countries, by far the most important of which was the United States. A United Nations resolution of June 27 called on UN members to assist the Republic of Korea, and several Western countries, including the United States, Britain and Australia, sent troops. China immediately denounced the resolution as illegal, and in October its troops began fighting on behalf of the Democratic People's Republic of Korea. This meant that Chinese troops and those of several Western countries were taking part on opposing sides. Each side declared the other to be the aggressor in Korea, but China also feared for its own security, and even accused the United States of air intrusions and the use of germ warfare in its northeast.

Several issues kept Sino-American relations at a low ebb in the late 1950s and early 1960s. These included a crisis in the Taiwan Straits between August and October 1958 and Tibet. The United States was among many countries condemning the Chinese for violating human rights in Tibet and suppressing the uprising there in March 1959, while China accused the United States of directly assisting the old ruling classes to mount the rebellion in the first place (see also Chapter 9).

France established full diplomatic relations at ambassadorial level in 1962, but the United States maintained its hostility towards the PRC for most of the 1960s. In the first instance, United States intervention in Vietnam (with combat troops from 1965 on) made relations with China even more bitter than in the preceding few years, since China supported the left-wing forces which were fighting against the United States. However, in contrast to the Korean War, Chinese troops never intervened in Vietnam, nor did United States ground troops actually invade North Vietnam; as a result, Chinese and American troops never fought against each other in Vietnam. For China, the poison tended to go out of relations with the United States as those with the Soviet Union worsened in the late 1960s.

It was during the 1970s that most of the capitalist countries and others friendly with them established diplomatic relations with the PRC. The United States president, Richard Nixon, visited China in February 1972, resulting in a vast improvement in China's image in the West. Early in 1979, to enormous fanfare, Deng Xiaoping visited the United States just after the formal establishment of relations between the two countries at ambassadorial level. This represented one of the most intense points of China's friendship with the West and hostility towards the Soviet Union.

During most of the 1980s, China proclaimed its foreign policy to be 'independent'. The Western countries and Japan were happy to contribute to China's modernization programs; consequently her overall relations with them remained generally positive. Economic and socio-cultural ties between China on the one hand, and the Western countries and Japan on the other, expanded to represent a substantial investment by each side in the other.

In the case of the United States, the major problem in the early 1980s remained the issue of Taiwan. China expressed extreme displeasure over the continuation of United States arms sales to Taiwan. In August 1982, a joint communiqué was signed in Beijing by Chinese and American representatives, in which the United States declared it would eventually cease the arms sales, but gave no timetable for so doing. Although the communiqué did not really resolve the issue, neither side chose to allow it to disrupt bilateral relations unduly.

In 1987, Tibet re-emerged as an issue in Sino-American relations. In September, during a visit to the United States, the Dalai Lama called for Tibet to be designated as a 'zone of peace' and denounced China's policies and actions there. Immediately afterwards, pro-independence disturbances broke out in Lhasa, and were suppressed by the Chinese authorities. The United States condemned China for human rights breaches, while China demanded that the United States stop interfering in its domestic affairs. A series of similar disturbances among the Tibetans followed over the following months, the worst occurrence being in March 1989. These events produced similar condemnations in the United States and counter-reactions from the Chinese government.

For Great Britain, Hong Kong was the main issue in relations with China in the 1980s. In September 1982, in response to a statement by British Prime Minister Margaret Thatcher that the treaties of the nineteenth century should continue to be regarded as valid, the Chinese Foreign Ministry reaffirmed its commitment to the reassertion of China's sovereignty over Hong Kong. In December 1984, Thatcher and Chinese Premier Zhao Ziyang signed the Sino-British Joint Declaration on Hong Kong, under which China would resume sovereignty over Hong Kong from July 1, 1997.

All Western and other advanced capitalist industrialized nations reacted with strong horror and condemnation to the Beijing massacre of early June 1989. Although none of them actually broke off diplomatic or economic relations, China was downgraded in their priorities and they took concrete measures of various kinds to show their disapproval, provoking pained and hostile reactions from China. (For further details, see Chapter 1, under *A. Foreign Affairs Events*, 1989.) Western and Japanese tourism to China declined sharply, and China's image in the West suffered severely. Human rights violations against pro-democracy dissidents were added to those against the Tibetans as a major issue in China's relations with the Western countries, and the United States in particular.

In an article on 'New China's Diplomacy: 40 Years On', marking the fortieth anniversary of the PRC's establishment in October 1989, the Minister of Foreign Affairs, Qian Qichen, claimed that China was still following a stand independent of the United States and the Soviet Union. He also attacked 'some Western countries' for regarding 'their values as absolute truth', and criticized them for interfering, exerting political pressure and applying economic sanctions: 'the Chinese people...will not submit to outside pressure,' he said.

CHINA AND THE UNITED NATIONS

A major factor in China's acceptance by many of the world's nations, especially those of the West, was its entry into the United Nations. In 1961 the United Nations General Assembly had adopted a resolution sponsored by the United States and four other countries designating the PRC's admission to occupy the China seat as an 'important question' requiring a two-thirds majority. This resolution, together with other factors, including the Cultural Revolution in China itself, had the effect of keeping the PRC out of the United Nations until October 25, 1971. On that day there were two votes on the China seat. One, concerning whether Taiwan's expulsion was an important question, was lost by fifty-nine votes to fifty-five, with fifteen abstentions. The other, the resolution calling for the restoration of the PRC's lawful rights in the United Nations and its related organizations, and for the immediate expulsion of Chiang Kaishek's representatives, was passed by seventy-six votes to thirty-five with seventeen abstentions.

Following this vote, formal decisions on the PRC's representation in the eight United Nations specialized agencies, as well as GATT and IAEA, were reached on the following dates:

- United Nations Education, Scientific and Cultural Organization (UNESCO)— October 29, 1971;
- Food and Agricultural Organization of the United Nations (FAO)—November 2, 1971;

- International Labour Organization (ILO)—November 16, 1971;
- General Agreement on Tariffs and Trade (GATT)—November 16, 1971;
- International Civil Aviation Organization (ICAO)—November 19, 1971;
- International Atomic Energy Agency (IAEA)—December 9, 1971;
- World Meteorological Organization (WMO)—February 24, 1972;
- Universal Postal Union (UPU)—April 13, 1972;
- World Health Organization (WHO)—May 10, 1972;
- Inter-Governmental Maritime Consultative Organization (IMCO)—May 23, 1972;
- International Telecommunication Union (ITU)—May 28, 1972.

China has taken an active role in the United Nations, including involvement in the UN's various councils and specialized agencies. It has participated in numerous United Nations-connected or sponsored international conferences and meetings, and has used the United Nations and associated international gatherings as a forum for its own policies on a wide range of international issues. On the whole, however, it has not attempted to assume a leadership role in the United Nations commensurate with its size or population.

CHINA AND NUCLEAR WEAPONS

China's reaction to the Partial Nuclear Test Ban Treaty of 1963 was negative. It advocated instead the total destruction of nuclear weapons. However, it carried out its own first nuclear test in October 1964, at the same time declaring that 'at no time and in no circumstances will China be the first to use nuclear weapons'. The Chinese government defended its nuclear program by arguing that it was necessary for China to secure itself against nuclear attack while the superpowers were still developing large nuclear arsenals.

At the Special United Nations General Assembly Session on Disarmament held in 1978, China's Foreign Minister Huang Hua repeated China's frequently stated position demanding the total destruction of nuclear weapons. He condemned both

superpowers for their nuclear (and other military) expansion and for hypocrisy in claiming to be maintaining peace, but his attacks on the Soviet Union were much more intense and hard-hitting than those on the United States.

In the 1980s China has stressed its demand that, since the two superpowers together possess 95 per cent of all the world's nuclear weapons, they should take the initiative to stop the arms race. China's reaction to the various steps taken by the Soviet Union and United States in this direction has been positive, but very low-key. Most importantly, it welcomed the signing of the Intermediate-range Nuclear Forces Agreement of December 1987 as a positive step towards reducing international tensions, but cautioned against overoptimism. On December 9, 1987, a Chinese Foreign Ministry spokesperson stated that the large size of the nuclear arsenals of the two superpowers 'remains a grave threat to the security of humanity, and the arms race is still far from being halted'.

China has continued to develop its own nuclear power capabilities. However, on March 21, 1986, in a speech given at a rally in Beijing to mark the United Nations' International Year of Peace, Premier Zhao Ziyang stated that 'China has not conducted nuclear tests in the atmosphere for many years and will no longer conduct atmospheric nuclear tests in the future'. In his article on 'New China's Diplomacy: 40 Years On', marking the fortieth anniversary of the PRC's establishment in October 1989, Foreign Minister Qian Qichen repeated China's claim to have respected and supported efforts to establish nuclear-free zones and peace zones. With regard to conventional weapons, he stated that China had taken the lead in lowering the rate of military expenditure, which he gave at 17.5 per cent of the 1979 state budget, but only 8 per cent of the 1988 budget.

CHINA AND THE KAMPUCHEA CONFLICT

The most important conflict with international dimensions in the East or South-east Asian region in the 1980s was over Kampuchea (Cambodia). On November 3, 1978, the Soviet Union and Vietnam signed their Treaty of Friendship and Co-operation, which Deng Xiaoping immediately denounced as a threat to China and to peace and security in the Asian–Pacific region. At the end of 1978, Vietnam, with Soviet approval and support, invaded Kampuchea and overthrew the Khmer Rouge régime of Pol Pot, which had very good relations with China. The new pro-Vietnamese régime, headed by Heng Samrin, was immediately opposed by China, which called for the withdrawal of Vietnamese troops and the reinstatement of the Khmer Rouge. A guerrilla war began against the Vietnamese, and the Kampuchean government which they supported. China believed a pro-Soviet Vietnam was a threat to her security, while Vietnam believed the threat China already posed to its security would be substantially increased by the return of the pro-Chinese Khmer Rouge in Kampuchea. In June 1982, three Kampuchean groups opposed to Vietnam formed a coalition, headed by Norodom Sihanouk, and continued to fight against the Vietnamese.

In the Sino-Soviet Joint Communiqué of May 18, 1989, which signalled the 'normalization' of relations between China and the Soviet Union, the two sides disagreed on some factors related to Kampuchea, but shared the concern that no civil war should follow the complete Vietnamese troop withdrawal planned to take place by the end of September 1989, 'and that future Kampuchea should be an independent, peaceful, neutral and non-aligned state'.

China's highest priority at all stages was the demand for the withdrawal of Vietnamese troops, but Vietnam wanted a guarantee that the Khmer Rouge would never return to power in their own right, an eventuality it believed would certainly follow a Coalition victory. China continued to provide military and other support to the Coalition, including the Khmer Rouge, and this was one of the main factors preventing a peaceful settlement of the conflict. According to the Vietnamese, all their troops were withdrawn from Kampuchea, as planned, by the end of September 1989, but China did not accept the claim and continued to press for total withdrawal, including verification by United Nations supervision.

THE SINO-VIETNAMESE WAR OF 1979

China was one of the main supporters of the Democratic Republic of Vietnam during the Vietnam War. However, in May 1978, each side began making hostile statements against the other over the issue of Chinese residents in Vietnam and the flight of many thousands of them to China. Public border clashes began in August 1978, and the Vietnamese invasion of Kampuchea at the end of the same year further poisoned relations.

On February 17, a large contingent of Chinese troops attacked Vietnamese territory. At the same time, the Chinese government issued a statement declaring that 'the Chinese troops are fully justified to rise in counterattack' against Vietnamese encroachments on Chinese territory. 'All we want is a peaceful and stable border,' the statement said. Not surprisingly, Vietnam immediately issued its own statement, denouncing China for starting a war of aggression. One of the clauses of the Soviet-Vietnamese Treaty of Friendship and Co-operation of November 1978 was that each side would take measures to eliminate any threat against the other. However, the Soviet Union took no concrete action against the threat to Vietnam.

The main battle was over the city of Langson, north-east of the Vietnamese capital Hanoi and very near the Chinese border. Chinese troops completed their occupation of the city on March 5 and on the same day the Chinese government stated that it had achieved its objectives in Vietnam and would withdraw. It repeated that 'all we want is a peaceful and stable border'. On March 16, the Chinese declared the withdrawal complete.

The Chinese troops suffered substantial casualties and, considering the might of China by comparison with Vietnam, did not perform particularly well, raising doubts about the effectiveness of China's military modernization. On the other hand, they did succeed in inflicting considerable economic and other damage on that part of Vietnam near the Chinese border. That China failed to secure 'a peaceful and stable border' is clear from the frequent later statements of violations of the border issued by both sides, especially in 1980.

Although negotiations between China and Vietnam began very soon after the war finished, they produced very little in the way of tangible results. As of early 1990, Vietnam continues to perceive China as a threat and, although no further full-scale wars have erupted between the two countries, their relations have remained very bad. Considering that the main roots of the conflict between the two countries in the late 1970s lay in the intensity of Sino-Soviet mutual antagonisms, which had largely disappeared by then, there was an irony in the persistence of Sino-Vietnamese hostility.

ALPHABETICAL LIST OF COUNTRIES WITH DIPLOMATIC RELATIONS WITH THE PEOPLE'S REPUBLIC OF CHINA

This list includes all those countries which, as of April 1990, had diplomatic relations with the PRC. In a few cases of countries which had once established relations, but had since broken them, the date of rupture is also given. In some instances, a further formal title is added for a country in order to distinguish among two or more rival claimants to government (as in Germany or Korea). This does not imply that the formal name of any country with which China holds diplomatic relations in 1989 is the same as it was when the relations were established. For example, China established diplomatic relations in 1950 with the Democratic Republic of Vietnam (North Vietnam) but the name of the united Vietnam with which diplomatic relations were held early in 1990 was the Socialist Republic of Vietnam.

The principal issue for China in the establishment of diplomatic relations has been the status of Taiwan, which both the CCP and Guomindang claim as a province of China. Neither is prepared to concede the possibility of two Chinas. This issue has assumed particular priority in the case of international bodies, such as the United Nations, and those countries— like the Western nations or Japan—which had strong and good relations with Taiwan until they recognized the PRC in the 1970s and which have continued to maintain flourishing unofficial and commercial relations since then. For this reason, comments are often made in the following list concerning a country's attitude to the Taiwan question.

Afghanistan—January 20, 1955

Albania—November 23, 1949

Algeria—December 20, 1958

Angola—January 12, 1983 (In the communiqué, Angola recognizes the PRC government as 'the sole legal government representing all the Chinese people, and that Taiwan is an inalienable part of the territory of the PRC'.)

Antigua and Barbuda—January 1, 1983 (In the communiqué, Antigua and Barbuda recognizes the PRC government as 'the sole legal government representing all the Chinese people, and that Taiwan is an inalienable part of the territory of the PRC'.)

Argentina—February 19, 1972 (In the communiqué, Argentina 'takes note' of China's position on Taiwan.)

Australia—December 21, 1972 (In the communiqué, Australia 'acknowledges (*chengren*) the position of the Chinese government that Taiwan is a province of China' and recognizes it as 'the sole legal government of China'.)

Austria—May 28, 1971 (In the communiqué, China 'respects the status of neutrality' and Austria recognizes the PRC government as 'the sole legal government of China', but there is no mention of Taiwan.)

Bangladesh—October 4, 1975

Barbados—May 30, 1977

Belgium—October 25, 1971 (In the communiqué, Belgium 'takes note' of China's position that Taiwan is 'an inalienable part of the territory' of the PRC and recognizes that the PRC government is 'the sole legal government of China'.)

Belize—March 6, 1987. On October 11, 1989, Belize established diplomatic relations with Taiwan; the PRC reacted by suspending diplomatic relations on October 23.

Benin—November 12, 1964

Bolivia—July 9, 1985 (In the communiqué, Bolivia recognizes the PRC government as 'the sole legal government of China' and Taiwan as 'an inalienable part of the territory' of the PRC.)

Botswana—January 6, 1975 (Botswana recognizes the PRC government as the 'sole legal government representing the entire Chinese people, and Taiwan province as an inalienable part of the territory' of the PRC.)

Brazil—August 15, 1974 (In the communiqué, Brazil recognizes the PRC government as 'the sole legal government' of the Chinese people and 'takes note' of China's reaffirmation that Taiwan is an inalienable part of its territory.)

Bulgaria—October 4, 1949

Burkina—September 15, 1973

Burma—*see* Myanmar

Burundi—December 21, 1963. Relations were suspended by Burundi on January 29, 1965, but restored on October 13, 1971.

Cambodia—see Kampuchea

Cameroon—March 26, 1971 (In the communiqué, China supports the policy of non-alignment of the Cameroon government, and Cameroon recognizes the PRC government as 'the sole legal government which represents the entire Chinese people' but does not specify Taiwan as an inalienable part of Chinese territory.)

Canada—October 13, 1970 (In the communiqué, Canada recognizes the PRC government as 'the sole legal government' of China and 'takes note' of China's position that Taiwan is 'an inalienable part of the territory' of the PRC.)

Cape Verde—April 25, 1976

Central African Republic—September 29, 1964. Relations were ruptured by the Central African Republic on January 6, 1966, but restored on August 20, 1976.

Chad—November 28, 1972

Chile—December 15, 1970 (In the communiqué, Chile recognizes the PRC government as 'the sole legal government' of China and 'takes note' of China's statement that Taiwan is an inalienable part of PRC territory.)

Colombia—February 7, 1980

Comoros—November 13, 1975 (The communiqué makes no reference to Taiwan.)

Congo (People's Republic)—February 22, 1964

Cuba—September 28, 1960

Cyprus—December 14, 1971 (date of the signature of the joint communiqué, issued on January 12, 1972, in which Cyprus recognizes the Chinese government as the sole legal government of the entire Chinese people but makes no reference to Taiwan.)

Czechoslovakia— October 6, 1949

Dahomey—November 12, 1964. Relations were ruptured on January 2, 1966, but resumed on December 29, 1972.

Denmark—May 11, 1950

Djibouti—January 8, 1979

Ecuador—January 2, 1980

Egypt—May 30, 1956

Equatorial Guinea—October 15, 1970 (In the communiqué, Equatorial Guinea recognizes the PRC government as 'the sole legal government of the entire Chinese people' but makes no reference to Taiwan.)

Ethiopia—November 24, 1970 (In the communiqué, Ethiopia describes the PRC government as 'the sole legal government representing the entire Chinese people' but makes no reference to Taiwan.)

Fiji—November 5, 1975 (In the communiqué, Fiji 'acknowledges' China's position on the status of Taiwan.)

Finland—October 28, 1950

France—January 27, 1964

Gabon—April 20, 1974 (In the communiqué, Gabon describes the PRC government as 'the sole legal government representing the entire Chinese people' but makes no reference to Taiwan.)

Gambia—December 14, 1974 (This state joined with Senegal as of February 1, 1982 to become Senegambia.)

Germany (Democratic Republic)—October 27, 1949

Germany (Federal Republic)—October 11, 1972 (The communiqué includes nothing about China's position on the two Germanies and nothing about Federal Germany's position on the status of Taiwan; there is not even any reference to the PRC government as the sole legal government of China.)

Ghana—July 5, 1960. Relations were suspended by Ghana on October 20, 1966, with China closing its embassy on November 5, 1966, but were resumed on February 29, 1972.

Greece—June 5, 1972 (In the communiqué, Greece 'takes note' of China's position that Taiwan is 'an inalienable part of the territory' of the PRC and recognizes that the PRC government is 'the sole legal government of China'.)

Grenada—October 1, 1985. On August 7, 1989, the Ministry of Foreign Affairs issued a statement suspending diplomatic relations with Grenada, after the government of Grenada had announced on July 19, 1989 that it had established diplomatic relations with Taiwan.

Guinea—October 4, 1959

Guinea–Bissau—March 15, 1974 (In the communiqué, Guinea–Bissau recognizes that the PRC government is 'the sole legal government of the entire Chinese people and that Taiwan province is an inalienable part of the territory of the People's Republic of China'.)

Guyana—June 27, 1972

Hungary—October 6, 1949

Iceland—December 8, 1971 (In the communiqué, Iceland 'takes note' of China's position that Taiwan is 'an inalienable part of the territory' of the PRC and recognizes that the PRC government is 'the sole legal government of China'.)

India—April 1, 1950

Indonesia—June 9, 1950. On October 9, 1967, the Indonesian government decided to declare an official suspension of diplomatic relations with the PRC; on October 31, 1967, a Chinese aircraft dropped all Indonesian Embassy staff in Jakarta and picked up its own Embassy staff, thus completing the rupture of Sino-Indonesian diplomatic relations. On August 8, 1990 China and Indonesia formally re-established diplomatic relations once again.

Iran—August 16, 1971 (Iran recognizes the PRC as the 'sole legal government of China'.)

Iraq—August 20, 1958

Ireland—June 22, 1979

Italy—November 6, 1970 (In the communiqué, Italy recognizes the PRC government as 'the sole legal government' of China and 'takes note' of China's statement that Taiwan is 'an inalienable part of the territory' of the PRC.)

Ivory Coast—March 2, 1983 (The Ivory Coast recognizes the PRC government as 'the sole legal government representing the entire Chinese people' and declares that it 'has taken note' of the Chinese government's statement that Taiwan is an inalienable part of PRC territory.)

Jamaica—November 21, 1972

Japan—September 29, 1972 (In the joint communiqué, signed the same day, Japan recognizes the PRC government as 'the sole legal government of China' and 'fully understands and respects' China's stand that Taiwan is an inalienable part of PRC territory.)

Jordan—April 7, 1977 (date of the signature of the joint communiqué, announced on April 14, 1977; Jordan 'recognizes the government of the People's Republic of China as the sole legal government

representing the entire Chinese people, and Taiwan province as an inalienable part of the territory of the People's Republic of China'.)

Kampuchea (Democratic)—July 19, 1958. China has continued diplomatic relations with the government of Norodom Sihanouk since his overthrow on March 18, 1970, including the Democratic Kampuchea with which he has been associated, nominally or otherwise, since its establishment following the seizure of Phnom Penh by the Khmer Rouge on April 17, 1975. China never recognized the Khmer Republic of Lon Nol, which came to power in Phnom Penh after Sihanouk's overthrow but was itself defeated in April 1975, nor the People's Republic of Kampuchea (renamed the State of Cambodia in 1989), which was established and based in Phnom Penh following a Vietnamese invasion of Kampuchea which took that city on January 7, 1979.

Kenya—December 14, 1963

Kiribati—June 25, 1980

Korea (Democratic People's Republic of)—October 6, 1949

Kuwait—March 22, 1971

Laos—April 25, 1961

Lebanon—November 9, 1971 (Lebanon 'takes note of' China's stand that Taiwan is an inalienable part of PRC territory and recognizes the PRC government as 'the sole legal government of China'.)

Lesotho—April 30, 1983 (In the communiqué, Lesotho 'recognizes that the government of the PRC is the sole legal government of China and that Taiwan is an inalienable part of the PRC'.) On April 2, 1990, Lesotho re-established diplomatic relations with Taiwan, following which the PRC decided on April 7 to break diplomatic relations with Lesotho.

Liberia—February 17, 1977. On October 2, 1989, Liberia announced its re-establishment of diplomatic relations with Taiwan, signing a joint communiqué to that effect on October 9. The PRC responded by announcing its suspension of diplomatic relations on October 10.

Libya—August 9, 1978

Luxembourg—November 16, 1972

Madagascar—November 6, 1972

Malaysia—May 31, 1974 (Malaysia recognizes the PRC government as the sole legal government of China and 'acknowledges' the PRC position that Taiwan is an inalienable part of PRC territory. The Chinese government considers that all persons who have acquired Malaysian nationality automatically forfeit Chinese nationality. China enjoins those in Malaysia who have retained Chinese nationality to abide by Malaysian law, 'to respect the customs and habits of the people there and live in amity with them'.)

Maldives—October 14, 1972

Mali—October 25, 1960

Malta—January 31, 1972

Mauritania—July 19, 1965

Mexico—February 14, 1972

Micronesia—September 11, 1989

Mongolia—October 16, 1949

Morocco—November 1, 1958

Mozambique—June 25, 1975

Myanmar—June 8, 1950

Namibia—March 22, 1990

Nepal—August 1, 1955

Netherlands—October 19, 1954, at chargé d'affaires level, raised to ambassadorial level on May 18, 1972. (In the communiqué, the Netherlands 'respects' the stand of the Chinese government that Taiwan is a province of the PRC and recognizes it as 'the sole legal government of China'.) On May 5, 1981, China downgraded the relationship to chargé d'affaires level; the Netherlands reciprocated on May 11, 1981.

New Zealand—December 22, 1972 (In the communiqué, New Zealand 'acknowledges' the position of the Chinese government that Taiwan is an inalienable part of PRC territory and recognizes it as 'the sole legal government of China'.)

Nicaragua—December 7, 1985 (Nicaragua recognizes the PRC government as 'the sole legal government of China' and Taiwan as an inalienable part of the territory of China.)

Niger—July 20, 1974 (In the communiqué, Niger recognizes the PRC government as 'the sole legal government representing the entire Chinese people, and Taiwan province as an inalienable part of the territory of the PRC'.)

Nigeria—February 10, 1971

Norway—October 5, 1954

Oman—May 25, 1978

Pakistan—May 21, 1951

Papua New Guinea—October 12, 1976 (The communiqué makes no mention of Taiwan, nor is there reference to the PRC government's being the sole legal government of China.)

Peru—November 2, 1971 (In the communiqué, Peru 'takes note' of China's position that Taiwan is 'an inalienable part of the territory' of the PRC and recognizes that the PRC government is 'the sole legal government of China'.)

Philippines—June 9, 1975 (The Philippines recognizes the PRC government as 'the sole legal government of China' and 'fully understands and respects' China's position that Taiwan is an integral part of China's territory. Both governments 'consider any citizen of either country who acquires citizenship in the other country as automatically forfeiting' the original citizenship.)

Poland—October 7, 1949

Portugal—February 8, 1979

Qatar—July 5, 1988

Romania—October 5, 1949

Ruanda—November 12, 1971 (In the communiqué, Ruanda recognizes the PRC government as 'the sole legal government of China', but makes no reference to Taiwan.)

San Marino—May 6, 1971

São Tomé and Principe—July 12, 1975

Senegal—December 7, 1971 (In the communiqué, Senegal recognizes the PRC government as 'the sole legal government of China', but makes no reference to Taiwan.) (*See also* under Gambia.)

Seychelles—June 30, 1976

Sierra Leone—July 29, 1971 (In the communiqué, Sierra Leone recognizes the PRC government as 'the sole legal government representing the entire Chinese people'.)

Somalia—December 14, 1960

Spain—March 9, 1973 (In the communiqué, Spain 'acknowledges the position of the Chinese government that Taiwan is a province of China'.)

Sri Lanka—February 7, 1957

Sudan—February 4, 1959

Surinam—May 28, 1976 (In the communiqué, Surinam recognizes the PRC government as 'the sole legal government' of China.)

Sweden—May 9, 1950

Switzerland—September 14, 1950

Syria—August 1, 1956

Tanzania—April 26, 1964 (China had previously established diplomatic relations with Tanganyika since its independence from Britain on December 9, 1961, and with Zanzibar since December 11, 1963, the day after its independence, before the unification of the two states into a United Republic on April 26, 1964.)

Thailand—July 1, 1975 (Thailand recognizes the PRC government 'as the sole legal government of China' and 'acknowledges the position of the Chinese government that there is but one China and that Taiwan is an integral part of Chinese territory'. 'Both governments consider anyone of Chinese nationality or origin who acquires Thai nationality as automatically forfeiting Chinese nationality. As for those Chinese residents in Thailand who elect to retain Chinese nationality of their own will, the Chinese government, acting in accordance with its consistent policy, will enjoin them to abide by the law of the Kingdom of Thailand, respect the customs and habits of the Thai people and live in amity with them.')

Togo—September 19, 1972 (In the communiqué, Togo recognizes the PRC government as 'the sole legal government of China'.)

Trinidad and Tobago—June 20, 1974 (The communiqué makes no reference to the Taiwan issue.)

Tunisia—January 10, 1964. Relations were formally ruptured on September 26, 1967, but resumed on October 8, 1971.

Turkey—August 4, 1971 (Turkey recognizes the PRC government as 'the sole legal government of China'; both sides undertake to 'facilitate the performance' of their diplomatic missions' functions. Turkey had earlier voted in the United Nations against the resolutions to place the PRC in the China seat there.)

Uganda—October 18, 1962

Union of Soviet Socialist Republics—October 3, 1949

United Kingdom of Great Britain and Northern Ireland—On June 17, 1954 both countries' governments agreed to send a chargé d'affaires to each other's capital. On March 13, 1972, both agreed to raise the status of their diplomatic relations to ambassadorial level. (In the communiqué, Britain 'acknowledges the position of the Chinese government that Taiwan is a province of China' and recognizes it as 'the sole legal government of China'.)

United States of America—January 1, 1979 (In the joint communiqué, issued on December 16, 1978 in Beijing, which was December 15 according to Washington time, the United States recognizes the PRC government as 'the sole legal government of China', but 'will maintain cultural, commercial, and other unofficial relations with the people of Taiwan'. In addition, the United States 'acknowledges the Chinese position that there is but one China and Taiwan is part of China'.)

Vanuatu—March 26, 1982 (In the communiqué, Vanuatu recognizes the PRC government as 'the sole legal government' of China, but makes no reference to Taiwan.)

Venezuela—June 28, 1974

Vietnam—January 18, 1950

Western Samoa—November 6, 1975 (In the communiqué, Western Samoa 'acknowledges' China's position on the status of Taiwan.)

Yemen (Arab Republic)—September 24, 1956

Yemen (Democratic People's Republic)—January 31, 1968

Yugoslavia—January 2, 1955

Zaire—February 20, 1961 (at which time the country was called Congo). Relations were ruptured on September 18, 1961, following the decision of Antoine Gizenga, who headed the China-recognized government based in Stanleyville, to join with the United Nations-supported government based in Leopoldville. Relations with China were re-established on November 24, 1972.

Zambia—October 29, 1964

Zanzibar—December 15, 1963 (*see also* under Tanzania)

Zimbabwe—April 18, 1980 (Chinese Foreign Minister Huang Hua attended the ceremony of April 17–18 declaring Zimbabwe independent of Great Britain.)

6 CHINA'S ECONOMY

INTRODUCTION

China is a poor country with an underdeveloped economy. It is still essentially agriculturally based, but in the last decade industry and commerce have advanced rapidly. In the past the economy has been affected by many political changes and upheavals, including rapid changes in policy. Since 1979, however, China has been attempting to reform the rather poorly functioning command economy that existed previously. This suffered from poor allocation of resources, a lack of incentives, irrational and arbitrary pricing, much waste of resources and a rigid and stultifying bureaucracy. As a result, the peasants and urban masses suffered a low standard of living. The recent economic history of China is the story of the effort to reform the centrally planned system, and of sometimes painful attempts to introduce market mechanisms. Many of the problems that have arisen, and the policy responses to these problems, have been caused by the co-existence of two systems: a planned and a market sector. There has been a 'stop–go' approach to development, with a push to establish a market in one area followed by a strategic retreat when problems have arisen, then by a further promotion later.[1]

TARGETS AND THE AIMS OF REFORM

The general aim of improving the economy has been carried out within a specific context of targets. Between 1957 and 1979, few reliable figures on economic growth were available from the PRC. From 1960 to 1979, China's leaders had stressed the practice of 'agriculture as the base, industry as the leading sector'. This indicated that the PRC was not following the Soviet-model economy, which gave priority to industrial development. On the basis of these criteria, when the World Bank Report *China, Long-term Development Issues and Options* was published in 1985, it seemed to indicate that, although the PRC was falling slightly behind industrial targets, its overall performance was fairly satisfactory, especially if compared with those of other emerging nations.

However, with the provision of more concrete figures over the last ten years, it became evident that earlier assumptions about China's economic targets were inaccurate. Despite the rhetoric about 'agriculture being the base', the fact of the matter is that most of the attention has been on industrial development, and from this perspective China's achievements, although still quite impressive, have fallen somewhat short of its objectives. From the newly furnished data for past economic targets and the degree of success of their achievement (see below), it has gradually become clear that the intent behind the economic reforms has been a radical reorganization of the economy and not just a minor readjustment, as some originally surmised.

Table 6.1 Sixth and seventh plans, and percentage annual average change in real terms

	Target 1981–85	Actual 1981–85	Target 1986–90
Gross industrial output*	4.0	12.6	7.5
Gross agricultural output*	4.0	8.0	4.0
National income	3.8	9.8	6.7
GDP	4.0	10.0	7.5
Grain output		3.4	2.3–3.5
Steel output		4.7	3.3–4.4
Coal output		6.5	3.3

*Rural industry included under GAO.

THE PROCESS OF REFORM

The implementation of a 'responsibility system' in agriculture began in 1979. Market elements were initially introduced into socialized agriculture and the system was then steadily extended until family

~ 156 ~

farming became the norm; eventually almost all agricultural communes were removed. Once agricultural reform was underway, an important meeting—the Twelfth National Party Congress—was held in 1982. This congress was originally to be convened in 1980, only three years after the previous congress in 1977 instead of the conventional five years, on the grounds that solutions were needed for several urgent problems:

- the determination of a long-term program for the development of the national economy;
- a decision on an economic system suited to the needs of the national economic development;
- decisions on an education plan and an education system to meet the needs of national economic development;
- solutions to a series of important problems in the political life of the Party and the state.[2]

In 1982 Hu Yaobang outlined China's economic policy in the section of his report to the Central Committee entitled: 'Bring About An All-Round Upsurge of the Socialist Economy'. According to the report, the economy's 'general objective' was to quadruple the gross annual value of industrial and agricultural produce from Rmb 710 billion in 1980 to Rmb 2800 billion in 2000. This contradicted the new line being espoused at the same time by Zhao Ziyang, which was designed to counteract the effects of using gross production value or GPV—'tonnage ideology', as it is called—as the main economic index. As early as 1979, Chinese economists began advocating the replacement of the GPV by the net production value (NPV): 'the GPV index figure includes not only the newly created production value (value added) of an enterprise, but also the value of all goods and services of ancillary industries employed by that particular enterprise'.

Bartke reports that GPV was seen by Zhao Ziyang in 1982 as 'detrimental to the efforts to reduce material consumption, prejudicial to the attempts to lower cost prices, and obstructive to the plans to introduce new technologies'. He notes, in further extracts from the 1982 report, that:

The sectors that are to play a major role in the development of the economy in the next 20 years are agriculture, energy, transport, education and science. During the next ten years,

as part of the overall plan for economic development, the aim is to create the necessary structural, organizational, and technological conditions for a great upsurge of the economy in the last decade of the century... Reform in the system of economic administration is only to be gradually introduced during the period of the 7th Five Year Plan (1986–1990). At the same time, the structure of the various economic sectors and the organizational structure of enterprises are to be further rationalized and the technical transformation of enterprises continued.

Four main principles for economic construction were outlined by the fourth session of the Fifth NPC that year (1982):

1. to concentrate funds on the development of key projects and to continue to improve the people's living standard;
2. to maintain the leading role of the state economy and to develop varied forms of economy;
3. to consolidate the leading position of the planned economy and the supplementary role of market regulation;
4. to maintain a position of self-reliance while espousing economic and technological exchanges with other countries.[3]

Figures for most major industries over the 1980s are shown below, but to put these in perspective it is important to understand a little of what has been happening to the economy during this important time. In the past, figures for China's economy were not always accurate, influenced as they were by the desires of cadres to prove their ability to attain, or even surpass, official targets. This trend was particularly marked during such periods as the Great Leap Forward (1958–60) and, more recently, the Cultural Revolution (1966–76), when official zeal to prove the correctness of the Party line of 'redness over expertness' resulted in vast discrepancies between actual and official production figures.

Added to this, the use of the 'gross production value' (GPV) and 'total social gross output value' (GOV: see Table 6.2) in calculating economic output produced much higher figures than the standard measure conventionally used in the West, the 'gross national product' (GNP). The use of the GPV

Table 6.2 Gross output value (in Rmb 100 million) in current prices

Item	1952	1957	1965	1978	1980	1981	1982	1983	1984	1985	1986	1987
Total social												
GOV*	1 015	1 606	2 695	6 846	8 532	9 072	9 966	11 125	13 166	16 588	19 066	23 083
GVIAO*	810	1 241	2 235	5 634	7 077	7 580	8 291	9 209	10 831	13 336	15 207	18 489
GVAO*	461	537	833	1 397	1 933	2 460	2 735	3 121	3 214	3 619	4 013	4 676
GVIO*	349	704	1 402	4 237	5 155	5 120	5 500	6 038	7 617	9 717	11 194	13 813
Light industry	225	387	723	1 826	2 431	2 781	2 919	3 135	3 608	4 610	5 330	6 656
Heavy industry	124	317	679	2 411	2 724	2 619	2 892	3 326	4 009	5 107	5 864	7 157

*GOV = gross output value; GVIAO = gross value industrial and agricultural output; GVAO = gross value agricultural output; GVIO = gross value industrial output.

actually discouraged efficiency, because the larger the workforce involved in production, the higher the GPV becomes. Of course, it could be argued that the bottom line of China's economic policy was not to achieve efficiency at the expense of job security, but rather to safeguard the workers' standard of living and right to work. However, the 'iron rice-bowl' system, as it was called, tended to make workers in the vastly overstaffed industries bored and complacent. At the same time, China's different scale of economic values and priorities made economic interaction with the West rather difficult, a problem reinforced by China's isolationist foreign policy and internal self-sufficiency. Because there are more stages of production in industry than in agriculture, the use of the gross concept also exaggerates the growth of industry relative to agriculture. However, despite these reservations, much real industrialization has occurred since 1949, as Tables 6.2 and 6.7 show. In just over four decades, China has developed a considerable industrial base.

If we deflate the gross output values in current prices shown in Table 6.2, we get an indication of the real changes that have occurred (see Table 6.3). After 1978, the real increase in GOV per annum (9.8 per cent) was much faster than that of the earlier period; while the growth of both agriculture and industry accelerated, it was agriculture that stood out (9.7 per cent per annum compared with 3.6 per cent earlier). Light industry also grew more quickly (10.7 per cent per annum) when compared both with its earlier performance (7.6 per cent) and with heavy industry (8.2 per cent), the result of government effort to promote light industry at the expense of the earlier-emphasized heavy industry, together with the opening of both new markets and greater opportunities.

With the decentralization and loosening of market controls, there has been a steady growth in prosperity, and hence more demand for consumer goods. The goods, however, have not always been there to supply the demand, leading to inflated prices. Present events can be seen as the result of tensions generated by efforts to reform the earlier command economy. This has created a stimulus to corruption and the 'dual-track' pricing system, with extensive opportunities for arbitrage between official and free-market prices for the same goods: these are just some

Table 6.3 Percentage change per annum in
gross output value, in constant 1952 prices

	1952–78	1979–87
GOV	6.8	9.8
GVIA	6.9	9.4
GVAO	3.6	9.7
GVIO	9.2	9.4
Light industry	7.6	10.7
Heavy industry	11.2	8.2

Note: Current price figures were deflated using the national index of retail prices.

of the many unforeseen consequences of deregulation. Market demand and inflation have been increasing gradually over the last ten years, but in 1988 the figures reached a new high. In 1988 it was revealed that the general level of inflation had reached 27.4 per cent, while for comestibles the level was 30–40 per cent, a jump caused by decontrol and anticipated decontrol of prices.

The skyrocketing prices have forced some consumer goods beyond the reach of ordinary people, creating a great deal of dissatisfaction about the drop in living conditions. An urban subsidy has been introduced to help counter the price rises, but it is too small to compensate fully. For some years the central government, worried about the size of the subsidy portion of total expenditure (over 20 per cent), has been trying to reduce it, so any large increase is precluded, and would in any case add to inflationary pressures unless spending elsewhere could be correspondingly reduced. Since the mid-1980s inflation has been the biggest socio-economic problem in China. Industrial production has still not been able to keep up with demand, partly due to a poor economic infrastructure, with insufficient transport to ensure a regular supply of raw materials to factories. This in turn has forced some factories to temporarily close down, thus exacerbating market shortages and pushing prices even higher. Corruption has become rampant among the higher echelons, with factory managers in regulated industries with high-level Party connections seeking to market their factory products on the open market at a huge profit. This has been particularly difficult to combat because of the degree of involvement at higher Party levels, and also because it is perceived that the salaries of Western managers of the joint ventures are many times higher than those of their Chinese counterparts.[4]

LI PENG'S ECONOMIC POLICY

Li Peng's response to the recent economic problems has been to rein in the economy more tightly, to limit joint ventures and to introduce new austerity measures. One series of policy guidelines he laid out tended to skirt around the question of price reform, instead identifying the main task as the improvement of the economic environment and rectification of the economic order—for instance, through reducing economic growth, curtailing capital investment and tightening fiscal and monetary controls. Yet even with the reimposition of centralized control on local construction projects and subsequent capital investment cuts, the industrial growth rate was not expected to slow down markedly until late 1989 or early 1990. Li Peng is also seeking to eliminate corruption and inefficiency. On the one hand, he is demanding a better quality of manufactured goods through the introduction of new technology, and on the other he is trying to promote more efficient use

of resources. Unfortunately, however, he has not yet produced any specific methods for doing this. One of his main tactics to reduce inflation is to increase the supply of consumer goods; even so, inflation did not officially fall beneath double figures in 1989. Stocks of consumer goods were allowed to dwindle faster than they were being replenished, in the hope of reducing demand and thus inflation, but in the long run the cure may prove worse than the ailment. A basic problem is the difficulty in restraining growth while at the same time stimulating the consumer goods industry. As a result of all this, China may now be entering a period of Brezhnev-type recession. Li Peng thinks he can 'turn the clock back', but perhaps he can only slow it down.

THE RECENT ECONOMIC SITUATION

As a result of the adoption of reformist policies and the rapid development of the economy, the composition of national income has altered. By 1987, agriculture, commerce and especially construction had increased their share of a larger output while industry (especially heavy industry) and transport had reduced theirs slightly. As measured in China, agriculture still makes up one-third of the economy, which is a notable reduction since 1952, although a slight increase since 1978; this is the result of agriculture performing better than industry since the reforms, despite problems with grain production in the second half of the 1980s.

Table 6.4 Composition of national income

Item	1952	1978	1987
Industry	19.5	49.4	45.7
Agriculture	57.7	32.8	33.8
Commerce	14.9	9.8	10.1
Construction	3.6	4.1	6.6
Transport	4.2	3.9	3.7

Following the inauguration of the 'open door' policy in 1979, a new era of prosperity was ushered in, with the introduction of joint ventures and foreign investment. Underlying this policy was the recognition that China's modernization required foreign capital and technology. Naturally, foreign businesspeople required an assurance of accurate accounting practice before they would invest their funds and much-needed expertise in China's industries, so this was one incentive to produce more accurate figures. China's entry into the World Bank in 1980 provided another. Officials wishing to borrow large sums through the International Monetary Fund discovered that terms were more favourable for less economically advantaged nations, so any exaggeration of figures would work to their detriment.

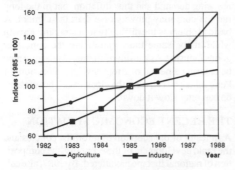

Figure 6.1 Production indices

After an initial acceleration in agricultural output following the reforms, increases could not be maintained. Once the existing slack, caused by earlier investment in large-scale projects without corresponding essential small-scale and local investment and the earlier lack of incentives to produce, had been taken up, it was impossible to maintain the momentum. Diminishing returns set in by the mid-1980s and agriculture began to languish.

AGRICULTURE

Agricultural growth was 3 per cent in 1988—1 per cent below the target—with serious shortfalls in grain and oil-bearing seed production. Production fell from 403 million tonnes in 1987 to 393.8 million tonnes, with wheat the hardest hit and rice also badly affected.

This was due mainly to the reluctance of peasants to commit the necessary land to meeting the state quota of 410 million tonnes. They preferred to plant cash crops, resulting in a 1.3 million hectare reduction of the area under grain production. Other contributory causes were severe frost, flooding and drought over some 51.9 million hectares, resulting in the loss of four million tonnes of output. As a result,

agricultural targets have been revised. The inability of the state to pay farmers in 1988 caused the use of unpopular promissory notes and IOUs, increasing the pressure on peasants to produce for the market.

Food shortages affected an estimated eighty million people in the winter of 1988–89, while another twenty million were considered to be in serious difficulties.

Agriculture: commodities

Prior to 1978, the output of important crops such as cotton, tea and sugar lagged badly, but with the reforms since 1978, the production of such crops has increased markedly. Despite this, a continuing problem is that annual outputs are subject to sharp fluctuations, caused mainly by the state setting prices for some items disproportionate to those for others and to the prices being obtained in the market. Unpredictable weather conditions have also been an occasional contributory factor.

Per capita output of cotton tended to stagnate until 1980; since then it has increased markedly (see Table 6.5). In 1988, cotton production fell by 1.3 per cent of the 1987 figures to 4.2 million tonnes, despite an increase in the sown area from 4.8 million hectares to 5.3 million hectares.

Per capita sugar production increased after 1952 but tended to fluctuate around the 2–2.5 kg per year mark until the 1980s; since that time it has doubled (see Table 6.6).

Tea production languished for decades, but again has benefited strongly from the adoption of market-oriented policies; per capita output in 1987 was five times that of 1965 and over twice that of 1978 (see Table 6.5).

Agriculture: essential agricultural produce

Grain production has suffered during the 1980s, largely because farmers have preferred to sow other crops that have higher prices, either set by the state or prevailing in the market. Although state quotas continue to be set, via contracts, surpluses can usually be freely sold, and cash crops such as fruit and vegetables command higher prices in the market than state set prices. By the 1980s, the annual output of grain per capita had risen strongly over the levels achieved in the 1970s, and peaked at 392 kg in 1984 (see Table 6.6).

Table 6.5 Selected commercial crop production in 10 000 tonnes (per capita in kilograms)

Item	1952	1957	1965	1978	1980	1981	1982	1983	1984	1985	1986	1987	1988
Cotton	130.4	164.0	209.3	216.7	270.7	296.8	360.0	460.0	625.8	414.7	354.0	425.5	420.0
Per capita	2.3	2.5	2.9	2.2	2.7	4.6	3.5	4.5	6.0	3.9	3.3	3.9	3.8
Tea	8.2	11.2	10.1	26.8	30.4	34.3	40.0	40.1	41.4	43.2	46.1	50.8	54.0
Per capita	0.1	0.2	0.1	0.2	0.3	0.5	0.4	0.4	0.4	0.4	0.4	0.5	0.5
Sugar cane	712.0	1039.0	1339.0	2112.0	2281.0	2967.0	3688.0	3114.0	3952.0	5154.0	5022.0	4716.0	4908.0
Per capita	12.3	16.1	18.5	21.9	23.1	29.6	36.3	30.3	38.0	49.1	47.1	43.8	44.8

Note   The figures for the items are in 10 000 tonnes, but the per capita figures are in kilograms. The categories in this table and Table 6.6 are used for convenience rather than strict accuracy, and to give some coherence to an otherwise overwhelming mass of data. For instance, it could be argued that such items as sugar or cotton are not necessarily consumer commodities, but producer goods; the definition depends more on the principal use to which the materials are put.

Table 6.6 Production of consumer essentials in 10 000 tonnes (per capita in kilograms)

item (per 10 000 t)	1952	1957	1965	1978	1980	1981	1982	1983	1984	1985	1986	1987	1988
Grain	16 392.0	19 505.0	19 453.0	30 477.0	32 056.0	32 502.0	35 450.0	38 728.0	40 731.0	37 911.0	39 151.0	40 200.0	39 401.0
Per capita	285.2	301.7	268.5	316.6	324.8	324.8	349.1	377.9	392.1	360.9	367.5	372.0	359.0
Oil-bearing crops	419.3	419.6	362.5	521.8	769.1	1 020.5	1 181.7	1 055.0	1 191.0	1 578.4	1 473.8	1 527.8	1 320.0
Per capita	7.3	6.5	5.0	5.4	8.0	10.2	11.6	10.3	11.5	15.0	13.8	14.1	12.0
Pork, beef and mutton	338.5	398.5	551.0	856.3	1 205.4	1 260.9	1 350.8	1 402.1	1 504.6	1 760.7	1 917.1	1 986.0	2 188.0
Per capita	5.8	6.2	7.6	8.9	12.2	12.6	13.3	13.7	14.4	16.8	18.0	18.4	20.0
Sugar	45.0	86.0	146.0	227.0	257.0	317.0	338.0	377.0	380.0	451.0	525.0	506.0	455.0
Per capita	0.8	1.3	2.0	2.4	2.6	4.9	4.9	3.3	3.7	4.3	4.9	4.7	4.2

Note: The figures for the items are in 10 000 tonnes, but the per capita figures are in kilograms

As in 1988, the 1989 grain target was set at 410 million tonnes, while the 1990 target of 450 million tonnes was downgraded to 425 million tonnes. Given the predicted population increase, food shortages may be expected to worsen, and prices to rise.

To help stimulate grain production, the state purchase prices for wheat and corn have been increased, and other incentives have been added. It is also expected that compulsory grain sowing and mandatory output quotas will increase the sown area and the grain output by 1.33 million hectares and five million tonnes respectively.

Oil-bearing crops are of great importance for Chinese cooking. The per capita output has risen markedly since the adoption of reformist policies and by 1985 was twice the 1952 level. However, a fall in the 1988–89 oilseed harvest was predicted, from 33.4 to 31.2 million tonnes, largely in soybeans. Failure to continue the increase in output of oil-bearing crops after 1985 has meant that sales of free market oils have been reduced in the three big municipal centres of Beijing, Shanghai and Tianjin, and China may soon be the biggest international buyer of vegetable oils, with imports being used to maintain the standard of living.

Sugar production fell in 1988 for the second time in the 1980s. As in the case of grain, the state price has been raised to stimulate production, with some success, as planted areas for cane and beet sugar rose in the late 1980s. However, demand continues to far outweigh supply, driving up prices (Rmb 3200 per tonne, compared with the state purchasing price of Rmb 120 per tonne).

In 1988 the total output of pork, beef and mutton was 21.9 million tonnes, nearly three million tonnes more than in 1987. Pork accounted for 91 per cent of meat production in 1988. As with grains, an increase in the state pork price brought output up to 19 million tonnes in 1988, 860 000 tonnes above the 1987 level. However, higher feed prices are resulting in escalating costs. China has found it increasingly difficult to increase its agricultural output generally since the mid-1980s (see Figures 6.2 and 6.3). Despite this, the standard of living has improved markedly for many in China although some people, frequently those in rural areas, have been left behind, and inflation has caused often-severe problems for urban residents.

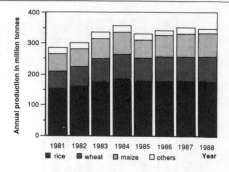

Figure 6.2 Cereals production

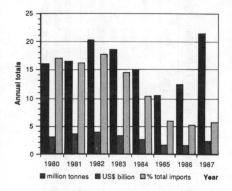

Figure 6.3 Net imports of cereals

Inflation seems an inescapable adjunct to the reform of a planned economy. Although a complex issue, in China inflation seems to be caused by several factors, including the government's failure to balance its budgets, an inability to reduce the high level of investment and to prevent provinces and other local units from investing, the creation of money by the banking system and trade credit. The money supply increased sharply during the 1980s, and control was difficult, owing to lack of experience of modern macroeconomic fiscal and monetary methods, the coexistence of planned and market sectors and an inability to control investment by such lower level bodies as provincial governments, cities and firms (see Figure 6.4).

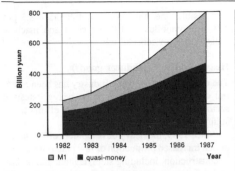

Figure 6.4 Money supply (M2)

Part of the measured price rise (see Figure 6.5) is caused by China having kept prices below market-clearing levels for decades. The removal of controls over some prices naturally led to substantial increases. The rising standard of living and increase in real demand have been caused partly by higher incomes and partly by running down private savings that in the past were maintained at substantial levels because there was little or nothing in the shops to tempt spending.

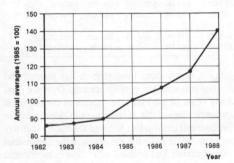

Figure 6.5 Consumer prices

INDUSTRY

In 1988 industrial production totalled Rmb 1215.5 billion (in constant 1980 prices). The highest percentage increase, of 18.8 per cent, was in the last quarter of the year; however, after peaking in October, the rate began to fall off as a result of the attempts to slow down the economy.

Statistics for consumer goods (such as everyday necessities) have been set out below separately from those for producer goods (those which are essential for manufacturing). Consumer goods are regarded as significant indicators for an economy of scarcity; in an economy where basic necessities are in short supply, increases in the supply of these goods are highly important. They also provide growing export earnings for China and are crucial in an export-promotion strategy of development. China does manage to export some producer goods, often to Third World countries, but the bulk of industrial exports are of light industrial goods.

The geographic location of industry has changed since the adoption of reformist policies in 1978. The earlier investment pattern gave priority to the centre and west of China in the provision of funds for investment; this starved the coastal areas, although they were responsible for accumulating much of the capital. Official policy now is to invest where it will do the most good (i.e. lead to further and faster development), rather than where it is most needed. This has considerably strengthened the coastal region. The five special economic zones (Shenzhen, Zhuhai, Shantou, Xiamen and Hainan), the fourteen cities and other areas marked out for special attention are all in coastal areas. In addition to this official policy, the increased freedom to produce and sell, both in agriculture and industry, has led to the spread of industry from the large cities, which the planners originally favoured, to medium and smaller ones. This is the result of several factors:

- the changes in agriculture and the release of some peasants, who have been encouraged to set up small firms;
- the freedom of firms to sell on the market once state quotas have been filled;
- allowing the unemployed to find work for themselves, either by setting up a firm or working for another; and
- the general ethos that no longer denies the pursuit of profit, so that the many new demands can be met by the mushrooming growth of firms.

Many rural townships have witnessed much construction work and experienced increases in industrial production.

Light industry

Light industrial output in China increased by 19 per cent in 1988, reaching Rmb 611.8 billion and surpassing heavy industrial output, which grew by only 16.4 per cent to reach Rmb 601.7 billion. Light industrial production has been stimulated in order to assist with the stepping-down of the inflationary spiral and to meet increased consumer demand.

At the same time, the government has been forced to cut growth in some consumer goods industries, because the level of demand is still far too high for the supply infrastructure, creating shortages and bottlenecks. In addition, there has been a heavy demand on such items as refrigerators and colour television sets as a hedge against inflation, resulting

was visible: the production of tractors (−8.3 per cent), automobiles (−11.0 per cent) and machine tools (−13.8 per cent) all fell.

Heavy industry (producer goods)

The development of heavy industry has been a central concern since 1949. A large heavy industrial sector now exists and, despite recent efforts to restrain it, continues to grow.

Since 1949, the heavy development effort has required increased production of raw materials needed in construction, including steel, cement and timber. In 1988 the output of steel and cement rose by 5.2 per cent and 9.1 per cent respectively, but timber output saw a fall of 1.7 per cent. Since 1949, China

Table 6.7 Consumer goods: household appliances, etc. (per 10 000 population)

Item	1952	1957	1965	1978	1980	1981	1982	1983	1984	1985	1986	1987
Bicycles	8.00	81.00	183.80	854.00	1 302.40	1 754.00	2 420.00	2 758.00	2 861.40	3 227.70	3 568.30	4 116.70
Cameras		0.01	1.72	17.89	37.28	62.30	74.23	92.60	126.18	178.97	202.54	256.70
Cassette recorders		0.50	16.50	74.30	154.60	347.10	497.70	776.40	1 293.10	1 756.80	1 978.00	
Refrigerators				0.30	2.80	5.56	9.90	18.85	54.74	144.81	225.02	401.34
Sewing machines	6.6	28.00	123.80	487.00	767.80	1039.00	1 286.00	1 087.00	934.90	991.20	989.40	970.00
Televisions			0.44	51.73	249.20	539.40	592.01	684.00	1 003.80	1 667.66	1 459.40	1 934.37
Colour sets				0.38	3.20	15.20	28.80	53.10	133.95	435.28	414.60	672.72
Washing machines			0.04	24.50	128.10	253.30	365.90	578.10	887.20	893.60	990.20	
Watches			0.04	100.80	351.10	2 215.50	2 872.00	3 301.00	3 469.00	3 798.20	5 431.10	7 317.40	6 142.40

in production growth rates of 86 per cent and 53 per cent respectively for these two items alone. In the case of television sets, shortages in the production of cathode ray tubes were predicted for 1989. Other examples of shortages which have produced bottlenecks in production in 1988, or which are potential future problem areas, include some foods (see under *Agriculture*); silk-weaving (essential for many fabrics); machine-made paper (essential for packaging); soda ash (essential for glass production); and rubber (essential for disposable rubber gloves). In 1989 the output of many industrial goods fell, including cloth (−1.0 per cent), bicycles (−11.3 per cent), colour television sets (−9.6 per cent), washing machines (−21.1 per cent) and refrigerators (−12.6 per cent). Among producer goods, a similar pattern

has cut down more trees than it has planted and timber supplies are getting scarcer. Over the first forty years of the PRC, the growth of the chemical industry allowed the development of chemical fibre production. In turn, this allowed the textile industry to grow, while reducing the pressure for the production of cotton, and enabled more land to be diverted to other uses. Chemical fertilizer production has expanded and assisted agriculture, and output rose by 5.7 per cent in 1988 to reach 17.7 million tonnes. The development of tractors and walking tractors (small tractors controlled by walking behind; the operator does not ride on the machine) has also been of value, although many large tractors are used as transport vehicles to take goods to market and are often not available for use in the fields. Agricultural machinery is still in very short supply and consequently techniques are labour intensive and old fashioned.

Economic development places great strains on the transport sector, which has long been a constraint, despite rapid increases in the output of locomotives and motor vehicles. Most long-distance transport is by rail, although the 1980s saw an acceleration in road vehicle production. In 1988, some 646 700 motor vehicles were produced, an increase of 37.1 per cent over the previous year.

Energy shortages are a feature of the Chinese economy and many factories are forced to stop work one or two days a week owing to power shortages.

Table 6.8 Heavy industrial production

Item (unit)	1949	1952	1957	1965	1978	1980	1981	1982	1983	1984	1985	1986	1987
Raw materials													
Steel (100 mill t)	16.0	135.0	535.00	1 223.0	3 178.0	3 712.0	3 560.0	3 716.0	4 002.0	4 347.0	4 697.0	5 220.0	5 628.0
Rolled steel (100 mill t)	13.0	106.0	415.00	881.0	2 208.0	2 716.0	2 670.0	2 902.0	3 072.0	3 372.0	3 693.0	4 058.0	4 386.0
Pig iron (100 mill t)	25.0	193.0	594.00	1 077.0	3 479.0	3 802.0	3 417.0	3 551.0	3 738.0	4 001.0	4 384.0	5 064.0	5 503.0
Cement (10 000 t)	66.0	286.0	686.00	1 634.0	6 524.0	7 986.0	8 290.0	9 520.0	10 825.0	12 302.0	14 595.0	16 606.0	18 625.0
Timber (10 000 m³)	567.0	1 233.0	2 787.00	3 978.0	5 162.0	5 359.0	4 942.0	5 041.0	5 232.0	6 385.0	6 323.0	6 502.0	6 408.0
Chemical derivatives													
Chemical fibres (100 mill t)	—	—	0.02	5.0	28.5	45.0	52.7	51.7	54.1	73.5	94.8	101.7	117.5
Chemical fertilizer (100 mill t)	0.6	3.9	12.90	103.7	763.9	999.3	985.7	1 021.9	1 109.4	1 221.0	1 143.8	1 159.2	1 342.3
Engines, engine-driven vehicles													
Locomotives (1)	—	20.0	167.00	146.0	521.0	512.0	398.0	486.0	589.0	658.0	746.0	818.0	909.0
Machine tools (10 000)	0.2	1.4	2.80	4.0	18.3	13.4	10.3	10.0	12.1	13.4	16.7	16.4	17.2
Mining equipment (10 000 t)	0.1	0.2	5.30	4.0	24.3	16.3	11.5	15.8	20.2	25.8	31.4	30.1	29.7
Motor vehicles (10 000)	—	—	0.80	4.1	14.9	22.2	17.6	19.6	24.0	31.6	43.7	37.0	47.2
Tractors (10 000)	—	—	—	1.0	11.4	9.8	5.3	4.0	3.7	4.0	4.5	2.9	3.7
Walking tractors (10 000)	—	—	—	0.4	32.4	21.8	19.9	29.8	49.8	68.9	82.3	77.5	110.6
Generators													
Generators (10 000 kw)	0.6 (1951)		19.8	68.3	483.8	419.3	139.5	164.5	274.0	467.4	563.6	722.4	941.1

Table 6.9 Energy production (in 10 000 tonnes standard fuel equivalent)

Item	1952	1957	1965	1978	1980	1981	1982	1983	1984	1985	1986	1987
Total energy	2 374	9 861	18 824	62 770	63 735	63 227	66 778	71 270	77 855	85 546	88 124	91 265
Of which, in percentages:												
Coal	96.7	94.9	88.0	70.3	69.4	70.2	71.2	71.6	72.4	72.8	72.4	72.6
Crude oil	1.3	2.1	8.6	23.7	23.8	22.9	21.9	21.3	21.0	20.9	21.2	21.0
Hydropower	2.0	2.9	2.6	3.1	3.8	4.2	4.5	4.8	4.5	4.3	4.3	4.4
Natural gas	—	0.1	0.8	2.9	3.0	2.7	2.4	2.3	2.1	2.0	2.1	2.0

The Chinese economy is coal-based and energy consumption generally is constrained by shortages of supplies. It is alleged that the 'gang of four' deliberately promoted the excessive use of oil as a fuel, and some firms have faced increased costs or supply problems as a result. Many of them have returned to using coal. China has made great efforts to develop its coal industry using extensive foreign capital, including Japanese and American, both for the mining itself (relatively little of which is mechanized) and also for the transport of coal to the coast. It is common to see stockpiles of coal near mines which cannot be transported to where it is needed. Coal washing, grading and sorting are also areas of great weakness. The production of petroleum increased 5.9 times between 1960 and 1970, 3.5 times between 1970 and 1980 and 1.3 times between 1980 and 1989—a slowing of the rate from the 1960s to the 1980s. However, in 1989 energy production continued to expand, despite the problems in both light and heavy industry.

The distribution of income has widened considerably. With the faster economic growth, increased opportunities to seek profits, the reduction in rigidities, the relaxation of rules and regulations in some sectors of the economy, and the coexistence of a planned and a market economy, some people have prospered greatly, though others have benefited little or not at all. Despite local variations, peasants who for a long time received little of the fruits of development have gained relative to urban workers. Others who have been able to take advantage of the changes include entrepreneurs, those in service industries, those dealing with foreigners and those who live and work in special economic zones. Those peasants living within half a day's journey of a town market, those with good land, those who work harder, those who are lucky with the weather and those who choose well which crop to sow have all done better than average. Certain provinces have also prospered more than others, and of the thirty provinces and autonomous regions, five now produce almost one-third of the national income.

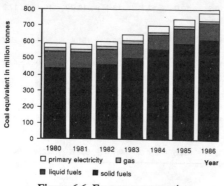

Figure 6.6 Energy consumption

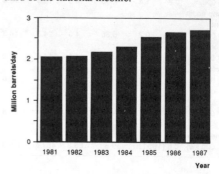

Figure 6.7 Petroleum production

EXPORTS AND IMPORTS

After 1949, China adopted a policy of import substitution, relying heavily on the Soviet Union for loans and the transfer of technology. This came to an abrupt halt in 1960, with the Sino-Soviet split. Despite a short period (1963–65) when China sought out foreign technology, there was relatively little interest in overseas trade. China entered a period of isolationism, sometimes seeming to border on autarky, which was to last until 1970 when a cautious movement back to the world began.

Before 1979 all Chinese foreign trade was centrally controlled and planned in the sense that, in any year, imports were allowed only up to the level of exports expected to be achieved. Foreign trade did not act as an engine of growth, but tended to be regarded as a surplus. With the control over imports, trade deficits—where imports exceed exports—were uncommon. Since then, foreign trade has been freed from total central control and trade deficits have increasingly become a problem.

These deficits are caused by several factors. On the import side, freedom to import has been exercised; the demonstration effect (seeing foreign consumption goods and living standards and emulating them) operates; the failure to control investment levels has added to import demands; and the real economic growth which has occurred sucks in imports. On the export side, China faces competition from other Third World countries and protective restrictions in many developed countries. In the mid-1970s it was rather confidently predicted that rising oil exports would pay for the modernization program; this failed to eventuate for two reasons. Firstly, the price of oil, which had risen sharply during the 1970s as a result of OPEC action, fell again during the 1980s; and secondly, the production of oil within China itself slowed down. A major attempt to find more large off-shore oil deposits, using foreign companies to explore, has essentially failed so far. It is probable that searching on-shore would have been much cheaper and used less resources, but China succeeded in transferring much of the cost to foreign companies. These provided most of the capital and all of the expertise in return for the promise of preferential treatment in sharing whatever was discovered.

The response by the government to the regular trade deficits has been to try to freeze import levels for a year or two, sometimes by banning the import of high-level consumer goods or by substantially raising the protective import duty.

In recent years, imports have outpaced exports, and the current account deficit for 1989 reached US$6.6 billion.

With a lessening comparative advantage in agricultural crops, owing to the population increase, together with limited agricultural land and the growth of industry, China has been a net importer of cereals for many years.

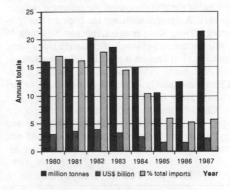

Figure 6.8 Net imports of cereals

Table 6.10 Principal exports and imports 1988

Exports		Imports	
Item	US$ billion	Item	US$ billion
Textiles, clothing and yarn	11.3	Machinery and transport equipment	16.7
Petroleum and related products	3.4	Telecommunications equipment	1.8
Vegetables, fruits and oilseeds	2.8	Vehicles	1.5
Machinery and transport equipment	1.7	Office machinery and data processors	0.7
Metal manufactures	1.0	Iron and steel	4.6
Cereals	1.0	Plastics	3.6

Table 6.11 Main destination/origin of exports/imports 1988

| Destinations of exports | | Origins of imports | |
Country, region	% of total	Country, region	% of total
Hong Kong and Macau	38.4	Japan	21.7
Japan	16.7	Hong Kong and Macau	20.0
United States	7.1	United States	12.0
Singapore	3.1	West Germany	6.2
Soviet Union	3.1	Canada	3.4
West Germany	3.1	Soviet Union	3.2

Imports are still heavily concerned with economic development and largely consist of machinery and raw materials or semi-finished products needed in the production process.

Many of China's exports are directed to Third World countries, but in an effort to close trade deficits, China is making significant attempts to establish export links with the developed world and also with rapidly growing areas such as Hong Kong, which re-exports a considerable amount. Trade with the Soviet Union has increased steadily since 1982.

China's trade with Hong Kong has grown sharply following the introduction of the reformist policies in 1978. A significant change has been the strengthening of Hong Kong as an entrepôt port for China. In 1970 China sold $43 worth of exports to Hong Kong for each $1 of imports it took; in 1978 the ratio was still 36:1, but by 1987 it had fallen to less than 2:1, as China substantially increased its purchases in and through Hong Kong.

China obtains many of its imports from the developed world, which can supply the machinery and equipment that the country needs, or food and raw materials to maintain the modernization and de-

velopment program. China typically runs a trade deficit with developed countries and finances this with earnings from exports to many Third World countries. The OECD countries exhibit the pattern of the developed world, and during the 1980s China has tried hard to narrow the trade imbalance by increasing exports substandially, but has not yet succeeded in closing the gap.

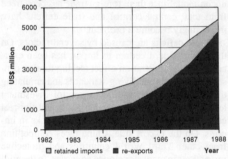

Figure 6.9 Hong Kong's imports from China

Table 6.12 Two-way trade in 1988

Main trading partners	Total trade (US$b)	% change over 1987
Hong Kong and Macau	29.6	30.3
Japan	19.0	15.3
EC	12.9	15.4
United States	10.0	27.2
Asean	5.9	33.6
Soviet Union	3.3	29.4
Canada	2.3	24.5
Australia	1.5	− 9.3
Romania	0.9	12.7
Czechoslovakia	0.8	44.6

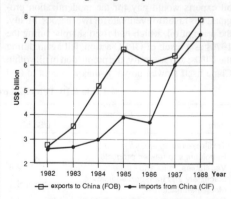

Figure 6.10 Trade with OECD

Japan, which once enjoyed a large trade surplus with China, has also recently seen this narrow, as the result of Chinese efforts to increase exports and to reduce reliance upon Japan.

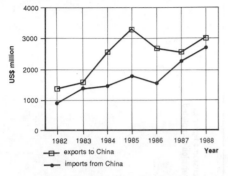

Figure 6.11 Trade with Japan

Although there are some sophisticated economists in China, those who decide economic policy still seem to think in excessively simple terms about trade deficits and attempt to balance on a bilateral basis wherever possible.

FOREIGN DEBT

China is well aware of the problems that some Third World countries have faced and has avoided falling into the debt trap. The debt–service ratio (interest and principal repayments as a percentage of the export of goods and services) has been kept below 10 per cent. According to the World Bank, at the end of 1987, external debt totalled US$30 227 million, and the terms of new commitments were generous: the rate of interest averaged 6.8 per cent and the term averaged fifteen years, with a four-year grace period before repayments commenced. Such figures are reasonably typical of the 1980s (see Table 6.13). The exis-

tence of these debts means that the published foreign exchange figures may be misleading; since 1986, total debts have exceeded total reserves and the gap has widened. As a result of the growing economic problems and balance of trade deficits, the value of the yuan, which is set by the state, has fallen during the 1980s.

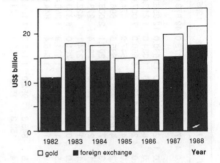

Figure 6.12 Reserves

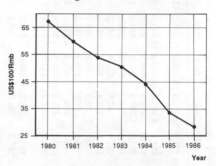

Note: Exchange rates calculated according to trade figures converted from US$ to Rmb by People's Bank of China and Bank of China

Figure 6.13 Exchange rate

Table 6.13 China's foreign debts

	1980	1981	1982	1983	1984	1985	1986	1987
Long-term debt (US$)	4 504.0	5 797.0	8 359.0	9 609.0	12 082.0	16 722.0	21 939.0	30 227.0
Debt-service ratio	4.6	6.9	7.3	7.5	6.5	6.3	7.9	7.1
Average term of new commitments								
Interest (%)	10.8	7.2	6.9	7.2	7.5	7.5	6.2	6.6
Maturity (years)	10.0	12.6	18.5	16.8	18.2	12.0	14.8	15.2
Grace period (years)	3.0	3.8	5.5	4.3	4.7	3.9	6.6	4.0
Grant element (%)	1.8	19.0	24.9	18.7	17.4	13.4	22.8	19.2

Table 6.14 Main indicators of the national economy

Item	Unit	1952	1957	1965	1978	1980	1981	1982	1983	1984	1985	1986	1987
Labour force (year-end)	10 000	20 729.0	23 771.0	28 670.0	39 856.0	41 896.0	43 280.0	45 706.0	46 004.0	49 873.0	49 873.0	51 282.0	52 783.0
Staff and workers state-owned units	10 000	1 603.0	3 101.0	4 965.0	9 499.0	10 444.0	10 940.0	11 281.0	11 515.0	11 890.0	12 358.0	12 809.0	13 214.0
average wage	Rmb	446.0	637.0	652.0	644.0	803.0	821.0	836.0	865.0	1 034.0	1 213.0	1 414.0	1 546.0
National income	Rmb 100 m	589.0	908.0	1 387.0	3 010.0	3 688.0	3 940.0	4 261.0	4 730.0	5 650.0	7 007.0	7 887.0	9 321.0
Per capita income	Rmb	104.0	142.0	194.0	315.0	376.0	396.0	423.0	464.0	547.0	674.0	746.0	868.0
Total foreign trade	US$ 100 m	19.4	31.0	42.5	206.4	378.2	440.2	416.3	436.2	535.5	696.0	738.5	826.5
	Rmb 100 m	64.6	104.5	118.4	355.1	563.8	735.3	772.0	860.1	1 201.1	2 066.7	2 580.4	3 084.2
Exports	US$ 100 m	8.2	16.0	22.3	97.5	182.7	220.1	223.5	222.3	261.4	273.5	309.4	394.4
Imports	US$ 100 m	11.2	15.0	20.2	108.9	195.5	220.1	192.8	213.9	274.1	422.5	429.1	432.1
Gross national product	Rmb 100 m	n/a	n/a	n/a	3 482.0	4 336.0	4 629.0	5 038.0	5 627.0	6 761.0	8 330.0	9 457.0	11 049.0
Revenue	Rmb 100 m	183.7	310.2	473.3	1 121.1	1 085.9	1 089.5	1 124.0	1 249.0	1 501.9	1 866.4	2 260.3	2 346.6
Expenditure	Rmb 100 m	176.0	304.2	466.3	1 111.0	1 212.7	1 115.0	1 153.3	1 292.5	1 546.4	1 844.8	2 330.8	2 426.9
Vol. of fixed assets and investments	Rmb 100 m	43.6	151.2	216.9	668.7	745.9	667.5	845.3	952.0	1 185.2	1 185.2	1 680.5	1 978.5
Retail prices index 1950 = 100		111.8	121.3	134.6	135.9	146.9	150.4	153.3	155.6	160.0	174.1	184.5	198.0

Notes:
1. All values in current year prices.
2. Up to 1980, total foreign trade exports and imports are MOFERT figures; 1981 on are customs figures.
3. 1981–83 commodities turned over include the number of main roads public transport vehicles completed.
4. Total value of commodities prices indices from 1950 taken as 100.
5. Staff and workers are white- and blue-collar workers.

7 POPULATION

TOTAL POPULATION

More people have lived under a single central government in China for much of that country's history than anywhere else on Earth. Since coming to power in 1949, the PRC government has reacted to this situation with a variety of policies, ranging from pride in the size of China's population during some periods to strong attempts to curb population growth rates at other times, especially during the 1980s.

The population of China remains predominantly rural. However, the urban/rural ratio has risen steadily since 1949, and gathered momentum in the 1980s.

A readjustment of the criteria for building towns in 1984 resulted in large numbers of newly built towns, which partly explains the sudden rise in the proportion of the urban population in that year shown in Table 7.1.[1] The figures in the table cover the thirty provinces, autonomous regions and province-level cities of the Chinese mainland. In the third column, 'urban/rural ratio', the urban population includes all those people living within areas under the jurisdiction of cities, while the rural population includes the population of counties, but not of towns.

Table 7.1 Total population figures

Year	Total population of PRC (in millions)	Male/female ratio (per cent)	Urban/rural ratio (per cent)	Growth rate over preceding year (per thousand)
1949	541.67	51.96/48.04	10.6/89.4	
1950	551.96	51.94/48.06	11.2/88.8	18.99
1951	563.00	51.92/48.08	11.8/88.2	19.60
1952	574.82	51.90/48.10	12.5/87.5	20.99
1953	587.96	51.82/48.18	13.3/86.7	22.85
1954	602.66	51.84/48.16	13.7/86.3	25.00
1955	614.65	51.75/48.25	13.5/86.5	19.89
1956	628.28	51.79/48.21	14.6/85.4	22.18
1957	646.53	51.77/48.23	15.4/84.6	29.05
1958	659.94	51.82/48.18	16.2/83.8	20.74
1959	672.07	51.91/48.09	18.4/81.6	18.38
1960	662.07	51.78/48.22	19.7/80.3	− 14.88
1961	658.59	51.44/48.56	19.3/80.7	− 5.26
1962	672.95	51.29/48.71	17.3/82.7	21.80
1963	691.72	51.37/48.63	16.8/83.2	27.89
1964	704.99	51.27/48.73	18.4/81.6	19.18
1965	725.38	51.18/48.82	18.0/82.0	28.88
1966	745.42	51.23/48.77	17.9/82.1	27.63
1967	763.68	51.22/48.78	17.7/82.3	24.50
1968	785.34	51.22/48.78	17.6/82.4	28.36
1969	806.71	51.18/48.82	17.5/82.5	27.21
1970	829.92	51.43/48.57	17.4/82.6	28.77
1971	852.29	51.41/48.59	17.3/82.7	26.95
1972	871.77	51.40/48.60	17.1/82.9	22.86
1973	892.11	51.42/48.58	17.2/82.8	23.33
1974	908.59	51.43/48.57	17.2/82.8	18.47
1975	924.20	51.47/48.53	17.3/82.7	17.18

(continued over)

Table 7.1 Total population figures (cont.)

Year	Total population of PRC (in millions)	Male/female ratio (per cent)	Urban/rural ratio (per cent)	Growth rate over preceding year (per thousand)
1976	937.17	51.49/48.51	17.4/82.6	14.03
1977	949.74	51.50/48/50	17.6/82.4	13.41
1978	962.59	51.49/48/51	17.9/82.1	13.53
1979	975.42	51.46/48/54	19.0/81.0	13.33
1980	987.05	51.45/48/55	19.4/80.6	11.92
1981	1000.72	51.48/48/52	20.2/79.8	13.85
1982	1015.41	51.52/48.48	20.8/79.2	14.68
1983	1024.95	51.58/48.42	23.5/76.5	9.40
1984	1034.75	51.63/48.37	31.9/68.1	9.56
1985	1045.32	51.67/48.33	36.6/63.4	10.22
1986	1057.21	51.65/48.35	41.4/58.6	14.78
1987	1072.40	51.67/48.33	37.1/62.9	18.10
1988	1096.14	51.1/48.9	n/a	14.94
1989 (April)	1100.00	n/a	n/a	—
1989 (end)	1111.91	n/a	n/a	14.39

The figures in Table 7.1 are based on the State Statistical Bureau's published figures,[2] and on the State Statistical Bureau's annual communiqués of China's socio-economic development. In the case of the three census years, 1953, 1964 and 1982, or the sample census year, 1987, they differ slightly from the figures given by the census, or sample census, for two reasons:

1. They are less precise.
2. They refer to the end of the year, whereas the census or sample census figures in each case refer to the middle of the year, specifically the midnight separating June 30 from July 1.

The sample census of 1987 was taken on the basis of a count done among 10 711 652 people—that is,

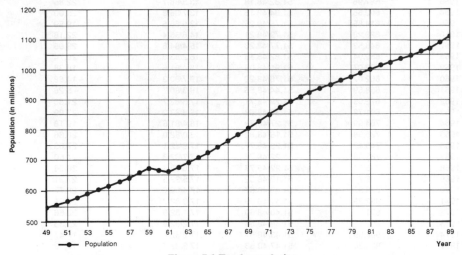

Figure 7.1 Total population

1 per cent of the total—chosen from 1045 counties or cities in all the then twenty-nine provinces, autonomous regions and cities under the control of the PRC government.

The Chinese government was extremely reticent about releasing population (and other) statistics from

In 1980, at the Third Session of the Fifth National People's Congress, Premier Hua Guofeng formally announced the policy of restricting each couple (except among the minority nationalities) to one child only, and to limiting the total population to 1.2 billion by the end of the twentieth century. For a

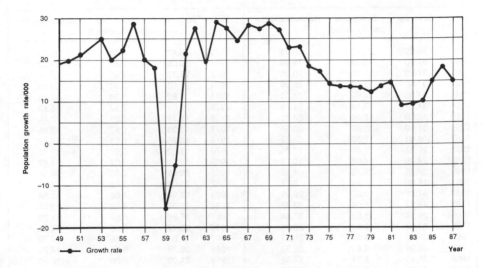

Figure 7.2 Population growth rate

the late 1950s until the end of the 1970s. Even the existence, let alone the results, of the 1964 census was not revealed until years after the event. Table 7.2 shows population figures in millions for some years; the direct sources of these figures are other than Chinese.[3]

Table 7.2 Selected population figures

1973	811	1981	985.0	1985	1042.0
1975	820	1982	1008.0*	1986	1050.0
1978	958	1983	1015.4	1987	1062.0
1979	971	1984	1034.5	1988	1087.0
				1989	1103.9

* Including residents of Hong Kong and Taiwan

The figures shown in this table are consistently lower than the official statistics, although the differences in the 1980s are not great.

while this policy succeeded to some extent in reducing the population growth rate, but from 1984 exemptions were increasingly allowed, especially for peasants whose first child was a girl. The lower population growth rate in the first half of the 1980s has consequently not been maintained in the second half. In the late 1980s, the Chinese government, even while reaffirming the one-child policy, issued statements conveying increasingly deep pessimism on the viability of the target of 1.2 billion by the end of the twentieth century, and announced that China was experiencing another baby boom.[4] On October 24, 1988, *People's Daily* reported that some provincial officials in charge of family planning policy had deliberately falsified the figures for 1987.

Most serious of all was the revelation made through a survey conducted by the State Statistical Bureau between January 1987 and October 1988 that 16.75

per cent of babies born in that period were not registered. In the cities the incidence of non-registration was 2.35 per cent, but in the countryside it was 31.85 per cent. This serious problem of under-registration indicates that the population figures for the last few

tions to the one child policy, point strongly to the widespread underreporting of female births'.[6]

The one-child-per-couple policy has caused underregistration and differential abortion, and contributed to the regrowth of female infanticide, largely

Table 7.3 Natural population growth rates

Year	Birth rate	Death rate (per thousand)	Natural increase	Year	Birth rate	Death rate (per thousand)	Natural increase
1949	36.00	20.00	16.00	1970	33.43	7.60	25.83
1950	37.00	18.00	19.00	1971	30.65	7.32	23.33
1951	37.80	17.80	20.00	1972	29.77	7.61	22.16
1952	37.00	17.00	20.00	1973	27.93	7.04	20.89
1953	37.00	14.00	23.00	1974	24.82	7.34	17.48
1954	37.97	13.18	24.79	1975	23.01	7.32	15.69
1955	32.60	12.28	20.32	1976	19.91	7.25	12.66
1956	31.90	11.40	20.50	1977	18.93	6.87	12.06
1957	34.03	10.80	23.23	1978	18.25	6.25	12.00
1958	29.22	11.98	17.24	1979	17.82	6.21	11.61
1959	24.78	14.59	10.19	1980	18.21	6.34	11.87
1960	20.86	25.43	− 4.57	1981	20.91	6.36	14.55
1961	18.02	14.24	3.78	1982	21.09	6.60	14.49
1962	37.01	10.02	26.99	1983	18.62	7.08	11.54
1963	43.37	10.04	33.33	1984	17.50	6.69	10.81
1964	39.14	11.50	27.64	1985	17.80	6.57	11.23
1965	37.88	9.50	28.38	1986	20.77	6.69	14.08
1966	35.05	8.83	26.22	1987	21.04	6.65	14.39
1967	33.96	8.43	25.53	1988	20.78	6.58	14.20
1968	35.59	8.21	27.38	1989	21.00	6.00	15.00
1969	34.11	8.03	26.08				

years are substantial undercounts.[5] However, as of September 1989, there had been no announcements of revisions in the population figures to take account of the implications of under-registration.

More accurate figures for the birth rates in 1986 and 1987 are 21.27 and 23.26 per thousand respectively. A province-by-province survey of sex ratios at birth, applying to the period January 1, 1986 to June 20, 1987, was carried out by the State Statistical Bureau. It found that 110.51 male infants were born for every 100 female infants. A normal sex ratio at birth varies from about 105 to approximately 107, but 110 is certainly too high. Three possible reasons present themselves: female infanticide, differential abortion and non-registration of female births. All three factors contribute, but according to Ellen Salem, 'the weight of evidence, and particularly the high incidence of abnormal sex ratios in high parity rural births, coupled with the gender-based excep-

because there is an extremely strong tradition in China of preferring male offspring to female, especially among peasants.

One factor making the task of supervising, let alone controlling, birth quotas very difficult is the existence of the 'floating' population. The first decade of reform after 1978 saw the movement around the country of about fifty million people. They included many women of child-bearing age who (or whose families) took advantage of the lack of permanent address to evade birth control authorities.[7]

In a statement issued some time after the population passed the 1.1 billion mark in the middle of April 1989, the State Statistical Bureau reaffirmed the family planning policy in strong terms. It pointed to two periods of rapid population expansion since 1949, between 1950 and 1957 and between 1962 and 1975, and predicted a third boom as unavoidable. It attacked the rural wish for large families and especially many sons, and criticized the lack of effective measures under the new economic system to control people who ignore the family planning policy. It also called for 'comprehensive measures' to bring down population growth, stating that these measures should include 'an effective educational campaign'; the enforcement of compulsory education; 'strict rules on the allowable age for births, marriages and the number of children'; fines for exceeding the allowable birth limit; implementation of the old-age pension system; and the provision of 'sufficient medical and technological means for birth control operation, especially for people in rural, outlying and backward districts'.[8]

POPULATION DENSITY

China may be the most populous country in the world, but it is not the most densely populated. The area of those territories currently ruled as part of the People's Republic of China totals 9.561 million square kilometres. The 1964 and 1982 censuses show a rise in the population density in the same territories from 72.65 persons to 105.46 persons per square kilometre. Population density is also extremely uneven, being heavily concentrated in the areas near the coast. In the three municipalities, seven provinces and one autonomous region nearest the coast, population density rose from 232.7 persons per square kilometre according to the 1964 census to 320.6 according to that of 1982. Between the same two censuses, the population density in the eighteen inland provinces and autonomous regions rose from 47.3 to 71.4 persons per square kilometre. In the sparsely populated autonomous regions and provinces of Tibet, Xinjiang, Qinghai, Gansu and Ningxia, the population density in 1964 was 5.94 persons per square kilometre, but this had risen to 9.87 by 1982.

POPULATION BY PROVINCE

There were thirty provinces or territories at province level in the PRC as of 1989. This number has varied slightly over the years—for example, Hainan was declared to be a province only in April 1988. Territories at province level include autonomous regions and certain municipalities. There are enormous variations in the population levels of China's provinces, with Sichuan having the largest population and Tibet the smallest.

Table 7.4 Census population by province

Province	1953	1964	1982
Beijing	2 768 149	7 568 495	9 230 663
Tianjin	2 693 831	part of Hebei	7 764 137
Hebei	35 984 644	45 687 781	53 005 507
Shanxi	14 314 485	18 015 067	25 291 450
Inner Mongolia	6 100 104	12 348 638	19 274 281
Liaoning	18 545 147	26 946 200	35 721 694
Jilin	11 290 073	15 668 663	22 560 024
Heilongjiang	11 897 309	20 118 271	32 665 512
Jehol*	5 160 822	—	
Shanghai	6 204 417	10 816 458	11 859 700
Jiangsu	41 252 192	44 504 608	60 521 113
Zhejiang	22 865 747	28 318 573	38 884 593
Anhui	30 343 637	31 241 657	49 665 947
Fujian	13 142 721	16 757 223	25 872 917 **
Jiangxi	16 772 865	21 068 019	33 185 471
Shandong	48 876 548	55 519 038	74 419 152
Henan	44 214 594	50 325 511	74 422 573
Hubei	27 789 693	33 709 344	47 804 118
Hunan	33 226 954	37 182 286	54 010 155
Guangdong	34 770 059	42 800 849	59 299 620
Guangxi	19 560 822	20 845 017	36 421 421
Sichuan	62 303 999	67 956 490	99 713 246
Xikang***	3 381 064	—	
Guizhou	15 037 310	17 140 521	28 552 942
Yunnan	17 472 737	20 509 525	32 553 699
Tibet	1 273 969	1 251 225	1 892 224
Shaanxi	15 881 281	20 766 915	28 904 369
Gansu	12 928 102	12 630 569	19 569 191
Qinghai	1 676 534	2 145 604	3 895 695
Ningxia	incl. with Gansu	2 107 490	3 895 576
Xinjiang	4 873 608	7 270 067	13 081 538
Others	11 743 320	3 361 655	—
People's Liberation Army	never announced	never announced	4 238 210
Total	582 603 417	694 581 759	1 008 180 738

* Jehol was abolished and parts of it merged with Hebei, Liaoning and Inner Mongolia in July 1955.
** This figure does not include the population of Quemoy and Matsu, under Guomindang control.
*** Xikang was merged into Sichuan in July 1955.

Some provincial boundaries have changed between these censuses, which explains some of the apparently unusually rapid or slow rates of growth.

The total figure from the 1964 census was announced in 1982 in conjunction with figures from the 1982 census. The figures given here are very slightly different from those originally announced for the 1982 census. These show a total figure for those territories under the control of the PRC government, including the army, of 1 008 175 288.

Map 7.1 Population density

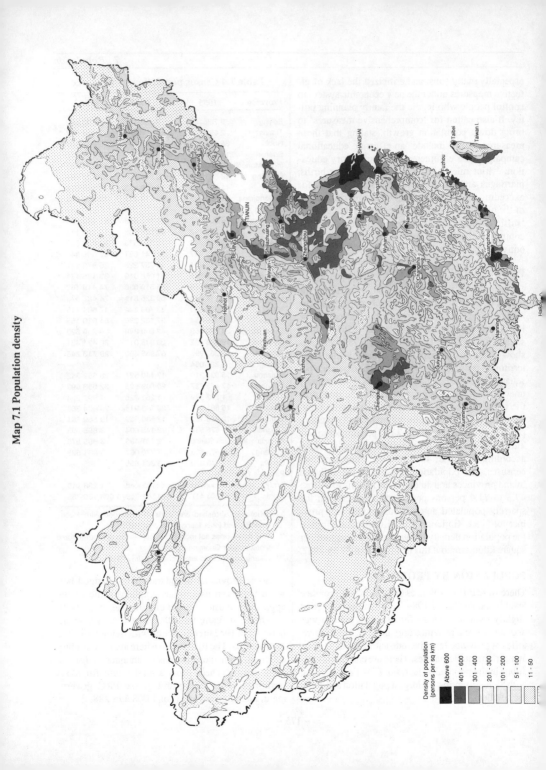

Density of population
(persons per sq km)

Above 600
401 - 600
301 - 400
201 - 300
101 - 200
51 - 100
11 - 50

Table 7.5 Figures from the sample census of 1987

Province	Number of households	Population	Sex ratio (Female=100)	Province	Number of households	Population	Sex ratio (Female=100)
Beijing	2 994 089	9 926 150	104.14	Henan	17 796 619	79 334 734	105.55
Tianjin	2 308 645	8 324 515	103.89	Hubei	12 111 832	50 580 806	106.50
Hebei	14 220 198	56 957 951	105.83	Hunan	14 858 500	57 826 065	108.76
Shanxi	6 687 083	26 908 122	110.28	Guangdong	14 154 444	64 472 237	106.25
Inner Mongolia	4 868 729	20 535 985	109.59	Guangxi	8 076 349	40 163 961	107.64
Liaoning	10 118 461	37 773 636	104.52	Sichuan	26 789 893	104 583 717	107.32
Jilin	5 726 739	23 363 983	105.04	Guizhou	6 017 388	30 513 897	105.34
Heilongjiang	8 102 864	33 639 815	104.91	Yunnan	7 214 588	35 129 988	103.53
Shanghai	3 801 850	12 495 087	101.30	Tibet	362 778	2 079 499	96.85
Jiangsu	17 236 785	63 480 088	104.36	Shaanxi	7 237 946	30 881 941	109.28
Zhejiang	11 672 963	41 211 921	107.74	Gansu	4 385 380	21 034 099	106.95
Anhui	12 783 857	52 866 217	108.41	Qinghai	834 970	4 175 345	104.97
Fujian	6 111 768	28 005 196	106.93	Ningxia	879 620	4 351 553	106.66
Jiangxi	7 562 209	35 589 531	107.32	Xinjiang	3 221 086	14 063 267	104.84
Shandong	19 603 742	78 894 784	104.38	Total	258 341 375	1 069 164 090	106.32

Table 7.6 Cities of over a million inhabitants

City	Population (in millions) End 1985	End 1986	City	Population (in millions) End 1985	End 1986
Shanghai (Shanghai)	6.98	7.10	Guiyang (Guizhou)	1.38	1.40
Beijing (Beijing)	5.86	5.97	Lanzhou (Gansu)	1.35	1.39
Tianjin (Tianjin)	5.38	5.46	Anshan (Liaoning)	1.28	1.30
Shenyang (Liaoning)	4.20	4.29	Qiqihar (Heilongjiang)	1.26	1.30
Wuhan (Hubei)	3.40	3.49	Hangzhou (Zhejiang)	1.25	1.27
Guangzhou (Guangdong)	3.29	3.36	Qingdao (Shandong)	1.25	1.27
Chongqing (Sichuan)	2.78	2.83	Fushun (Liaoning)	1.24	1.27
Harbin (Heilongjiang)	2.63	2.67	Fuzhou (Fujian)	1.19	1.21
Chengdu (Sichuan)	2.58	2.64	Changsha (Hunan)	1.16	1.19
Xi'an (Shaanxi)	2.33	2.39	Shijiazhuang (Hebei)	1.16	1.19
Zibo (Shandong)	2.30	2.33	Nanchang (Jiangxi)	1.12	1.19
Nanjing (Jiangsu)	2.25	2.29	Jilin (Jilin)	1.14	1.17
Taiyuan (Shanxi)	1.88	1.93	Baotou (Inner Mongolia)	1.10	1.12
Changchun (Jilin)	1.86	1.91	Huainan (Anhui)	1.07	1.09
Dalian (Liaoning)	1.63	1.68	Luoyang (Henan)	1.05	1.06
Zhengzhou (Henan)	1.59	1.61	Ürümqi (Xinjiang)	1.00	1.04
Kunming (Yunnan)	1.49	1.52	Ningbo (Zhejiang)	1.02	1.03
JInan (Shandong)	1.43	1.46	Datong (Shanxi)	1.00	1.02
Tangshan (Hebei)	1.39	1.41	Handan (Hebei)	0.96	1.01

THE LARGEST CITIES

In China, population figures for cities include those people within a fixed administrative area, which covers only the 'urban areas' (*shiqu*) of the city. The list in Table 7.6 shows the province or autonomous region of the relevant city in parentheses. Although the three most populous cities are province-level administrative areas in their own right, the administrative area counted for the Shanghai, Beijing and Tianjin figures in Table 7.6 represents only the 'urban areas' of these cities; this is much smaller than the area for the province-level municipalities of the same name, which explains why the populations given below are so much smaller than in the sample census provincial figures of 1987 shown in Table 7.5.

THE AGE OF THE CHINESE POPULATION

China's is a fairly young population.[9] Just over one-third of the population was under fifteen years of age in 1982, which was proportionately higher than in the countries of Western or Eastern Europe, or in any of the other advanced industrialized countries of the West or Japan in the early 1980s. It was, however, low when compared with the countries of the Third World, including India, Indonesia, the Philippines, Thailand and Egypt.

AGE STRUCTURE OF THE CHINESE POPULATION

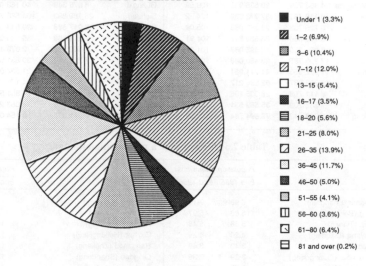

Under 1 (3.3%)
1–2 (6.9%)
3–6 (10.4%)
7–12 (12.0%)
13–15 (5.4%)
16–17 (3.5%)
18–20 (5.6%)
21–25 (8.0%)
26–35 (13.9%)
36–45 (11.7%)
46–50 (5.0%)
51–55 (4.1%)
56–60 (3.6%)
61–80 (6.4%)
81 and over (0.2%)

Figure 7.3
Age structure,
1953 census

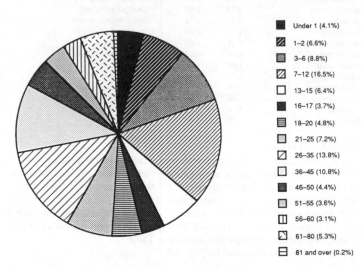

Under 1 (4.1%)
1–2 (6.6%)
3–6 (8.8%)
7–12 (16.5%)
13–15 (6.4%)
16–17 (3.7%)
18–20 (4.8%)
21–25 (7.2%)
26–35 (13.8%)
36–45 (10.8%)
46–50 (4.4%)
51–55 (3.6%)
56–60 (3.1%)
61–80 (5.3%)
81 and over (0.2%)

Figure 7.4
Age structure,
1964 census

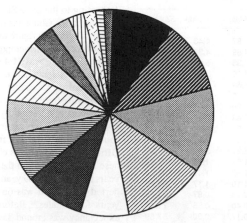

Legend:
- 0–4 (9.43%)
- 5–9 (11.03%)
- 10–14 (13.13%)
- 15–19 (12.49%)
- 20–24 (7.41%)
- 25–29 (9.22%)
- 30–34 (7.27%)
- 35–39 (5.40%)
- 40–44 (4.82%)
- 45–49 (4.72%)
- 50–54 (4.07%)
- 55–59 (3.38%)
- 60–64 (2.73%)
- 65–69 (2.12%)
- 70–74 (1.43%)
- 75 and more (1.35%)

**Figure 7.5
Age structure,
1982 census**

Table 7.7 Census of 1982

Age	Total persons	Percentage	Male	Female	Sex ratio
0–4	94 704 361	9.43	4.88	4.55	107.14
5–9	110 735 871	11.03	5.68	5.35	106.18
10–14	131 810 957	13.13	6.76	6.37	106.04
15–19	125 366 344	12.49	6.36	6.13	103.64
20–24	74 363 020	7.41	3.77	3.63	103.83
25–29	92 563 882	9.22	4.76	4.46	106.53
30–34	72 958 237	7.27	3.78	3.48	108.29
35–39	54 221 629	5.40	2.85	2.56	111.34
40–44	48 437 943	4.82	2.57	2.25	114.23
45–49	47 403 331	4.72	2.50	2.22	112.28
50–54	40 815 501	4.07	2.14	1.92	111.63
55–59	33 894 327	3.38	1.74	1.63	106.67
60–64	27 362 204	2.73	1.37	1.36	100.41
65–69	21 260 370	2.12	1.01	1.10	91.74
70–74	14 348 045	1.43	0.64	0.79	81.32
75–79	8 617 043	0.86	0.35	0.51	68.29
80–84	3 704 605	0.37	0.13	0.23	57.39
85–89	1 088 295	0.11	0.03	0.07	46.14
90–94	218 046	0.02	0.01	0.02	37.60
95–99	35 294	—	—	—	43.68
100 and over	3 851	—	—	—	41.79
Unknown	771	—	—	—	89.43
Total	1 008 152 137	100.00	51.52	48.48	106.27

Table 7.8 Sample census of 1987

Age	Percentage	Male	Female	Sex ratio
0–4	9.30	4.87	4.43	109.95
5–9	9.07	4.69	4.38	107.19
10–14	10.39	5.35	5.04	106.18
15–19	11.95	6.10	5.89	103.66
20–24	11.38	5.69	5.68	100.19
25–29	6.96	3.56	3.40	104.70
30–34	8.40	4.29	4.11	104.27
35–39	6.68	3.43	3.26	105.13
40–44	4.93	2.55	2.39	106.71
45–49	4.40	2.29	2.11	108.45
50–54	4.32	2.24	2.08	107.32
55–59	3.70	1.92	1.78	107.48
60–64	2.99	1.52	1.47	102.84
65–69	2.27	1.10	1.17	94.15
70–74	1.61	0.74	0.87	84.74
75–79	0.95	0.40	0.55	71.43
80–84	0.47	0.17	0.30	57.89
85–89	0.15	0.05	0.10	45.61
90–94	0.03	0.01	0.02	38.18
95–99	0.01	—	—	36.80
100 and over	—	—	—	60.69

LIFE EXPECTANCY IN CHINA

According to the State Statistical Bureau, the average lifespan in China has now reached 68.92 years, a surprisingly high figure for a country with China's level of economic development. In 1981 the average lifespan in towns was 71.4 years, while it was 70.85 for urban residents and 67.17 for rural dwellers.[10] Judith Banister states that: 'Life expectancy at birth in China rose from only about 24 years in 1929–31 to approximately 63 years by the mid–1970s and, by 1981, to around 66 years. According to official sources, it has risen still further in recent years.'[11] Official Chinese sources claimed in 1988 that Chinese life expectancy in the period 1970–75 was 67 years for males and 69 years for females, while in the period 1980–85 it was 66 years for males and 69 years for females.[12] Before 1949 the average life expectancy was around 35 years. The 1988 official claim for the infant mortality rate in 1981 was thirty-five per thousand.[13]

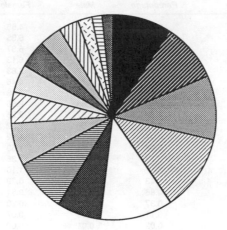

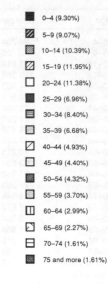

0–4 (9.30%)
5–9 (9.07%)
10–14 (10.39%)
15–19 (11.95%)
20–24 (11.38%)
25–29 (6.96%)
30–34 (8.40%)
35–39 (6.68%)
40–44 (4.93%)
45–49 (4.40%)
50–54 (4.32%)
55–59 (3.70%)
60–64 (2.99%)
65–69 (2.27%)
70–74 (1.61%)
75 and more (1.61%)

**Figure 7.6
Age structure,
1987 sample census**

Table 7.9 Reported male and female life expectancy, 1957–81

Year	Total	Males	Females
1957	57.00	—	—
1973–75	65.81–66.20	63.62	66.31
1975	68.25	67.17	69.32
1978	68.28	66.95	69.55
1979	Over 70	68.00	70.00
1981	67.88	66.43	69.35

Note: This table is taken from Judith Banister, *China's Changing Population* (Stanford University Press, Stanford, 1987), p. 86. The figures themselves derive from a range of Chinese sources, except for the 1973–75 figures which are calculated by Judith Banister, Victoria Ho and Frank Hobbs based on Cancer Epidemiololgy Survey date.

Table 7.10 Life expectancy (selected dates)

Year	Life expectancy	Year	Life expectancy
1976	62	1981	68
1982	65	1983	69
1984	65	1985	65
1986	64	1987	66
1988	66	—	—

Note: This table is taken from successive *Asia Yearbooks* which, for population figures, are themselves based on the United Nations Statistical Yearbooks, the Population Reference Bureau, Inc. in Washington DC, *Far Eastern Economic Review* correspondents and other sources.

Table 7.11 China's population, cultivated land and grain

Year	Population (millions)	Cultivated land (million mu)	Per capita share (mu)	Grain yield (kg per mu)	Per capita output (kg)
1741	143.41	588	4.1	140	574
1840	412.81	842	2.1	150	over 300
late 1940s	455.59	1275	2.7	110	around 300
1952	574.82	1860	3.2	90	around 280
1962	672.95	1820	2.7	90	240
1979	975.42	1810	1.8	180	340
1985	1 050.44	1450	1.4	260	365

Note: *Beijing Review* XXXII, 23 (June 5–11, 1989), p. 26, itself based on *Zhongguo renkou bao (China's Population)*, March 31, 1989.

LAND, GRAIN AND POPULATION

Population pressure on China's available land resources has intensified since the relatively prosperous period of the mid-eighteenth century. The figures in Table 7.11 show that even by 1985, the year after the record grain harvest, the average per capita share of grain per *mu* was well below what it had been around the middle of the eighteenth century.

EMPLOYMENT AND POPULATION

The majority of working Chinese are still involved in various branches of peasant employment. However, the proportion fell substantially in the 1980s due to the growth of the new towns. Tables 7.12 and 7.13 give some idea of the changes which took place in China's employment structure in the 1980s.

Table 7.12 China's population by employment according to the 1982 census

Employment, trade, profession	Number of persons	Proportion of total	Male (per cent)	Female (per cent)
Peasant, pasture, forestry, fishery	384 155 030	73.66	53.75	46.25
Mining and timber industries	8 401 845	1.61	80.64	19.36
Electricity, gas and water production and supply	1 500 343	0.29	74.06	25.94
Manufacturing industry	61 668 204	11.83	55.90	44.10
Geological prospecting and exploration	824 043	0.16	77.93	22.07
Building industry	11 009 419	2.11	81.13	18.87
Communications, transport, post and telecommunications	8 980 972	1.72	77.12	22.88
Commerce, food industry, goods supply and marketing	15 507 928	2.97	56.76	43.24
Residence and public utilities management, residents service industry	2 441 405	0.47	55.13	44.87
Medicine, physical culture and social services	4 101 355	0.79	51.87	48.13
Education, culture and the arts	12 382 079	2.37	64.62	35.38
Scientific research and technology service	1 202 272	0.23	63.36	36.64
Finance and insurance	1 022 975	0.20	68.06	31.94
State organs, political parties and mass groups	8 018 546	1.54	79.55	20.45
Others	289 202	0.05	63.25	36.75
Total	521 505 618	100.00	56.31	43.69

Table 7.13 China's population by employment at the end of 1986

Employment, trade, profession	Number of persons (millions)	Percentage
Peasant, pasture, forestry, fishery, water conservation	313.11	61.06
Industry	89.80	17.51
Geological prospecting and exploration	1.05	0.21
Building industry	22.71	4.43
Communications, transport, post and telecommunications	13.05	2.54
Commerce, food industry, goods supply and marketing	24.85	4.85
Residence and public utilities management, residents and consultative service industry	5.04	0.98
Medicine, physical culture and social services	4.82	0.94
Education, culture, the arts, broadcasting and television	13.24	2.58
Scientific research and technology service	1.52	0.30
Finance and insurance	1.52	0.30
State organs, political parties and social groups	8.73	1.70
Others	13.38	2.61
Total	512.82	100.00

8   GAZETTEER

This section provides an overview of China's main geographical divisions and, within these, its provinces and their cities, especially capital cities. Information is given on history, economic geography, population and the principal features of interest of each province or city, including natural topographical features and climate, and man-made objects of interest. Some information is also provided on the climate, significant features and history of provincial capitals, and other places of special historical interest are also noted.

CLIMATE

Data presented show the approximate climatic situation at the beginning and middle of each year. Unless otherwise stated in brackets, the information includes temperatures in degrees celsius for January and July, generally the coldest and hottest months respectively; rainfall in millimetres for January and June, usually the driest and wettest months respectively; and hours of sunshine for December and May, generally the sunniest and dullest months respectively.

ECONOMIC GEOGRAPHY

A general overview of the economic base of each province/municipality/ autonomous region is presented, followed by a listing of the region's main products grouped roughly, according to generic order, under industrial manufacturing materials and manufactured products, naturally derived products and agricultural produce.

POPULATION

The population of each province or province-level administrative unit given in this chapter is based on the 1987 sample census. In the case of cities, the population of the 'urban areas' (*shiqu*) is given where it is 500 000 or larger. These figures also follow the sample census of 1987.[1]

PRINCIPAL TOPOGRAPHICAL FEATURES

Mountain ranges

Himalayas (8848 m)
Karakorum (8611 m)
Kunlun (7724 m)
Pamir (7579 m)
Hengduan (7556 m)
Tianshan (7435 m)
Nyainqentanglha (7111 m)
Gangdise (7095 m)
Qiangtang Plateau (6596 m)
Tanggula (6137 m)
Qilian (5826 m)
Altai (4374 m)

Rivers

Yangzi River (Changjiang) (6300 km)
Yellow River (Huanghe) (5464 km)
Heilongjiang (within PRC) (3101 km)
Pearl River (Zhujiang) (2210 km)
Liaohe (1390 km)
Haihe (1090 km)
Huaihe (1000 km)

Lakes

Poyang (Jiangxi: 3583 km²)
Dongting (Hunan: 2824 km²)
Taihu (Jiangsu: 2425 km²)
Qinghai (Qinghai: 4584 km², saltwater)
Nam Co (Tibet: 1925 km², saltwater)

NORTH CHINA

Beijing municipality (previous names Cambaluc or Khanbaliq, City of Khan; Beiping; Peking)

Climate: temp.: −3.7°C and (Jun.) 25.3°C; rain: 0 mm and 203 mm; sun: 149 hrs and 286 hrs

Population: 9 926 150

Population of 'urban areas': 6 710 344

Economic geography: Beijing is China's capital, and is also the nation's political and cultural centre. In economic terms, its total industrial output was ranked second highest among China's major cities in 1975. Beijing has good transport facilities, and is an important communications and aviation centre for China. In the western hills around the city there are rich mineral reserves—mainly non-metals. Beijing is noted for traditional handicrafts including cloisonné enamels, ivory and jade carvings, carpets and silk flowers.

Products: Second largest producer of mining equipment; third largest producer of motor vehicles; largest producer of plastics and third largest producer of colour televisions; third largest producer of herbal medicines; significant producer of grapes, walnuts and milk.

Features and history: Tian'anmen Square, Palace Museum, Temple of Heaven, Summer Palace, Ming Tombs, Great Wall of China. Beijing is among the most ancient cities in the world. In the wave of Mongol invasions which destroyed the Northern Song Dynasty, the city became the secondary capital of the Khitans' Liao Dynasty 907–1115 and the capital of the Jurchens' Jin Dynasty 1115–1234. Destroyed in the thirteenth century, it was restored as the capital of the Mongol Yuan Dynasty in 1261–1368 by Khubilai Khan. It was re-established as the Han capital in 1421 by the third Ming emperor, Yongle, during whose reign the Imperial Palace or 'Forbidden City' was constructed. The city was taken over by the Manchu Qing Dynasty in 1644. The Summer Palace was built by Dowager Empress Cixi; the Second Summer Palace, Yuanmingyuan, constructed in Graeco-Roman style, was destroyed by western invaders in 1860. The Great Wall, now partially restored at Badaling, was originally built in small sections in the fifth century BC, and first linked by Qinshi Huangdi in the third century BC. Like the present-day Imperial Palace, the remaining wall is the result of Ming restoration.

Tianjin municipality

Climate: temp.: −3.2°C and 25.9°C; rain: 0 mm and 187 mm; sun: 136 hrs and 264 hrs

Population: 8 324 515

Population of 'urban areas': 5 543 775

Economic geography: Tianjin is a large commercial and industrial centre also known by the romanized name of Tientsin. The city is still one of northern China's most important trading ports, and is a transport centre where imports and exports are handled. Links with other parts of China are good. Since 1949, Tianjin has become an industrial centre, with a wide range of industry and products, including a large textile industry and a machine-building industry. The municipality's main mineral resources are salt, petroleum and natural gas, with Tianjin being one of China's main producers of sea salt. There are also other mineral resources.

Products: Second largest producer of soda ash; second largest producer of bicycles; third largest producer of sewing machines and cameras; important producer of shellfish.

Features and history: Although ravaged in July 1976 by the Tangshan earthquake, Tianjin's architecture still retains many distinctive features with its blend of Western and Chinese styles. Examples include the Friendship Club and former English Country Club. Restaurants offer fresh seafood, and the Viennese coffee shop Qishilin (Kiesling's) is a well-known landmark.

Hebei province

Topographical features: North China Plain, 1 500 000 km² of highly fertile loess or yellow earth plateau up to 100 m deep; Huanghe in south

Population: 56 957 951

Population of main cities: Tangshan—1 435 585; Shijiazhuang—1 218 738; Handan—1 027 814; Zhangjiakou—643 941; Baoding—601 384

Economic geography: Hebei province is best known for its vast mineral resources and high level of agricultural production, particularly grain farming. More than eighty minerals have been discovered in the province, and there are extensive reserves of coal. Since the founding of the PRC, industry has developed considerably, and the province is now an important producer of coal, petroleum, iron, steel and textiles. The electricity, machine-building, chemical and several light industries are also significant.

Products: Main producer of salt; third largest producer of beer; significant grain producer: third largest producer of corn, and fourth largest of wheat; third largest producer of cotton and peanuts; fourth largest producer of walnuts; significant producer of sesame; third largest fruit producer: main producer of pears, third largest of apples, and fourth largest of grapes; significant producer of mutton, fish and shellfish.

Capital: Shijiazhuang

Climate: temp.: (Feb.) –0.6°C and 26.5°C; rain: 3 mm and (Jul.) 116 mm; sun: (Oct.) 125 hrs and (Apr.) 252 hrs

Features and history: Shijiazhuang was a small village of little significance until industrialization brought the Beijing–Hankou (Wuhan) railway at the beginning of this century. It was the communist capital for the period 1947–49, between the fall of Yan'an to GMD forces and the capture of Beijing by the communists. There are few sites of historical interest, apart from a military cemetery with a pair of twelfth century Jin Dynasty bronze lions. In nearby Zhengding is Longxing Temple, featuring a tenth century statue of Guanyin, the Goddess of Mercy.

Other places of interest:
Chengde, previously Jehol or Warm River—resort of Manchu emperors. The Kangxi Emperor constructed the palace to blend in with the natural scenery, and around it the Qianlong Emperor added eight temples, seven of which still remain.

Beidaihe—On Bohai Gulf, this Western-style seaside resort was built at the turn of the century.

Shanhaiguan—An ancient walled town at the eastern end of Great Wall with a gate, built in 1639, inscribed 'First Pass under Heaven'.

Shandong province

Topographical features: Mountainous region bordering the Bohai and Yellow Seas

Population: 78 894 84

Population of main cities: Zibo—2 372 496; Jinan—2 144 236; Zaozhuang—1 644 607; Taian—1 352 892; Qingdao—1 296 738; Weifang—1 073 066; Jining—792 881; Yantai—756 923; Dongying—557 082

Economic geography: Shandong province is rich in mineral resources, and is an important energy-producing area of China. Ore deposits include coal, iron, petroleum, gold, diamonds and aluminium; the province also exports oil and coal. Other industries include iron and steel, chemicals, textiles and pottery and china manufacture. Shandong's machinery industry produces motor vehicles, trains, power machines and mining equipment. The province also has China's highest output of fertilizer.

Products: Main producer of generators and cement; second largest producer of crude oil; third largest producer of soda ash; third largest producer of electric irons; third largest producer of yarn and cloth; second largest producer of salt; third largest producer of machine-made paper and board, and cigarettes; significant producer of beer; third largest grain producer: main producer of corn, second largest of wheat and soybeans; main producer of cotton and oil-bearing crops, especially peanuts; second largest producer of tubers; second largest fruit producer: main producer of apples and second largest of pears and grapes; important producer of tobacco and silkworm cocoons; third largest producer of aquatic products and marine products specifically: third largest producer of marine crustacea and significant producer of ocean fish, largest producer of algae, significant producer of freshwater products, including all types of shellfish; significant meat producer, including pork, and third largest producer of mutton; significant milk producer.

Capital: Jinan

Climate: temp.: 0.1°C and 28.2°C; rain: 0.3 mm and (Aug.) 98 mm; sun: 143 hrs and 296 hrs

Features and history: Lying in the foothills of the Li Mountains, just south of Huanghe, Jinan offers evidence of neolithic settlement. The present-day architecture is strongly influenced by early twentieth century German occupation. Jinan is notable for its many pavilions and teahouses overlooking a variety of springs, pools and lakes. In nearby mountain caves, including those of One Thousand Buddha Mountain, are found Buddhist carvings dating back to the Northern Wei Dynasty of the sixth century.

Other places of interest:

Taishan—Some 1500 m high, this is one of China's five sacred mountains and a site of imperial sacrifices to heaven. It rises impressively from the surrounding plain, with many shrines and temples dedicated to the Daoist deity, Princess of Coloured Clouds. Some 7000 carved steps lead to the main temple at the summit. At the mountain's foot is the enormous Confucian temple Tai Miao.

Qufu—Birthplace of Confucius and capital of the ancient state of Lu, containing a major Temple to Confucius.

Qingdao—An early twentieth century German coaling station on the southern Shandong Peninsula, and also a popular seaside resort, Qingdao is now Shandong's main industrial city. The Germans also founded the Qingdao (Tsingtao) Brewery here.

Henan province

Topographical features: Huanghe, with its fertile loess, forms part of the northern border.

Population: 79 334 734

Population of main cities: Zhengzhou—1 581 483;

Luoyang—1 089 653; Pingdingshan—866 187; Kaifeng—647 760; Xinxiang—558 797; Anyang—557 842; Jiaozuo—535 013

Economic geography: Henan is another province which has undergone major industrial development since the founding of the PRC. Its industries include metallurgy, coal, machine-building, power, chemicals, textiles and paper-making. Luoyang, a machine-building centre, is home to China's largest tractor plant, bearings plant and mining machinery factory. Henan has abundant mineral resources, with prospective coal reserves of 100 billion tonnes. The Xiaoqinling gold mines are among China's largest, and the province's bauxite deposits rank second in the country. Thanks to the Beijing–Guangzhou railway, and other railway lines, Henan is one of China's major communications centres.

Products: Second largest producer of coal and tractors; main producer of machine-made paper and board, and of cigarettes; significant grain producer and main producer of wheat; significant producer of hemp, cotton and oil-bearing crops: second largest producer of sesame and third largest of peanuts; second largest producer of tobacco; significant producer of walnuts, lacquer and fruit: third largest producer of grapes; main beef producer and significant mutton producer.

Capital: Zhengzhou

Climate: temp.: 0.8°C and 27.4°C; rain: (Feb.) 0.2 mm and 74 mm; sun: (Nov.) 129 hrs and 285 hrs

Features and history: Zhengzhou has been a site of continuous settlement for over 3500 years, and was the second capital of the Shang Dynasty (c. 1500–1066 BC). Remains of the Shang city walls and dwellings are still visible in the eastern suburbs, and the Henan Provincial Museum preserves evidence of early settlement. In 1910, foreign industrial expansion brought railways to Zhengzhou, which was the site of a bloody strike by Beijing–Hankou railway workers in 1923. In 1937 severe flooding was caused and thousands of lives lost when the GMD breached the Huanghe dyke 32 km north-east of the city to repel the Japanese invasion; order was not restored to the river until 1947. The city again sustained heavy damage over the following two years, during the civil war, and has since been rebuilt as a modern industrial centre. People's Park separates the old and new areas.

Other places of interest:

Luoyang—Now the home of China's best tractors, this ancient city was the Chinese capital for nine dynasties, 1027 BC–937 AD: it was the principal capital of the Zhou Dynasty (770–256 BC) and the Eastern Han (AD 25–220). Luoyang contains China's earliest Buddhist temple, White Horse Temple, whose original buildings dated from the first century, and Longmen Buddhist caves, including 1352 caves carved out during the Northern Wei Dynasty, 493–543, and Fengxian Temple Cave, dating from 672–75, containing fine Tang sculpture.

Anyang—Although now a modern industrial city, the nearby village of Xiaotun is the site of ancient Yin, the Shang Dynasty capital c.1400–1050 BC. The royal palace and tombs, workshops and houses have been excavated, and oracle bones and tortoise shells furnishing evidence of early Chinese script have been uncovered.

Kaifeng—Formerly the capital of seven dynasties and the Northern Song capital, Kaifeng is now Henan's agricultural centre. Many Shang Dynasty bronzes have been uncovered here. After sacking by Jurchens caused the flight of the Song court to the south in AD 1126, the city lost its prominent position. Sites of interest include the Old Music Terrace, or Yuwangtai; Xiangguo Si, a monastery founded in the sixth century and restored during the Qing Dynasty which contains a fine statue of Guanyin; and the Dragon Pavilion, site of a Ming Dynasty palace.

Shaolin Monastery—Reputedly founded in the fifth century by an Indian monk, Shaolin has long been a monkish training ground for the local version of martial arts. It has been almost destroyed several times, but a few original buildings still remain intact.

Shaanxi province

Topographical features: In the north-west, Huanghe, with its tributary Wei River, forms the borders of Shaanxi, Shanxi and Henan. Shaanxi was the site of China's capitals for the first 2000 years of its

recorded history. Huashan, one of China's five sacred mountains, rises 2135 m above the confluence of the Huanghe, Wei and Luo Rivers.

Population: 30 881 941

Population of main cities: Xi'an—2 576 926; Xianyang—683 289

Economic geography: Shaanxi is one of China's important machine-building centres, producing high-voltage transmission and transformation equipment, turbine blowers and turbine compressors, petroleum and coal mining equipment and motors, among other things. The Guanzhong area is also one of the country's main textile bases, producing both cotton and woollen textiles. The province has seen rapid development in the electronics industry, and there is also an important coal industry, with extensive coal deposits and other mineral deposits, including molybdenum, aluminium, vanadium, mercury and nickel.

Products: Main producer of lacquer and third largest of walnuts; significant producer of silkworm cocoons, grapes and milk.

Capital: Xi'an, previously Chang'an

Climate: temp.: 1.4°C and 26.6°C; rain: 1 mm and (Sept.) 122 mm; sun: 63 hrs and 162 hrs

Features and history: Xi'an was the capital of the Tang Dynasty. Evidence of stone age settlement has been found at nearby Banpo. The tomb of the first emperor to unite China, Qinshi Huangdi, with its 6000 terracotta warriors, was found in Xi'an. With the founding of the Han dynasty and establishment of trade with imperial Rome, the city evolved into a major trading centre on the Silk Road. A strong Moslem flavour is still evidenced in the local style of dress and in the spicy kebabs and noodles sold at roadside stalls. After the fall of the Tang, Xi'an declined in importance. The Shaanxi Provincial Museum contains a unique collection of neolithic stone carvings and bronze Han bas-relief steles. Big Goose Pagoda, dating from 652, and the Ming Dynasty Bell Tower and Drum Tower are also notable. To the north-west of the city, the tomb of the second Tang emperor, Zhao Ling, is approached through an avenue of gigantic guardian figures and spirits.

Other places of interest:

Yan'an—Situated on the Yan River, northern Shaanxi, this was the site of the Communist Chinese headquarters 1936–47, when caves were cut out of the cliffs as dwellings.

Shanxi province

Topographical features: Huanghe forms the south-western border.

Population: 26 908 122

Population of main cities: Taiyuan—1 975 957; Datong—1 037 859; Jincheng—633 110

Economic geography: Shanxi is a centre of heavy industry, with one of the biggest iron and steel complexes in the country, mainly engaged in producing special steels of various types and steel plates. There is also a major machine-building industry, producing hoisting equipment and machinery for mining, spinning and weaving, and steel-rolling. The province has vast mineral resources, and its reserves of coal and aluminium rank first in the country, with proven coal deposits of 200 billion tonnes and proven aluminium deposits of over 300 million tonnes—more than a quarter of the country's total. Shanxi's proven reserves of titanium rank second in China.

Products: Main producer of coal, about one-quarter of China's total; second largest producer of coke.

Capital: Taiyuan

Climate: temp.: –5.2°C and (Aug.) 29°C; rain: 0 mm and 45 mm; sun: 113 hrs and (Jun.) 259 hrs

Features and history: Located at the northern end of Taiyuan Basin on Shanxi Plateau, Taiyuan was previously a strategic city with a turbulent history as the guardian of the western approach to the North China Plain. Historical sites include Chongshan Temple and Shanxi Provincial Museum. The Jin Ancestral Temple, dating back to the fifth century, is located 26 km from Taiyuan.

Other places of interest:

Datong—Originally a trading centre near the Great Wall, Datong is now in the middle of the coal mining areas on the railway line between Beijing and Inner Mongolia, and was the centre of China's steam locomotive industry. Of historical interest are the Ming Dynasty Nine Dragon Screen, Guanyin Temple with its Three Dragon Screen and the Upper and Lower Huayan Temples.

Yungang—This is the site of fifty-three Northern Wei Buddhist caves cut mainly AD 460–93, with a 17 m statue of Sakyamuni, representing the earliest collection of Chinese Buddhist stone figures.

NORTH-EAST CHINA (previously Manchuria)

Heilongjiang province

Topographical features: Manchurian plateau; Heilongjiang (Sungari River)

Population: 33 639 815

Population of main cities: Harbin—3 911 572; Qiqihar—1 325 644; Daqing—879 591; Yichun—835 314; Jixi—823 138; Mudanjiang—654 380; Hegang—612 144; Jiamusi—586 828

Economic geography: The largest province (as opposed to autonomous region) in China, Heilongjiang is also the most favourable for the development of agriculture. A government plan to build most of the country's state farms here has led to the establishment of over 870 state farms, more than 100 of them on a large scale. Like other northern provinces, Heilongjiang has an abundance of mineral resources. There are major deposits of oil, coal and natural gas, together with good deposits of gold, copper, lead, zinc and other minerals. Since the founding of the PRC, Heilongjiang has established itself as an important industrial centre, with a range of industries including coal, oil, timber and machinery, all using advanced technology. The Sanjiang Plain and Songnen Plain, once known as the Great Northern Wasteland, now form one of China's major cereal-producing regions. Heilongjiang also contains China's largest forestry centre, and is one of the key areas for animal husbandry, particularly horses, oxen, sheep and deer.

Products: Main producer of crude oil and natural gas; third largest producer of coal; main producer of tractors, over one-third of China's total, and rolling stock; second largest producer of beer; main producer of timber; significant grain producer: main producer of soybeans and fourth largest producer of corn; main producer of beetroot; important producer of hemp, tobacco and shellfish; main producer of milk.

Capital: Harbin

Climate: temp.: –20.2°C and 20.2°C; rain: 3 mm and (Aug.) 225 mm; sun: (Jan.) 152 hrs and 284 hrs

Features and history: Harbin offers neo-classical Russian architecture, including an Orthodox Russian cathedral. Ice-sculptures and ice-sports on the river are popular in winter. Originally a fishing village, Harbin developed into a city when the Siberia–Vladivostok railway was built last century, during the Russian occupation.

Jilin province

Topographical features: Hilly region

Population: 23 363 983

Population of main cities: Changchun—2 002 054; Jilin—1 199 445; Hunjiang—692 212

Economic geography: Since 1949, Jilin's industry has developed greatly and is now based on machine building, basic chemicals and optical instruments. The province is one of China's chief producers of optical instruments, and its papermaking industry is second in the country. Jilin's favourable agricultural conditions have made it a granary for north-east China, with major cereal crops being rice, maize, sorghum and millet. Jilin is also a major soybean producer, and an important forestry zone. The province is known for its production of 'the three treasures of north-east China'—ginseng (the province produces 80 per

cent of China's ginseng exports), sable fur and pilose antlers.

Products: Main producer of ferro-alloy; second largest producer of motor vehicles; second largest producer of timber and corn; and fourth largest of soybeans.

Capital: Changchun

Climate: temp.: –17.1°C and 21.6; rain: 2 mm and (Jul.) 444 mm; sun: 153 hrs and 285 hrs

Features and history: Changchun became the capital of the Japanese puppet state of Manzhouguo or Manchuria, 1933–45, and retains some evidence of its previous grandeur in former administrative buildings now used by Jilin University.

Other places of interest:
Changbai Nature Reserve—This is China's second largest reserve, in which is situated Lake Tian, or Lake of Heaven, a volcanic crater lake.

Liaoning province

Topographical features: Liaodong Peninsula; Manchurian plateau

Population: 37 773 636

Population of main cities: Shenyang—4 368 271; Dalian—2 276 451; Anshan—1 326 826; Fushun—1 294 712; Benxi—858 507; Jinzhou—807 006; Fuxin—704 378; Dandong—608 451; Liaoyang—597 821; Yingkou—525 729

Economic geography: Liaoning is highly developed in industry, and is the centre of China's iron and steel-making industry. Industries involve nonferrous metals, fuel, electricity, machine-building and oil processing. The province is also China's major manufacturer of heavy industrial products. Light industry is also well developed, with products including bicycles, textiles, wristwatches, televisions, radios and sewing machines. Abundant mineral resources include iron ore, making up a quarter of China's total, and talcum and boron, which are the largest deposits in the country. The coast provides abundant sea-salt resources, and the seas are a major fishing ground.

Products: Main producer of steel, about one-fifth of China's total: rolled steel, pig iron, coke, soda ash; third largest producer of natural gas and crude oil; main producer of mining equipment, metal-cutting machine tools and a.c. motors; second largest producer of locomotives; third largest producer of washing machines and watches; third largest producer of chemical fibres; main beer producer; significant producer of silkworm cocoons; significant producer of fruit: second largest producer of apples and third largest of pears; significant marine producer: main producer of shellfish, second largest producer of seaweed.

Capital: Shenyang (previously Mukden)

Climate: temp.: −11.9°C and 23.2°C; rain: (Feb.) 2 mm and (Jul.) 287 mm; sun: 113 hrs and 265 hrs

Features and history: Shenyang is the communications centre of the extreme north-east (formerly Manchuria), situated in the largest heavy industrial province, Liaoning. Liaoning Exhibition Hall displays its accomplishments. The city was the original Manchu capital of Mukden, with the Imperial Palace built 1625–36, before the move to Beijing with the establishment of Qing Dynasty, 1644.

Other places of interest:
Lüda—Formed from agglomeration of the naval base of Lüshun, formerly also called Port Arthur, and Dalian, this is an important industrial port still exhibiting evidence of earlier Japanese and Russian occupation. It is spaciously laid out with beaches and parks, and contains a large Museum of Natural History.

NORTH–NORTH-WEST CHINA

Gansu province

Topographical features: Principally desert and mountain. The Huanghe flows through the province.

Population: 21 034 099

Population of main cities: Lanzhou—1 416 130; Tianshui—982 958

Economic geography: Heavy industry is central to the economy of Gansu province, with metallurgical, petroleum, chemical, power, machine-building and coal mining industries dominating. The most important area of the metallurgical industry in Gansu is the non-ferrous metals sector. Oil prospecting, drilling and refining equipment is produced by the province's machine-building industry. Gansu has rich mineral deposits, with nickel, copper, lead and zinc reserves amongst the largest in China. The province also has China's largest sulphur nickel mine. Light industry consists of food processing, textiles, leather-making, medicine and paper making. Extensive grassland areas are the basis for animal husbandry of cattle, sheep, horses, donkeys, mules, camels and pigs. The best-known Gansu livestock are the Hequ horses and Gansu plateau fine-wool sheep.

Products: Largest producer of woollen carpets; significant producer of pears and walnuts.

Capital: Lanzhou

Climate: temp.: –4.9°C and (Aug.) 20.9°C; rain: 0 mm and 109 mm; sun: 68 hrs and 213 hrs

Features and history: Lanzhou is a major new industrial city of the north-west, located at the centre of the railway system.

Other places of interest:

Binglingsi Caves—These 116 caves and niches were carved out, generally during the Tang Dynasty, on Huanghe above Lanzhou.

Buddhist caves at Maijishan, 'Corn Rick Mountain'—Containing clay and stone figures and wall paintings, these caves were excavated between the Northern Wei and Song dynasties.

Jiayuguan—This is the westernmost outpost of the Great Wall, with a Ming Dynasty gatepost, located on the Silk Road.

Inner Mongolian autonomous region

Topographical features: The Mongolian Steppes extend from the Altai Mountains in the west to the Manchurian plateau in the east.

Population: 20 535 985

Population of main cities: Baotou—1 133 725; Chifeng—915 616; Hohhot—828 255

Economic geography: With 30 per cent of China's pasture (about 88 million hectares), the Inner Mongolian autonomous region is a major livestock breeding area. The main animals are sheep, cattle, horses and camels, with several breeds very highly regarded. Other branches of agriculture include grain and cash crop production. The region is rich in minerals, and is ranked first in the

world in rare earth metals and niobium deposits, first in China in natural soda deposits, and amongst the first few in the country in coal deposits. Industry has developed since the autonomous region was set up, and now includes iron and steel, coal, electricity, timber, machine-building, chemicals, electronics, building materials and other sectors.

Products: Third largest producer of timber; significant grain producer: third largest producer of corn and largest producer of soybeans; second largest producer of beetroots; significant meat and dairy producer: second largest producer of mutton and milk, and third largest of beef.

Capital: Hohhot

Climate: temp.: –11°C and 22.7°C; rain: 0 mm and 83 mm; sun: 146 hrs and (Jul.) 307 hrs

Features and history: Hohhot is a relatively new settlement to the south of the Daqing Mountains. It is the site of the tomb of Han Dynasty princess Wang Zhaojun, sent to marry a Xiongnu chieftain in 33 BC.

Other places of interest:

Baotou—The largest city in Inner Mongolia, Baotou was greatly expanded after the founding of the PRC. It is now an industrial centre with iron and steel works. Nearby is the eighteenth-century Tibetan monastery of Wudangzhao.

Xinjiang Uygur autonomous region

Topographical features: Tianshan Mountains; Lake of Heaven in mountains below Mt Bogda, 100 miles south-east of Ürümqi, Turpan (Turfan) Basin 160 m below sea level; arid desert region

Population: 14 063 267

Population of main cities: Ürümqi—1 055 852; Shihezi—543 431

Economic geography: Xinjiang is one of China's chief pastoral areas, with a tradition of animal husbandry, particularly in sheep and horse production. The region is rich in minerals, with deposits including oil, coal, gold, mica, jade and asbestos. The Tarim and Junggar basins have large areas of oil-containing structures with high pressure and good yields. Crops include cereal crops and long-staple cotton. Xinjiang has built up an industrial system including a range of industries such as petroleum, coal mining, iron and steel and machine building.

Products: Main producer of grapes; third largest of beetroots; important producer of cotton; main producer of mutton; fourth largest of milk.

Capital: Ürümqi

Climate: temp.:–11.7°C and 24.9°C; rain: (Feb.) 4 mm and (Sept.) 46 mm; sun: 111 hrs and (Aug.) 327 hrs

Features and history: Ürümqi developed as Xinjiang's most modern city with the completion of the railway in 1963, but it also has Islamic and early twentieth-century Russian architecture.

Other places of interest:

Turpan—Historically a centre of Buddhism, Turpan contains the One Thousand Buddha Caves, which once rivalled Dunhuang. It is also a centre of Islam, with the Imin Minaret and Mosque dating from 1776. Turpan Basin, nicknamed 'the Oven', experiences temperatures of 48°, and Lake Aydingkol in its centre, at 154 m below sea level, is the second lowest land place on earth. Irrigation enables extensive fruit production, including grapes and melons. Gaochang and Jiaohe were flourishing centres on the Silk Road, the former with a population of 50 000 during the Tang Dynasty, but abandoned in the fourteenth century; and the latter with a population of 6000, flourishing between the second and fourteenth centuries.

Ningxia Hui autonomous region

Topographical features: Arid desert and mountains

Population: 4 351 553

Population of main city: The population of the 'urban areas' of the largest city, Yinchuan, is 433 621.

Economic geography: Ningxia has a long tradition of agriculture, and is China's chief producer of sheep fleeces. The Yinchuan plain has also become an important base for commercial cereals production in north-west China. Crops include wheat, rice, sorghum, maize, millet and broom corn millet. The area also has abundant aquatic products. Mineral deposits include coal, phosphorus, petroleum, salt, iron and chromium. There are large reserves of coal, and a coal industry base has been established along the Helan mountain ranges. The power industry has also seen rapid development since 1949. Other industries include machine building, metallurgy, chemical, petroleum and electronic industries.

Products: No major products; some grain, beetroots, fruit, freshwater fish.

Capital: Yinchuan

Climate: temp.:–7.1°C and 23.3°C; rain: 0 mm and (Aug.) 56 mm; sun: 157 hrs and 290 hrs

Features and history: Yinchuan was the Western Xia capital in the eleventh century, with the Drum Tower in the city centre and streets radiating outwards from this. Beita, the Northern Pagoda or Haibaota, and Chengtian Xita, the Western Pagoda, are two sites of interest; the former, with its monastery, dates from the fifth century.

Other places of interest:

Gunzhongkou—In the vicinity of this mountain resort near Mt Helan are the twin pagodas, Baisikou Shuangta, and the Western Xia Mausoleum.

Qingtongxia—Contains a group of 108 dagobas dating from the Yuan dynasty.

Zhongwei—A market town on the railway line 167 km south-west of Yinchuan, Zhongwei features Gao Miao, a temple dedicated to Buddhism, Daoism and Confucianism, whose fifteenth century buildings, destroyed several times, have since been partially restored.

CENTRAL CHINA

Jiangsu province

Topographical features: Lake Taihu: 2425 km²

Population: 63 480 088

Population of main cities: Nanjing—2 390 681;

Yancheng—1 286 499; Wuxi—878 000; Suzhou—736 246; Xuzhou—855 654; Changzhou—633 083

Economic geography: Both industry and agriculture play an important part in Jiangsu's economy. The province's industry encompasses a range of fields, with textiles, light industry, electronics, chemicals and machine-building important. Jiangsu's chemicals, silk reeling and silk textiles are especially significant. The cultivation rate of land in the province is 60 per cent, with a wide variety of crops. The province is a very important grain producer, with cereal crops accounting for 70 per cent of cultivated land—especially rice, wheat and barley. Jiangsu is also an important cotton-producing area.

Products: Main producer of sulphuric acid; second largest producer of chemical fertilizer; second largest producer of a.c. motors; third largest producer of mining equipment and metal-cutting machine tools; main producer of radios and second largest producer of television sets, electric fans, cameras and recorders; third largest producer of bicycles and refrigerators; main producer of woollen goods, cloth and yarn; second largest producer of chemical fibres; third largest producer of edible vegetable oil; second largest grain producer: third largest producer of rice and wheat; important producer of soybeans and tubers; third largest producer of cotton and silkworm cocoons; third largest oil-bearing crop producer: third largest producer of rapeseed and important producer of peanuts; fourth largest producer of pears and important producer of grapes; significant producer of fish and shellfish: main producer of freshwater shellfish, and second largest of freshwater fish; main meat producer: second largest producer of pork, and significant producer of mutton.

Capital: Nanjing, previously called Jiankang and Jinling

Climate: temp.: 2.4° C and (Aug.) 26.9° C; rain: (Feb.) 4 mm and 199 mm; sun: (Nov.) 107 hrs and 255 hrs

Features and history: Nanjing is the more-than-2000 years-old capital of eight dynasties, including (for about half a century) the Ming Dynasty. After the suppression of the Taiping Heavenly Kingdom during the Qing Dynasty, the Ming city walls and the tomb of Ming founder Hongwu, although still extant, were severely damaged. Also of interest are Xuanwu Lake, Linggu Monastery, Sun Yatsen Mausoleum and Qixia Mountain.

Other places of interest:

Yangzhou—Founded 400 BC and situated on the Grand Canal, this city was famed for its scholarship, because its scenic attractions tempted many scholars to retire there. Its elegantly carved, narrow canal-side dwellings, reminiscent of Holland or Venice, have escaped modernization, even since the advent of the railway and subsequent decline of the canal in importance.

Suzhou—Founded around 600 BC by the King of Wu on the shores of Lake Taihu, Suzhou, like Yangzhou, was an important trading centre on the Grand Canal, especially for silk, for which it remains famous. The city is the site of 107 beautiful gardens created by retired scholars; of six remaining open to the public, the most famed is that of the Master of Fishing Nets. Other attractions are Tiger Hill, the birthplace of Suzhou's founder; the Tang Dynasty Bridge with fifty-three arches, a museum and the Silk Embroidery Institute.

Anhui province

Topographical features: The province is divided into three sections by the Huaihe running southwest to north-east across north-western end, and the Changjiang running roughly parallel across south-eastern end. Huangshan, or the 'Yellow Mountains', standing 1830 m, are composed of seventy-two peaks.

Population: 52 866 217

Population of main cities: Huainan—1 111 161; Hefei—927 013; Bengbu—638 699; Wuhu—516 648; Huaibei—513 841

Economic geography: Anhui has some important mineral reserves, with proven coal deposits amounting to 22.3 billion tonnes (half the total in east China), iron reserves amounting to 2.4 billion tonnes (ranked first in east China) and copper reserves ranked second in east China. The province has an industrial system comprising coal mining, metallurgy, electricity generation, machine-building, chemicals, building materials, textiles, food processing and other industries. Anhui is also an important agricultural area, with some significant rice-producing areas, and commodity cereal production. Tea is also produced in certain areas of the province, and Anhui has the largest freshwater fish-farming area in China.

Products: Significant grain producer: third largest producer of soybeans, and also producer of rice, wheat and tubers; fourth largest producer of oil-bearing crops: second largest producer of rapeseed and third largest of sesame; main producer of hemp; third largest of pine resin; fourth largest of tea; significant producer of silkworm cocoons, pears and grapes; second largest producer of marine shellfish; significant producer of freshwater products: second largest producer of freshwater crustacea.

Capital: Hefei

Climate: temp.: 3.1° C and (Aug.) 27.1° C; rain: (Feb.) 4 mm and (Jul.) 239 mm; sun: (Nov.) 115 hrs and 258 hrs

Features and history: A small market town prior to 1949, Hefei is now a modern industrial centre and home of the National Science and Technology University. Anhui Provincial Museum contains a 2000-year-old jade burial costume.

Other places of interest:
Huangshan—One of China's five sacred mountains, Huangshan's scenic grandeur has been renowned throughout history. The most famous of its peaks are Lotus Flower Peak, Bright Summit and Heavenly Capital.

Hubei province

Topographical features: Mountainous areas interspersed with large areas of alluvial lowlands, lakes and rivers, including Changjiang

Population: 50 580 806

Population of main cities: Wuhan—3 571 168; Xiaogan—1 227 538; Jingmen—973 451; Ezhou—851 445

Economic geography: Hubei's economy has both an industrial and an agricultural base, and the province is rich in minerals. These include gypsum, with the highest output in China, iron, copper and several others. Hubei's industries include iron and steel, machine-building, building materials, ship-building, instrument making and textiles, with several heavy industrial enterprises being of national significance. The province's agriculture has characteristics of both the north and south, with crops including rice, wheat, maize, Chinese sorghum and sweet potatoes. The Jianghan plain is one of China's most important rice and wheat areas, and Hubei's output of ramie ranks amongst the first in China. Hubei is also a major freshwater produce centre, exporting a large output of fish fry each year. It is also an important area for forest reserves.

Products: Third largest producer of steel, and main producer of rolled steel; second largest producer of pig-iron; main producer of motor vehicles; third largest producer of tractors; second largest producer of herbal medicine; significant producer of grain, including rice, and of cotton, tea, citrus fruit and pears; main producer of sesame, and second largest of hemp and lacquer; third largest producer of freshwater products, including second largest production of fish and all types of shellfish; important meat producer, including pork.

Capital: Wuhan

Climate: temp.: 4.6° C and (Aug.) 27.9° C; rain: (Feb.) 10 mm and (Jul.) 226 mm; sun: (Mar.) 114 hrs and 251 hrs

Features and history: Wuhan is actually composed of three cities on the confluence of the Changjiang and Han Rivers: Hankou, Hanyang and Wuchang. Hankou, on the north bank of the Han River, is a modern commercial city displaying some colonial-style buildings and boulevards. Hanyang, on the south bank of Han River, is built in more traditional style, and affords a panoramic view of the rivers from Tortoise Hill, the site of the temple of Yu. It also contains a monastery with 500 statues of Sakyamuni's disciples. Wuchang, on the east bank of the Changjiang, is an old Han city with many features of historical interest. On Snake Hill are found a stone terrace, site of the Yellow Crane Pavilion; Yuan Dynasty stupa; and the headquarters of the 1911 Revolution. East Lake is the site of many temples and pagodas; Hubei Historical Museum is also situated here.

CENTRAL–SOUTH CHINA

Hunan province

Topographical features: Alluvial lowlands dissected by rivers and lakes, including Dongting Lake, 2824 km², the second largest freshwater lake in China.

Population: 57 826 065

Population of main cities: Changsha—1 226 819; Hengyang—630 695; Xiangtan—629 468; Zhuzhou—527 110

Economic geography: Hunan is a major centre of China's non-ferrous metallurgical industry. Its reserves of non-ferrous metals and rare metals occupy an important place in the national economy, with rich stibium reserves and major lead, zinc, mercury and kaolin deposits. The province has approximately ninety large non-ferrous metallurgical enterprises. Hunan is one of China's major grain suppliers. Its chief cereal crop is rice, and it also has one of the largest outputs of ramie in China. Tea is another major product and Hunan is also well known for its pigs and pig products.

Products: Third largest producer of chemical fertilizer; third largest producer of locomotives and second largest producer of rolling stock; fourth largest grain producer; main producer of rice; significant producer of sugar cane, tobacco, lacquer, fruit; third largest producer of citrus fruit and second largest producer of tea; third largest producer of tung-oil seed; important producer of aquatic products, including marine shellfish; third

largest producer of freshwater fish; and significant producer of all types of shellfish; second largest meat producer, including pork.

Capital: Changsha

Climate: temp.: 5.6° C and 28.2° C; rain: (Aug.) 2 mm and (Apr.) 187 mm; sun: (Apr.) 54 hrs and 198 hrs

Features and history: Changsha is divided by the Xiang River, which has formed a long sandbank or 'changsha' at that point. On the sandbank is found Juzi Zhou Tou Memorial Pavilion in memory of Mao Zedong, who received his education here. Yuelu Hill offers panoramic views of city, now dominated by modern architecture, although it dates back to Warring States Period, as part of the Kingdom of Chu. The provincial museum contains treasures from the Western Han tomb of Mawangdui. Puppet shows are a feature of modern Changsha.

Zhejiang province

Topographical features: Part of fertile Yangzi Basin

Population: 41 211 921

Population of main cities: Hangzhou—1 291 623; Ningbo—1 048 493; Huzhou—985 489; Jiaxing—708 994;Zhoushan—652 234; Wenzhou—543 900

Economic geography: Industry in Zhejiang is mainly light and small scale, with the silk textiles, papermaking and wine-making industries important to China's economy. Zhejiang is known as 'the home of silk' and has established a comprehensive silk production system. Most of the yellow rice wine of China is produced in the province. The high-grade industrial paper made in Zhejiang holds a leading position in China. The province has quite rich non-metallic mineral reserves, with deposits of fluorine ranking first in the country. Zhejiang has a high level of agricultural production. The diverse economy includes farming, forestry, animal husbandry and fishery. Rice is the primary crop, and silk and tea are also important.

Products: Second largest producer of generators and metal-cutting machine tools; main producer of washing machines; second largest producer of refrigerators, electric irons and aluminium household utensils; third largest producer of electric fans; main producer of silk; third largest producer of woollen goods; main producer of canned food; largest producer of tea, a quarter of China's total output; second largest producer of silkworm cocoons; significant fruit producer: fourth largest producer of citrus fruit; important producer of rice, hemp, sugar cane, walnuts and milk; second largest aquatic producer; and main producer of marine produce specifically; also significant producer of freshwater produce, including fish and shellfish.

Capital: Hangzhou

Climate: temp.: 4.3° C and 28.4° C; rain: 14 mm and 210 mm; sun: (Jan.) 157 hrs and 231 hrs

Features and history: Situated on the Grand Canal between West Lake and Qiantang River, it is said of this city with its lovely scenery, 'Above is Heaven; below are Hangzhou and Suzhou'. Hangzhou has been one of China's principal silk producers since the Tang Dynasty, and Hangzhou Silk Printing and Dyeing Complex is the largest in China. Hangzhou is the home of two great poets, Bai Juyi and Su Dongpo. During the sixth century, when there were settlements on surrounding hills, West Lake was a shallow bay in Qiantang River which gradually became silted up. After AD 610, when the Grand Canal reached Hangzhou, the city's development began, and Hangzhou finally became the capital of the Southern Song Dynasty, 1138–1279. In the thirteenth century Marco Polo described it as the most prosperous city in the world. However, it declined in importance from the Ming Dynasty onwards. Much of the city, together with hundreds of Buddhist monasteries and temples on surrounding hillsides, was devastated either as a result of the suppression of the Taiping Heavenly Kingdom in the nineteenth century, or during the PRC's early history. Restoration and reafforestation of West Lake, with its numerous islands and surrounding pagodas and temples, has since been successfully accomplished. The Pagoda of Six Harmonies and Lingyin Temple date from 970 and 326 respectively. Nearby is the West Lake

People's Commune, where Dragon Well tea is grown.

Other places of interest:
Shaoxing—This was the birthplace of China's most famous modern writer, Lu Xun, whose deeds are enshrined in the Lu Xun Museum. Attractions include old wood and stone buildings, including canalside dwellings similar to those in Suzhou, and the original wineshop used by Lu Xun as the setting for his story *New Year Sacrifice*, where famous Shaoxing wine is still served. Shaoxing was also the home of China's early female revolutionary, Qiu Jin, whose house is now a museum. Outside the town are found the temple and tomb of Yu the Great, the semi-mythical founder of the Xia Dynasty, twenty-first to sixteenth centuries BC.

Jiangxi province

Topographical features: Fertile alluvial lowlands, lakes and rivers; bounded by Changjiang in north

Population: 35 589 531

Population of main cities: Pingxiang—1 328 187; Nanchang—1 259 728; Xinyu—635 032; Jingdezhen—589 643

Economic geography: Jiangxi has a diverse range of products, including minerals, fine porcelain and agricultural products. The province has the second largest wolfram reserve in China, accounting for half the country's wolfram exports, and its copper reserves rank first in China. Tantalum and nickel are also important minerals. The province's porcelain, made at Jingdezhen, is world famous and the city is known as 'the capital of porcelain'. Agriculture is important to Jiangxi's economy, and the province is one of China's commodity grain-producing centres. The most important crop is rice. Jiangxi is one of China's main tea-growing areas and is also an important timber-producing area, with more than 60 per cent of its total area covered by forests.

Products: Second largest producer of ferro-alloy and third largest producer of generators; significant producer of rice, sugar cane, tea and citrus fruit; third largest producer of marine shellfish, and significant producer of freshwater produce, including fish and all types of shellfish; significant producer of forestry products: second largest producer of tea-oil seed and fourth largest of pine resin.

Capital: Nanchang

Climate: temp.: 5.9° C and 29° C; rain: (Dec.) 14 mm and 370 mm; sun: (Apr.) 83 hrs and (Aug.) 296 hrs

Features and history: Nanchang was the birthplace of the PLA following the uprising led by Zhou Enlai and Zhu De in 1927.

Other places of interest:
Lushan—one of China's five sacred mountains, Lushan's cluster of peaks rises to 1475 m above Lake Poyang and Changjiang, with the resort town of Guling at 1098 m. Here can be seen the Daoist Cave of Immortality, a sub-alpine Botanical Garden and the former residence of Chiang Kaishek.

Shanghai municipality

Climate: temp.: 3.3° C and 27.5° C; rain: 13 mm and 296 mm; sun: (Nov.) 106 hrs and 230 hrs

Population: 12 495 087

Population of 'urban areas': 7 217 737

Economic geography: Shanghai is China's most powerful industrial centre. It is primarily a centre of industrial processing, with a good balance of large and small enterprises, and of light and heavy industries. Enterprises in Shanghai generally have a high level of scientific and technological expertise. Major industries are steel, metallurgy, chemicals, machine building, shipbuilding, electronics, instruments and meters, textiles and handicrafts. Products of the city's chemical industry include sulphuric acid, caustic soda, chemical fertilizers, medicines, pesticides, chemical fibres, synthetic rubber and plastics. The electronics industry produces complete sets of electronic instruments,

meters and computers. Light and textile industries are well developed and the output of products such as television sets, bicycles and sewing machines accounts for between 10 and 30 per cent of China's total. Agriculture remains important on the city's outskirts, with rice, wheat, cotton, rape and vegetables being the main crops.

Products: Second largest producer of steel and rolled steel; third largest producer of pig-iron, coke and ferro-alloy; third largest producer of a.c. motors and fourth largest producer of metal-cutting machine tools; main producer of bicycles, nearly one-fifth of China's total; television sets, nearly a quarter of China's total; sewing machines, nearly one-third of the total; cameras and electric irons; second largest producer of colour televisions, radios, washing machines and watches; largest producer of chemical fibres; second largest producer of plastics, yarn, cloth and woollen goods; significant producer of fish, shellfish and milk.

Features and history: Five thousand years old, Shanghai began as a small trading centre on Huangpu, or Whampoa, Creek. It was of little import until the nineteenth century establishment of Western treaty ports, and it is now China's largest city and industrial centre, and the country's principal port. The architecture of Nanjing Road and the waterfront area, or Bund, still display marks of the International Concession, while the still-popular Jinjiang Hotel is found in the French quarter. In the old Chinese quarter is found the Yu Garden, dating from the Ming Dynasty, and the Huxingting Teahouse, while the Longhua Pagoda and Jade Buddha Temple date back to the Song and Qing Dynasties respectively. From twentieth-century China, the Lu Xun Museum, Residence and Tomb, commemorating China's greatest modern writer, and the Shanghai Art Museum and Children's Palace are notable features.

SOUTH CHINA

Guangdong province

(Note that the information under Guangdong province includes the island of Hainan, which was detached from Guangdong and upgraded as another province in April 1988—see Chapter 1, under *B. Domestic Political Events*, 1988.)

Topographical features: Coastal province with rich alluvial valleys and plains

Population: 64 472 237

Population of main cities: Guangzhou—3 417 112; Zhanjiang—967 886; Shantou—786 660

Economic geography: Guangdong is an important centre of light industry, leading the country in the production of sugar, canned food, ceramics, dry batteries and arts and crafts. Food processing is the province's major industry, and Guangdong is China's principal sugar producer. Other products include umbrellas, salt, paper, textiles, knitwear, sewing machines and bicycles, all of which are produced in large quantities. Heavy industries include iron and steel, electricity, rubber, machinery, petroleum, coal, chemicals, non-ferrous metals and shipbuilding. Guangdong is also known for its rich underground mineral deposits of rare and non-ferrous metals. There are rich iron ore reserves, oil shale deposits and offshore oilfields. Guangdong's handicrafts, including ivory and jade carvings, are famous. The Pearl River delta is one of China's three major silk-cocoon producing centres, and Guangdong is the country's major cultivator of tropical and sub-tropical plants and China's largest producer of fruit, including bananas, pineapples, oranges and litchi. Fishery is also an important industry.

Products: Second largest producer of sulphuric acid and third largest producer of cement; major producer of colour televisions, refrigerators, electric fans, watches, aluminium household utensils; second largest producer of sewing machines; third largest producer of television sets and radios; fourth largest producer of washing machines; third largest producer of silk, and significant producer of silkworm cocoons; main producer of sugar (over one-third of China's total) and sugar cane, herbal medicine and fruit: main producer of bananas, over three-quarters of China's total, and second largest producer of citrus fruit; important producer of rice, tubers, tea, oil-bearing crops: second largest producer of peanuts; main producer of rubber, over two-thirds of China's total; and second largest of pine resin; main producer of aquatic products: largest and second largest producer of freshwater and marine products respectively; main producer of ocean and freshwater fish, and significant producer of all types of shellfish; second largest producer of freshwater crustacea; significant meat producer, including pork.

Capital: Guangzhou, or Canton

Climate: temp.: (Feb.) 13.1° C and (Aug.) 29.3° C; rain: 1 mm and (Jul.) 267 mm; sun: (Apr.) 48 hrs and (Sept.) 225 hrs

Features and history: Situated on the Pearl River estuary, Guangzhou was already a thriving port, with Arab traders among its populace, by the Tang Dynasty: Huaisheng Mosque, built in 627, is China's oldest mosque. From the sixteenth century until the signing of the Treaty of Nanjing in 1842, as the only Chinese port open to European traders, Guangzhou flourished. In 1840, the Opium Wars started here, and after the treaty was signed, Guangzhou lost its unique status and some of its importance. However, Guangzhou's modern World Trade Fair illustrates the continuing importance of international trade to the city. The Cantonese supported their local leader, Sun Yatsen, in the 1911 Revolution, and Sun Yatsen Memorial Hall is located here. Mao Zedong and Zhou Enlai's efforts to educate Guangdong peasants later in the 1920s are commemorated by the National Peasant Movement Institute. Other interesting features are the History Museum, Hualin Temple, Temple of Six Banyan Trees and Guangxiao Monastery. Nearby are Shamian Island, still retaining evidence of its foreign occupation; White Cloud Mountain Park; Seven Star Crags; and Foshan or 'Buddha Mountain'.

Other places of interest:
Shenzhen, Shantou, and the Hainan and Zhuhai Special Economic Zones.Hong Kong and Macao adjoin the province.

Guangxi Zhuang autonomous region

Topographical features: Limestone karst formations

Population: 40 163 861

Population of main cities: Nanning—998 737; Liuzhou—679 267

Economic geography: Prior to the founding of the PRC, Guangxi was industrially underdeveloped, but has made considerable progress over the past four decades. Heavy industry includes machine building, non-ferrous metallurgy, power generation, chemical, coal, iron and steel and cement, while light industry includes sugar refining, paper-making, cannery and tannery plants. Sugar refining is important, as Guangxi is one of the leading sugar producers in China. Agriculture is central to the autonomous region's economy, with rice being the major cereal crop, together with maize, sweet potato and wheat. The southern part of Guangxi is a major tropical and subtropical plant development area. This autonomous region is known for its fruits and also has a forestry industry and fishery.

Products: Third largest producer of rolling stock; second largest producer of canned food, sugar and sugar cane; significant fruit producer, including citrus fruit, and second largest producer of bananas; second largest producer of rubber, and third largest of tea-oil seed; significant producer of aquatic products, and marine products specifically, including fish and crustacea.

Capital: Nanning

Climate: temp.: (Feb.) 12.9° C and (Aug.) 28.7° C; rain: 8 mm and 416 mm; sun: (Feb.) 51 hrs and (Aug.) 228 hrs

Features and history: Of comparatively little significance before the present century, Nanning has now become an important light industrial centre on the Yong River.

Other places of interest:
Guilin—On the Li River, founded in the third century BC by Qinshi Huangdi, with the establishment of nearby Ling Canal, Guilin has long been known for its limestone karst scenery, including, in the town centre, Solitary Beauty Peak. At the base of Fubo Hill, on the Li River, are found caves with Tang and Song Buddhist carvings. Reed Flute Cave and Seven Star Cave are also of interest.

Yangshuo—Eighty kilometres upstream from Guilin, Yangshuo, perched high on rocky cliffs above the river, is a frequent destination of tourist boats travelling up the Li River. Stone steps lead up cliffs to the old town with its still-thriving marketplace and an ancient stone washpool in its centre.

Fujian province

Topographical features: Extremely mountainous, with narrow but fertile river valleys

Population: 28 005 196

Population of main cities: Fuzhou—1 236 560; Xiamen—569 757

Economic geography: Fujian's industries have developed in low-technology areas such as sugar, paper, canned food, plastics, pottery and porcelain. More than 60 per cent of the province's total output value comes from this sector. Other industries include coal mining, cement, electricity and timber processing. Handicrafts are another important industry. The province has a wide range of mineral deposits, and salt is produced along the coastal areas. Fujian produces mainly grain crops, with rice as the staple. Grains account for more than 80 per cent of the total sown area. The province is also one of the sugar-producing areas of China, and a major tea-producing area. Fruits, including tropical fruits, are an important product. The province is one of the China's four largest forestry areas.

Products: Third largest producer of sugar, sugar cane and bananas; fourth largest of rubber; significant producer of tea and pears; significant producer of aquatic products, including marine products: third largest producer of fish, and significant producer of crustacea, third largest producer of seaweed, and a significant producer of freshwater shellfish.

Capital: Fuzhou

Climate: temp.: (Feb.) 9.1° C and 29° C; rain: 6 mm and 226 mm; sun: (Nov.) 74 hrs and (Jul.) 243 hrs

Features and history: On the banks of the Min River, surrounded by hills such as the famous Drum Hill, Fuzhou was a thriving trading centre by the thirteenth century, with Moslem, Jewish and Christian traders among its populace. Mosques and temples to Ma Zu, the goddess of the sea, abound.

Other places of interest:
Xiamen Special Economic Zone, previously known as Amoy—On the coast at the mouth of the Jiulong River, Xiamen was established during the Ming Dynasty, and during the following Qing Dynasty became the stronghold of Ming loyalist buccaneer Koxinga. The Overseas Chinese Museum is of interest.

SOUTH-WEST CHINA

Sichuan province

Topographical features: Fertile plains; Changjiang runs across south-eastern corner through Changjiang Gorges; Mt Emei.

Population: 104 583 717

Population of main cities: Chongqing—2 888 519; Chengdu—2 694 265; Suining—1 216 388; Leshan—1 049 615; Zigong—940 290; Mianyang—870 516; Guangyuan—831 638; Deyang—782 224; Panzhihua—560 628

Economic geography: Sichuan is the most important new industrial centre in south-west China. Its industries include metallurgical, power generation, coal, petroleum, chemicals, machine-building, building materials, forestry, food processing, textiles, tannery and paper-making operations. Machine-building is the largest of these, with iron and steel also important. Well known for its mineral resources, Sichuan has the second largest deposits of natural gas in China, has a quarter of China's phosphorus deposits, and has the highest ranking output of salt in China. The province also has important asbestos and mica deposits. Sichuan produces 10 per cent of China's total cereals output. Its production of rice is ranked among the first in China, and its wheat, maize and sweet potato production is also important to China's economy. Its sugar cane production ranks second in China. Sichuan has one of the three major afforested areas in the country, as well as one of the five largest grassland pastures, making animal husbandry important. Sichuan leads China in pig production.

Products: Main producer of natural gas, and chemical fertilizer; third largest producer of sulphuric acid; fourth largest producer of coke; second largest producer of silk and machine-made paper and board; main producer of edible vegetable oil; second largest producer of salt; third largest producer of canned food; main grain producer: second largest producer of rice, significant producer of wheat and corn, and main producer of tubers; second largest producer of oil-bearing crops; third largest producer of hemp and tea; significant producer of sugar cane and tobacco; fourth largest fruit producer: largest citrus fruit producer, and significant producer of pears; main producer of silkworm cocoons and tung-oil seed; fourth largest producer of lacquer; and significant producer of walnuts; significant producer of aquatic products, especially freshwater fish; major meat producer: largest producer of pork, and second largest of beef, significant producer of mutton, and third largest producer of milk.

Capital: Chengdu, formerly Jinjiangcheng

Climate: temp.: 6.4° C and 25.5° C; rain: (Dec.) 3 mm and (Jul.) 216 mm; sun: (Nov.) 48 hrs and (Aug.) 166 hrs

Features and history: Dating back 2500 years, Chengdu was a minor town during the Warring States Period, rising to prominence as the capital of the state of Shu during the Three Kingdoms Period. During the Eastern Han Dynasty it was named Jinjiangcheng, or Brocade City, as the silk industry flourished here. The city was devastated during the thirteenth century by Mongols after Sichuanese resistance to their invasion. In the seventeenth century Chengdu was briefly the headquarters of an independent Sichuanese state. It was also one of the last GMD strongholds in the 1940s. Interesting sights in or near Chengdu include Wuhou Temple, commemorating Zhuge Liang, Shu's great military leader, the home of the great poet, Du Fu, Riverview Pavilion Park, the vice-regal Summer Palace, destroyed during the Cultural Revolution and recently restored, and Green City Mountain, with its monasteries, temples and pavilions.

Other places of interest:

Leshan—This is the home of great modern writer and scientist Guo Moruo, where the world's largest stone Buddha is found, carved in cliffs above the Min River.

Mt Emei—This is one of China's five sacred mountains, with many Buddhist monasteries.

Chongqing or Chungking—Originally a village of houses on stilts, built at confluence of Changjiang and Jialing River, Chongqing became the Nationalist headquarters during the Japanese occupation and is now a modern city. Zhou Enlai's former home is here, and nearby in Red Crag Village are the headquarters of the Eighth Route Army from the Sino-Japanese War. Scenic sights include Beiwenquan and Nanwenquan parks, as well as Jinyunshan.

Changjiang Gorges—Trips by steamer from Chongqing to Wuhan, stopping at the town of Wanxian, reveal towering cliffs as vessels pass through Qutang, Wushan and Qiling gorges.

Yunnan province

Topographical features: A central limestone plateau with Lake Dianchi, China's sixth largest freshwater lake, in the middle. Changjiang forms part of the northern border.

Population: 35 129 988

Population of main city: Kunming—1 547 191

Economic geography: Yunnan has rich mineral deposits, with reserves of tin, lead and zinc which rank first in China. Proven coal deposits total more than 14 billion tonnes, and there are rich marble deposits. Industries established since 1949 include mining, metallurgy, power, coal, chemicals, machine building, building materials, food processing, textiles, electronics and paper making. The most important of these is the nonferrous metal industry. The province has a complex cultivation system and a wide variety of crops, although rice production accounts for half of its total cereals output. Yunnan is famous for its tea. The northern part of the province is a major forestry area, while the southern section is an important production base for tropical and subtropical crops and fruit.

Products: Largest tin producer; second largest producer of cigarettes; and main tobacco producer; main producer of walnuts; second largest of rubber; and significant producer of lacquer; fourth largest producer of sugar cane and bananas; significant producer of tea and pears; and freshwater crustacea.

Capital: Kunming, also known as City of Perpetual Spring

Climate: temp.: 7.5° C and (Jun.) 20.5° C; rain: (Feb.) 0 mm and 400 mm; sun: (Jul.) 79 hrs and (Jan.) 199 hrs

Features and history: Kunming was founded in the Han Dynasty, with many temples dating from the Yuan; the Golden Temple on Phoenix Song Hill dates from Ming times. On the shores of nearby Lake Dianchi is the Western Garden, and in the cliffs above the lake is the Dragon Gate, surmounted by two Yuan Dynasty temples, the Huating and Taihua Temples.

Other places of interest:

Stone Forest—Found in Lu'nan Yi autonomous county 120 km from Kunming, this 30 metre high karst 'forest' is composed of jagged limestone columns interspersed with lakes.

Xishuangbanna Dai autonomous prefecture—This area features tropical forests with sixty species of mammals, including elephants and gibbons, and 400 types of birds, situated on the Burmese–Lao border. Due to its location, its populace consists of members from ten different minority groups.

Guizhou province

Topographical features: Karst limestone formation

Population: 30 513 897

Population of main cities: Liupanshui—1 683 583; Guiyang—1 431 074

Economic geography: Guizhou's mineral deposits play an important part in the province's economy and industry. Coal deposits are widespread and phosphorus deposits rank third in China, as do aluminium deposits. The province also has the largest mercury deposit in the country. Guizhou's industry, which only began to see rapid development in the 1960s, consists mainly of coal, metal-lurgical, chemical, machine-building and power industries, with coal being the key sector. The province is one of China's most important metal-lurgical bases for non-ferrous metals. Light industries and winemaking are significant, with the province producing the world-famous Maotai spirit. Rapeseed output ranks among the top in China, while sugar cane is the province's principal sugar crop. Guizhou is also one of China's important fir-tree producers.

Products: Annual output of mercury and cinnabar accounts for 70 per cent of China's total; significant producer of cigarettes, textiles, paper, fur, leather and silk cloth; third largest producer of tobacco and lacquer; and significant producer of walnuts.

Capital: Guiyang

Climate: temp.: (Feb.) 5.3° C and 23.3° C; rain: (Dec.) 3.3 mm and 223 mm; sun: (Feb.) 24 hrs and (Aug.) 159 hrs

Features and history: Guiyang is an industrial city with little of interest, apart from the Ming Dynasty Hongfu Monastery, Kanzhu Pavilion and Nanjiao Park.

Other places of interest:

Huangguoshu Falls—Near Anshun, these falls, 50 m wide and with a drop of 70 m among cave-riddled cliffs, are China's most famous.

TIBET AND QINGHAI

Tibetan autonomous region

Topographical features: The Himalayan Mountains, including Qomolangma (Mt Everest), the world's highest mountain, are along the south-western border; Yarlung Zangbo River (India's Brahmaputra) with its watershed in the Himalayas, flows south through the region; Lake Nam Co, 1940 km², a saltwater lake.

Population: 2 079 499

Population of main cities: The largest city is Lhasa, the 'urban areas' of which have a population of 117 679.

Economic geography: Before the 1960s there was no real industry apart from handicrafts; however, approximately 600 small and medium-sized enterprises now produce some of the industrial products required by the region. Industries include coal mining, power, chemicals, machine building, building materials, textiles and leather processing. Tibet has reserves of ferrochrome, copper, borax and salt that are amongst the largest in China, and also has abundant geothermal resources. Agriculture is the mainstay of Tibet's economy, with highland barley the principal grain crop. Peas, broad beans, wheat, buckwheat, rice and winter highland barley are other crops. Animal husbandry is important to the Tibetan economy, with the main livestock being sheep and yaks. The region's dense primeval forests form one of the important natural forest zones in China.

Products: Significant producer of beef, mutton and milk.

Capital: Lhasa

Climate: temp.: (Dec.) – 0.7° C and (May) 17.3° C; rain: 13 mm and 296 mm; sun: 254 hrs and 295 hrs

Features and history: Lhasa is Tibet's main religious and administrative centre, 3540 m above sea level. The city has suffered considerable depredation since Chinese occupation in 1950, including the destruction of the Ganden Monastery, although much has since been restored. After the 1959 rebellion, the Fourteenth Dalai Lama, Tibet's traditional temporal and spiritual ruler, fled to India. In 1980, following a decade of repression during the Cultural Revolution, more lenient policies towards Tibet were announced, but 1987 and 1989 saw further disturbances and riots. The Potala Palace is the former seat of the Dalai Lama. A palace was first constructed on this site by Tibet's first recorded ruler, King Songtsan Gambo, 617 650, whose successors ruled until the mid-ninth century, when Buddhists took over the

leadership of government and, in the fifteenth century, installed the Dalai Lama on the throne. Modern Potala, a thirteen-storey structure built by the Fifth and Sixth Dalai Lamas, consists of White and Red Palaces, built in 1653 and 1693 respectively. There are three main monasteries: Jokhang, from the seventh century; and Sera and Drepung, from the fifteenth century.

Other places of interest:

Xigaze or Shigatse—This is Tibet's second city and home of the second most revered leader after the Dalai Lama, the Bainqen Lama, whose seat is Tashi Lumpo, a monastery built in 1447.

Gyangze or Gyantse—Also an important religious centre, Gyangze is Tibet's third city.

Qinghai province

Topographical features: Lake Qinghai, 4585 km², saltwater; north-west, Qaidam Basin, 240 500 km² of desert and saltmarsh; north-east, Qinghai (Kokonor) Basin; south, Qinghai Plateau, 4000 m above sea level and source of Changjiang and Yellow River

Population: 4 175 345

Population of main city: Xining—622 761

Economic geography: Minerals are very important to Qinghai's economy, with lake salt, sylvite, magnesia, salt, lithium, iodine, natural sulphur, bromine, limestone, quartz and asbestos ranking first in the country and several others being of national importance. There was no industry before 1949, but industries which have developed over the past four decades include metallurgy, coal mining, machine-building, textiles, chemical, petroleum and other industries. Animal husbandry is important, since Qinghai has more than 33 million hectares of pasture land, making it one of China's five largest pastoral areas. Sheep and cattle are the main livestock and Qinghai is one of China's major horse producers.

Products: Fourth largest producer of mutton and significant producer of beef and milk.

Capital: Xining

Climate: temp.: –7° C and 16.9° C; rain: 0.2 mm and 96 mm; sun: 171 hrs and (Aug.) 260 hrs

Features and history: As a trading centre only recently developed into a modern city, Xining has little to offer of historical or architectural interest.

Other places of interest:

Taersi or Kumbum Monastery—China's largest Tibetan Buddhist monastery, almost a town in its own right, is located a short distance from Xining, with ancient temple buildings, stupas and shrines and a small market complex. Two special features are a courtyard dominated by lifelike carved heads representing those animals especially sacred to the region's Tantric Buddhism; and butter sculptures given as offerings.

9 CHINA'S MINORITY NATIONALITIES

INTRODUCTION

Officially, China still adopts Stalin's definition of a nationality: a historically constituted community of people having a common territory, a common language, a common economic life and a common psychological makeup which expresses itself in a common culture. In the 1980s the Chinese government recognized fifty-six nationalities in China, the majority Han grouping and fifty-five minority nationalities.

These fifty-six are extremely diverse. Some of the minorities, including the Hui and Zhuang, are very similar to the Han; others are very different, for instance, the Turkic peoples of the west such as the Uygurs or Kazakhs, or the Iranian Tajiks. The minority nationalities occupy about 60 per cent of China's territory, including, above all, the vast western areas.

Chinese policy officially opposes forced assimilation and allows autonomy to the minority nationalities, so that they can retain their own characteristics. Under this policy, the government has set up numerous autonomous areas throughout China. The policy's real effect, however, can best be described as integration.

Both policy and reality are fiercely opposed to outright secession, which the government has suppressed brutally on several occasions. Chapter 1 lists such occasions under the years 1959, 1987 and 1989, among others. Most of the minorities have succeeded in integrating reasonably well with the Han, but independence or secessionist movements and wishes have remained strong among a few, particularly the Tibetans. Ethnic dissent among some nationalities could easily develop as an issue in the coming years.

THE POPULATIONS OF THE NATIONALITIES

Excluding members of the army, the total population of the minority nationalities in the three censuses was: July 1, 1953—35 320 360, or 6.06 per cent of China's total population; July 1, 1964—39 993 046, or 5.76 per cent of the total; and July 1, 1982—67 238 983, or 6.7 per cent of the total. The sample census taken on July 1, 1987 showed that the minority nationalities represented 8 per cent of the total population.[1]

In the 1953 census, the Han accounted for 547 283 057 people. Forty-one minority nationalities were specified, with a total population of 34 247 718 people. There were 1 072 642 people belonging to unspecified minorities. Fourteen minority nationalities had populations of half a million or more. These were: Zhuang—6 611 455; Hui—3 559 350; Uygurs—3 640 125; Yi—3 254 269; Miao—2 511 339; Tibetans—2 775 622; Mongolians—1 462 956; Manchus—2 418 931; Bouyei—1 247 883; Koreans—1 120 405; Dong—712 802; Yao—665 933; Minjia (Bai)—567 119; and Kazakhs—509 375.

Table 9.1 Census populations of the nationalities, 1964 and 1982

Nationality	Population (1964 census)	Population (1982 census)	Increase (percentage)	Nationality	Population (1964 census)	Population (1982 census)	Increase (percentage)
Han	651 296 368	936 703 824	43.82	Daur	63 595	94 126	48.01
Zhuang	8 402 483	13 383 086	59.28	Jingpo	57 891	92 976	60.61
Hui	4 488 015	7 228 398	61.06	Mulam	52 949	90 357	70.65
Uygurs	4 000 402	5 963 491	49.07	Sibe	33 451	83 683	150.17
Yi	3 388 940	5 453 564	60.92	Salar	34 680	69 135	99.35
Miao	2 788 800	5 021 175	80.05	Blang	39 411	58 473	48.37
Manchus	2 700 725	4 304 981	59.40	Gelo	26 852	54 164	101.71
Tibetans	2 504 628	3 847 875	53.63	Maonan	22 419	38 159	70.21
Mongolians	1 973 192	3 411 367	72.89	Tajiks	16 236	26 600	63.83
Tujia	525 348	2 836 814	439.99	Pumi	14 298	24 238	69.52
Bouyei	1 351 899	2 119 345	56.77	Nu	15 047	22 896	52.16
Koreans	1 348 594	1 765 204	30.89	Achang	12 032	20 433	69.82
Dong	838 254	1 426 400	70.16	Ewenki	9 695	19 398	100.08
Yao	857 866	1 411 967	64.59	Jing	4 293	13 108	205.33
Bai	709 673	1 132 224	59.54	Uzbeks	7 717	12 213	58.26
Hani	630 245	1 058 806	68.00	Benglong or Deang	7 261	12 297	69.36
Kazakhs	491 867	907 546	84.51	Juno	—	11 962	—
Dai	536 399	839 496	56.51	Yugurs	5 717	10 568	84.85
Li	439 587	887 107	101.80	Bonan	5 125	9 017	75.94
Lisu	270 976	481 884	77.83	Drung	3 090	4 633	49.94
She	234 320	371 965	58.74	Oroqen	2 709	4 103	51.46
Lahu	191 241	304 256	59.10	Tatars	2 294	4 122	79.69
Va	200 295	298 611	49.09	Russians	1 326	2 917	119.98
Shui	156 388	286 908	83.46	Gaoshan	366	1 650	350.82
Dongxiang	147 460	279 523	89.56	Hezhen	718	1 489	107.38
Naxi	157 862	251 592	59.37	Moinba	3 809	1 140	−70.07
Tu	77 484	159 632	106.02	Lhoba	—	1 066	—
Kirghiz	70 175	113 386	61.58	Others	17 706	799 705	4416.58
Qiang	49 241	102 815	108.80	Indeterminate	15 802	—	—

The original 1982 census figures show an 'indeterminate' population about 80 000 greater than that shown in the 'others' category in the later and more highly processed figures for the same census. Some 'indeterminate' persons had clearly been allocated to a nationality in the later analysis. To determine precisely to which nationality a person belongs may be difficult in some instances—for example, in the case of the children of mixed marriages. There has also been some reallocation among nationalities. For instance, the figures for the Moinba and Lhoba are very much higher in the original version than the later version of the 1982 census: the original figures show 6248 for the Moinba and 2065 for the Lhoba. Substantial groups have been reallocated, probably to the Tibetan or the Han nationalities.

In the 1964 census, there were 183 nationalities registered, among which the government recognized only fifty-four. Of the remaining 129 nationalities, seventy-four were considered to be part of the officially recognized fifty-four, twenty-three were classified as 'other nationalities' and the remaining thirty-two were classified as 'indeterminate'.

The order given in Table 9.1 is by size according to the 1982 census. Other than natural increase, the most important reason for the population growth among the minority nationalities between the 1964 and 1982 censuses was the re-registration of people as members of minority nationalities. The best illustrative example of this is the Tujia, who are not very different from the Han. The 439.99 per cent average growth rate is largely explained by Han people simply reregistering as Tujia, an action which brought with it personal social benefits. The large rise in the proportion of the minority nationalities between 1982 and 1987 (6.7 to 8 per cent) is also mainly due to the re-registration of significant numbers of Han people as members of minority nationalities, although it also relates to the substantial (though not total) exemption of members of minority nationalities from the family planning policy. There are no 1964 figures for the Juno and Lhoba because they were not then recognized as minority nationalities. The figures do not include Taiwan province, where there is, for instance, a substantial Gaoshan community.

The figures for the Tibetan populations given by exile communities also differ substantially from the official Chinese figures.[2] The reasons for the decline in the Tibetan population between the 1953 and 1964 censuses are highly controversial. There are two likely explanations. The first is that the population was continuing a decline which had been occurring for centuries as the result of a high proportion of the population being in the monastic estate. Secondly, the 1959 rebellion and its suppression caused a large number of refugees to leave China, as well as some deaths. The Legal Inquiry Committee of the International Commission of Jurists carried out two investigations,[3] which suggested that breaches of human rights may have occurred on a scale which could have affected Tibetan demography in the period between 1953 and 1960. On the other hand, a Chinese analysis of the lower count of Tibetans in 1964 than in 1953 suggested primarily that the 1953 census overcounted the Tibetans. The figure for Tibet itself was based on estimates given to the central government by the local regime, which was still dominated by the old rulers. These exaggerated the population figures because they followed the principle that 'the larger the population the greater the power'.[4]

MINORITY NATIONALITIES BY PROVINCE

The following list gives population figures for minority nationalities in those provinces or autonomous regions which had minority populations of one million or more according to the 1982 census.[5]

Inner Mongolian autonomous region

The minority population was 2 996 380, 15.5 per cent of the total. The most populous minorities were:

Mongolians	2 489 780	Hui	169 096
Manchus	236 390	Daur	58 611

Ewenki	18 139	Oroqen	2 055
Koreans	17 564		

Xinjiang Uygur autonomous region

The minority population was 7 795 148, or 59.6 per cent of the total. The most populous minorities were:

Uygurs	5 949 661	Tajiks	26 484
Kazakhs	903 370	Uzbeks	12 433
Hui	570 788	Manchus	9 137
Mongolians	117 460	Daur	4 369
Kirghiz	112 979	Tatars	4 106
Sibe	27 364		

Guangxi Zhuang autonomous region

The minority population was 13 936 254, or 38.3 per cent of the total. The most populous minorities were:

Zhuang	12 332 098	Hui	19 279
Yao	863 407	Jing	9 845
Miao	338 014	Yi	4 676
Dong	229 589	Shui	4 032
Mulam	88 753	Gelo	974
Maonan	37 906		

Ningxia Hui autonomous region

The minority nationality population was 1 244 224, or 31.9 per cent of the total. The most populous minorities were:

Hui	1 235 207	Mongolians	859
Manchus	7 085		

Tibetan autonomous region

The minority population was 1 800 673, or 95.2 per cent of the total. The principal minority nationalities were:

Tibetans	1 786 544	Lhoba	2 023
Moinba	6 193	Hui	1 788

Qinghai province

The minority population was 1 535 727, or 39.4 per cent of the total. The most populous minorities were:

Tibetans	754 254	Mongolians	50 456
Hui	533 750	Manchus	3 048
Tu	128 930	Kazakhs	1 497
Salar	60 930		

Yunnan province

The minority nationality population was 10 318 998, or 31.7 per cent of the total. The minorities were:

Yi	3 354 993	Tibetans	95 915
Bai	1 121 051	Jingpo	92 915
Hani	1 058 416	Blang	58 318
Zhuang	888 159	Pumi	24 169
Dai	836 089	Nu	22 859
Miao	752 226	Achang	20 412
Lisu	466 909	Benglong	12 275
Hui	438 883	Juno	11 966
Lahu	304 059	Shui	6 301
Va	298 510	Mongolians	6 233
Naxi	236 409	Bouyei	4 721
Yao	147 208	Drung	4 592

Guizhou province

The minority population was 7 425 537, or 26 per cent of the total. The most populous minorities were:

Miao	2 588 277	Shui	274 856
Bouyei	2 100 121	Hui	100 058
Dong	849 124	Gelo	51 204
Yi	563 747		

Sichuan province

The minority population was 3 661 277, or 3.7 per cent of the total. The most populous minorities were:

Yi	1 525 713	Miao	358 129
Tibetans	922 024	Qiang	102 513
Tujia	595 349		

Gansu province

The minority population was 1 548 975, or 7.9 per cent of the total. The most populous minorities were:

Hui	950 974	Manchus	8 499
Tibetans	304 540	Bonan	8 325
Dongxiang	237 858	Mongolians	6 226
Tu	12 567	Salar	5 116
Yugurs	10 227	Kazakhs	2 367

Jilin province

The minority population was 1 827 659, or 8.1 per cent of the total. The most populous minorities were:

Koreans	1 103 402	Hui	110 673
Manchus	517 276	Mongolians	93 038

Heilongjiang province

The minority population was 1 608 838, or 4.9 per cent of the total. The most populous minorities were:

Manchus	908 910	Daur	30 192
Koreans	431 140	Sibe	2 621
Hui	126 427	Oroqen	2 031
Mongolians	96 532	Hezhen	1 387

Hunan province

The minority population was 2 193 429, or 4.1 per cent of the total. The most populous minorities were:

Miao	761 754	Zhuang	14 194
Tujia	744 701	Uygurs	4 446
Dong	318 411	Li	3 544
Yao	273 878	Manchus	2 456
Hui	67 205		

Hubei province

The minority population was 1 778 772, or 3.7 per cent of the total. The most populous minorities were:

Tujia	1 486 698	Hui	70 516
Miao	179 075	Dong	21 808

Guangdong province

The minority population was 1 060 131, or 1.8 per cent of the total. The most populous minorities were:

Li	810 379	Hui	10 849
Yao	95 801	Manchus	4 427
Zhuang	86 169	She	3 205
Miao	41 431	Jing	1 130

Due to availability, the original 1982 census figures have been used in this list, not the later and more reliable ones presented in the census figures at the beginning of this chapter. This explains, for example, how the above list can claim 2023 Lhoba and 6193 Moinba in the Tibetan autonomous region, whereas the national census figures at the beginning of the chapter are only 1066 for the Lhoba and 1140 for the Moinba.

AUTONOMOUS AREAS

PRC minority nationality policy encourages the establishment of autonomous areas at several levels: autonomous regions, equivalent in level to provinces; prefectures; and counties, or banners. (See the section *The Government* in Chapter 2 for more detail about this.) Table 9.2 lists China's autono- mous regions, together with the autonomous prefec- tures, counties and banners. Capitals are given for autonomous regions and autonomous prefectures.[6]

Table 9.2 PRC autonomous areas

Name	Province (or autonomous region)	Date of establishment
1. Inner Mongolian autonomous region (capital Hohhot)		May 1, 1947
2. Xinjiang Uygur autonomous region (capital Ürümqi)		October 1, 1955
3. Guangxi Zhuang autonomous region (capital Nanning)		March 15, 1958
4. Ningxia Hui autonomous region (capital Yinchuan)		October 25, 1958
5. Tibetan autonomous region (capital Lhasa)		September 9, 1965
6. Yanbian Korean autonomous prefecture (capital Yanji)	Jilin	September 3, 1952
7. Exi Tujia–Miao autonomous prefecture (capital Enshi)	Hubei	December 1, 1983
8. Xiangxi Tujia–Miao autonomous prefecture (capital Jishou)	Hunan	September 20, 1957
9. Hainan Li–Miao autonomous prefecture (capital Tongshen)	Hainan	July 1, 1957
10. Ganzi Tibetan autonomous prefecture (capital Kangding)	Sichuan	November 24, 1950
11. Liangshan Yi autonomous prefecture (capital Xichang)	Sichuan	October 1, 1952
12. Ngawa Tibetan autonomous prefecture (capital Maerkang)	Sichuan	January 1, 1953
13. South-east Guizhou Miao–Dong autonomous prefecture (capital Kaili)	Guizhou	July 23, 1956
14. South Guizhou Bouyei–Miao autonomous prefecture (capital Duyun)	Guizhou	August 8, 1956
15. South-west Guizhou Bouyei–Miao autonomous prefecture (capital Xingyi)	Guizhou	May 1, 1982
16. Xishuangbanna Dai autonomous prefecture (capital Jinghong)	Yunnan	January 24, 1953
17. Dehong Dai–Jingpo autonomous prefecture (capital Luxi)	Yunnan	July 24, 1953
18. Nujiang Lisu autonomous prefecture (capital Liuku)	Yunnan	August 23, 1954
19. Dali Bai autonomous prefecture (capital Dali)	Yunnan	November 22, 1956
20. Diqing Tibetan autonomous prefecture (capital Zhongdian)	Yunnan	September 13, 1957
21. Honghe Han–Yi autonomous prefecture (capital Gejiu)	Yunnan	November 18, 1957
22. Wenshan Zhuang–Miao autonomous prefecture (capital Wenshan)	Yunnan	April 1, 1958
23. Chuxiong Yi autonomous prefecture (capital Chuxiong)	Yunnan	April 15, 1958
24. South Gansu Tibetan autonomous prefecture (capital Hezuo)	Gansu	October 1, 1953
25. Linxia Hui autonomous prefecture (capital Linxia)	Gansu	November 19, 1956
26. Yushu Tibetan autonomous prefecture (capital Yushu)	Qinghai	December 25, 1951
27. South Qinghai Tibetan autonomous prefecture (capital Gonghe)	Qinghai	December 6, 1953
28. Huangnan Tibetan autonomous prefecture (capital Tongren)	Qinghai	December 22, 1953
29. North Qinghai Tibetan autonomous prefecture (capital Menyuan Hui autonomous county)	Qinghai	December 31, 1953
30. Guoluo Tibetan autonomous prefecture (capital Maqen)	Qinghai	January 1, 1954
31. West Qinghai Mongolian–Tibetan autonomous prefecture (capital Delingha)	Qinghai	January 25, 1954
32. Bayingolin Mongolian autonomous prefecture (capital Korla)	Xinjiang	June 23, 1954
33. Bortala Mongolian autonomous prefecture (capital Bole)	Xinjiang	July 13, 1954
34. Kizilsu Kirghiz autonomous prefecture (capital Artux)	Xinjiang	July 14, 1954
35. Changji Hui autonomous prefecture (capital Changji)	Xinjiang	July 15, 1954
36. Ili Kazakh autonomous prefecture (capital Gulja)	Xinjiang	November 27, 1954
37. Mengcun Hui autonomous county	Hebei	November 30, 1955
38. Dachang Hui autonomous county	Hebei	December 7, 1955
39. Harqin Left Wing Mongolian autonomous county	Liaoning	April 1, 1958
40. Fuxin Mongolian autonomous county	Liaoning	April 7, 1958
41. Qian Gorlos Mongolian autonomous county	Jilin	September 1, 1956
42. Changbai Korean autonomous county	Jilin	September 15, 1958

(continued over)

Table 9.2 PRC autonomous areas (cont.)

Name	Province (or autonomous region)	Date of establishment
43. Dorbod Mongolian autonomous county	Heilongjiang	December 5, 1956
44. Jingning She autonomous county	Zhejiang	December 21, 1985
45. Changyang Tujia autonomous county	Hubei	December 8, 1984
46. Wufeng Tujia autonomous county	Hubei	December 12, 1984
47. Tongdao Dong autonomous county	Hunan	May 7, 1954
48. Jianghua Yao autonomous county	Hunan	November 25, 1955
49. Chengbu Miao autonomous county	Hunan	November 30, 1955
50. Xinhuang Dong autonomous county	Hunan	December 5, 1956
51. Liannan Yao autonomous county	Guangdong	January 25, 1953
52. Lianshan Zhuang and Yao autonomous county	Guangdong	September 26, 1962
53. Ruyuan Yao autonomous county	Guangdong	October 1, 1963
54. Longsheng Multinational autonomous county	Guangxi	August 19, 1951
55. Jinxiu Yao autonomous county	Guangxi	May 28, 1952
56. Rongshui Miao autonomous county	Guangxi	November 26, 1952
57. Sanjiang Dong autonomous county	Guangxi	December 3, 1952
58. Du'an Yao autonomous county	Guangxi	December 15, 1955
59. Bama Yao autonomous county	Guangxi	February 6, 1956
60. Fangcheng Multinational autonomous county	Guangxi	May 1, 1958
61. Longlin Multinational autonomous county	Guangxi	January 1, 1953
62. Fuchuan Yao autonomous county	Guangxi	January 1, 1984
63. Luocheng Mulam autonomous county	Guangxi	October 1, 1984
64. Muli Tibetan autonomous county	Sichuan	February 19, 1953
65. Maowen Qiang autonomous county	Sichuan	July 7, 1958
66. Xiushan Tujia–Miao autonomous county	Sichuan	November 7, 1983
67. Xiyang Tujia–Miao autonomous county	Sichuan	November 11, 1983
68. Ebian Yi autonomous county	Sichuan	October 5, 1984
69. Mabian Yi autonomous county	Sichuan	October 9, 1984
70. Pengshui Miao–Tujia autonomous county	Sichuan	November 10, 1984
71. Qianjiang Tujia–Miao autonomous county	Sichuan	November 13, 1984
72. Shizhu Tujia autonomous county	Sichuan	November 18, 1984
73. Weining Yi–Hui–Miao autonomous county	Guizhou	November 11, 1954
74. Songtao Miao autonomous county	Guizhou	December 31, 1956
75. Sandu Shui autonomous county	Guizhou	January 2, 1957
76. Zhenning Bouyei–Miao autonomous county	Guizhou	September 11, 1963
77. Ziyun Miao–Bouyei autonomous county	Guizhou	February 11, 1966
78. Guanling Bouyei–Miao autonomous county	Guizhou	December 31, 1981
79. Yuping Dong autonomous county	Guizhou	November 7, 1984
80. Eshan Yi autonomous county	Yunnan	May 12, 1951
81. Lancang Lahu autonomous county	Yunnan	April 7, 1953
82. Jiangcheng Hani–Yi autonomous county	Yunnan	May 18, 1954
83. Menglian Dai–Lahu–Va autonomous county	Yunnan	June 16, 1954
84. Gengma Dai–Va autonomous county	Yunnan	October 16, 1955
85. Ninglang Yi autonomous county	Yunnan	September 20, 1956
86. Gongshan Drung–Nu autonomous county	Yunnan	October 1, 1956
87. Weishan Yi–Hui autonomous county	Yunnan	November 9, 1956
88. Lunan Yi autonomous county	Yunnan	December 31, 1956
89. Lijiang Naxi autonomous county	Yunnan	April 10, 1961
90. Pingbian Miao autonomous county	Yunnan	July 1, 1963
91. Hekou Yao autonomous county	Yunnan	July 11, 1963
92. Cangyuan Va autonomous county	Yunnan	February 28, 1964
93. Shuangjiang Lahu–Va–Blang–Dai autonomous county	Yunnan	December 30, 1985
94. Weixi Lisu autonomous county	Yunnan	October 13, 1985

Table 9.2 PRC autonomous areas (cont.)

Name	Province (or autonomous region)	Date of establishment
95. Jingdong Yi autonomous county	Yunnan	December 20, 1985
96. Jinggu Dai–Yi autonomous county	Yunnan	December 25, 1985
97. Puer Hani–Yi autonomous county	Yunnan	December 25, 1985
98. Yangbi Yi autonomous county	Yunnan	November 1, 1985
99. Luquan Yi–Miao autonomous county	Yunnan	November 25, 1985
100. Jinping Miao–Yao–Dai autonomous county	Yunnan	December 7, 1985
101. Ximeng Va autonomous county	Yunnan	March 5, 1965
102. Nanjian Yi autonomous county	Yunnan	November 27, 1965
103. Mojiang Hani autonomous county	Yunnan	November 28, 1979
104. Xundian Hui–Yi autonomous county	Yunnan	December 20, 1979
105. Yuanjiang Hani–Yi–Dai autonomous county	Yunnan	November 22, 1980
106. Xinping Yi–Dai autonomous county	Yunnan	November 25, 1980
107. Tianzhu Tibetan autonomous county	Gansu	May 6, 1950
108. North Gansu Mongolian autonomous county	Gansu	July 29, 1950
109. Dongxiang autonomous county	Gansu	September 25, 1950
110. Zhangjiachuan Hui autonomous county	Gansu	July 6, 1953
111. South Gansu Yugur autonomous county	Gansu	February 20, 1954
112. Aksay Kazakh autonomous county	Gansu	April 27, 1954
113. Jishi shan Bonan–Dongxiang–Salar autonomous county	Gansu	September 30, 1981
114. Menyuan Hui autonomous county	Qinghai	December 19, 1953
115. Huzhu Tu autonomous county	Qinghai	February 17, 1954
116. Hualong Hui autonomous county	Qinghai	March 1, 1954
117. Xunhua Salar autonomous county	Qinghai	March 1, 1954
118. Henan Mongolian autonomous county	Qinghai	October 16, 1954
119. Yanqi Hui autonomous county	Xinjiang	March 15, 1954
120. Qapqal Sibe autonomous county	Xinjiang	March 25, 1954
121. Mori Kazakh autonomous county	Xinjiang	July 17, 1954
122. Hoboksar Mongolian autonomous county	Xinjiang	September 10, 1954
123. Taxkorgan Tajik autonomous county	Xinjiang	September 17, 1954
124. Barkol Kazakh autonomous county	Xinjiang	September 30, 1954
125. Oroqen autonomous banner	Inner Mongolia	October 1, 1951
126. Ewenki autonomous banner	Inner Mongolia	October 1, 1951
127. Morin Dawa Daur autonomous banner	Inner Mongolia	August 15, 1958

Under the policy of autonomy, the minority nationalities should hold effective control in their own areas. One implication is that cadres in minority nationality areas should, as far as possible, belong to the relevant minorities. In 1982, the State Nationalities Affairs Commission reported that there were 1.03 million cadres from the minority nationalities. By the end of 1988, there were about 1.84 million minority cadres; it was claimed that this figure was 33 times greater than in 1950 and 1.2 times greater than in 1978.[7]

SOME ECONOMIC AND CULTURAL INDICATORS IN NATIONALITY AREAS

The minority nationalities' economic development and standard of living have both improved dramatically under the PRC. Agricultural, and especially industrial, production growth rates have been high. However, the improvements have been uneven, and the gap between the regions near the coast, inhabited mainly by the majority Han nationality, and the western regions, where many of the minorities live, has widened. Growth in education and culture has also been generally impressive. However, in the early 1980s the proportion of minority students to the total relevant population was still below the national average, except among the Mongolians and Koreans.[8]

Map 9.1 Distribution of minority nationalities

Table 9.3 Economic figures for nationality areas

	1952	1965	1978	1984	1985	1986
Grain (millions of tonnes)	15.82	22.17	31.24	41.15	40.06	40.65
Cotton (thousands of tonnes)	31.40	88.70	59.70	209.20	193.60	224.00
Large livestock (millions)	24.39	33.73	38.07	44.63	47.49	49.51
Sheep (millions)	40.30	85.95	95.80	96.89	97.57	99.88
Pigs (millions)	11.37	21.51	32.60	40.47	45.33	48.69
Steel (thousands of tonnes)	—	394.00	1 285.00	1 978.00	2 325.00	2 481.00
Pig iron (thousands of tonnes)	9.00	558.00	1 682.00	2 150.00	2 581.00	2 951.00
Raw coal (millions of tonnes)	1.78	20.29	60.81	69.93	85.97	88.76
Raw oil (thousands of tonnes)	52.00	973.00	5 777.00	7 046.00	8 049.00	8 616.00
Electricity (millions of kwh)	80.00	3 340.00	17 400.00	26 570.00	38 900.00	40 080.00
Railways (thousands of km)	3.787	n/a	9.018	12.10	12.50	12.60
Roads (thousands of km)	25.90	125.50	208.00	235.40	254.10	250.90
Hospital or sanitorium beds (thousands)	5 .711	93.23	224.40	285.10	294.90	301.00
Hygiene technical personnel (thousands)	17.90	156.90	279.40	406.90	423.70	435.90

Table 9.4 Figures on minority nationality education and culture (1000s)

	1952	1965	1978	1983	1985	1986
Minority students						
Tertiary level	2.9	21.9	36.0	59.6	94.1	101.4
Secondary level	92.0	390.7	2 526.2	1 911.8	2 448.7	2 775.8
Primary level	1 474.2	4 350.0	7 685.6	8 129.0	9 548.1	10 337.3
Minority teachers						
Tertiary level	0.623*	3.311	5.876	10.791	12.775	14.236
Secondary level	2.7	16.1	116.9	114.8	140.3	156.8
Primary level	59.8*	133.2	310.2	344.9	397.8	421.3
Volumes published in minority languages	6 612	24 800	31 790	33 580	36 290	36 350
Magazines published in minority languages (volumes)	1 686	2 680	3 130	6 160	10 350	10 850
Newspapers published in minority languages (issues)	29 333	39 550	70 720	79 270	114 020	75 610

* 1953 figures

CHARACTERISTICS OF CHINA'S MINORITY NATIONALITIES[9]

Achang

The Achang are mountain farmers. Some groups believe in primitive spirits and practise ancestor worship, while others believe in Hinayana Buddhism.

Bai

A Tibeto-Burman people, the Bai were a major ethnic grouping and cultural elite in the Nanzhao kingdom which dominated the region to China's south-

west from the seventh century until 902. They are rice-growers, whose religions include worship of 'local tutelary spirits', shamanism, Buddhism and Daoism. The Bai have close cultural ties with the Han, and are among the most acculturated of China's minority nationalities.

Benglong

The Benglong speak a south Asian language close to that of the Va. They are subsistence farmers and are culturally similar to the Burmese. Some Benglong follow a form of Hinayana Buddhism.

Bonan

The Bonan are culturally close to the Hui. They speak a Mongolian language and are Islamic.

Blang

The Blang speak a Mon–Khmer language, and their culture is closely related to those of nearby Burma (Myanmar) and Laos. They are farmers, with an economy based on shifting cultivation. The main traditional religions are Hinayana Buddhism, polytheism and ancestor worship. Some people speak Thai, Va or Chinese.

Bouyei

The Bouyei have a similar way of life to the Miao and their language is closely related to those of the Zhuang and Dai. They practise polytheism and ancestor worship.

Dai

The Dai, who have a close affinity with the Thais, were one of the main ethnic groups dominating the Nanzhao kingdom (seventh century to 902). They are Hinayana Buddhists and their arts include colourful dancing and singing.

Daur

The traditional occupations of the Daur are grain and vegetable farming and animal husbandry; they also rely on logging, hunting and fishing. This nationality has a strong spoken-language and cultural affinity with the Mongolians. There is a rich oral literature, but no written script. The main religion is shamanism.

Dong

The Dong trace their origins back to about the third century BC. They speak a Thai language and have a close affinity with the Thais. Dong architecture features covered bridges and multi-storey drum towers.

Dongxiang

The Dongxiang are closely related to the Mongolians. They speak a Mongolian language and are Islamic.

Drung

These farmers speak a Tibeto-Burman language closely related to Jingpo. Their traditional religion is nature worship, with belief in spirits, but there are also some Christians within the nationality group.

Ewenki

The Ewenki are a Tungus people who speak a Tungus language. Their religions include animal and ancestor worship, shamanism and lama Buddhism. Once migrant hunters, the Ewenki have led a more settled life over the past forty years; however, they still hunt, breed deer, tend flocks and farm.

Gaoshan

The aboriginal mountain people of Taiwan, the Gaoshan are millet farmers and hunters. Until the early 1900s the Gaoshan were headhunters. They speak a Malay–Polynesian language and believe in polytheism and ancestor worship, although some are Christians.

Gelo

The Gelo are mountain subsistence farmers and hunters. A Gelo language exists but few use it, instead communicating in Chinese, Miao, Yi and Bouyei.

Hani

The Hani are subsistence farmers who speak a Tibeto-Burman language. They practise polytheism and ancestor worship.

Hezhen

Among China's smallest minority nationalities, the Hezhen speak a Manchu–Tungus language. They are farmers who concentrate on rice growing. Their religion is based on nature worship and shamanism. Their main art form is sung folk narrative.

Hui

The Hui are Moslems who can trace their origins to the seventh century, when Arab and Persian merchants settled in China. They are involved in many occupations, with the Hui working as shop and restaurant keepers, artisans and peasants. The Hui culture is basically the same as that of the Han. Nationality members speak and write Chinese. Territorially they are very scattered.

Jing

The Jing cultivate rice and are good fishermen. They

have their own language, but many now speak Cantonese. The Jing are descendants of Vietnamese migrants who arrived in China from the fifteenth century on. Some are Daoists and a few Catholics.

Jingpo

The Jingpo live along the Burma border and speak a Tibeto-Burman language closely related to Drung. The main traditional religion is polytheism, but some practise Christianity.

Juno

Subsistence farmers, renowned for their fine, colourful fabrics, the Juno speak a Tibeto-Burman language. The Juno are the latest minority nationality to have been classified as such. Their traditional religion is nature and ancestor worship.

Kazakh

Renowned for their horsemanship, the Kazakhs keep Bactrian camels and are wandering herders of goats and sheep. The Kazakh language has two scripts, one based on Arabic, the other on Latin. Kazakh people are mainly Moslems, but shamanism still survives.

Kirghiz

The Kirghiz are pastoral wanderers and herders of goats and sheep. They are a Turkic people who speak a Turkic language. Most are Islamic, but a few are lama Buddhists.

Korean

Korean migration into Manchuria dates from the seventeenth century, but did not occur in sizeable numbers until the nineteenth. The Koreans are mainly rice growers, but have also joined China's industrialization. This nationality's culture and language are the same as in Korea.

Lahu

The Lahu have their own language, which belongs to the Yi branch of the Tibeto-Burman languages, but most Lahu speak Chinese or Thai due to a close association with the Han and Dai peoples. They lacked a written script until 1957. Some Lahu practise nature and ancestor worship, but Mahayana Buddhism and Christianity are also found.

Lhoba

The Lhoba speak a Tibetan language, but do not have their own script. Their traditional religion is nature worship. The Lhoba are currently the least populous of all China's nationalities.

Li

Natives of Hainan Island, the Li have a long history of rebellion against the Chinese authorities, and in 1943 rose against the Guomindang government. They believe in polytheism and nature worship.

Lisu

Subsistence farmers, the Lisu have arranged, monogamous marriages, but rather free love before marriage. Their language belongs to the Yi branch of the Tibeto-Burman family.

Manchu

Once herders and hunters, the Manchus trace their origins back some 3000 years. They conquered China in the seventeenth century and adopted Chinese manners, language and culture to such an extent that little survives of their own distinctive culture. Very few now speak the Manchu language. The Manchus formerly practised shamanism and ancestor worship. Territorially they are the least concentrated of all minorities in China.

Maonan

The Maonan share a love of festivals and colourful dress with the Zhuang, and speak a related language. They are farmers who grow millet and buckwheat.

Miao

The Miao are one of the most ancient of China's nationalities, tracing their origins back more than 4000 years. Prior to modernization of farming methods they grew millet and buckwheat using the slash-and-burn method. The Miao language has three main dialects, but there was no unified written script until 1956. Religions include nature and ancestor worship and Christianity.

Moinba

The Moinba are mountain herders. They have a way of life, culture and language similar to the Tibetans and are lama Buddhists.

Mongolian

The Mongolians once ran a gigantic empire, founded in 1206 by Chinggis Khan, which covered most of the Eurasian continent. The Mongolian language belongs to the Altaic family; there are many mutually understandable dialects. The Mongolian script, still in use in the PRC, dates at least from the early thirteenth century. The main religion is lama Buddhism. Mongolians were traditionally nomadic (some still are), living in hide and felt tents called yurts. However, they are increasingly becoming settled and even urban dwellers. Industry is well developed among the Mongolians.

Mulam

The Mulam are an agricultural people with a self-sufficient village economy. Religions include Buddhism and Daoism. The Mulam language is related to that of the Dong and Chinese characters are used.

Naxi

The Naxi speak a language belonging to the Yi branch of the Tibeto-Burman family. Traditional religions include the national worship of Dongba, lama Buddhism and Daoism. Most Naxi follow a patriarchal family system, but one section of the nationality is matriarchal.

Nu

Farmers who are closely related to the Tibetans, the Nu speak a Tibeto-Burman language. Some follow lama Buddhism, while others are nature worshippers or Christians.

Oroqen

A Tungus people who speak a Tungus language, the Oroqen were once semi-nomadic, living in birch and hide tents. They are now more settled and work as hunters, herders of deer and farmers.

Pumi

The Pumi speak a language related to Tibetan and have a similar lifestyle to Tibetans, but only part of the nationality accepts lama Buddhism; the others have a polytheistic religion and sacrifice to their ancestors.

Qiang

Closely related to Tibetans and speaking a similar language, the Qiang are herders and farmers. They are, however, polytheists, nature worshippers and shamanists, not lama Buddhists.

Russian

Almost all of China's Russian population arrived in the north-east and Xinjiang after the Russian civil war of 1918–22. Culturally and linguistically they are the same as in Russia.

Salar

Islamic Turkic speakers living in a semi-desert area, the Salar are herders of sheep and some cattle. Their diet consists largely of steamed buns and a variety of noodles made of highland barley, wheat and buckwheat.

She

The She language belongs to the Miao branch of the Miao–Yao family. The origins of the She are unclear, but probably date back to the seventh century. Some are Buddhists, while others are polytheists or ancestor worshippers.

Shui

The Shui have a language close to that of the Dong. Most are nature worshippers, but some are Catholics.

Sibe

The Sibe speak a Manchu–Tungus language. They traditionally lived in the north-east of Liaoning with the Manchus, but in 1764 many were moved to the west as border guards on the Russian frontier, where a portion of the Sibe population still lives. They are traditionally polytheistic.

Tajik

Of Iranian stock, the Tajiks speak an Iranian language and believe in Islam. By means of extensive irrigation, they grow rice, wheat, fruit and cotton; some are herders. Houses are built of wood and stone, with square flat roofs.

Tatar

The Tatars are Islamic Turkic speakers and farmers. Their diet includes round cakes, with the outside crisp and inside soft. They also eat cheese, dried apricots and rice.

Tibetan

Prior to the implementation of 'democratic reforms' in 1959, Tibet was a theocratic state. The Tibetans have a highly distinctive culture, mainly based on lama Buddhism, and a rich written and oral literature. They are farmers of barley, peas and tubers and herders of yaks, sheep and goats. They are also the only one of China's minority nationalities to have created a tradition of drama independently of the Han people.

Tu

The Tu trace their origins to the thirteenth century. They speak a Mongolian language and are related to the Mongolians. They have two dialects and a rich oral literature. Originally pastoralists, they have practised agriculture for several centuries. Most believe in lama Buddhism, but some still adhere to polytheistic beliefs.

Tujia

The Tujia farm rice and corn, collect fruit and fell trees for lumber. They are good at handicrafts; and in many ways are very similar to the Han people.

Uygur

A Turkic people who ran a major empire centred on what is now Mongolia from 744 to 840, the Uygurs converted to Islam over several centuries. They grow fruit, wheat, cotton and rice through irrigation. Uygur customs, culture and art are similar to those of other Turkic people and they excel in music, song and dance. The Uygur language belongs to the Turkic group of the Altaic family of languages.

Uzbek

The origins of the Uzbeks go back to the fourteenth century. They are Islamic Turkic speakers and farm-ers with dress and food very similar to those of the Uygurs.

Va

The Va speak a Mon–Khmer south Asian language. Most are nature worshippers, but some are Hinayana Buddhists or Christians.

Yao

The Yao farm sweet potatoes, maize and rice. They have recently developed hydroelectric power and in-creased irrigation. There are several different mutu-ally incomprehensible Yao languages, and Chinese or Zhuang are often used for communication. Tradi-tional religions include nature worship, ancestor worship and Daoism.

Yi

The Yi speak a Tibeto-Burman language and have their own script. They once had a reputation as fierce warriors and those in Liangshan, Sichuan formerly had a heavily stratified slave system. They are poly-theists, and also have a long tradition of Buddhism, with Daoism and Christianity introduced later.

Yugur

Descended from the Uygurs of the ninth century, the Yugurs are Turkic speakers. They are herders and farmers, with a few hunting as a sideline. Most practise lama Buddhism.

Zhuang

The Zhuang are the most populous of China's minor-ity nationalities, and one of the best integrated with the Han. Zhuang origins go back well before the time of Christ. They speak a language related to Thai, but many speak Chinese. The Chinese written language was formerly used, but in 1955 a Zhuang written language based on Latin letters was devised. Relig-ions include Buddhism, Daoism, ancestor worship and Christianity.

10 EDUCATION

BACKGROUND TO EDUCATION IN CONTEMPORARY CHINA

Since before the PRC was established, universal education has been a central goal of CCP policy. Prior to 1949, the great majority of the population (more than four-fifths according to CCP sources, but very much less than that according to GMD sources) was illiterate.

Education was a high priority for the CCP, and has remained so; however, periodic conflict within the Party about the function of education saw major shifts in policy between 1949 and the late 1980s. Initially, China depended heavily on the Soviet Union for educational policy and techniques. Political movements such as the 1957 Anti-Rightist movement, and the Great Leap Forward which followed, disrupted progress in education—the former attacking students and teachers for their 'expert' stance; the latter placing more emphasis on political attitudes and participation in manual labour than on formal education.

During the Cultural Revolution, the educational structure of the preceding period was labelled 'revisionist' and virtually destroyed. However, the period also saw a considerable expansion of secondary school enrolments, as the figures in Tables 10.3 and 10.4 show.

The current attitude is that education should be geared towards China's modernization. Education has regained a central position in government policy, with public expenditure increasing and a number of legislative measures coming into force to establish a national system which retains sufficient flexibility to adapt to local needs and conditions. During the 1980s the trend was increasingly towards downplaying the ideological content of education, especially at tertiary level. However, this trend changed dramatically after the Beijing massacre of June 1989.

In April 1986, the National People's Congress adopted a law stipulating nine-year compulsory education in the cities and developed areas by 1990 and almost everywhere by the end of the twentieth century. The nine years or so are preceded by three years of pre-school education and are followed by an optional three years of senior secondary education and then tertiary or technical education.

Pre-school education is widely available to children aged between three and six years. Areas covered include hygiene, physical education, moral education, language, general knowledge, basic mathematics, music and art. A large part of pre-school education is concerned with moral and social training. Most kindergartens offer full-time care for children, and many are boarding schools, run on a weekly basis or for even longer periods of time, with children returning home for weekends or holidays.

Primary school education—which approaches being universal except in very remote areas—may be either a six-year or five-year system, with the latter commonly found in rural areas, where children begin school at seven years of age rather than six. The dropout rate is relatively high in rural areas. Subjects taught to primary school children are moral education, Chinese, science, arithmetic, geography, history, physical education, music and painting.

Outside the formal school system, particularly in the large cities, a network of children's centres and children's 'palaces' provides additional educational and recreational activities for children. Alternative education systems include part-time schools, mobile schools and alternate day schools, many of them found in the minority nationality areas.

The first three years of secondary education are part of the compulsory education system. In 1985, some 70 per cent of children attended at this level. The number moving into senior middle school education is naturally much lower.

Table 10.1 Student enrolments 1989 (millions)

Primary schools	125.4
Secondary schools	57.5
Universities	2.1

Note: From *Asia Yearbook 1990* (Far Eastern Economic Review, Hong Kong, 1990), p. 6. This item and State Statistical Bureau, comp., *Zhongguo tongji nianjian (Statistical Yearbook of China)* are the main sources for this chapter, especially *Statistical Yearbook of China1988.*

Table 10.2 Overall student enrolment as percentage of population

	1949	1952	1957	1965	1978	1980	1981	1982	1983	1984	1985	1986	1987
Students as % population	4.76	9.47	11.11	18.09	22.28	20.78	19.55	18.58	17.91	17.93	17.81	17.61	17.12
% student population													
Primary	94.60	93.90	89.50	88.60	68.50	71.60	73.60	74.40	74.10	73.10	71.80	70.50	69.60
Secondary	4.90	5.80	9.90	10.90	31.10	27.80	25.70	25.00	25.30	26.20	27.30	28.50	29.30
Tertiary	0.50	0.30	0.60	0.50	0.40	0.60	0.70	0.60	0.60	0.70	0.90	1.00	1.10

Table 10.3 Primary and secondary school enrolments (10 000s)

	1952	1957	1965	1978	1980	1981	1982	1983	1984	1985	1986	1987
Primary schools												
	52.7	54.7	168.2	94.9	91.7	89.4	88.1	86.2	85.4	83.2	82.1	80.7
Students	5 110.0	6 428.0	11 621.0	14 624.0	14 627.0	14 333.0	13.972.0	13 578.0	13 557.0	13 370.0	13 182.0	12 836.0
Enrolling	1 149.0	1 249.0	3 296.0	3 315.0	2 942.0	2 749.0	2 672.0	2 544.0	2 473.0	2 298.0	2 258.0	2 095.0
Percentage	22.5	19.4	28.4	22.7	20.1	19.2	19.1	18.8	18.2	17.2	17.1	16.3
Continuing	n/a	n/a	n/a	9 221.0	9 609.0	9 515.0	9 319.0	9 039.0	9 084.0	9 056.0	8 882.0	n/a
Percentage				63.0	65.7	66.4	66.7	66.6	67.0	67.7	67.4	
Graduating	n/a	n/a	n/a	2 088.0	2 076.0	2 069.0	1 981.0	1 995.0	2 000.0	2 016.0	2 043.0	n/a
Percentage				14.3	14.2	14.4	14.2	14.7	14.8	15.1	15.5	
Secondary schools												
	0.6	1.2	8.1	16.5	12.5	11.3	10.8	10.5	10.4	10.5	10.5	10.5
Students	314.5	708.1	1 431.8	6 637.2	5 677.8	5 014.6	4 702.8	4 634.1	4 860.9	5 092.6	5 321.6	5 403.1
Enrolling	174.6	261.6	673.0	2 743.6	2 011.8	1 810.5	1 726.9	1 700.4	1 713.4	1 789.8	1 824.4	1 834.2
Percentage	55.5	36.9	47.0	41.3	35.4	36.1	36.7	36.7	35.2	35.1	34.3	33.9
Continuing	n/a	n/a	n/a	1 491.1	1 955.8	1 803.7	1 721.4	1 728.1	1 868.4	1 914.3	2 000.3	n/a
Percentage				22.5	34.4	36.0	36.6	37.3	26.3	27.3	37.6	
Graduating	n/a	n/a	n/a	2 402.5	1 710.2	1 400.4	1 254.5	1 205.6	1 279.1	1 388.5	1 496.9	n/a
Percentage				36.2	30.1	28.0	26.7	26.0	26.3	27.3	28.1	

Table 10.4 Specialized secondary school enrolments by type of institution (students in 10 000s)

	1952	1957	1965	1978	1980	1981	1982	1983	1984	1985	1986	1987
Total no. schools	1710.0	1320.0	1265.0	2760.0	3069.0	3132.0	3076.0	3090.0	3301.0	3557.0	3782.0	3913.0
% technical	48.1	48.7	70.2	59.9	54.1	55.0	57.4	60.0	64.3	67.6	66.5	72.9
% teacher training	51.9	51.3	29.8	40.1	45.9	45.0	42.6	40.0	35.7	32.4	33.5	27.1
Total no. students	63.6	77.8	54.7	88.9	124.3	106.9	103.9	114.3	132.2	157.1	175.7	187.4
% technical	45.7	62.0	71.7	59.5	61.2	59.1	60.4	60.2	61.3	64.2	65.2	65.3
% teacher training	54.3	38.0	28.3	40.5	38.8	40.9	39.6	39.8	38.7	35.8	34.8	34.7
No. enrolling	35.1	12.3	20.8	44.7	46.8	43.3	41.9	47.8	54.6	66.8	67.7	71.5
% technical	48.1	48.8	70.2	60.0	54.1	55.0	57.5	60.0	64.3	67.8	66.5	67.8
% teacher training	51.9	51.2	29.8	40.0	45.9	45.0	42.5	40.0	35.7	32.2	33.5	32.2
No. continuing	n/a	n/a	n/a	26.1	17.0	20.4	24.5	28.9	34.7	40.7	50.2	n/a
% technical				69.7	84.1	73.0	64.1	56.4	57.1	58.7	61.2	
% teacher training				30.3	15.9	27.0	35.9	43.6	42.9	41.3	38.8	
No. graduating	n/a	n/a	n/a	18.1	60.5	44.6	37.5	37.6	42.9	49.6	57.8	n/a
% technical				43.6	60.3	54.3	61.3	63.3	61.1	64.7	67.3	
% teacher training				56.4	39.7	45.7	38.7	36.5	38.9	35.3	32.7	

LITERACY

According to the 1964 census, 38.1 per cent of the population aged twelve years or over was illiterate or semi-literate. By 1982, the rate had dropped to 23.5 per cent, which compares very well with the only other Third World country of similar size, India, which has an illiteracy rate of 64 per cent. Since then, if the official figures for primary school attendance were wholly reliable, a continued fall in the illiteracy rate should have been the predictable outcome, but extrapolating from a figure for literacy in 1988 given in a Hong Kong source, the rate of illiteracy had actually risen to 26.7 per cent by that year.[1] The introduction of the responsibility system in the countryside and the reversion to semi-privatized forms of land tenure have contributed to this situation. The incentive for peasants to send their children to school has decreased with the growing imperative to employ as many family members as possible as labourers, and because of the increasing requirement for parents to pay education fees.

For those members of China's population who are city dwellers, or who live in the coastal provinces or more developed areas of the interior, nearly universal primary school education has been achieved, however, and the goal was to make junior middle school universally available by 1990. For the just under half of the population living in less developed towns and rural areas, the goal is to achieve universal primary school education, while for the underdeveloped remainder, elementary education is to be spread as far as possible. The birth-control policy of the past decade should mean that it will now be possible, in the urban areas, to concentrate more on improving the quality of primary and secondary education. In the countryside, however, the introduction of the responsibility system has provided a disincentive to rural workers to send all their children to school.

Table 10.5 Enrolment rates

	1952	1957	1965	1978	1980	1981	1982	1983	1984	1985	1986	1987
No.children	6 642.0	8 078.0	11 603.0	12 131.0	12 220.0	12 019.0	11 763.0	11 251.0	10 669.0	10 362.0	10 068.0	9 751.0
No.enrolled	3 268.0	4 987.0	9 830.0	11 584.0	11 478.0	11 176.0	10 958.0	10 578.0	10 170.0	9 943.0	9 702.0	9 477.0
% enrolled	49.2	61.7	84.7	94.0	93.0	93.0	93.2	94.0	95.3	95.9	96.4	97.2

Table 10.6 Primary and secondary student enrolment per 10 000 population

	1949	1952	1957	1965	1978	1980	1981	1982	1983	1984	1985	1986	1987
Primary	450	889	994	1602	1526	1489	1439	1381	1326	1310	1278	1242	1192
Secondary	23	55	110	197	693	578	503	465	453	470	487	501	502

Table 10.7 Primary and secondary school teachers (10 000s)

Education Department	435.8	(53.3%)
Other departments	64.6	(7.9%)
Collective-run schools	316.7	(38.8%)

Table 10.8 Student–teacher ratio, primary and secondary schools

	1949	1952	1957	1965	1978	1980	1981	1982	1983	1984	1985	1986	1987
Primary schools													
No. teachers (per 10 000)	83.6	143.5	188.4	385.7	522.6	549.9	558.0	550.5	542.5	537.0	537.7	541.4	543.4
No. students/teacher	29.2	35.6	34.1	30.1	28.0	26.6	25.7	25.4	25.0	25.2	24.9	24.3	23.6
Secondary schools													
No. teachers (per 10 000)	8.3	13.0	29.3	70.9	328.1	317.2	300.9	287.1	282.7	282.1	296.6	311.5	326.6
No. students/teacher	15.3	24.2	24.2	20.2	20.2	17.9	16.7	16.4	16.4	17.2	17.2	17.1	16.5

TERTIARY EDUCATION ENROLMENTS

Since Deng Xiaoping's accession to power in 1978, there has been an attempt to reform the higher education system, previously handicapped by political struggles, as part of the push to modernize China. The reintroduction of examination-based selection procedures for higher studies has helped to achieve this. Previously, the system was hindered by a tendency to select undergraduates for their political background rather than their academic performance, a trend which, unfortunately, is now seeing a resurgence with Deng's announcement that the selection of candidates for study overseas will be on the basis of their 'loyalty' to China.

The percentage of the population attaining higher education in China is very low compared with other similar Third World countries. In 1985, only 2 per cent of the population between the ages of 20 and 24 was enrolled in higher education, compared with an average of 5 per cent for low-income countries in general. This is partly the result of the disruptive influence of the Cultural Revolution decade.

Table 10.9 Tertiary enrolments (students in 10 000s)

	1952	1957	1965	1978	1980	1981	1982	1983	1984	1985	1986	1987
No. of institutions	201	229	434	598	675	704	715	805	902	1016	1054	1063
Students	19.1	44.1	67.4	85.6	114.4	127.9	115.4	120.7	139.6	170.3	188.0	195.9
Enrolling	7.9	10.6	16.4	40.1	28.1	27.9	31.5	39.1	47.5	61.9	57.2	61.7
Percentage	41.4	24.0	24.3	46.8	24.6	21.8	27.3	32.4	34.0	36.3	30.4	31.5
Continuing	n/a	n/a	n/a	37.0	72.3	54.3	50.4	52.9	63.0	69.1	77.6	n/a
Percentage				43.2	63.2	42.5	43.7	43.8	45.1	40.6	41.3	
Graduating	n/a	n/a	n/a	8.5	14.0	45.7	33.5	28.7	31.6	39.3	53.2	n/a
Percentage				9.9	12.2	35.7	29.0	23.8	22.6	23.1	28.3	

KEY TERTIARY INSTITUTIONS

Some ninety-eight universities in China were officially designated as 'national keypoint (*zhongdian*) universities' among the 675 tertiary institutions in existence in 1980, but these figures have fluctuated up and down over the decade. Originally it was envisaged that this group of keypoint universities should receive special attention in terms of teaching resources, level of scholarship among their students and funding priorities. But by 1980 the group was considered to have grown too unwieldy for the sort of concentrated approach originally envisaged, so it was announced that a smaller number of 'keypoints among the keypoints' would be selected for this purpose. This elite group is identical with the list of twenty-six universities singled out as the recipients of the first World Bank loan to China. The ninety-seven current keypoint universities, with the twenty-six specially designated universities marked by an asterisk, are as follows:

Anhui province

*Chinese Science and Technology University, Hefei; Hefei Polytechnical Institute

Beijing

Beijing College of Traditional Chinese Medicine; *Beijing University; *Beijing Agricultural University; Beijing Institute of Agricultural Machinery; Beijing Institute of Aeronautics; Beijing Institute of Chemical Technology; Beijing Institute of Foreign Languages; Beijing Institute of Foreign Trade; Beijing Institute of Forestry; Beijing Institute of International Relations; Beijing Institute of Iron and Steel Technology; Beijing Institute of Physical Culture; Beijing Institute of Posts and Telecommunications; Beijing Institute of Technology; *Beijing Medical College; Beijing Normal University; *Beijing Teachers' Training University; Central Conservatory of Music; Central Nationalities Institute; China Capital Medical University; North China Communications University; People's University of China; *Qinghua University

Fujian province

*Xiamen University

Gansu province

*Lanzhou University

Guangdong province

*South China (Huanan) Institute of Technology, Guangzhou; South China Institute of Agriculture, Guangzhou; *Zhongshan University, Guangzhou; Zhongshan Medical College, Guangzhou

Hebei province

North China Institute of Agricultural Machinery; North China Institute of Electrical Power

Heilongjiang province

Daqing Petroleum Institute, Anda county; Harbin Naval Engineering Institute; Harbin Institute of Technology; Northeast China Heavy Machinery Institute, Qiqihar

Hubei province

Central China Institute of Agriculture, Wuhan; *Central China (Huazhong) Institute of Technology, Wuhan; *Wuhan University; Wuhan Institute of Building Material Industry; Wuhan Institute of Geodesy, Photogrammetry and Cartography; Wuhan Institute of Geology; Wuhan Institute of Water Conservancy and Electric Power

Hunan province

Central–South China Institute of Mining and Metallurgy, Changsha; Changsha Institute of Technology; Hunan University, Changsha; Xiangtan University

Inner Mongolian autonomous region

University of Inner Mongolia, Hohhot

Jiangsu province

East China Institute of Engineering, Nanjing; East China Institute of Water Conservancy, Nanjing; Nanjing Institute of Aeronautics; Nanjing Institute of Meteorology; Nanjing Institute of Technology; *Nanjing University; Zhenjiang Institute of Agricultural Machinery

Jiangxi province

Jiangxi Communist Labour University, Nanchang

Jilin province

Changchun Geological Institute; Jilin Polytechnical Institute, Changchun; *Jilin University, Changchun

Liaoning province

*Dalian Institute of Technology; Dalian Marine College; Fuxin Mining Institute; Northeast China Institute of Technology, Shenyang; Shenyang Institute of Agriculture

Shaanxi province

Northwest China College of Light Industry, Xianyang; Northwest China Institute of Agriculture, Xi'an; Northwest China Institute of Technology, Xi'an; Northwest China Institute of Telecommunication Engineering, Xi'an; Northwest China University, Xi'an; *Xi'an Communications (Jiaotong) University

Shandong province

East China Petroleum Institute, Kenli county; Shandong College of Oceanography, Qingdao; *Shandong University, Jinan

Shanghai

*East China (Huadong) Teachers' Training University; *Fudan University; *Shanghai Communications (Jiaotong) University; Shanghai First Medical College; Shanghai Institute of Chemical Technology; Shanghai Institute of Foreign Languages; Shanghai Textile College; Tongji University

Shanxi province

Shanxi Agricultural University, Taiyuan

Sichuan province

Chengdu Institute of Telecommunication Engineering; Chengdu University of Science and Technology; China Mining Institute, Hechuan county; Chongqing Institute of Architectural Engineering; *Chongqing University; Sichuan Medical College, Chengdu; *Sichuan University, Chengdu; Southwest China Communications University, Emei county; Southwest China Institute of Political Science and Law, Chongqing

Tianjin

*Nankai University; *Tianjin University

Xinjiang Uygur autonomous region

Xinjiang University, Ürümqi

Yunnan province

Yunnan University, Kunming

Zhejiang province

*Zhejiang University, Hangzhou

TERTIARY EDUCATION ENROLMENTS AND GRADUATES BY FIELD OF STUDY

Tables 10.10 and 10.11 reveal a particularly marked decline in engineering, an ideologically 'safe' subject, since it was at the height of its popularity during the Cultural Revolution decade, despite the official rhetoric regarding the importance of technical skills for industrial modernization. A similar trend is evident in another important area, agriculture; this may be linked with the perception that agricultural labour is less profitable than industrial enterprises, and with the consequent migration of rural dwellers into urban areas. Medicine has also lost its appeal, while, perhaps due to the intellectual broadening and spirit of inquiry which emerged in China through the early 1980s, the liberal arts and sciences have flourished. Again, with the re-emergence of a positive attitude towards capitalism in the atmosphere of intense economic debate of the past decade, interest both in economics per se, and as an entrée to a business career, has grown, making it the most significant area of expansion over this period.

Not revealed by the tables, but also significant, has been the re-establishment of an interest in law and politics, the former stimulated by the need for Chinese lawyers to negotiate with foreign firms and both motivated, no doubt, by the need for competent international negotiators to handle the legal and political aspects of China's intended resumption of sovereignty over Hong Kong in 1997. This area, which originally had captured 2 per cent of student enrolments, but in which enrolments had ceased completely by 1970, attracted 2.3 per cent of enrolments in 1986.

Table 10.10 Number (in 1000s) and percentage of enrolments by field of study

	1952	1957	1965	1978	1980	1981	1982	1983	1984	1985	1986	1987
Engineering	66.6	163.0	295.3	287.6	383.5	461.4	398.3	418.5	479.5	580.2	645.1	686.3
Percentage	34.8	37.0	43.8	33.6	33.5	36.1	34.5	34.7	34.4	34.1	34.0	35.0
Agriculture and forestry	15.5	39.9	63.2	61.6	82.2	92.5	75.8	81.5	92.6	106.0	112.4	111.7
Percentage	8.1	9.0	9.4	7.2	7.2	7.2	6.6	6.8	6.6	6.2	6.0	5.7
Medicine	24.8	49.1	82.9	113.0	139.6	159.0	164.0	140.1	143.9	157.4	170.3	182.2
Percentage	12.9	11.1	12.3	13.2	12.2	12.4	14.2	11.6	10.3	9.2	9.1	9.3
Pedagogy	31.6	114.8	94.3	249.9	338.2	321.4	289.4	313.3	361.8	425.0	481.8	508.0
Percentage	16.5	26.0	14.0	29.2	29.6	25.1	25.1	26.0	25.9	25.0	25.6	25.9
Economics and finance	22.0	12.0	18.1	18.2	37.1	47.9	56.0	71.1	97.4	147.5	169.4	180.4
Percentage	11.5	2.7	2.7	2.1	3.2	3.7	4.9	5.9	7.0	8.7	9.0	5.8
Liberal arts	13.5	19.6	46.0	46.2	58.1	69.1	59.7	67.9	89.1	126.8	128.1	113.4
Percentage	5.0	6.5	9.2	7.5	7.3	7.8	7.0	6.6	6.2	5.7	5.4	5.8
Natural sciences	9.6	28.7	62.2	64.2	83.7	99.8	81.1	79.8	86.9	97.7	102.2	106.6
Percentage	7.0	4.5	6.8	5.4	5.1	5.4	5.2	5.6	6.4	7.4	6.8	5.4
Other*	7.7	14.0	12.4	15.6	21.5	28.5	29.7	34.6	44.4	62.4	70.7	70.2
Percentage	4.1	3.2	1.8	1.8	1.9	2.2	2.6	2.9	3.2	3.7	4.0	3.6

*Physical culture, art, politics and law

Table 10.11 Number (in 1000s) and percentage of graduates by field of study

	1952	1957	1965	1978	1980	1981	1982	1983	1984	1985	1986	1987
Engineering	10.2	17.2	80.3	56.5	44.2	12.2	172.2	111.4	97.5	97.7	119.2	156.1
Percentage	31.9	30.6	43.3	34.3	30.2	8.7	37.7	33.2	34.0	30.9	30.3	29.3
Agriculture and forestry	3.2	3.9	18.9	16.5	5.3	8.8	38.1	19.3	18.5	20.7	26.0	31.3
Percentage	10.0	6.9	10.2	10.0	3.6	6.3	8.3	5.8	6.4	6.5	6.6	5.9
Medicine	2.6	6.2	22.0	27.5	17.7	9.5	26.0	55.5	31.9	29.2	27.9	32.1
Percentage	8.1	11.0	11.9	16.7	12.1	6.8	5.7	16.6	11.1	9.2	7.1	6.0
Pedagogy	3.1	15.9	29.0	35.4	61.9	103.4	129.5	90.1	84.8	94.1	117.4	163.3
Percentage	9.7	28.3	15.7	21.5	42.4	74.1	28.3	26.9	29.6	29.7	4.4	3.1
Economics and finance	7.3	3.7	2.1	1.6	1.3	2.1	13.1	13.0	15.0	24.1	32.7	53.9
Percentage	22.8	6.7	1.1	1.0	0.9	1.5	2.9	3.9	5.2	7.6	8.3	10.1
Liberal arts	1.7	4.3	8.3	11.8	6.2	1.2	27.4	17.8	14.4	22.5	34.6	49.1
Percentage	5.3	7.7	4.5	7.2	4.2	0.9	6.0	5.3	5.0	7.1	8.8	9.2
Natural sciences	2.2	3.5	20.7	12.7	8.4	2.0	40.7	21.0	18.0	18.5	21.6	24.7
Percentage	6.9	6.2	11.2	7.7	5.7	1.4	8.9	6.3	6.3	5.8	5.5	4.6
Other*	1.8	1.5	4.3	2.5	1.7	0.4	10.2	7.1	6.9	9.6	13.3	21.2
Percentage	5.7	2.7	2.3	1.5	1.2	0.3	2.2	2.2	2.4	3.0	3.4	4.0
Total	32.0	56.2	185.5	164.6	146.6	139.6	457.2	335.3	286.9	316.4	392.8	531.9

*Physical culture, art, politics and law

Table 10.12 Tertiary student enrolment per 10 000 population

	1949	1952	1957	1965	1978	1980	1981	1982	1983	1984	1985	1986	1987
Students (per 10 000 pop.)	2.2	2.3	6.8	9.3	8.9	11.6	12.8	11.4	11.8	13.5	16.3	17.7	18.2

Table 10.13 Student–teacher ratio, tertiary institutions

	1949	1952	1957	1965	1978	1980	1981	1982	1983	1984	1985	1986	1987
No. teachers (per 10 000 pop.)	1.6	2.7	7.0	13.8	20.6	24.7	25.0	28.7	30.3	31.5	34.4	37.2	38.5
No. students/teacher	7.3	7.1	6.3	4.9	4.2	4.6	5.1	4.0	4.0	4.4	5.0	5.1	5.1

Table 10.14 Full-time teachers in tertiary institutions by field of study, 1987

Discipline	Professor	Assoc. prof.	Lecturer	Teacher	Assistant	Total
Engineering	3 676	19 973	39 067	5 436	37 979	385 352
Agriculture and forestry	985	3 751	6 148	622	7 801	19 307
Medicine	2 779	6 121	9 821	1 409	12 521	32 651
Pedagogy	127	590	1 057	597	2 078	4 449
Economics and finance	472	2 142	4 231	2 222	8 334	17 401
Liberal arts	1 709	13 114	28 908	8 675	34 862	87 268
Natural sciences	2 125	14 391	32 329	4 923	29 940	83 708
Physical culture, art, politics, law	634	4 384	10 993	3 765	14 661	34 437
Total	12 507	64 466	132 554	27 649	148 176	385 352

Table 10.15 Postgraduate enrolments

	1952	1957	1965	1978	1980	1981	1982	1983	1984	1985	1986	1987
Total no.												
students	2 763.0	3 178.0	4 546.0	10 934.0	21 604.0	18 848.0	25 847.0	37 166.0	57 566.0	87 331.0	110 371.0	119 248.0
Enrolling	1 785.0	334.0	1 456.0	10 708.0	3 616.0	9 363.0	11 080.0	15 642.0	23 181.0	46 871.0	41 310.0	38 759.0
Percentage				97.9	16.7	49.7	42.9	42.1	40.3	53.7	37.4	
Continuing	n/a	n/a	n/a	86.0	6 319.0	5 427.0	10 270	18 768.0	17 381.0	23 510.0	41 666.0	n/a
Percentage				0.9	29.2	28.8	39.7	50.5	30.2	26.9	37.8	
Graduating	n/a	n/a	n/a	140.0	11 669.0	4 058.0	4 497.0	2 756.0	17 004.0	16 950.0	27 395.0	n/a
Percentage				1.3	54.0	21.5	17.4	7.4	29.5	19.4	24.8	

Table 10.16 Postgraduate training: number of units

	1965	1978	1980	1981	1982	1983	1984	1985	1986	1987
Tertiary institutions	134	208	316	338	330	345	358	388	395	408
Chinese Academy of Sciences	81	73	89	98	111	115	116	119	121	113
Chinese Academy of Social Sciences		18	21	1	1	1	1	1	1	1
State Council ministries and commissions	19	71	102	101	134	162	161	173	177	177
Provincial, regional and municipal scientific research institutes			58	55	57	57	60	59	61	56
Total	234	370	586	593	633	680	696	740	755	755

Table 10.17 Adult school enrolments (in 10 000s)

	1982	1983	1984	1985	1986	1987
Primary level courses	756.6	817.2	932.2	833.8	1 261.4	1 351.8
Literacy	390.0	528.7	608.8	519.0	353.3	247.8
Primary education	360.6	288.5	323.4	314.8	232.1	173.7
Technical					676.0	930.3
Secondary level schools	1080.4	974.8	598.7	547.0	806.6	1 047.0
Technical and training					442.4	736.3
Middle	635.0	644.5	516.0	412.3	213.0	142.5
Secondary technical	445.4	330.3	82.7	134.7	151.2	168.2
Tertiary level universities and colleges	66.2	92.6	129.3	172.5	185.6	185.8
Colleges						
Pedagogical	5.2	6.3	16.4	24.7	26.0	25.1
Management cadres		0.2	1.5	4.0	5.6	5.6
Universities						
Correspondence and evening	20.8	27.3	32.2	50.3	59.5	64.6
White- and blue-collar worker and peasant	14.4	17.4	19.3	26.1	34.1	33.9
Radio and TV	25.8	41.4	59.9	67.4	60.4	56.7

Table 10.18 Female participation in education (in 10 000s)

Level of institution	No. and % female students			No. and % female teachers		
	1985	1986	1987	1985	1986	1987
Primary school	5 986.2	5 950.0	5 821.8	212.8	218.6	222.5
Percentage	44.8	45.1	45.4	39.6	40.4	40.9
Agricultural and vocational middle schools	95.4	111.1	116.3	3.5	4.3	5.1
Percentage	41.6	43.4	43.5	24.8	26.2	27.6
Regular secondary schools	1 893.1	1 987.9	2 018.6	74.4	78.1	82.8
Percentage	40.2	40.7	40.8	28.1	28.3	28.9
Specialized secondary schools	60.7	77.0	84.9	5.7	6.6	7.4
Percentage	38.6	43.8	45.3	32.8	34.2	35.2
Tertiary institutions	51.1	47.9	64.7	9.2	10.2	10.7
Percentage	30.0	25.5	33.0	26.7	27.4	27.8
Total	8 086.5	8 173.9	8 106.3	305.6	317.8	328.5
Percentage	43.4	43.7	44.0	35.2	35.7	37.8

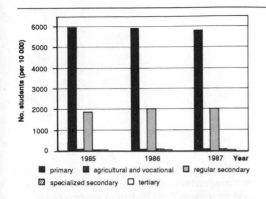

Figure 10.1 Female student enrolments

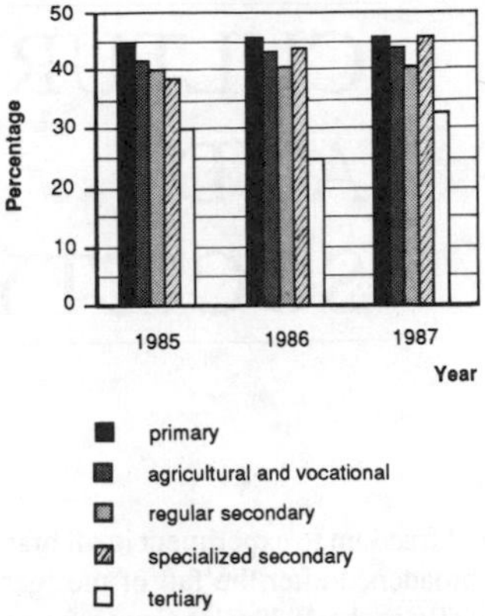

Figure 10.2 percentage of female students

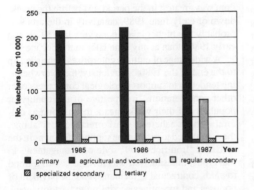

Figure 10.3 Female teachers

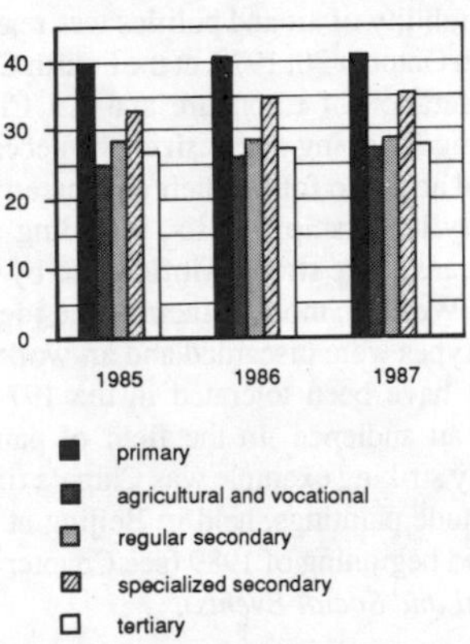

Figure 10.4 Percentage of female teachers

11 CULTURE AND SOCIETY

CULTURE

The degree of freedom to experiment in all branches of the arts broadened after the fall of the 'gang of four', especially in the 1980s, leading to far greater variety compared with the Cultural Revolution decade of 1966 to 1976. The downgrading of Mao Zedong and his ideas in 1981 meant that his theories on the arts were reinterpreted and his insistence on the inseparability of art and politics was rejected. In a speech on October 30, 1979, at the Fourth Congress of the Federation of Literature and Art Circles of China, Deng Xiaoping emphasized the necessity for writers and artists to follow their own creative spirit under Party leadership. Artists, including painters and musicians, were strongly influenced by foreign, especially Western, models, themes and ideas. Earlier stereotypes were discarded and art works which would not have been tolerated in the 1970s were permitted an audience. In the field of painting, a particularly striking example was China's first exhibition of nude paintings, held in Beijing at the end of 1988 and beginning of 1989 (see Chapter 1 under *E. Cultural and Social Events*).

On the other hand, the degree of freedom was still not comparable to that found in Western countries, and the stress on Party leadership was never relaxed. Especially during political campaigns, such as the one against 'spiritual pollution' late in 1983 (see Chapter 1 under *B. Domestic Political Events*), authors and artists remained likely to find their work banned. On the whole, although the degree of freedom was greatest in the period just before the crackdown of early June 1989, creativity in the arts was probably at a higher level in the very late 1970s and early 1980s than at any time later in the decade.

A wide range of cultural enterprises flourished up to the end of the 1980s. Previously, the overwhelming tendency to support ideological correctness over other considerations, irrespective of the quality or popularity of their work, meant that as long as cultural workers adhered to the correct ideological line, they continued to receive the support of their unit: the so-called 'iron rice-bowl' style of management. In the 1980s, this situation was reversed, with a trend towards contractual agreements, and the payment of bonuses and incentives according to performance.[1]

Table 11.1 Cultural institutions

	1952	1957	1965	1978	1980	1981	1982	1983	1984	1985	1986	1989
Cultural halls	2430	2748	2598	2748	2912	2803	2925	2946	3016	2965	2993	3002
Public libraries	83	400	577	1256	1732	1787	1889	2038	2217	2344	2406	2507
Museums	35	72	214	249	365	383	409	467	618	711	777	958
Performing arts troupes	2084	2884	3458	3150	3533	3483	3460	3444	3397	3317	3195	2864

Note: The statistics in Tables 11.1, 11.2, 11.3 and 11.4 come from State Statistical Bureau, comp., *Zhongguo tongji nianjian 1987 (Statistical Yearbook of China 1987)* (Statistical Press of China, Beijing, 1987), pp. 813–15; State Statistical Bureau, comp., *Zhongguo tongji nianjian 1986 (Statistical Yearbook of China 1986)* (Statistical Press of China, Beijing, 1986), p. 779.

Literature and publishing

Of the many forms of literature, those which figure prominently in post-1976 China include the full-length and short novel, the short story, poetry and reportage. All were severely affected by the severe steotypes imposed by the ideological constraints and political repression of the Cultural Revolution decade, but recovered during the new period following the death of Mao Zedong in 1976.

Literary journals which had been forced to close by the Cultural Revolution began reappearing in 1976. Soon afterwards, new journals began publication in substantial numbers. Numerous examples include *People's Literature* and *Poetry*, both of which were revived after long breaks early in 1976, and *Harvest* and *The Present*, which reappeared and began publication in 1976 and 1979 respectively (see Chapter 1, under *E. Cultural and Social Events*, 1976 and 1979).

A number of full-length novels were published in the 1950s and early 1960s. A few, such as Haoran's *The Bright Golden Road*, appeared during the Cultural Revolution decade (see Chapter 1, under *E. Cultural and Social Events*, 1972), but in general the period was notable for the paucity and low standard of its novels.

The most famous writers of the 1980s in China are probably still those of the older generation, such as Ba Jin and Ding Ling (for information on whose careers see Chapter 3). Both suffered severely as a result of the political machinations of the Cultural Revolution and, when rehabilitated, spent more time on official duties than on literature. Although they both continued to write, their later output was neither great nor distinguished, and their main works still belong to the pre-1949 period. Literature is now mainly the province of the younger generations.

In the early years after the revival of literature in the late 1970s, a major theme was the suffering caused by the Cultural Revolution. This was called 'the literature of the wound' after the short story 'The Wound' by Lu Xinhua (b. 1954), published in August 1978. Its theme is a young woman who refuses to have anything to do with her mother during the Cultural Revolution for political reasons. When the mother is rehabilitated, her daughter returns to her repentant, but arrives at her bedside just after she dies.

Among the most distinguished writers of the 1980s was Wang Meng, whose short novel, *The Butterfly,* published in 1980, was innovative for its impressionism in a literary context where it was assumed that narrative, not atmosphere, was the essential hallmark of a good short story or novel. (On Wang Meng's career and works, see Chapter 3.) The range of themes and characterization expanded and broadened rapidly in the fiction of the 1980s.

In poetry, Ai Qing was was very active until denounced as a rightist in 1957. He was attacked during the Cultural Revolution, but since the death of Mao Zedong has continued to write, as well as carry out official duties. (On Ai Qing's career see Chapter 3.) However, the most innovative and interesting poets are very much younger than Ai Qing. A prominent example is Zhao Zhenkai (born 1949), whose penname is Bei Dao. He is a fiction writer as well as a poet (for example, see Chapter 1, under *E. Cultural and Social Events, 1979*). His lyrical poetry is concerned with the 'search for truth' and the concept of confinement, rather than liberation. Since it is thus distinctly critical of the socialist order, authorities have attacked his work as nihilist. Like many of China's most innovative writers of the 1980s, Bei Dao has now left China to live in the West.

The best reportage writer of the 1980s is probably Liu Binyan (see Chapter 3 for his biography). Liu's works come to grips with the major social problems of China in a daring and uncompromising way. He was among those expelled from the CCP for 'bourgeois liberalization' early in 1987.

In general, the literary world expressed strong support for the pro-democracy movement of April to June 1989, so the crackdown which followed it had a highly deleterious impact on Chinese literature. The most obvious sign of this was the dismissal of the liberal novelist Wang Meng as Minister of Culture in September (see Chapter 1, under *D. Appointments, Dismissals, etc.*)

Although figures cannot show quality, those in Table 11.2 certainly suggest that, in terms of quantity and variety, the 1980s have seen a tremendous increase in publishing.

Table 11.2 Number of publications (titles)

	1952	1957	1965	1978	1980	1981	1982	1983	1984	1985	1986
Books	13 692	27 571	20 143	14 987	21 621	25 601	31 784	35 700	40 072	45 603	51 789
New titles	7 940	18 660	12 352	11 888	17 660	19 854	23 445	25 826	28 794	33 743	39 426
Magazines	354	634	790	930	2 191	2 801	3 100	3 415	3 907	4 705	5 248
Newspapers	296	364	343	186	188	242	277	340	458	698	791

Table 11.3 Categories and print-runs, 1986

	Titles	Volumes printed (millions)
Books other than textbooks		
Philosophy and social science	6 502	230
Culture and education	10 892	1 340
Literature and the arts	7 417	170
Natural science, technical	10 893	140
Children's and youth books	3 448	200
Charts and maps	5 393	630
Textbooks		
University level	2 740	70
Technical secondary	998	40
Secondary school	952	860
Primary school	1 294	1 440
Spare-time education	265	10
Others	995	n/a

In 1985, there were 374 publishing companies (employing 29 262 people), 180 printing houses (with a staff of 133 897 people) and 113 006 bookshops (employing 146 052 persons). In 1986 there were 395 publishing companies (employing 32 039 people), 179 printing houses (136 432 people) and 112 292 bookshops (149 943 people).

The theatre

The 1980s saw a flowering in the Chinese theatre. In the spoken drama *(huaju)* there was a good deal of experimentation, a prime early example being *Warning Signal* by Gao Xingjian (see Chapter 1, under *E. Cultural and Social Events*, 1982). Bai Fengxi exemplified feminist drama through such works as *A Friend Comes in Time of Need*, 1983. In addition to substantial Western influence in Chinese spoken drama, great Western dramas were performed in China. Arthur Miller directed his own *Death of a Salesman* (see Chapter 1, under *E. Cultural and Social Events*, 1983) and a Shakespeare festival was held in 1986, featuring some performances by Chinese companies in English, some in Chinese translation and some adapted into Chinese traditional regional styles, for example, *Othello* as a Peking Opera.

Following its total suppression during the Cultural Revolution, traditional theatre returned with renewed vigour in the late 1970s and 1980s. The drama form called 'newly written historical dramas' *(xin bian lishi ju)*, which uses largely traditional style, died during the Cultural Revolution but was revived in the late 1970s. Among the most distinguished and innovative of the playwrights of 'newly written historical dramas' in the 1980s was Wei Minglun, whose works include the Sichuan dramas *The Scholar of Bashan* and *Pan Jinlian*. Another very fine example of innovative 'newly written historical dramas' is *The Spirit of Daming* by Qi Zhixiang and others (see Chapter 1, under *E. Cultural and Social Events*, 1983, 1984 and 1986).

The crackdown following the Beijing massacre of early June 1989 severely hampered the creativity and freedom of dramatists. On the other hand, socially critical and experimental, but essentially non-political, spoken dramas continued to be performed, such as *Fire God and Autumn Girl (Huoshen yu Qiunü)* by Su Lei. A good 'newly written historical drama' which premiered late in 1989 in Beijing was Sun Yuexia's *Hualong dianjing (Painting Dragons and Filling in Eyes)*. It concerns one of China's most famous emperors, Li Shimin, and is set in the year 627. Pure traditional drama flourished as strongly as ever in the aftermath of the crackdown.

Table 11.4 Performing arts troupes: organizations and personnel

	1982		1985		1986	
	Organizations	*Personnel*	*Organizations*	*Personnel*	*Organizations*	*Personnel*
Spoken or children's drama troupes	105	11 560	103	10 681	100	10 325
Song drama, dance drama troupes	165	24 649	204	25 600	226	27 439
Symphony orchestras, choruses	11	1 966	18	2 387	20	2 590
Cultural work troupes, propaganda teams, caravan troupes	584	25 206	517	18 122	502	18 626
Traditional drama troupes	2 269	150 119	2 167	129 459	2 061	137 788
Balladry, acrobatics, puppetry troupes, etc.	326	16 034	308	13 631	286	13 420
Theatres	1 426	17 901	1 673	21 974	2 036	37 197
Arts creation organizations	440	2 492	354	2 340	314	2 412
Arts research organizations	79	1 820	112	2 698	137	2 608
Arts exhibition organizations	27	1 065	21	834	21	1 059
Performance companies	n/a	n/a	n/a	n/a	153	1 295
Others	181	3 093	269	3 013	118	3 431
Total	5 613	255 905	5 746	230 739	5 974	258 190

A nationwide survey of 2524 professionally performed dramas in twenty-nine cities in 1980 showed 1786 traditional dramas, 232 newly or recently written or rearranged dramas on historical themes, 186 dramas in traditional style but on modern themes, 176 spoken dramas, seventy-six song dramas (*geju*, operas influenced by the Western style or Western operas), sixty-three shadow plays and puppet plays and five foreign dramas arranged in traditional Chinese style.[2]

Although there was incomparably more innovation and freedom in the 1980s than in any earlier period, considerable restrictions still applied. For some of the best troupes, the greater importance of the box office led to a much more interesting performing arts diet. On the other hand, quality has often not always been the workers' highest consideration, and has sometimes suffered as a result of commercialization. Of course, quality is extremely difficult to evaluate: the value systems of powerful conservative, but not necessarily informed, pressure groups within society can easily turn out to be much more important than artistic professionalism. Perhaps it would be fair to argue that, although the drama

productions of the 1980s have been the best in the history of the PRC, standards have not risen as much as the freer climate of the decade might have permitted.

The cinema

The 1980s have also been by far the best and most innovative period in PRC history for the cinema. The decade produced the 'fifth generation' of film-makers who were prepared to tackle sensitive political, social and historical issues with some independence of Party dictates. For this reason, they have often irritated and angered the cultural authorities, and the cinema has suffered as much as any art form from the political changes following June 1989.

An early and excellent representative example of the work of the 'fifth generation' is the Guangxi Studio's 1984 film *Yellow Earth*, directed by Chen Kaige. It challenges the orthodox interpretation of the impact of the CCP on tradition and the peasantry in the late 1930s in the area near Yan'an, where the CCP had its headquarters. In his authoritative work on Chinese cinema, Paul Clark described it simply as 'the best film China had produced since 1949'.[3]

Table 11.5 The cinema industry: numbers of studios and films*

	1952	1957	1965	1978	1980	1981	1982	1983	1984	1985	1986
Film studios	4	11	16	12	17	19	19	19	20	20	20
Feature films	4	40	52	46	82	105	112	127	144	127	134
Arts films	2	5	21	26	32	33	33	37	37	45	46
Science and education films	41	84	240	289	337	277	284	343	387	357	383
Documentaries	157	272	378	203	269	276	259	344	399	419	417
Total number of films	204	401	691	564	720	691	688	851	967	948	980

*These numbers include only State Council-approved studios or films produced in them.

Table 11.6 The cinema industry: organizations and personnel

	1982		1985		1986	
	Organizations	Personnel	Organizations	Personnel	Organizations	Personnel
Film studios	19	15 028	35	17 000	36	17 677
Film processing units	5	2 121	5	2 000	4	2 661
Film distribution and projection management organizations	4 432	56 228	5 733	65 000	6 276	65 810
Cinemas and cinema–theatres	12 297	127 394 *	15 374	128 000	15 363	140 101
Open halls, clubs	n/a	n/a	2 986	32 000	2 995	33 540
Projection teams	143 650	403 375	149 666	269 000	141 389	251 809
Internal halls, clubs	n/a	n/a	14 801	41 000	13 482	35 681
Cinema machine production, production and spare parts units	n/a	n/a	38	4 000	14	1 061
Others	n/a	n/a	31	2 000	9	1 256
Totals	160 403	604 146	188 669	560 000	179 568	549 596

*These figures include open halls and clubs.

Cultural and sporting organizations

The lists of cultural and sporting organizations below are representative rather than comprehensive. For brevity, the prefix 'China' or 'All-China' has generally been omitted elsewhere in the text where the names of these organizations appear.

Main museums
Palace Museum; Museum of Chinese History; Museum of the Chinese Revolution; Chinese People's Revolutionary Military Museum; National Art Gallery

Main literary, artistic and mass media organizations
All-China Journalists' Association; China Confederation of Societies of Journalism; China Federation of Literary and Art Circles; China Film Art Research Centre; China PEN Centre; China Society for the Study of Traditional Opera; Chinese Acrobatics Association; Chinese Artists' Association; Chinese Association of Ballad Singers; Chinese Association of Popular Science Editors and Journalists; Chinese Calligraphers' Association; Chinese Dancers' Association; Chinese Dramatists' Association; Chinese Evening Paper Workers' Association; Chinese Film Artists' Association; Chinese Graphic Artists' Association; Chinese Musicians' Association; Chinese Photographers' Association; Chinese Publishers' Association; Chinese Sports Writers' Association; Chinese Television Artists' Association; Chinese Writers' Association; Journalism Education Society; National Legal News Reporters' Association; Society for Research into Traditional Operas on Modern Themes; Society for Study of Children's

Drama; Society for Study of Modern Drama; Society for Study of Painting and Calligraphy of the Aged; Society for Study of Picture-books; Television Drama Art Committee

Publishing and media groups
Central Newsreel and Documentary Film Studio; China News Service; Chinese People's Literature Publishing House; Commercial Press; Foreign Languages Press; Friendship Publishing House; International Cultural Publication Corporation; Language and Literature Publishing House; People's Fine Art Publishing House; People's Publishing House; Xinhua Bookstore; Xinhua Publishing House

Main sporting organizations
1990 Asian Games Organizing Committee; All-China Sports Federation; Angling Association; Archery Association; Athletics Association; Badminton Association; Baseball Association; Basketball Association; Billiard and Snooker Association; Bowls Association; Boxing Association; Bridge Association; Chess Association; Chinese Chess (*Weiqi*) Association; Chinese Olympic Committee; Cycling Association; Equestrian Association; Fencing Association; Fin-swimming Association; Football Association; Golf Association; Gymnastics Association; Handball Association; Hockey Association; Ice-hockey Association; International Chess Association; Judo Association; Kite-flying Association; Martial Arts (*Wushu*) Association; Middle School Sports Association; Model Ship Sports Association; Modern Pentathlon and Biathlon Association; Motorboat Association; Motorcycle Association; Mountaineering Association; Petanque Association; Rowing Association; Shooting Association; Shooting Association; Skating Association; Ski Association; Snowmobile Association; Softball Association; Sports Acrobatics Association; Sports Aviation Association; Sports Navigation Association; Sports Radio Contest Association; Swimming Association; Table-tennis Association; Taiwan Provincial Sports Liaison Office; Tennis Association; Toboggan Association; University Sports Association; Volleyball Association; Water-skiing Association; Weightlifting Association; Winter Sports Association; Wrestling Association; Yachting Association

SOCIETY[4]

Marriage and the family

Families, and children in particular, have traditionally played an extremely important part in Chinese social life: children, especially male children, were needed to carry on the ancestral line, assist the peasant on his holding and provide for the parents in their old age. Since the inception of the PRC, and particularly with the establishment of the commune system, there was an increasing emphasis on replacing old Confucian values and ideas of family with modern ones, but children have continued to be very important.

Up to the end of the Cultural Revolution decade, divorce was extremely rare. Yet this hitherto almost unknown phenomenon has now become a recognizable, even if socially unacknowledged, feature of Chinese life. In 1986 the divorce rate was one in 17.4; while there were 8 822 935 registered marriages, there were 505 675 divorces. This appears to be more closely related to recent economic pressures on people in general than to any specifically urban problems as, contrary to perceptions of urban life in the West, the three largest population centres actually have a lower than average divorce rate (See Table 11.7).

Table 11.7 Marriage and divorce in China's three municipalities 1986

Municipality	Marriages	Divorces	Ratio
Beijing	142 466	7 270	1:19.6
Tianjin	103 802	3 982	1:26.1
Shanghai	189 359	8 776	1:21.6

Juvenile delinquency

According to the juvenile crime expert Shao Daosheng, at the conclusion of the Cultural Revolution there were over twenty million people unemployed, the majority of them youths whose education had been interrupted. They formed criminal gangs whose power is still largely unchecked. Shao claims that illiterate or partly illiterate people make up one-third of China's population, and clearly this section of the population has been more vulnerable to recent economic pressures. The increased pace of industrial development in China, and the introduction of Western industrial practices without compensatory protective measures such as a fully developed national social security system (see below) or free trade unions, has exacerbated the plight of the urban poor and itinerant workers in the special economic zones. A growing proportion of juvenile crime is the partial result of this situation.

Table 11.8 Medical statistics (1000s)

	1952	1957	1965	1978	1980	1981	1982	1983	1984	1985	1986
Total medical personnel	690.0	1 039.0	1 532.0	2 464.0	2 798.0	3 011.0	3 143.0	3 253.0	3 344.0	3 411.0	3 507.0
Doctors	358.0	411.0	510.0	610.0	709.0	806.0	860.0	901.0	921.0	938.0	960.0
Western medicine	52.0	74.0	189.0	359.0	447.0	516.0	557.0	588.0	597.0	602.0	619.0
Traditional Chinese medicine	306.0	337.0	321.0	251.0	262.0	290.0	303.0	313.0	324.0	336.0	341.0
Nurses	61.0	128.0	235.0	407.0	466.0	525.0	564.0	596.0	616.0	637.0	681.0
Total medical institutions	39.0	123.0	224.3	169.7	180.6	190.1	193.4	196.0	198.3	200.9	203.1
Hospitals	3.5	4.2	42.7	64.4	65.5	65.9	66.1	66.7	67.2	59.6	59.7

Table 11.9 Medical institution statistics

	1949	1965	1975	1980	1982	1982/1949 ratio
Hospitals	2 600	42 711	62 425	65 450	66 149	25.4
Sanatoria	30	887	297	470	593	19.8
Clinics, outpatient departments	769	170 430	80 739	102 474	113 916	148.1
Disease prevention and cure stations	11	822	683	1 138	1 272	115.6
Epidemic prevention stations	—	2 499	2 912	3 105	3 271	—
Maternal and child care stations	9	2 795	2 025	2 610	2 645	293.9
Medical inspection stations	1	131	310	1 213	1 186	1 186.0
Medical research institutes	3	94	141	282	294	98.0
Total	3 670	224 266	151 733	180 553	193 438	52.7

Table 11.10 Hospital bed statistics

	1949	1965	1975	1980	1982	1981/1949 ratio
Number of beds	80 000	765 558	1 598 232	1 982 176	1 053 836	13.2
Urban	59 867	457 662	637 416	767 794	832 418	13.9
Rural	20 133	307 896	960 816	1 214 382	1 221 420	60.7
Beds per thousand population	0.15	1.06	1.74	2.02	2.03	13.5
Urban	0.63	3.78	4.61	4.70	4.76	7.6
Rural	0.05	0.51	1.23	1.48	1.46	29.2

Table 11.11 Nutritional intake per day

	1952	1978	1982	1983	Percentage increase 1983/1952
Calories	2270.0	2311.0	2779.0	2877.4	26.76
Animal	111.0	142.0	214.7	225.9	103.51
Vegetable	2159.0	2169.0	2564.3	2651.5	22.81
Cities	—	2715.0	3087.9	3182.5	—
Countryside	—	2224.0	2707.2	2805.9	—
Protein (gm)	69.6	70.8	80.5	82.8	18.97
Animal	3.1	4.0	5.7	6.2	100.00
Vegetable	66.5	66.8	74.8	76.6	15.19
Cities	—	81.6	85.8	87.5	—
Countryside	—	68.5	79.3	81.7	—
Fat (gm)	28.3	29.9	44.4	47.2	66.78
Animal	10.6	13.9	21.1	22.1	108.49
Vegetable	17.7	16.0	23.3	25.1	41.81
Cities	—	49.0	70.6	74.9	—
Countryside	—	25.7	38.3	40.7	—

A 1990 figure from the Editorial Research Department of *Asiaweek* Limited ranked a series of selected Asian–Pacific regions or countries in order of the daily calories consumed by each person. The list down to China, followed by three other important nations, with the daily calories in parentheses, was: New Zealand (3463), Australia (3326), South Korea (2907), Japan (2864), Hong Kong (2859), Brunei (2850), Singapore (2840), Taiwan (2749), Malaysia (2730), China (2630), Indonesia (2579), India (2238) and Bangladesh (1927).[5]

The disabled

The first national census of the disabled revealed in 1987 that forty-nine out of every 1000 people were handicapped. The 51.6 million disabled represented just under 5 per cent of the population. Of these people, 17.7 million suffered speech or hearing defects, 7 million eyesight defects and 10.2 million some mental defect.

Table 11.12 Mortality rates from ten major diseases 1986

Disease	% of total urban deaths			% of total rural deaths		
	Total	Male	Female	Total	Male	Female
Heart disease	23.03	21.04	25.08	24.49	22.46	26.89
Cancer	21.15	24.17	17.58	15.18	17.11	13.16
Cerebrovascular disease	21.11	20.59	21.63	15.65	15.10	16.30
Respiratory disease	8.88	8.42	9.55	5.46	5.75	5.11
Digestive disease	4.21	4.38	4.08	4.21	4.38	4.08
Trauma	4.11	4.86	3.25	3.62	4.64	2.41
Tuberculosis	1.72	2.17	1.36	3.45	4.03	2.78
Urinary disease	1.63	1.34	1.72	1.26	1.36	1.15
Toxicosis	1.62	1.56	1.95	3.86	3.22	4.60
Neonatal disease	1.49	1.57	—*	2.14	2.31	1.94

*Not one of ten major causes of female urban mortality.

Table 11.13 Employment of the disabled 1981–85

	1981	1982	1983	1984	1985
Number employed	61 291	64 091	66 423	72 208	80 876
% increase over previous year	—	4.6	3.6	8.7	12

Welfare

Industrial workers receive pensions and sick pay through their trade unions, which are responsible for what limited social security exists. Non-union members do not qualify. While the PRC has no fully developed social security system, there is some provision for relief in cases of regional problems or in extreme cases of personal hardship, such as widows, retired war veterans and the severely disabled. This is provided in the form of the five guarantees, or *wubao*, for basic existence.

There are two levels of aid: state, or *guojia,* and collective/local, or *minban.* Aid is granted at state level for the relief of widespread rural poverty in designated poor areas; to some categories of disadvantaged individuals in rural areas, in the form of the five guarantees; or as urban relief funds and subsidies. Aid is granted at the local level for the relief of individuals in poor urban households; and to retired workers, in some cases as a percentage of their former wage or, in others, as quota relief funds. In 1986 a total of Rmb 4 246 445 000 yuan was paid in social welfare relief funds, a 17.34 per cent rise over the 1985 figure, of which state allocations constituted Rmb 2 662 735 000 yuan, or 62.7 per cent, and collective funds Rmb 1 583 710 000 yuan, or 37.3 per cent.

Table 11.14 Distribution of subsidies and relief funds 1985–86 (per 1000 persons)

Type of funds	1985	1986
State subsidies and relief funds		
Rural		
Poor household relief funds	38 004	39 902
Five guarantees of existence (relief funds)	226	220
Urban		
Poor household relief funds and subsidies	182	356
Local subsidies and relief funds		
Rural		
Five guarantees of existence (subsidies)	1 976	1 919
Workers' relief funds*		
40% of original wages	245	253
Quota relief funds	289	280
Other*		
Urban relief funds and subsidies	3 587	6 311
*Unspecified whether state or local		

~ 236 ~

APPENDIX

SELECTION OF ACRONYMS

Following is a list of acronyms or abbreviations in common current usage, not necessarily appearing in this book, which apply to Chinese economic corporations, banks and other organizations. Those acronyms listed in the front of this book have not been repeated.

ACFIC Economic Service Centre
China Industrial and Commercial Economic Service Centre

ARTCHINA
China National Arts and Crafts Import and Export Corporation

BBT
Beijing Book Traders

BEBIC
Beijing Ever-Bright Industrial Company

BFSU
Beijing Foreign Studies University

BOC
Bank of China

BPIEC
Beijing Publications Import and Export Corporation

CAFIU
Chinese Association for International Understanding

CAS
Chinese Academy of Sciences

CASS
Chinese Academy of Social Sciences

CAST
Chinese Association for Science and Technology

CATIC
China National Aero-Technology Import and Export Corporation

CCECC
China Civil Engineering Construction Corporation

CCPA
China Committee of the Publishers' Association

CCPIT
China Council for Promotion of International Trade (China Chamber of International Commerce)

CCTV
China Central Television

CEIEC
China National Electronics Import and Export Corporation

CEROILFOOD
China National Cereals, Oil and Foodstuffs Import and Export Corporation

CGWIC
China Great Wall Industry Corporation

CHICICON
China Civil Engineering Construction Corporation

CHINAFILM
China Film Corporation

CHINAPEACE
Chinese People's Association for Peace and Disarmament

CHINASTAMP
China Stamp Company

CHINATEX
China National Textiles Import and Export Corporation

CHINSURCO
China Insurance Company Ltd

CHPN
China Henan Native Produce I/E (Group) Corporation

CIBTC
China International Book Trading Corporation (Guoji Shudian)

CITIC
China International Trust and Investment Corporation

CITS
China International Travel Service

CLSS
China Library Science Society

CMC
Central Military Commission

CMEC
China National Machinery and Equipment Import and Export Corporation

CMIC
China Machine-Building International Corporation

CNAAA
China National Amateur Athletics Association

CNABSIEC
China National Animal Breeding Stock Import and Export Corporation

CNCCC
China National Chemical Construction Corporation

CNEIC
China Nuclear Energy Industry Corporation

CNFTSC
China National Foreign Trade Storage Corporation

CNIC
China North Industry Corporation

CNOOC
China National Offshore Oil Corporation

CNPIEC
China National Publications Import and Export Corporation

CNPITC
China National Publishing Industry Trading Corporation

CNTIC
China National Technical Import Corporation

COBDC
China Overseas Building Development Company

COC
Chinese Olympic Committee

COMPLANT
China National Complete Plant Export Corporation

COSC
China Ocean Shipping Company

CPAP
Chinese People's Armed Police

CPBS
Central People's Broadcasting Station

CRIPST
China Research Institute of Printing Science and Technology

CSCEC
China State Construction Engineering Corporation

CSSC
China Sports Service Company or China State Shipbuilding Corporation

CSTC
China Shipbuilding Trade Company

CSTIND
Commission for Science, Technology and Industry for National Defence

CSIMC
China Scientific Instruments and Materials Corporation

EQUIPEX
China National Machinery and Equipment Export Corporation

GDL
General Department of Logistics

GACA
General Administration of Civil Aviation

INSTRIMPEX
China National Instruments Import and Export Corporation

MACHIMPEX
China National Machinery Import and Export Corporation

MINMETALS
China National Metals and Minerals Import and Export Corporation

MOFERT
Ministry of Foreign Economic Relations and Trade

MRC
Military Regional Command

NLC
National Library of China

NORINCO
China Northern Industrial Corporation

OCIC
Overseas Chinese Investment Corporation

OCC
Overseas Chinese Committee

PENAVICO
China Ocean Shipping Agency

PICC
People's Insurance Company of China

PUBLIMEX
China National Publications Import and Export Corporation

SBT
Shanghai Book Traders

SC
State Council

SCNPC
Standing Committee of the National People's Congress

SEZ
Special Economic Zone

SGAEC
State General Administration of Exchange Control

SIEC
State Import–Export Commission

SINOCHART
China National Chartering Corporation

SINOCHEM
China National Chemicals Import and Export Corporation

SINOPEC
China Petrochemical Company

SINOTRANS
China National Foreign Trade Transportation Corporation

SITCO
Shanghai Investment and Trust Corporation

SPC
Supreme People's Court

SPP
Supreme People's Procuracy

SSTC
State Science and Technology Committee

TAIPINGINC
Tai Ping Insurance Company

TECHIMPORT
China National Technical Import and Export Corporation

TLIP
China National Light Industrial Products Import and Export Corporation, Tianjin Branch

ZLIPIEC
Zhejiang Light Industrial Products Import and Export Corporation

NOTES

CHAPTER 1

1. The sources are numerous, especially Colin Mackerras, with the assistance of Robert Chan, *Modern China, A Chronology from 1842 to the Present* (Thames and Hudson, London, 1982). For the whole period covered here a very useful general source has been Li Shengping a.o. comp., *Dictionary of Modern Chinese History (Zhongguo xiandai shi cidian)* (China International Broadcasting Press, Beijing, 1987). For the period since the early 1960s or late 1950s respectively the regular 'Quarterly Chronicle and Documentation' in *The China Quarterly*, published by the Contemporary China Institute, School of Oriental and African Studies, London, and Beijing Review, an English-language weekly published by Beijing Review in Beijing, China are valuable. For the years since 1979 the *Chinese Encyclopedic Yearbook 1980 (Zhongguo baike nianjian)* (Chinese Encyclopedia Press, Beijing and Shanghai, 1980 and later years) has been particularly useful and for those since 1977 John L. Scherer (ed.), *China, Facts and Figures Annual* (Academic International Press, Gulf Breeze, Florida, 1978 and later years) is recommended.

CHAPTER 2

1. State Statistical Bureau, comp., *Zhongguo tongji nianjian 1987 (Statistical Yearbook of China 1987)* (Statistical Press of China, Beijing, 1987), p. 4.
2. The main sources are Edward J. Epstein in *Far Eastern Economic Review* CXXXIX, 12 (March 24, 1988), pp. 81–2; *Beijing Review* XXXI, 16 (April 18–24, 1988), pp. 7–8; and *Beijing Review* XXXII, 21 (May 22–8, 1989), p. 8.
3. *China Daily*, September 8, 1986, p. 4.
4. The main sources include Epstein in *Far Eastern Economic Review* CXXXIX, 12 (March 24, 1988), pp. 81–2 and The Chinese Academy of Social Sciences, ed. for Pergamon Press by

C. V. James, *Information China, The Comprehensive and Authoritative Reference Source of New China, Vol. 2* (Pergamon Press, Oxford and New York, 1989), pp. 428–33
5. This is based on a report by the British Broadcasting Corporation's Tim Louard, broadcast over the Australian Broadcasting Corporation's program *World Roundup* on December 13, 1988, itself claiming to be based on *Shanghai Evening News (Shanghai wanbao)*.

CHAPTER 3

1. There are several major biographical works, of which Wolfgang Bartke, *Who's Who in the People's Republic of China*, 2nd edn (K. G. Saur, Munich, New York, London, 1987) and Wolfgang Bartke and Peter Schier, *China's New Party Leadership: Biographies and Analysis of the Twelfth Central Committee of the Chinese Communist Party* (M. E. Sharpe, Armonk 1985) are excellent for the 1980s. For information on the earlier period see also Donald W. Klein, and Anne B. Clark, *Biographic Dictionary of Chinese Communism, 1921–1965*, 2 vols (Harvard University Press, Cambridge, Mass., 1971). For official positions and similar material, Malcolm Lamb, *Directory of Officials and Organisations in China, 1968–1983* (Contemporary China Centre, Australian National University, Canberra, 1983) has proved very helpful. The sources listed for the chronology in Chapter 1 are also useful for the biographical material in the present chapter.

CHAPTER 6

1. There are no absolutely guaranteed, hard-and-fast economic statistics covering the entire history of the PRC since its inception in 1949 up to the present. However, for this publication the most up-to-date and reliable sources available have been used. The Economist Intelligence

Unit's *Country Report* and *Country Profile* have provided an invaluable source of background information to supplement the rather drily-presented data in the Statistical Yearbook of China. Other publications have also proved useful, and a special section is given over to the economy in Chapter 4. Additionally, the following are those sources used most frequently in preparing the material for this chapter: Bartke, Wolfgang and Schier, Peter, *China's New Party Leadership: Biographies and Analysis of the Twelfth Central Committee of the Chinese Communist Party* (M. E. Sharpe, New York, 1985; *China, North Korea Country Report No. 1 & 2*, The Economist Intelligence Unit, London, 1989; *Country Profile: China, North Korea*, The Economist Intelligence Unit, London, 1988–89; *Asia Yearbook* (Far Eastern Economic Review, Hong Kong, 1989); Hu Qiaomu and others, comp., *Zhongguo baike nianjian (Encyclopedic Yearbook of China)* (Encyclopedic Press of China, Beijing, Shanghai, successive years); Scherer, John L. (ed.), *China Facts and Figures Annual* (Academic International Press, Gulf Breeze, Florida), Vols. 7–11; State Statistical Bureau, comp., *Zhongguo tongji nianjian (Statistical Yearbook of China)* (Statistical Press of China, Beijing, 1981–88); *World Bank, World Debt Tables* (World Bank, 1989).

2. Bartke and Schier, *China's New Party Leadership*, p. 15.
3. ibid., pp. 29–31.
4. 'Dual-track' problems are pinpointed in the article 'The ten-year reform ideological conflict: views on a few controversial issues' ('Dui shinian gaige fansizhong yixie zhengyi wenti de kanfa') by Zhao Lükuan and Yang Tiren in Shanghai's *World Economic Herald (Shijie jingji daobao)* No. 420 (December 5, 1988).

CHAPTER 7

1. The following are the main general sources, in order of importance, for the figures in this chapter: State Statistical Bureau Office of Population Statistics, *Zhongguo renkou tongji nianjian China Population Statistics Yearbook 1988* (Zhanwang Press, Beijing, 1988); State Statistical Bureau, comp., *Zhongguo tongji nianjun*

(Statistical Yearbook of China) (Statistical Press of China, Beijing, 1981–88); and *Asia Yearbook* (Far Eastern Economic Review, Hong Kong, successive years).

2. Especially those given in *China Population Statistics Yearbook 1988*, p. 198.
3. They derive from the successive *Asia Yearbooks*, themselves based on the *Far Eastern Economic Review's* own sources, the United Nations Statistical Yearbooks, and a range of other sources.
4. See *Beijing Review* XXXII, 11 (March 13–19, 1989), p. 4.
5. See Ellen Salem in *Far Eastern Economic Review* CLXIII, 9 (March 2, 1989), p. 63.
6. *Far Eastern Economic Review* CXLIII, 9 (March 2, 1989), p. 64.
7. See *Beijing Review* XXXI, 3 (January 18–24, 1988), p. 8.
8. See *Beijing Review* XXXIII, 7 (February 12–18, 1990), pp. 22–4.
9. The sources for the material on age structure are: *Statistical Yearbook of China 1983*, pp. 110–11 and *China Population Statistics Yearbook 1988*, pp. 477–81 and 54–7.
10. Cited in *Zhongguo laonian (Old Age in China)* (November 11, 1988), itself cited in *Beijing Review* XXXII, 12 (March 20–26, 1989), p. 29.
11. See Judith Banister, 'The Aging of China's Population', *Problems of Communism* XXXVII, 6 (November–December 1988), p. 62.
12. *China Population Statistics Yearbook 1988*, p. 856.
13. *China Population Statistics Yearbook 1988*, p. 857.

CHAPTER 8

1. The source for the population figures is State Statistical Bureau Office of Population Statistics, *Zhongguo renkou tongji nianjian China Population Statistics Yearbook 1988* (Zhanwang Press, Beijing, 1988), pp. 156–96.

CHAPTER 9

1. The main source for the population figures is the State Statistical Bureau Office of Population Statistics, *Zhongguo renkou tongji nianjian (China Population Statistics Yearbook 1988)* (Zhanwang Press, Beijing, 1988), pp. 273, 391,

545. There are conflicts among the sources for the 1964 and 1982 censuses, but this source is preferred as being the most thorough and up-to-date tabulation of the data. There are the original, less well processed and less reliable figures for the 1964 and 1982 censuses in State Statistical Bureau, comp., *Zhongguo tongji nianjian 1983 (Statistical Yearbook of China 1983)* (Statistical Press of China, Beijing, 1983). See also Chen Yongling, et al., comp., *Minzu cidian (Nationalities Dictionary)* (Shanghai Lexicographical Press, Shanghai, 1987), pp. 1255–7; Editorial Committee of the China Official Yearbook, *The China Official Yearbook 1985/6* (Salem International Publications, Hong Kong), p. 13; and Charles E. Greer (ed.), *China Facts & Figures Annual, Volume 11, 1988* (Academic International Press, Gulf Breeze, Florida, 1989), pp. 337–8.

2. For an account and analysis of various claims of the population of Tibet, see A. Tom Grunfeld, *The Making of Modern Tibet* (M. E. Sharpe, Armonk, Zed Books, London, 1987), pp. 218–22.

3. These were published as *The Question of Tibet and the Rule of Law* (International Commission of Jurists, Geneva, 1960) and *Tibet and the Chinese People's Republic* (International Commission of Jurists, Geneva, 1960).

4. See Zhang Tianlu, *Xizang renkou de bianqian (Changes in the Population of Tibet)* (The Tibetan Studies Press of China, Beijing, 1989), pp. 9–10.

5. The source for these figures is *The China Official Yearbook 1985/6*, pp. 10–13.

6. The main source for this list is Chen Yongling et al., comp., *Minzu cidian*, pp. 1258–63. See also Shi Zhengyi et al., comp., *Minzu cidian (Nationalities Dictionary)* (Sichuan Nationalities Press, Chengdu, 1984), pp. 400–403, and The Chinese Academy of Social Sciences, edited for Pergamon Press by C. V. James, *Information China, The Comprehensive and Authoritative Reference Source of New China Volume 3* (Pergamon Press, Oxford, New York, 1989), pp. 1280–81.

7. *China Daily*, August 26, 1982, p. 3, and 9 November 1989, p. 1.

8. The main sources for the figures in the following tables are *Zhongguo tongji nianjian 1986 (Statistical Yearbook of China 1983)* (Statistical Press of China, Beijing, 1986), pp. 81–2; and *Zhongguo tongji nianjian 1983 (Statistical Yearbook of China 1983)* (Statistical Press of China, Beijing, 1987), pp. 79–80. See also *The China Official Yearbook 1985/6*, p. 13.

9. The main sources for the information in this section are Baoerhan et al., comp., *Zhongguo da baike quanshu, minzu (The China Encyclopedia, Nationalities)* (China Encyclopedia Press, Beijing, Shanghai, 1986); Chen Yongling et al., comp., *Minzu cidian*; and Shi Zhengyi et al., comp., *Minzu cidian*, especially pp. 404–10. See also Lunda Hoyle Gill and Colin Mackerras, *Portraits of China* (University of Hawaii Press, Honolulu, 1990), pp. 122–8.

CHAPTER 10

1. *Asia Yearbook* 1989 (Far Eastern Economic Review, Hong Kong, 1989), p. 6.

CHAPTER 11

1. For the application of this new system to the theatre arts see Colin Mackerras, 'Modernization and Contemporary Chinese Theatre: Commercialization and Professionalization', in Constantine Tung and Colin Mackerras (eds), *Drama in the People's Republic of China* (State University of New York Press, Albany, 1987), pp. 184–9.

2. See the extensive lists in *Zhongguo xiju nianjian 1981 (Chinese Theatre Annual)* (Chinese Theatre Press, Beijing, 1981), pp. 296–303.

3. Paul Clark, *Chinese Cinema, Culture and Politics since 1949* (Cambridge University Press, Cambridge, 1987), p. 179. The sources for the following tables on cinema are State Statistical Bureau, comp., *Zhongguo tongji nianjian 1984 (Statistical Yearbook of China 1984)* (Statistical Press of China, Beijing, 1984), p. 505, *Statistical Yearbook of China 1986*, pp. 777–9, and *Statistical Yearbook of China 1987*, pp. 818, 812.

4. The two main sources for the section on society are *Statistical Yearbook of China 1987* and Scherer, John (ed.), *China Facts and Figures Annual* (Academic International Press, Gulf Breeze, Florida).

5. *Asiaweek* XVI, 12 (March 23, 1990), p. 13.

INDEX